DAILY
WITH THE
KING

by
W. Glyn Evans

MOODY PUBLISHERS
CHICAGO

ISBN: 0-8024-1725-6
ISBN-13: 978-0-8024-1725-1

We hope you enjoy this book from Moody Publishers. Our goal is to provide high-quality, thought-provoking books and products that connect truth to your real needs and challenges. For more information on other books and products written and produced from a biblical perspective, go to www.moodypublishers.com or write to:

Moody Publishers
820 N. LaSalle Boulevard
Chicago, IL 60610

15 17 19 20 18 16 14

Printed in the United States of America

My heart overflows with a good theme;
I address my verses to the King;
My tongue is the pen of a ready writer.

Psalm 45:1

This luminous psalm expresses the majesty of God,
the glory of His Son, and the beauty of His bride.
These are objectives of this book, also.
With such glorious themes to write about,
why should not the heart of the psalmist,
and this writer, overflow!

IN APPRECIATION

Special Thanks is due my office staff
for their assistance in the preparation of the manuscript:
Ruth Crane, Linda Fitzgerald, and Mary Spitz.
God will not forget their "labour of love" (Hebrews 6:10, KJV)

FOREWORD

Most of us are very thirsty. We live in a dry world where daily living leeches the vitality and the enjoyment of our days. Glyn Evans has prepared a refreshment, a delightful concoction of tonics for the spirit. They are designed to be habit-forming, a daily pick-me-up, but they also have a cumulative effect. I find myself a more consistent disciple of our Lord.

Glyn is a choice friend from Wheaton College days, and I always knew he was reflective by nature. But not until I began to drink from his well of daily devotionals did I comprehend the fertility of his heart. He has the rare gift of plucking a choice truth from the biblical text and preparing it for common what-I-need-now consumption. The same truth may have washed over me before, but Glyn's gentle mist reaches my underside and I am renewed.

The art of presenting God's Word tastefully and accurately, so that it has early morning appeal requires a mind attuned to the spirit and alert to breakfast table lethargy. Daily maintenance is the "biggie" in Christian living; here is one of the best tools I have ever used.

HOWARD G. HENDRICKS
Chairman, Center for Christian Leadership
Dallas Theological Seminary

JANUARY 1
Owning Nothing, Enjoying Everything

I will settle things with You, Lord, once and for all concerning my rights and responsibilities. To accept Jesus as my Savior means I resign all rights to justify my sin before You; Jesus does that for me. But to accept Jesus as my Lord means I resign all rights to myself—my time, my talents, my future, my all.

That is where my difficulty is—resigning myself. To surrender my rights to myself means surrendering my rights to my reputation (He "made himself of no reputation," Philippians 2:7, KJV); surrendering my rights to choose my place of service (He "set His face to go to Jerusalem," Luke 9:51); surrendering my rights to my possessions (He had "no place to lay his head," Luke 9:58, NIV); surrendering my rights to make demands (He "came not to be ministered unto, but to minister," Matthew 20:28, KJV); surrendering my rights to privacy and immunity from the needs of others (He said, "They need not depart; give . . . them to eat," Matthew 14:16, KJV).

When I became a Christian I thought, *How wonderful to be rid of the burden of sin's responsibility!* But when I became a disciple, Jesus put another burden upon me; the burden of others. The second burden took away all my rights, and a person without rights is a slave (He "took on the nature [form] of a slave," Philippians 2:7, Williams).

Most of the time when I am touchy, irritable, or peevish (if it is not physical), it is because I have reclaimed what I thought I had surrendered to Jesus, for these are the feelings of one whose claim is threatened. My job then is to re-surrender as quickly as possible and quitclaim my possessions. I rejoice that I am an "all things new" person, made so because I have become a "new creation" in Christ (2 Corinthians 5:17, Berkeley).

"Rest in the Lord and wait patiently for Him; do not fret because of him who prospers in his way, because of the man who carries out wicked schemes" (Psalm 37:7).

JANUARY 2
The Lord of What Is to Come

Lord, I know You can save me from my sins, but can You save me from myself? God can save me from the effects of my hate, but can He save me from being hateful? Can He change me so that I am no longer stingy, suspicious, jealous, cruel, and moody? If salvation means anything, it must work where sin begins, not merely where it ends.

Lord, that is what Jesus came to do—to change people, not just their record books. He came to erase the criminal's record; but, even more, He came to erase the criminal's repeatability. He not only came to clear the criminal in court, but to keep him out of court thereafter.

"Thou art Simon . . . thou shalt be called Cephas, . . . a stone" (John 1:42, KJV). By that statement Jesus showed Himself to be the Lord of what is to come. Changeable men are transformed into firm, rocklike men. He did not say, "You are Simon the sinner; you shall become Simon the saint." Simon became a rock.

That is the wonderful thing about Jesus—He sees us not as we are but as what we can become. Even more, He is able to change us from what we are into what He sees us capable of becoming.

I am a planned-for-the-future man. I am destined for God's eternal drama. The eyes of the all-seeing Sculptor have scanned me and set me aside for developing. Lord, now I see what You meant when You said, "He has . . . set eternity in their heart" (Ecclesiastes 3:11). We are being made for tomorrow, for the future, for eternity. To look within ourselves now and be discouraged is to miss it all. God, You look at us in your tomorrow and rejoice over us as one finding great spoil.

"And do not be conformed to this world, but be transformed by the renewing of your mind, that you may prove what the will of God is, that which is good and acceptable and perfect" (Romans 12:2).

JANUARY 3
Formulas Are to Be Avoided

I will avoid the pitfall of being a formula Christian. I am surrounded by literature that promises me the secret of victory, as if God can be reduced to a method. Everywhere I turn I discover "steps to this" and "steps to that." Christians who are privileged to share a new insight of God are quick to build it into a formula.

I must avoid all that. I must keep in mind Paul's expression: "O the depth of the riches both of the wisdom and knowledge of God! How unsearchable are his judgments, and his ways past finding out!" (Romans 11:33, KJV).

God will not let Himself be boxed into a recipe. How often I have discovered that when I attempted to use someone else's formula, it did not work for me. God's dealings with us are strictly personal. There are general principles, of course, but the application is *ad hominem* ("to the man"). That's why someone else's spiritual secret is a mystery to me.

Neither can I say with Archimedes, "I have found it!" God's timely deliverance for me today will not necessarily be His deliverance tomorrow. God is constantly trying to tell me that He will not be nailed down. Yet I find something in my nature that keeps on trying to do that very thing. Why do I feel I have to manage God? Is there a little god within me who must have his property, his domain, his castle?

God will disappoint my every effort to corner Him, for He will be servant to no man. Even those who know Him best find Him a stranger at times. That is why my warmest prayer sometimes will meet the coldest response and my deepest need will go unsatisfied. Not often, of course, but often enough to remind me that God must be God. Yet, through it all, "I will never leave thee" (Hebrews 13:5, KJV) rings loud and clear. That is because God's stake in my salvation is great.

"Oh, the depth of the riches both of the wisdom and knowledge of God! How unsearchable are His judgments and unfathomable His ways!" (Romans 11:33).

JANUARY 4
The Cult of Success

I will always allow God His sovereign right of refusal. I am sure God has promised me many things, but I also am aware that God's right to be God is greater than my claim on those blessings. When I read, "With long life will I satisfy him, and shew him my salvation" (Psalm 91:16, KJV), I am comforted. But when I read of those who were "stoned, . . . sawn asunder, . . . tempted, . . . afflicted, tormented" (Hebrews 11:37, KJV), I am confused. Jesus Himself did not enjoy long life.

The psalmist reminds me that if I delight in the Lord and meditate on His Word, "whatsoever [I do] shall prosper" (Psalm 1:3, KJV). The "cult of success" takes a promise like this and makes it absolute. Then I have problems, because believers in God are not always the richest, healthiest, most favored people on earth. In fact, they are the opposite.

My comfort does not lie in things, even spiritual things. I cannot rejoice in a miraculous answer to prayer today and think I will always get the same kind of answers. My comfort lies in the acceptance of God's right to do as He wills with me, even though what He wills may seem contradictory to His promises.

Since I cannot fathom God, I must trust Him. I am encouraged to trust Him, not because He promises me things, but because He is good, holy, fair, and does what is right. In other words, I can trust His Word because I can trust His character. Jesus is my example, for He trusted the character of His heavenly Father implicitly, completely, and thoroughly. That is why He obeyed His Father's will so unswervingly, even though it meant a cross. Yet I must remember that my trust in God will never be betrayed, misplaced, or denied. He who magnifies His Word above His name (see Psalm 138:2, KJV) will see that it is not.

"Then the Lord passed by in front of him and proclaimed, 'The Lord, the Lord God, compassionate and gracious, slow to anger, and abounding in lovingkindness and truth'" (Exodus 34:6).

JANUARY 5
The Eternal Adventure

I will, by God's grace and power, keep the center of my life adjusted strictly to God's will, and let God keep the periphery any way He desires. *(surrendered)*

I will seek holiness (which results in wholeness), without which no man can see the Lord, at all times. Wholeness is God-centeredness, the "one thing needful," the "one thing I desire and seek after," the "one thing I do."

I will not pray for peace, power, success, or fruit, for they are by-products of a relationship, not its conditions. They are God's responsibility, not mine.

Neither will I seek promotion, honors, recognition, or acclaim, for they also are by-products and therefore outside my sphere. Nor will I resent others to whom God gives these tokens, but I will praise God that His will has been done in them.

I will no longer strive ambitiously for ends, for God's purpose is process, not destiny. I never hope to arrive but rather to continue with God in an eternal adventure, the result of which is a continual knowing of Him who is the "end" God seeks for me.

I will accept the fact that the self-life is not only displeasing to God; it is His enemy. When self reigns, I am at war with God, and that leads to frustration, anxiety, and misery. I will therefore crucify the self-life and be at peace with God.

I will realize that when all is said and done, I owe my daily overcoming to this one, solid fact: "Christ lives in me" (Galatians 2:20). Therefore, I can say honestly, "Thanks be to God, who gives us the victory through our Lord Jesus Christ" (1 Corinthians 15:57).

"No one can serve two masters; for either he will hate the one and love the other, or he will hold to one and despise the other. You cannot serve God and mammon" (Matthew 6:24).

JANUARY 6

The Shame of the Cross

I will learn to accept, and even enjoy, God's humiliating me. I must learn that God disciplines me by embarrassing me. He did that with Simon Peter. "Get behind Me, *Satan!*" (Matthew 16:23, italics added). If I do not shame myself, that is, if I do not sense my need to the point where I feel shame, God will do it for me. To feel shame is really to judge myself; and Paul says if I do not judge myself, God will have to do it for me (1 Corinthians 11:31–32).

To be ashamed before God is painful; to be put to shame by God is more painful; but the worst pain is to be put to shame by the world. God wants to hurt me to correct me, so the world will never be able to get a lick at me. Now I know what Paul meant in 2 Corinthians 7:8–10 about godly sorrow working repentance.

God put Jesus to shame and grief (Isaiah 53:10), but not for Himself; it was for me. There was nothing in Jesus that shame could improve. His shame was my shame, in order that I might improve. The shame of the cross is constantly being worked out in me daily. If I accept it, then I enjoy Isaiah's word, "He who believes . . . [on Him] . . . will not be ashamed" (28:16, Amp.).

It does me good to wear sackcloth occasionally. I need to sit in the ash pile. God has no spoiled children, and He applies the rod as often as I need it to learn. If He shames me, it is because He loves me. He decrees that good will come of me, that His image will be formed in me. To that end, He shames me into sonship, but only that His eternal glory may radiate from me, for what son is there who is not disciplined by his father (Hebrews 12:7)? God is treating me as a son (v. 6). Hallelujah for the rod!

"It is for discipline that you endure; God deals with you as with sons; for what son is there whom his father does not discipline?" (Hebrews 12:7).

JANUARY 7
Becoming Angry with God

I must realize that unless I get angry with God occasionally my dedication is not worth a wooden nickel. Jeremiah got so frustrated with God that he said God was like a "deceptive [changeable] brook" (Jeremiah 15:18, NIV). Further, he vowed he would not prophesy for Him any longer (20:7–9). The only person who never got angry with God was Jesus, and that was because He understood His heavenly Father so perfectly. Anger is a sign of two things: I do not understand, but I care. God would rather have me angry with Him than indifferent to Him.

I must be certain, however, that my anger is not peevishness, like Jonah's. Peevishness says, "God won't let me have my way." Concerned anger says, "I can't see the relationship between what God says He will do and what He is doing." David's frustration with God because of the death of Uzzah is a lesson to me (2 Samuel 6:6–20). David was angry because he sensed a contradiction in God, righteousness versus grace. That is the way it is with me. When God becomes angry with me, it is because of my sin and rebelliousness; when I become angry with Him, it is because of His righteousness, which I think is rigid.

God is not shocked by my occasional anger. But I must be quick to confess it. Chronic anger will lead me to cynicism, which God hates. Confessing my anger is a sign of faith. It says, "I don't understand any better, but I trust God anyhow." I must never assume that because I get angry with God I am a poor believer. On the contrary, it is a sign of a developing relationship with Him. If I am always correct with God, I do not know Him personally. When I am free to become angry, I am free to become myself. And being myself, I am free to grow toward Him. That is the key: to keep growing toward "the stature of the fulness of Christ" (Ephesians 4:13, KJV).

"Do not be eager in your heart to be angry, for anger resides in the bosom of fools" (Ecclesiastes 7:9).

JANUARY 8
The De-nesting Process

I will accept God's "de-nesting" of me without remonstrance. To be de-nested by God is a sign that He feels I am reaching a level of maturity. As a new Christian I am given personal, fatherly attention by God for my growth's sake. A new convert receives the quickest, fullest answers to prayers of any Christian. Later on, God will seem to ignore my prayers. That is because He feels that now I am beyond the need for assurance; I can rely on His naked Word.

My first real shock as a Christian comes when I begin to feel the de-nesting process. I am like a child being weaned. God no longer seems close, familiar. The "joy of . . . salvation" (Psalm 51:12) dims and may return only periodically. Feeling must give way to faith; dependence to independence. God begins to put me in alien hands, even Satan's (cf. Job 2:6). He calls in other teachers to perfect my growth. Even Jesus was not exempt. He was put "into the hands of men" (Matthew 17:22), not for His own sake, but for mine. His de-nesting began with the incarnation and ended with His burial. But the process for Him was nothing other than self-sacrificial. Mine is always educational.

The de-nesting process goes on throughout life. That is why I can never have absolute tranquillity here. The moment I learn my lesson in one pair of hands, God farms me out to another. The important thing is my growth; what I *feel* is unimportant. God looks for the image of Christ in me, not for my comfort. I may feel very upset, discomposed, fruitless, and aimless, and yet He rejoices because He finds Jesus in me. It is a mark of tremendous growth when I see God rejoicing and can rejoice with Him. It is positively thrilling to realize I can rejoice the heart of God.

"The eternal God is a dwelling place, and underneath are the everlasting arms" (Deuteronomy 33:27).

JANUARY 9
The Success of Obedience

I must learn what Jesus learned: to be "obedient unto death" (Philippians 2:8, KJV). All true obedience is unto death. That is a reversal of the world's standard. "I will obey *if*" is what the world says. The *if* means there must be a happy ending. Anyone will meet conditions, even drastic ones, if he gets his own way in the end. But that is not the obedience of Christ. His example was, "I will obey *regardless*." For Him, the "regardless" was not a heavenly deliverance but a cross.

True obedience is always successful. It always accomplishes God's will. It is immaterial to me whether my cancer is cured, my promotion achieved, or my loved one saved. If I have obeyed, that is enough. I am successful. Beyond that, it is God's business. If I insist on a happy, selfish outcome, then I am meddling. The instant I obey, success is automatic—God's success, not mine. Therefore, obedience carries in itself its burst of praise. I am jubilant, not because my ship has come in, but because it has gone out. Maybe I will never see it again, but that is beside the point. The point is, I have launched it unto God and now He is responsible. So I praise God because He is working and I rest in His activity.

I must be careful to obey for obedience's sake, and to love obedience for the Lord's sake. What a level to live on, loving it for His sake! In this I have the example of my Master, who said, "I delight to do your will, my God" (Psalm 40:8, TLB).

"Trust in the Lord with all your heart, and do not lean on your own understanding. In all your ways acknowledge Him, and He will make your paths straight" (Proverbs 3:5–6).

JANUARY 10
Justified Before God

I will realize that the war with my self-life is daily, even hourly. I cannot reach a state in which the war ends and I am permanently delivered. Not in this life. The self-life is natural to human beings, and after each victory over self, the old tendency begins to turn me back to the fleshpots. It is an everlasting war, a relentless struggle, a continuous fight. But it is not hopeless. Christ imparts His life to neutralize the self-life; and as I trust Him, He puts it to death. But I must keep trusting Him to keep putting it to death, or else it will return to damage me.

I will always be prepared to justify my attitudes, motives, and behavior before God. Instant confession is my means of keeping myself clean in the light. I must keep short accounts with God and be ready to give an explanation to Him on demand.

I will not demand that God explain Himself to me at any time, for this is characteristic of the unregenerate man. I must be willing to let God be unreasonable, in my view, if necessary, because He is not concerned with my understanding but with my faith. The unregenerate man sees contradiction in the world and demands that God justify Himself before him; the believing man makes no such demand but believes God supremely. He is only concerned with keeping himself justified before God.

I will endure hardness as a good soldier of Jesus Christ. The soldier executes the will of his officer. This means the soldier must be other-directed and other-compelled. To look inward is fatal to the man of war, but to look upward is both his salvation and joy. I will at all times seek to "please Him who called me to be a soldier" (see 2 Timothy 2:4).

"So let us know, let us press on to know the Lord. His going forth is as certain as the dawn; and He will come to us like the rain, like the spring rain watering the earth" (Hosea 6:3).

JANUARY 11
People Are Redeemable

I must learn to distinguish between "human nature" and "people." Jesus did not trust human nature, for "He Himself knew what was in man" (John 2:25). Paul said he had "no confidence in the flesh [human nature]" (Philippians 3:3). Further, he said he did not want to know people according to the laws of human nature (2 Corinthians 5:16). I must pattern my relationships to people as Jesus did.

But that is where I fail. How can I distrust human nature without rejecting people? How can I love someone whose nature I cannot trust?

I have to bring a third person into the relationship. It must be a triangle. I must never relate to anyone without including Jesus in the relationship. If I do, I will either become disappointed or suspicious. I must realize that while human nature is not redeemable, people are. God cannot save human nature, but He can save a person from his nature. "God so loved the world"—the world of people, not the principle of human nature.

If I expect too much of my loved ones and friends, I will be disappointed. But I can expect infinities of them if I am trusting Jesus in them. It is "Christ in you" who is "the hope of glory" (Colossians 1:27). I must always look at people—enemies, friends, family—not as "you" but as "Christ in you." Then my enemies will not become threats and my loved ones will not become snares.

Lord, I need to keep my temper and feelings out of the way and let nothing interfere with "Christ in them," which gives me hope for what would be a hopeless task otherwise. The potential person, not the real, is my goal; and the potential keeps me from groveling in despair.

"Therefore from now on we recognize no man according to the flesh; even though we have known Christ according to the flesh, yet now we know Him thus no longer" (2 Corinthians 5:16).

JANUARY 12
Good in Others

I will acknowledge that to be easily hurt, offended, intimidated, alarmed, or upset is really a manifestation of the self-life; it is because I am not getting my own way, or I am not accorded the place I think I deserve, or I am not given the share I think I am entitled to. To feel forever cheated, deprived, alienated, or isolated is to taste what the unregenerate man will taste forever—hell.

Christ died not only to forgive my sins but to break sin's hold on me. Why should He bind the strong man only to release him to renew his attacks on me? To indulge sin is to forfeit one of God's richest privileges, the personal power of the cross in my life. The power of the cross and the power of sin are mutually exclusive; one or the other dominates me.

I will look for good in others, but I will not be surprised if I find evil. If I find evil, I will not feel personally rebuffed, as in the case of a friend who has failed me, or someone who has not lived up to my expectations. To feel rebuffed or hurt in such cases is an expression of the self-life. I will accept human beings as I find them—persons capable of redemption but just as capable of evil—and I will accord them the same treatment as Christ did. He did not rely on them, but neither did He exclude them. He was not personally hurt by rejection, only sorry for the rejecter. He was not vengeful or vindictive toward those who hurt Him. He gladly forgave and kept offering forgiveness. When He saw a glimmer of faith and love, He rejoiced.

The glory of Christian discipleship is to see the miracle of the emerging person, "the new man in Christ," and to realize I have had a part in his newness under the hand of God. Then I am able to say with Christ, "I and the children God has given me" (Hebrews 2:13, Berkeley).

"Now those who belong to Christ Jesus have crucified the flesh with its passions and desires. If we live by the Spirit, let us also walk by the Spirit" (Galatians 5:24–25).

JANUARY 13
God and Nothing

I will make You the basis of my trust, Lord. I will accept Your demolition of my security, even though it is painful. When I was a young Christian I thought everything was God—and. It was God—and blessing; God—and power; God—and fruitfulness. Now I see that everything is just God—and nothing.

Now I fully understand why God tested Abraham's faith by telling him to sacrifice Isaac (Genesis 22). God gives, but He also takes away. He *must* take away. God will not have me trusting anything other than Himself, not even a good, lovely thing like Isaac. God gives me vibrant health, then He takes it away and leaves me weak and clinging. Why? To show me where my ultimate trust should be. No sooner do I find something in which I can boast than God takes away the object of my boasting. Not bad things, but good things! Sermons, books, and articles tell me constantly that the Christian life is the greatest, the most exciting, the most rewarding life available. But they miss the point! They tell me God *adds* so much to me. As a result, my Christian life can become a shambles through false expectancy. What really happens is that God *takes away* so much. He continually removes from my life everything that would make me earthbound, self-dependent, or experience centered.

Why were so many of the Corinthian Christians "weak . . . sickly . . . and [dead]" (1 Corinthians 11:30, KJV)? Because a *thing* had come between them and God. God will tolerate no "thing" between Himself and me—even so dear a thing as my "Isaac." But He will take nothing away without adding the larger dimension of Himself to take its place. Once I have given my dearest to Him, I will hear Him say, "Now I will *really* bless you" (see Genesis 22:17).

"Yet those who wait for the Lord will gain new strength; they will mount up with wings like eagles, they will run and not get tired, they will walk and not become weary" (Isaiah 40:31).

JANUARY 14
Using, Not Possessing, Things

I vow to my God that I will no longer practice *accumulation* but *dissemination*. The world and the flesh are always after me to gather in, to collect, to secure myself against illness, old age, catastrophe, and death. Jesus sent His disciples out with the word: "[Take] neither gold, nor silver, nor copper in your purses, nor a bag . . . neither two coats, neither shoes, not yet a staff" (Matthew 10:9–10, NSRB). Strange equipment for His spiritual army! And yet, how wise! The soldier who enters a battle overloaded is already defeated.

I must learn to use things without possessing them, as Paul did (2 Corinthians 6:10). I am to seek first the Kingdom of God and His righteousness, then I will not need to worry about my daily necessities. God gives me *things* to use and to enjoy, not to idolize.

When I can no longer use something, I must give it to someone who can. Jesus was the great "giver-upper." When He died He owned nothing.

I must beware the world's cry, "You need this or that or the other thing." The world is always telling me what I need; and if I listen to such talk, I will accumulate forever and yet never find satisfaction. How can the world tell the disciple what his needs are? Only the great Pioneer of all disciples can do that (Hebrews 12:1).

How true was Bunyan's picture of Vanity Fair. The main street was covered with stalls, each one possessing an attractive ware, and each stall keeper rushed out into the street to drag customers in to buy. The world cries, "Buy, buy, buy!" But the wise pilgrim will move right along, never daunted, never turned aside.

Only in Christ is there sanity, and only the pilgrim is wise. Paul's word to Timothy was: "God has . . . given us a spirit of . . . power and love and discipline" (2 Timothy 1:7). What a heartening word of healing in a broken world!

"But seek first His kingdom and His righteousness; and all these things shall be added to you" (Matthew 6:33).

JANUARY 15
To Obey Is Better

I will realize that God expects only one thing of me—obedience. This obedience must be prompt and entire. I must leave no "bleating sheep" around. I must not try to develop faith, love, or hope, for these things are elements of obedience. Nor must I try to develop spiritual power, for this is the result of obedience. Obedience is my concern; the results of obedience are God's concern. Obedience is God's way of testing my discipleship; therefore, God's commands may sometimes seem strange to the natural mind. I must obey God's commands as literally as possible; there can be no "spiritualizing away" what God tells me to do.

I will accept Christ as my life as well as my Savior. He is the way, indeed, but He is also the way-shower. He shows me the life that pleases the Father, and thus I can avoid the mistakes of the opposite kind of life. He died for my sins, but this was only to make way for the goal He has for me—His life in me. It is life, not death, that God is interested in. Whenever death occurs it is only a means to an end, and the only life that pleases the Father is that which the Son exhibited on this earth. Being "saved by His life" (Romans 5:10) is literally and necessarily true. Christ's life is the absolute antithesis of the self-life. As I lift up my life to Christ's, I can immediately see my raggedness against His perfection. Then there must be confession of sin and surrender to that life. Then I please the Father also. "Christ who is my life" is more than a motto, a catchword. It is a glorious reality, for Christ makes me more alive than any other person can. And the life He gives me carries me forward with its inborn drive to glory (Colossians 1:27).

"Behold, to obey is better than sacrifice, and to heed than the fat of rams" (1 Samuel 15:22).

JANUARY 16
A Pocket Full of Holes

Lord, do I have pockets full of holes (Haggai 1:6, TLB)? Am I praying more but enjoying it less? Am I forever sowing but never reaping? You have said, "Seek ye first the kingdom of God, . . . and all these things shall be *added*" (Matthew 6:33, KJV, italics added). Lord, that is my trouble. I have been thinking too much about material things, such as savings, insurance, and retirement. You have made it clear, Lord, that it is in not thinking about those things that they are guaranteed to me.

Lord, I need heaven's economics. There is no supply and demand law in heaven, because there is no limit to the supply. My need is supplied "according to His riches in glory" (Philippians 4:19), not according to a finite amount.

Lord, teach me the mystery of the feeding of the five thousand. I have always thought it meant that Jesus is the Son of God. Now I see it means more than that. The multiplying is one of heaven's mysterious laws in which the spiritual is tapped for the sake of the material. How shrewd and sharp Satan was when he said to Jesus, "Command that these stones become bread!" (Matthew 4:3, ASV). He was right when he said (or implied) Jesus could make bread out of anything; but he was wrong when he, not the Father, issued the command.

Lord, I am surrounded by infinite, mighty resources, invisible perhaps to me, but always at Your fingertips, ready for instant conversion into the material for my benefit—if I should ever need them. So, Lord, keep me from worrying about things in which the natural man puts his trust. Poor man, his visible means of support is pitifully frail! God, let me never think myself poor like that! May I always be grounded in Philippians 4:19.

"And God is able to make all grace abound to you, that always having all sufficiency in everything, you may have an abundance for every good deed" (2 Corinthians 9:8).

JANUARY 17
Loving God's Best

I will put myself under the questions of Christ, one of which is, "Lovest thou Me?" This question was first addressed to a disciple who momentarily misplaced his affections. Christ is very jealous of my love and feels rejected when it is spent on the world. I cannot take my love for granted, for it dies from lack of nourishment. It must pass the test: "Do you love Me *more than these?*" (John 21:15, italics added). It is well that Jesus left the object indefinite when addressing Simon, for his "these" were different than mine.

Men usually love things or beings because of value received. I am to love Christ because of His nature, His character, His being. I must love Him because I see spiritual beauty in Him, because in Him are perfect morality and purity. To love Him, therefore, is to show affinity with God, who also loves the same things that are found in Christ, and in such perfection that He can say, "In whom I am well-pleased" (Matthew 3:17). To love the world is to choose the less than perfect, the less than highest, and therefore to cross swords with God, who says the highest is Christ. No wonder God says the worldly Christian is a spiritual adulterer!

The language of love is, "What more have I to do with idols?" (Hosea 14:8). The result of love is discrimination, for we cannot love two objects equally. Yet loving Christ means more, not less, love to others because God has "poured out his love into our hearts by the Holy Spirit" (Romans 5:5, NIV). I positively cannot love Jesus Christ with all my heart while I love others less than myself.

"And though you have not seen Him, you love Him, and though you do not see Him now, but believe in Him, you greatly rejoice with joy inexpressible and full of glory" (1 Peter 1:8).

JANUARY 18
The Simple Life

Dear Lord, I will try by Your help to live the simple life. Kierkegaard said the pure life was the single life, willing one thing. Distraction is my enemy, and the world's function is to distract me. Jesus teaches me to have a "single eye," which I understand to be an eye fixed on a single goal or object. Purity is allowing no distractions. There is a carelessness about the simple life. It allows for steadfastness and concentration.

The longer I live the more I realize that the Kingdom of Heaven must be "taken by force." To enter the Kingdom is the easiest thing of all, but to let the Kingdom enter me is the most difficult. Why did Jesus call John the Baptist one of the greatest? I think it was because of his single-mindedness. John did not know diversion. He was like an arrow.

Some things I do in the Christian life are effortless—preach a sermon, lead a soul to Christ, write an article. Other things—vastly more important—are so difficult they command my whole strength and time—learn about God, know God, imitate and obey God. Those are the abiding things, like faith, hope, and love.

God, You never told me how hard the way was. You let me find that out for myself. If I had known, I never would have followed. But having begun, I cannot turn back. That backward road leads to nowhere and to nothingness. To go forward is hard but it promises its reward. "That I may know Him" was Paul's cry (Philippians 3:10). So it is mine. Life's greatest reward is to know Him! The joy of the captured heart! There is no elation like that of knowing I am claimed, I am included, I am purposed. The rejoicing of Luke 15 is not only over the lost one who has been saved, but also the saved one who has been reclaimed.

"But Jesus said to him, 'No one, after putting his hand to the plow and looking back, is fit for the kingdom of God'" (Luke 9:62).

JANUARY 19
To Be or Not to Be Ambitious

I must refuse all attempts at being ambitious, especially spiritually ambitious, which can be my greatest stumbling block. A Christian often gladly surrenders the ambition to be rich, famous, and powerful, and thinks himself a favorite of God. But he often retains ambitions that are just as disabling, such as the ambitions to be the most powerful preacher, to win the most souls, to write the most influential books, or to be the greatest spiritual leader. He justifies those ambitions because they are "for the Lord's sake," but in reality they are self-centered. They are no different, except in dress, from the ambitions of the unregenerate man.

A true disciple has no personal ambitions whatever. He is not concerned with ambitions; they are not germane to his function in God's Kingdom. To have any kind of ambition for oneself is to indicate a mind independent of God. To do God's will is the disciple's function, and God does not always make His will clear beforehand. It is worked out in clarity but not clearly predicted before the "working out." So I always must keep my life open and clean for the Lord to write in His will. Having personal ambition is writing my own will for myself.

Thank God I need not direct my paths, for He has promised to do that (Proverbs 3:6). Once I surrender my ambition, He will often say, "Go up higher" (Luke 14:10, KJV). But going up higher means nothing to the man of God unless his Lord makes it the expression of His will. He rejoices in the will of God for its own sake, not for any personal gain that may come out of it.

"But you, are you seeking great things for yourself? Do not seek them" *(Jeremiah 45:5)*.

JANUARY 20
Destroying God's Image in Others

Lord, I will learn the reconciliation of the heart. I do not get along with people, not because of their words or ways, but because of my heart. Jesus said, "Why do you think evil in your hearts?" (Matthew 9:4, Berkeley). I meet with failure when I attribute evil motives to people's actions. I say, "He said, but he *meant*." What I do not realize is that what I *think* he meant is nothing more than my suspicious nature at work. "Love *thinks* no evil" (1 Corinthians 13:5, author's trans.). When Christ possesses my mind, His total love pushes out the dark and suspicious sides of my mind.

Lord, when will I realize that to judge (attribute improper motives to) my brother means that I am doing You as well as him a disservice? I am destroying Your image in him, for I must believe that You are working in him as well as in me. Judging others is the grossest form of self-worship. It says God is working in only *me*.

Lord, teach me what Jesus said about the mote and the beam. I see motes in others because I have beams in my own eyes. If I truly saw the evil in my own heart, I would not condemn; I would confess. I see now what Paul meant when he said, "To the pure, all things are pure" (Titus 1:15). My faultfinding means I have more to learn, more to grow, and more to do.

Lord, let me not be guilty of murder—murdering Your image in others by defaming their actions. I vow to look for Christ in others, as Bishop Whipple, a missionary to the American Indians, did, and let my relationship to Him condition my relationship to my brothers. When I do this I will be surprised to find two things: first, the increasing ministry I have to others; and second, "the beauty of the Lord our God" will be upon me just as really as I see His beauty in others (Psalm 90:17, KJV).

"But you, why do you judge your brother? Or you again, why do you regard your brother with contempt? For we shall all stand before the judgment seat of God" (Romans 14:10).

JANUARY 21
Dust Between the Toes

I must avoid being a "no part with Me" disciple (John 13:8). This kind of disciple has not merely sinned; he has remained unconscious of sinning. There is no hypocrisy here, certainly not deceit, but simple carelessness or ignorance. But Christ is strict about the matter, and if Simon Peter feels that a little dust between the toes is insignificant, then he will hear the Lord say, "You have no part with Me."

Having no part in Christ means that His *blessing* power turns to *pleading* power. The flow of one stream must stop and the flow of the other must be turned on. This means a loss of efficiency as the outflowing virtue of Christ is temporarily checked. If I have no part *in* Christ, those around me will have no part *of* Christ. It is essential to God that He has channels through whom to work; it is also essential, as Jesus made clear, that those channels be clean (Isaiah 52:11).

Having no part in Christ also means that His *showcase* becomes a *confessional* box (Job 1). I am no longer on display, no longer pointed to, until I have allowed Him to wipe off the last trace of mud. God's pride in me has turned to grief over me (Ephesians 4:30); and until I grieve like-mindedly with Him, I cannot expect to be "daily His delight" (Proverbs 8:30).

Jesus exposed Simon Peter's slovenliness, but only because Peter had exposed the Lord to shame. Happily, Peter immediately dipped his feet and removed the irritation between himself and Christ. "Now ye are clean" (John 15:3, KJV) is a statement of fact but also of pleasure—the exquisite pleasure of Jesus Christ when He makes us one with Him in spiritual purity. Once again we have "part in Him." Then comes His peace, which is His very own (John 14:27), and His joy, which is always full (John 15:11).

"But put on the Lord Jesus Christ, and make no provision for the flesh in regard to its lusts" (Romans 13:14).

JANUARY 22
Enduring Contradictions

I will promise to learn what Jesus experienced, the "contradiction of sinners against himself" (Hebrews 12:3, KJV). So often my best friends become a "snare" (Matthew 16:23, Berkeley). Jesus had to suffer the contradiction of Simon Peter against Himself. What harder trial than to have your most loyal supporter unconsciously become your worst enemy? But Jesus "endured" it (Hebrews 12:3, KJV).

This is where I fail so often. I do not endure. When opposed by a brother, I feel sorry for myself, lash out in anger, or shrug the whole thing off with a moral philosophy, "That's the way things are." How much better for me to learn something from the contradiction. Why should I waste a valuable commodity like a contradiction when it has so many educational benefits for me?

To be contradicted means I can shape my brother, my opponent, and he can shape me. It is a diamond cutting a diamond. God does not send me contradictions to harass me (only Satan harasses; God always disciplines and educates). He sends those contradictions because there is still something in my character (lack of patience, maybe?) that needs His correction. And likewise my contradictor has a defect that God intends to correct.

Lord, teach me how to endure, as Jesus did. Teach me that snares and obstacles, traps and offenses are only means of reaffirming my ministry to which You have called me. If I keep my eye on the goal as Jesus did (Hebrews 12:1–2), I will endure. Maps and snares never bother the disciple who is steadfastly looking at his Pioneer and Guide. When the "contradicted One" is in me and is in control, He will enable me to cut through the forests of contradictions like an experienced woodsman. He has gone before me. Now He turns to give me what He has—the life of unruffled trust.

"Therefore, gird your minds for action, keep sober in spirit, fix your hope completely on the grace to be brought to you at the revelation of Jesus Christ" (1 Peter 1:13).

JANUARY 23
Skinned Shins and Bruised Knees

Lord, do I know You as my stumbling stone or my building stone? If I am not properly related to You, I will surely stumble over You, as Peter did (Matthew 26:31). How often You have been offensive to me, Lord, when I wanted my own way. You offended me when I wanted to choose certain friends, or other things that the flesh craved, and You would not allow it.

There is only one place for the foundation stone, or the cornerstone. If it is not in its proper place, I will only stumble over it repeatedly. I find that when I do not put You in Your proper place, the result is pain.

Your cross, Lord, is often offensive to me, just as it was to Peter. I often crave a "glory" religion, a religion of feeling, fame, joy, and happiness. I do not like a "cross" religion, the drudgery and misery of dealing with people deep in their sins and failures. I do not like saying no to myself, I do not like being put on the cross. Peter wanted a kingdom and position and power. So do I. He could not bear to see it all go down the drain via the cross. How often he hurt himself stumbling over You!

Yet I read, "Who for the joy . . . before Him endured the cross" (Hebrews 12:2). Jesus found joy in that miserable cross, while I shun it. Not only that, but via the cross He found victory, sitting at God's right hand. God will not deny me victory or power (He desires that for me), but He says I will get these things only by enduring the cross. So if I keep bumping up against God, something is wrong with me. If my feet are bruised it is because I am rebelling, not submitting. But if I submit, the joy of the cross will see me through many a dark day. This joy is not the cross itself, but its aftermath, for God always deals with ends—final realities—not routes to them. I look for God's end, my "posterity" (Psalm 37:37), through my cross today.

"And he who does not take his cross and follow after Me is not worthy of Me" (Matthew 10:38).

JANUARY 24
His Burden Is Light

Have I ever really felt the "burden of the Lord"? If I have, there will be times when I will be sick and tired of the Lord's work and wish that I had never heard of His name. Lord, I have felt that way at times. I have sometimes felt ashamed when preaching, not of *how* I preached but of *what*. The gospel sometimes has embarrassed me, and I longed to be free from having to care for people and from having to announce a message that begins with human sin.

The Lord's "burden" is heavy, not as heavy as my sin burden, perhaps, but heavy just the same. Yet the Lord's "woe" is even heavier. "Woe is me if I do not preach the gospel," said Paul (1 Corinthians 9:16). How could Jesus say, "My yoke is easy, and my burden is light" (Matthew 11:30, KJV)? A "burden" by definition cannot be light (easy). He was the only Spokesman for God who never complained about the burden. It does me no good to say, "But He was God!" He was man, too, and in becoming man He set aside all the privileges of Deity.

No, I think the answer is that Jesus' manhood was whole. He never knew deviation or exception. He willed one will with the Father *always*. But I am plagued with vacillation—one day feeling so spiritual I could give my body to be burned, and the next day resenting the phone call that drew me from my bed in the middle of the night.

My message is a burden because it demands consistency and total dedication from me. It would be intolerable unless He who found His burden so light helped me. But He assures me that though the rivers swell, they will not drown me; and though the fires rage, I will not be consumed (Isaiah 43:2). That is the glory of the disciple of Christ; he is burdened only to fly, and he is put to death only to live.

"I know, O Lord, that a man's way is not in himself; nor is it in a man who walks to direct his steps" (Jeremiah 10:23).

JANUARY 25
God the Multiplier and Diminisher

Lord, I promise to accept You as my diminisher as well as my multiplier. How often I have rejoiced in the word, "He turneth the wilderness into a standing [pool of] water" (Psalm 107:35, KJV)! Even more, I have rejoiced in seeing that very thing happen. Modern Israel is a demonstration of that word. And spiritually, many hearts and lives are testimony to it.

That is what You did for me, Lord, when I first heard Your name and gave my heart to You. The barren wilderness became green as the water of life started to trickle through my life. Fruit and flowers began to grow, and people began to notice and comment on them. That was the delightful life, and it still is when Your water makes my life green and beautiful.

But just as You multiply, so You can diminish. Just as You make me heavy with fruit, so You can dry me up like a desert skeleton. "He turneth rivers into a wilderness, and the [fountains] into dry ground" (Psalm 107:33, KJV).

God diminishes me when I turn away from Him and seek other gods, such as fame, wealth, pleasure, and pride. I may be pleasant, like Naomi, but if I move from God's land to Moab, the place of idols, my name will quickly become Marah ("bitterness"). I must remind myself of the many others in the Bible whom God diminished, such as Herod, Sennacherib, Nebuchadnezzar, Gehazi, Pharaoh, and Ananias and Sapphira.

And yet, if I stay myself continually upon Him, He will multiply the little that I have. My barrenness will give way to fertile fields, and my puny strength will chase a thousand. I will be able to say with David, "By You [my God] I can run through a troop, and by my God I can leap over a wall" (Psalm 18:29, Amp.). Lord, let me never know You as my diminisher, but always as my multiplier. You are sufficient for this, Lord; no one else is.

"I will go before you and make the rough places smooth; I will shatter the doors of bronze, and cut through their iron bars" (Isaiah 45:2).

JANUARY 26
Living in God's Present Time

I will no longer serve the clock but, rather, the timeless plan of God. To be continually wrapped up in time, always conscious of it, hoping or yearning for some future thing while dreaming joyously of some past thing, is frustration. I must be past as well as the future, and live in the present. I must do this because I now *am* my past, those experiences have already worked themselves into my life, so it is foolish to try to scrape out the honey that has already been eaten and become part of me.

I cannot dwell on the future, because I do not know what God has in store for me; so dwelling on it is fantasy, and fantasy is not reality. But the present is real, alive, active, important. To miss God's purpose for me today is to cripple my future as well as to neutralize the beneficial lessons of the past.

To be confined to a time clock is to tell God when to work. Schedules have their place, but God operates independently of them. However, I must be sure I have God's reason, not a fleshly one, for interrupting a time schedule.

The only schedule I must keep is a "day" schedule, even as one was kept by Jesus, who worked "the works of Him who sent [Him], as long as it [was] day" (John 9:4). I must remember that God does not publish His schedules (except rarely); therefore, I must live by faith. Faith says, "Lord, You have Your *eye* on my schedule and Your *hand* on me; You will bring us together." Faith, when it is strong, already rejoices that this eventual meeting is an accomplished fact!

"But do not let this one fact escape your notice, beloved, that with the Lord one day is as a thousand years, and a thousand years as one day" (2 Peter 3:8).

JANUARY 27
The Faces We Wear

L ord, what kind of a face am I wearing right now? Help me to realize that whatever kind it is, that's what You are reflecting back to me. Teach me carefully what David meant when he said,

> With the merciful, You are merciful,
> With the perfect, You are perfect,
> With the pure, You are pure,
> And with the stubborn, You are stubborn.
> Psalm 18:25-26 (author's trans.)

My face determines You, Lord, just as a child's face determines the mother or father. When the child has hurt himself and turns a piteous face toward his mother, instant pity is the result. But when the child grows sullen and rebellious and throws a surly look toward his mother, look out! I see now what C. S. Lewis meant when he was trying to be reconciled to God through Christ and God said to him, "Wipe that look off your face!" God will not be reconciled with surly birds.

How do I see my own face? How do I know what mood I am wearing? I must look continually into the Word of God, the "mirror" that reminds me of what kind of man I am. I am the greatest of fools if I lose contact with my face, if I imagine myself to be one thing while the mirror tells me I am something else.

Lord, not only You but my friends and neighbors are constantly scanning my face to see what news there is in the heart. Does my face tell them of a Christ who is abundantly able, or do they see a Christ still lying in the tomb? How thrilling it is to realize that Christ's face can be seen in me (2 Corinthians 4:6). If He is alive in my heart, my face will be alive with His glory; if He rules me inwardly, He will shine from me outwardly. Jesus Christ is my spiritual cosmetic.

"Thus says the Lord, 'Let not a wise man boast of his wisdom, and let not the mighty man boast of his might, let not a rich man boast of his riches'" (Jeremiah 9:23).

JANUARY 28
Christ's Love Need

Lord, I promise from now on to be more sensitive to Your love need. I have been selfish in this, thinking only of *my* love need and how I could satisfy it. I have bent myself in prayer before You, begging for conscious evidence, however slight, of Your love for me. How one-sided!

I hear You say, "Do you love Me . . . ?" (John 21:15) and wonder why You ask, You who know all things. Now I see what You mean: "I know you love Me; now, demonstrate it, evidence it." Love is never satisfied with abstractions, only personal tangibles. "Give Me a drink," You ask (John 4:7). You know that inwardly I am giving You something to drink all the time, but still You demand that I do it outwardly. A startling thought: the all-sufficient One asks that I make Him complete. The Lover needs loved ones; the Savior needs sinners; the worshiped One needs worshipers. I am not sure I understand this, Lord, but if it is not true, then John 3:16 is a meaningless hoax.

When I was a younger Christian, Lord, I thought my love for You must be proved by exploits. Now I realize that You are far more concerned with my fellowship. "Remember Me." Not "Die for Me" or "Risk for Me," but simply "Remember Me." Love's requirement is ridiculously simple. "Just be there for Me." How often, Lord, have I brought my grocery list to You instead of simply opening the door and letting You come in to sup with me and I with You! Even though You are in heaven, glorified, You still have need to sit down with me and become one with me in personal fellowship. Now I understand what You meant when You said, "The Lord's portion is His people" (Deuteronomy 32:9). Holiness is Your greatest *requirement*, but Your people are Your greatest *delight*. Lord, help me to delight You with a hundred ways of expressing my love for You.

"Keep yourselves in the love of God, waiting anxiously for the mercy of our Lord Jesus Christ to eternal life" (Jude 21).

JANUARY 29
The Soldier's Will Is the Key

I will be soldierly at all times. The chief requirement of the soldier is the surrender of his will. Other things are irrelevant. The disposition of his time, his duties, and his responsibilities is entirely in the hands of his commander, and they are not his business. If Christ has my will, He will also have my body, my mind, my strength, my ambitions, my inclinations, my attitudes, in short, my all. The will is the key. When I am tempted it is in the will that the victory will be won or lost. Temptation gives me alternatives: I can submit and lose or resist and win. There is ample power for either. Christ gives me power to resist; my old nature gives me power to submit. But the key is the will. If I will to resist, Christ will empower me as He has promised; if I will to submit, I only need to let the old nature take over. Whoever has my will is my master. I therefore must decide daily, hourly: shall Christ have my will, or shall it be some other master? The decision is instantaneous; the results are eternal.

My hope is based on the twofold action of God: "God . . . is at work in you, both to will and to work for His good pleasure" (Philippians 2:13). While God does not make up my mind, He strengthens my resolve. Even more, He brings my resolution to a finished product "for His good pleasure." Thus, I can honor the Lord's intent and say, "It can be done."

"Suffer hardship with me, as a good soldier of Christ Jesus" (2 Timothy 2:3).

JANUARY 30
The Image of Himself in Us

He shall see of the travail of his soul, and shall be satisfied" (Isaiah 53:11, KJV). Lord, what is the travail of Your soul? I used to think it was Your sufferings on Calvary, the nails and the thorns. I am sure that is a very basic part of it, but I also think there is more. The mother travails to bring her baby into the world, then she travails a lot more to bring that infant to maturity. True of all mothers, but how much truer of God, who brings forth spiritual children!

I know You travail for me, Lord, but my question is: Are You satisfied with Your work? Has Your travail for me—Your crossly sufferings, Your painstaking discipline, Your heartfelt concern—been in vain? Has every correction turned out wrong? Is my heart as unmoved as when You first began to chip away at it?

You said, "Ephraim is a flat cake not turned over" (Hosea 7:8, NIV). Lord, am I, like Ephraim, an unfinished product, an embarrassment to You, a repeated failure who cannot seem to make the grade? Can You display me proudly as You did Job, "Hast thou considered my servant Job?" (Job 1:8, KJV).

I once heard a mother scold her son for a disobedience. She said to him, "How can I be so proud of you one moment and so ashamed of you the next?" That spoke to my heart. Certain words in the Bible cause me fear: "marred" (Jeremiah 18:4, KJV); "castaway" (1 Corinthians 9:27, KJV); "ashamed" (1 John 2:28, KJV). These have been written, Lord, that I may take Your travail for me with utmost seriousness and realize that to be a disciple of Jesus is not playing games. But "You are my hope; O Lord God" (Psalm 71:5, Amp.) that I will "never be put to shame" (v. 1). I trust You to "increase my . . . honor" (v. 21) by building me into the image of Your Son.

"But we all, with unveiled face beholding as in a mirror the glory of the Lord, are being transformed into the same image from glory to glory, just as from the Lord, the Spirit" (2 Corinthians 3:18).

JANUARY 31
When to Sit Still

Lord, there are times when I must be a "Do Nothing" disciple. Those times are when everyone else is scurrying about in a frenetic and distracted manner. Sometimes true spiritual strength, as Isaiah says, is to "sit still" when the emergency arrives (Isaiah 30:7, KJV).

As You know, Lord, it takes an enormous amount of strength to be inactive when such inactivity, to the natural mind, is irrational. How irrational (seemingly) was Moses' command, "Stand still, and see the salvation [deliverance] of the Lord" (Exodus 14:13, KJV). To do nothing when the enemy was pursuing so hotly was the height of foolishness! Yet Moses' command was a shrewd understanding of what an emergency was.

Lord, an emergency does not mean disaster to a disciple; it means a crossroads. The emergency means God's word is vitally at stake. The emergency gives rise to the question, "Is your God . . . able . . . ?" as King Darius asked Daniel in the lions' den (Daniel 6:20, Amp.). The den was not Daniel's death chamber but his pulpit. There God's word was vindicated.

When Gladys Aylward, a missionary to China, was summoned by the prison warden to stop the convicts from rioting in Yengchang, it was an emergency—a call to put God's Word to the test. Was God able to protect His servant as she stood in front of the murderous prisoners? God was! And by that "emergency" God's Word had free course from then on in that Chinese city.

There were times when Jesus opened His mouth and taught marvelously. But there were other times when He "gave . . . no answer" (John 19:9). So there are times when I must make no excuse, cite no reason, but just sit. This is what it means to "be still, and know that I am God" (Psalm 46:10, KJV).

"For thus the Lord God, the Holy One of Israel, has said, 'In repentance and rest you shall be saved, in quietness and trust is your strength'" (Isaiah 30:15).

FEBRUARY 1
Spiritual Education

I will give attention to proper spiritual education. I will realize that a liberal arts education, while fine in itself, is of no value to me in seeking the secret things of the Most High. Man by his reason did not find God, says Paul. The gospel is foolish to the learned man; spiritual things are so much spinach also. Only God can teach spiritual lessons to His children, and those lessons are learned by the inner working of the Holy Spirit. To depend upon such things as reason, investigation, research, analysis, and comparison to learn God's ways is folly. A moment of the Holy Spirit's illumination will reveal what man can never discover by the natural tools of learning.

Reading the Bible, therefore, is a spiritual exercise, as much a part of the heart as the head; as much to do with character as brain. Bible study is the total person coming into alignment with the Holy Spirit, not a separatistic brain figuring out the problems of the text. Man cries for understanding, but there is no understanding apart from illumination, and no illumination apart from the Spirit. When He reveals truth, the Bible becomes amazingly relevant, not distant and historic. He makes the Bible a now thing, its message as pertinent as if my problem just now came to heaven's attention. I see myself there in that Book, my problem as clearly identified as if God wrote it purposely into the Bible for my benefit, and the answer as personal as a direct word from Him.

Jeremiah saw the spiritual meaning of God's word: "Thy words were found and I ate them, and Thy words became for me a joy and the delight of my heart" (Jeremiah 15:16). When the Bible is my food, joy, and delight, it means I have gone past the intellectual to the spiritual comprehension of the Bible and have encountered a living Person.

"For who has known the mind of the Lord, that he should instruct Him? But we have the mind of Christ" (1 Corinthians 2:16).

FEBRUARY 2
Life Between Brackets

Lord, You are teaching me that I must always live my life between brackets. No condition of my life is ever permanent. God brings about every condition; He also ends every one. If I am in sorrow today, God will bring me out of it tomorrow. If I am blessed with material things today, that does not mean I can expect to be rich tomorrow.

Why does God give us changing, altering conditions? I think it is to give us balance. God does not want one-track minds in His Kingdom. Too much wealth leads us to "trust in uncertain riches" (1 Timothy 6:17, KJV). Too much sorrow leads us to despair. The combination is just right. The land to which the Israelites were traveling was "a land of hills and valleys" (Deuteronomy 11:11). There cannot be hills without valleys.

That comforts me, Lord. The distressing situation that nags and embarrasses me today must give way to something better (or at least different). Patience says, "Wait, God will set it right." The ecstasy of God's blessings must be received with a sober thought; tomorrow it will be gone.

Now I see what Your Word means when it says Moses "endured, as seeing him who is invisible" (Hebrews 11:27, KJV). It is in seeing the invisible One that I keep myself in perfect balance. I cannot *endure* seeing my brief, ever changing circumstances. I can endure only by looking to the One who ends those circumstances at will. Lord, my vow is this: I will patiently look to the only constant and reality in my life—God Himself. Then I will understand what the psalmist said: "The Lord will perfect [bring to terminus] that which concerneth me" (Psalm 138:8, KJV).

"And you shall remember all the way which the Lord your God has led you in the wilderness these forty years, that He might humble you, testing you, to know what was in your heart, whether you would keep His commandments or not" (Deuteronomy 8:2).

FEBRUARY 3
Riding in Christ's Procession

I will not steal from Jesus Christ the position that is rightfully His, the position of conqueror. My place is to ride in the train of His triumph, to ride *behind* Him as His captive. I realize now that I have often tried to mount His chariot and push Him out, taking the honor and glory for myself. I have not always been content to be His captive; I have tried to be His successor.

Being a captive is not a glorious thing in itself. It is not the limelight or the chief place. All the glory goes to the Conqueror. My function as a captive is to show the glories of the Conqueror, to display to the world the principles of His triumph in me. To do that I must constantly let Him have center stage. If I pout because I have failed, because I am not recognized, because my expectations did not materialize, I am really challenging the right of Jesus Christ to ride in the lead chariot. I am crying for the spotlight to search me out and bathe me.

I must learn that God does not make captives to glory in them, but to make captives whose very presence enhances the conquering power of His Son. Only in this way do I become "a sweet savor of Christ" to God (2 Corinthians 2:15, NSRB). If I enhance myself, it is not a sweet savor but something nauseating to Him.

If I want to join the praise of heaven, it must be on the basis of "Worthy is the Lamb" (Revelation 5:12). That is the heart of it: worthiness. It is not only that Jesus is my Lord, but He is *worthy* to be Lord. When I see this, I will not have to wait to get to heaven to throw my crown at His feet; I will do it now in anticipation—and do it gladly because of His worthiness.

"But thanks be to God, who always leads us in His triumph in Christ, and manifests through us the sweet aroma of the knowledge of Him in every place" (2 Corinthians 2:14).

FEBRUARY 4
Thinking Rich

Lord, I promise that by Your help I will never poor-mouth You again. Most of Your children do not need a dose of poverty; they need a dose of faith.

"All things are yours," You told us through Paul (1 Corinthians 3:21, KJV). But most of the time I have not believed this word. I have lived as a pauper, a beggar, in spite of what You distinctly said, "The Lord . . . daily loadeth us with benefits" (Psalm 68:19, KJV).

I have often come to the end of the day feeling distressed and unhappy. My talk before the group fell flat; my visit to a spiritually hungry soul was fruitless; a prominent Christian did not call on me for prayer—worse, he did not even remember my name; and the expected letter did not arrive.

So I tossed on my bed, feeling cheated, left out, denied. Lord, is this the portion You had for me?

You have tried to teach me, Lord, that all things are mine in Christ. Also, You have tried to teach me that You select the daily portion meant personally for me from the great storehouse of "all things." What a rebel I am, Lord! My nightly unhappiness is simply childish rebellion against Your portion for me during that day. I need to master the idea that what happens in my life each day is what You send. It is Your portion, wrapped in the ribbons of love. Each day yields what You send and I cannot lose it. Nothing planned for me is denied me. Whatever arrives is heaven's recipe.

Yet You have said, "All things are yours." In Christ, I am heir to the universe. I vow to remember my wealth and think rich. I vow to remember that my daily portion, whether bitter or sweet, is given by Your love and cannot be lost. I will receive all that Christ has for me. This, Lord, will banish the inferiority and bring quiet acceptance.

"Correct me, O Lord, but with justice; not with Thine anger, lest Thou bring me to nothing" (Jeremiah 10:24).

FEBRUARY 5
Seeing the Invisible

Teach me, Lord, that spiritual maturity is all a matter of directness. The child depends upon its mother for food, warmth, protection, and speech. All of this is indirection. Maturity means directly assimilating what I need.

Jesus is my example here. "I have food to eat of which you know nothing" (John 4:32, Amp.). What food? The food of direct partaking. Out of the spiritual realm Jesus appropriated nourishment, and by faith He was fed.

I sometimes feel jealous of the disciple John's faith. "He saw and believed" (John 20:8). What did John see? Nothing! Yet he believed. Lord, I desire to see beyond the tangible, as John did, to the spiritual and, seeing that, to believe. My sight is so short, so powerless. It cannot escape space and time; it is trapped by the fleshly veil. If I could only see that heaven is not far away, that God is not remote, that divine resources are not hopelessly beyond me, but near, realizable, and available.

The more I think about it, Lord, the more I realize that great saints live in another world, feed on another food, see intangible things, and believe that which is plainly rubbish to the world. Like Moses, they constantly see the "invisible." And like all powerful saints, they realize the spiritual and bring it into actuality. Jesus, the King of saints, did this when He fed the five thousand.

The heroes of faith (Hebrews 11) were people who lived in another world; but they maintained contact with this world in order to provide for earthlings the fruit of that other, more real, world.

So today, Lord, You are looking for spiritual heroes again. The world needs them so desperately. How I long to be one of them!

"While we look not at the things which are seen, but at the things which are not seen; for the things which are seen are temporal, but the things which are not seen are eternal" (2 Corinthians 4:18).

FEBRUARY 6

Holy Carefreeness in Love

Lord, I promise to love You with a holy carefreeness. I promise it will not be a measured, dosed-out thing. "Love never falls short" (1 Corinthians 13:8, author's trans.). The Pharisees' rigid rules-and-regulations devotion was not love of You; it was love of themselves.

Love is not love unless it results in abandon. That is why Jesus highly praised Mary's offering of perfume that she poured over His feet. A waste? Never! An abandonment! If Mary had calculated her offering to an exact dose, it would not have been love; it would have been ostentation.

"Perfect love casts out fear" (1 John 4:18). If I am afraid of God, I do not love Him. When I am afraid to offend God, I am thinking of myself, not Him; therefore, my love has evaporated. Lovers of God have a characteristic childlike boldness that is all innocency. A stranger approaches a king with timid deference, while the king's son strides into his presence.

I see now what Ezekiel's river was (Ezekiel 47). The river flowed from the Temple with increasing depth—ankle-deep, knee-deep, loin-deep, then deep enough to swim. Lord, You want me to be a swimming Christian, abandoned to You in love so that I am carried away by it. Only twice in His earthly ministry did Jesus call attention to giving—once when the widow gave her two mites, and again when Mary emptied her jar over His feet.

The measured, careful, calculated gift is not a love action; it is a duty. How shameful to be loved out of duty! If I am concerned with niceties, I am not concerned with God, only with my reputation. Love "does not seek its own [reputation]" (1 Corinthians 13:5). I want to love You with abandon, Lord, and thus show how completely worthy You are of my love. I want to love You to shamelessness, the same kind of shamelessness that put You on a tree for me.

"And this I pray, that your love may abound still more and more in real knowledge and all discernment" (Philippians 1:9).

FEBRUARY 7
The Spared Self

I promise with Your help not to spare myself, Lord. How loathsome this self-saving is to You is clearly indicated in the words of Jesus to Peter. When Peter said to Him, "Never, Lord! . . . This [the cross] shall never happen to you!" (Matthew 16:22, NIV), Jesus turned very forcibly to His disciple and said, "Get behind Me, Satan!" (v. 23, NIV).

Self-pity is of Satan. I think I can see why, Lord. Self-pity is a wall of defense around the "self" in which the self is defended against everyone—including God. If Jesus had pitied Himself, He would never have gone to the cross. If I pity myself, I will never submit to the lethal principle of God's will and, therefore, never become the means of life to others.

Self is like Ananias keeping back part of the money he had promised to give to the Lord (Acts 5:1–2). Self is forever telling me to keep back a part of myself. It considers total dedication to God a "waste" (Mark 14:4, KJV). In the language of Jesus' bystanders, it begs Him to come down from the cross and save Himself (Mark 15:30).

I must understand, of course, that self-pity is not the same thing as self-preservation. Accepting Jesus as my sin-bearer is self-preservation, the noblest thing I can do. Resting when I am weary and going on a vacation when I need a change are forms of self-preservation and are wise.

There is no cure for self-pity except in death—spiritual death. And spiritual death comes to the one who says yes to God in whatever He wants to do with him. It is impossible to say yes to God and pity myself at the same time. It is my choice to make. When I say yes to Him, He responds with an almighty yes to me, and I rise from the death of crucifixion into newness of life.

"I have been crucified with Christ; and it is no longer I who live, but Christ lives in me; and the life which I now live in the flesh I live by faith in the Son of God, who loved me, and delivered Himself up for me" (Galatians 2:20).

FEBRUARY 8
God's Word About Our Bodies

I will strive to ignore feelings. Spiritual ecstasies are helpful, and even necessary, to the babe in Christ because he has not learned to walk by faith. But God is most honored when I simply take Him at His word, not when I am looking for spiritual dessert. If I do not have spiritual ecstasies, therefore, it is because God thinks I am capable of the strong meat of faith and obedience.

And those other feelings—fear, anxiety, doubt, worry—I must nail to the cross. Since they are mostly products of my body—its glands, blood, and digestion—to listen to them is to be earthy and animal. I cannot reason with them any more than I can reason with undigested potatoes. I can only ignore them, force my mind to think of better things, and know that God is far greater than a gland, a stomach, or a corpuscle.

It really boils down to this: Shall I listen to God's Word about myself or to my body's word about myself?

Victory comes when I deliberately say to my body: "I ignore you!" and when I say to my soul, "Hope you in God" (Psalm 42:5, Amp.). When I hope in God I am deliberately cutting past my moods, which ebb and flow, to a solid anchor, an unchangeable mooring. Not to have moods, of course, is not to be human; but to succumb to my moods is certain defeat. Hoping in God is a timeless remedy for a temporary mind-set.

"Therefore we do not lose heart, but though our outer man is decaying, yet our inner man is being renewed day by day" (2 Corinthians 4:16).

FEBRUARY 9
Praise and Belief Go Hand in Hand

I promise to value praise more than before. Praise is the natural outgrowth of trust. The one who truly believes will automatically praise God. Before, I thought praise should come *after* the act was done. I asked, God answered, so I praised. But this is weak, sickly praise. Jesus thanked His Father before He raised Lazarus. I should look at problems, difficulties, impossibilities, and then praise God ahead of time for the opportunity of glorifying His name. If Romans 8:28 is still in the Bible, and believable, then praise should characterize my life.

Difficulties, to the Christian, are only miracles that have not yet happened. Faith cannot tell time very well. To say we should praise only after the miracle has occurred makes no sense to faith. Faith means God *will* just as much as God *has*.

So if I am to always believe, then I should always praise, since perfect trust eliminates worry and anxiety and fills me with good feelings.

To live a life full of praise, I must thank God for evil circumstances as well as thank Him when I am in evil circumstances. The difference is whether I am going to endure evil or make it a vehicle of blessing. The Bible tells me that God is not complacent about evil, but He uses it for a greater good.

When God surrounds me with harassments, He is preparing me for a breakthrough to victory and growth that He could not accomplish in any other way. So, in a sense, evil circumstances are my friends and I should welcome them as much as David welcomed the lion and the bear, which made him ready for Goliath. If I welcome them, I will praise; and if I praise, they are no longer my enemies but my conquests. Therefore, as James advises, I will "rejoice and jump for joy" when surrounded by impossibilities (James 1:2, author's trans.).

"Praise the Lord! For it is good to sing praises to our God; for it is pleasant and praise is becoming" (Psalm 147:1).

FEBRUARY 10
Yielding to God's Claims

I will be a *methodist* in the true sense of the word. The psalmist said: "I will pay my vows unto the Lord now in the presence of all his people" (Psalm 116:18, KJV). God calls for my vows every once in a while, even as He called for Abraham's Isaac. The vow is one of "test and response" by which God continually proves my love for and faith in Him.

However, I must beware of being legalistic. I must not surrender anything God has not claimed. God claims definite parts of me when He feels I am ready for the discipline of giving them up. It is my job to go about my business till He puts in a claim. Then I am to respond with alacrity.

That is the truly disciplined life: yielding a claim instantly, without question or hesitation. I believe no life amounts to anything in His service until it is disciplined. The disciplined man does not spend his time thinking how much he can get; he keeps watching for God's signal to pay the vow and then he leaps to do it.

Paying the vow must be done with the "sacrifice of thanksgiving" (Psalm 116:17). I must be extremely grateful that God puts a claim against me. I also must realize that when God puts in a claim, He plans to reward the one who responds, not necessarily with riches, health, and comfort, but with what is more important—spiritual power and effectiveness.

God is unhappy with me when He has to tell me twice about giving up a claim. If He asks for my money, He should not have to ask me again. Once yielded, I should never remind God of a claim or keep needling Him about how much I have sacrificed. It is no sacrifice to give up peanuts for gold nuggets. I must therefore "*bind* the . . . sacrifice with cords to the horns of the altar" (Psalm 118:27, italics added). It is in the binding that my life abounds.

"Then Jesus said to His disciples, 'If anyone wishes to come after Me, let him deny himself, and take up his cross, and follow Me'" (Matthew 16:24).

FEBRUARY 11

Fussiness About Time

I will try to be less earthy and more heavenly in my attitudes. Worldliness is being earthbound, a substitution of the heavenly for the here and now. Earthiness is expressed in many ways, such as time, place, property, money, and pleasure. I cannot free myself physically from these restraints, but I must do so spiritually. The Bible tells me I must live in the heavenlies, where Christ now is "seated at the right hand of God" (Colossians 3:1). This means a substitution of heaven's ways for earth's ways.

Concerning time, I must be heavenly minded, not earthly minded. My daily life involves the clock; and the more I bind myself to it, the less I follow the heavenly schedule. The only clock Jesus paid any attention to was the clock of His Father's will (John 9:4). This must be my clock. If I am rigid with a schedule, fussy about being late, worried because I have wasted time, anxious for a certain moment to arrive, distressed because I have missed my plane, I am not yielding to my Father's timetable. I must press on to the place where "time shall be no more." If I am occupied with time, it means something is amiss in my spirit. The person who is absolutely at peace pays no attention to time.

Jesus said, "My time is not yet come: but your time is always ready" (John 7:6, KJV). Jesus had no schedule; He just did His Father's will as it was impressed upon Him; but His friends were schedule-bound. I am constantly faced with an alternative: shall I obey God or the clock? To do the latter is to be locked into earthiness, a quality Jesus never manifested. Idleness is not a matter here, for God's will never means idleness. When I deeply abide in Jesus, time will cease to be, just as really as if I were already in heaven.

"So teach us to number our days, that we may present to Thee a heart of wisdom" (Psalm 90:12).

FEBRUARY 12

Competition with Others

I must beware of one of Satan's subtlest traps—competing with others. Jesus knew nothing of competition; He only knew service. Too often I am like the disciples, striving who should be greatest (Luke 22:24) and forgetting that the greatest of all is he who washes the feet of others.

Competition is really warfare, and the only competitor I have is myself. Competition is a Pandora's box that releases a number of negative feelings toward others. This must be discouraged. But I must encourage negative feelings toward my own pride, laziness, self-will, love of praise, and unwillingness to put myself out for others. I must avoid the religion of comparison, for God's plan for me is as individual and distinctive as the formation of a snowflake. A true disciple compares himself with himself, and he is able to say, "The Lord has enabled me to grow in that particular discipline."

Competition is one of Satan's flaws. The moment God said to him, "Have you considered [seen] My servant Job? For there is no one like him" (Job 1:8), Satan was in a fit to bring Job down. Satan could not stand God's praise of Job; he wanted it himself. Whenever I am tempted to pattern my life or behavior after someone else, I must hear Jesus say: "What is that to you? You follow Me!" (John 21:22).

Competition ceases the moment I follow Paul's advice: "Give preference to one another in honor" (Romans 12:10). This kind of striving is for the lowest, not the highest, place. Imagine that, striving for the humblest spot! Yet wasn't this the path chosen by Jesus, who "humbled himself . . . even [to] the death of a cross" (Philippians 2:8, KJV)? Lord, give me excellent marks in thus following *You!*

"For consider Him who has endured such hostility by sinners against Himself, so that you may not grow weary and lose heart" (Hebrews 12:3).

FEBRUARY 13
The Wounds of God

I will respond to Your "hurtings" with grace and, yes, gratitude. Too often I look upon God as the mender of broken hearts and the binder-up of our wounds. He does this, thank God. But He also breaks hearts and causes wounds.

Can I forget how Jacob went away limping from wrestling with the Lord (Genesis 32:30–31)? Do I limp where God has touched me? Even His wounds were inflicted for my sake, not His. He needed no correction or discipline, but I needed an infinite amount, so much that it was impossible for me to measure up. So Jesus stood in for me and bore the wounds that I should have borne.

In the meantime, God hurts, wounds, and stings until He lays bare the very inmost secrets of our hearts, challenging us to a stronger, fiercer love for Him.

When Jesus asked Peter, "Lovest thou me?" He hurt him. Peter was "grieved" over that question (John 21:17). Has the Lord ever grieved me? If I have never experienced His grieving, correcting, rebuking, or chastening, I know very little of Him.

We have been lulled to sleep on easy believism and cheap grace. It is so easy to mentally accept certain doctrines without allowing them to filter down into the daily living of life. God wants crucified men, not merely men who believe in the cross. He looks longingly for servants who say, "I love [You], . . . I will not go out free" (Exodus 21:5, KJV).

Lord, are my ears pierced, my heart broken? Do I limp because of my thigh? The wounds of the Christian are God's applause for a life well lived. Are You applauding me, Lord?

"For those whom the Lord loves He disciplines, and He scourges every son whom He receives" (Hebrews 12:6).

FEBRUARY 14
Proving God

I promise to fulfill my function as a "prover of God." That is every Christian's function, regardless of his occupation or spiritual gift. A prover of God brings God out of the Bible and makes Him alive today.

God loves to be proved. "Prove me *now*" (Malachi 3:10, KJV, italics added). "Ask a sign for yourself from the Lord" (Isaiah 7:11). He knows that each generation is born skeptical. The Bible must be reborn to every generation. God must break out of print into live action and re-create Bible scenes and activities. Just as God wrote the Bible, so He must repeat the Bible in us. That is why He needs Abrahams, Gideons, Davids, and Pauls today. In short, He needs God-provers.

George Mueller said he began his orphan home in Bristol for one purpose, "To prove God in our day as formerly." Exactly! So with us.

Proving God, however, is not easy. It involves the impossible. You do not prove God when you pray for a healing that will occur naturally. Or when you ask God for $10,000 when you already have $20,000 in the bank. Proving God is asking Him to cure the *incurable*. It is asking Him to give you $10,000 when you have nothing.

But who is sufficient for those heroics? Isn't life fairly humdrum and prosaic? Doesn't God come in the "still small voice" (1 Kings 19:12, KJV)?

If so, there is something wrong with our faith. If Satan is still alive, if sin is still man's habit, and if disease, hunger, and death still stalk, then God must find "provers." He needs the ordinary man who has extraordinary faith.

The question is, am I willing to risk embarrassment and failure to be a prover of God? That is the nub of it all—to dare God and risk everything on His simple Word. Provers of God are always winners with God.

"Ascribe to the Lord the glory of His name; bring an offering, and come into His courts" (Psalm 96:8).

FEBRUARY 15
Sacrificial Preaching

L ord, am I a Christian by indoctrination or revelation? If I am merely parroting truths that have been dictated to me, woe is me and woe is any congregation that listens to me.

When Christ met Paul on the Damascus road, He revealed Himself to His former enemy. Afterward Paul did not confer with flesh and blood but escaped into the desert to receive further revelation (Galatians 1:15–17). Later, when he emerged to preach Christ, it was an incarnational message he preached, not one learned at the foot of a teacher.

All divine knowledge is received inwardly. Christian education has its place, but only to make Christ's revelation to me *possible*. It cannot make that revelation *actual*. Too many Christians are around today who have taken on the culture of Christ without taking in His person. What is worse, too many spokesmen for Christ in the world are like the disciples before Pentecost—surrounded by Christ but not invaded by Him. After Pentecost the disciples did not need to be taught; they only needed opportunity to release what had been revealed. What had formerly been meaningless words now became truths that seared their hearts.

If Jesus did not dare to speak from Himself (John 7:17), how dare I? If Jesus spoke only what was revealed to Him by the Father (John 7:16), how can we possibly preach anything unless it is revealed to us? What we need in our pulpits are men who talk about God based on firsthand knowledge. God revealers will never lack an audience. I will do what Habakkuk did: "Station myself on the [watch] tower, and watch to see what He will say to me" (Habakkuk 2:1, Berkeley). It is what God says to me that becomes the message people longingly desire.

"Then the Lord stretched out His hand and touched my mouth, and the Lord said to me, 'Behold, I have put My words in your mouth'" (Jeremiah 1:9).

FEBRUARY 16
Learning How to Lose

Lord, I will try to learn the lesson You have been teaching me all my Christian life—how to lose. The Christian life is the life of great losses. The natural man always wants to come in first; the true disciple of Jesus learns how to come in last.

Look how Jesus lost. He lost the confidence of John the Baptist (Matthew 11:3); He lost many disciples (John 6:66); He lost his dignity, respect, and clothing (Matthew 27:29, 35); and most important, He lost His life.

Look how Paul lost. "For [Christ's] sake I have lost everything" (Philippians 3:8, Amp.). That "everything" included his life.

I will never amount to anything for Christ until I attend my own funeral. A disciple is like a house in a cyclone; every part gets blown away bit by bit until there is nothing left but the foundation. Then God builds a new structure. The trouble with me—and with most Christians—is that I want to live; I dislike dying. Paul said something profound about that: "Death works in us" (2 Corinthians 4:12). Lord, there have been many times when death did not work in me at all.

This is difficult to understand, Lord. I thought at first that the Christian life was verve, joy, vitality, victory, and an eternity of heavenly ecstasy. That is the way You treated me at first. Then the stripping began. What a list! Friends, health, ambitions, loved ones, and even common, human desires. God's plan for my life seems at times to be a story without a plot. God my Friend has often seemed to be God my enemy.

I am thankful for Him through whom all the promises of God are "yes" (2 Corinthians 1:20). When I deliberately make my life a no for His sake, He responds by making it a victorious yes.

"And let the favor of the Lord our God be upon us; and do confirm for us the work of our hands; yes, confirm the work of our hands" (Psalm 90:17).

FEBRUARY 17
Everyone Needs a Burning Bush

I will not forget, Lord, what the burning bush means. What did it mean to Moses? Exactly what You said it would mean: "This will be the sign to you that it is I who have sent you" (Exodus 3:12, NIV).

A sign! How many times, Lord, have You spoken to me through a sign? Possibly none of them was as dramatic and arresting as a bush that burned and yet was not consumed. But signs nevertheless. For the important thing about a sign is not what it is but what it points to. And Your signs have pointed me to the same all-powerful One as the burning-bush sign pointed Moses. The God of the burning bush was to become the God of the Exodus. And the God of the Exodus became the God of the Red Sea deliverance.

Moses was able to do such marvelous exploits because he believed in that kind of a God. And he believed in that kind of God because of what he saw at the burning bush. The burning-bush experience created a *foundation* for Moses' faith. If God could do *that*—

All of God's actions for us are designed to build a platform underneath our faith. That is why I must have a personal burning bush. Someone else's experience is valuable to me only as an incentive. But that incentive does nothing for me inwardly unless it leads me to a burning-bush experience in which spiritual reality becomes conviction.

Every child of God needs his burning bush, the place where God is so real he can no longer doubt, no longer equivocate, no longer rebel. He will never be the same person afterward. His remaining life may have its share of trials, burdens, and afflictions, as did Moses', but it also will have its victories and triumphs. The burning bush tells us of a God who is so real that He dares us to doubt.

"For I am confident of this very thing, that He who began a good work in you will perfect it until the day of Christ Jesus" (Philippians 1:6).

FEBRUARY 18

God Moves in a Circular Way

Lord, I promise I will not balk any longer at Your "circles." In my Western way of thinking, I have always assumed that God moved in a straight line. But years of studying God's Word and ways have taught me that He always moves in a circle. That is why God is often mysterious, perplexing, and dark to me. Once I learn the secret of His circles, all becomes clear.

Look at Joseph. God promised him power and authority in his dreams; yet instead of directly fulfilling the promises, God led him to slavery and to prison, the very opposite. Why? Because God's dealings with us, like the lines of space He created in the universe, are circular.

Even Jesus was treated in this circular way. He left the Father's home to go out to mankind, down through the cross to the tomb, then back up and home again. This history is clear to everyone. What is not clear is that God uses the same route for all of us.

Why does God deal with us in circles? Why does He promise us things, then deny them? Why does He cause us to hope, then give us disappointment?

Because God is in the business of making *saints*, not programs. To develop spiritually involves outgrowing things that are no good for us and implanting things that are necessary. That takes time.

We are all on a circle, at one point or another. The apogee is the most distressful time because there *everything* seems to have gone wrong. But that point, also, is the greatest time to trust because it starts the turn back. Lord, let me never give up too soon!

What encourages me immensely is that God constantly supervises my journey on the circle. At whatever point I may be, He knows. His determination is to bring me "home." And that will be my greatest exulting!

"And we know that God causes all things to work together for good to those who love God, to those who are called according to His purpose" (Romans 8:28).

FEBRUARY 19

How Not to Fear Judgment

Lord, I will give attention to Your reminding me that eternity is *now*. I have been bombarded by announcements that in the "sweet by and by" all things will be settled and I shall reach my rest and reward. But that is only partly true. Unless I make the right decisions and direct my feet properly now, there will be no sweetness in my by-and-by.

The old statement "Heaven and hell are right here on earth" is not totally true. But it is partly true. Hell is simply the ultimate confirmation of sin, and sin can be confirmed in this life as well as the next. So can godliness. As Oswald Chambers said, "The penalty of sin is confirmation in sin." If I allow hardness and perverseness to set in, sin begins its confirming work immediately. Only the blood of Christ and the indwelling Holy Spirit can stop, turn, and reverse sin's deadly work. That is why a once-for-all decision, in which I rest upon one moment's experience for a lifetime, is dangerous. I must engage in a daily, moment-by-moment walk with Christ if I am to avoid the deathly hardening of sin. The cross of Christ is sufficient for me only as I make it efficient in my life.

Should I, as a Christian, fear death? What is death? What else but God's servant who brings home the ones who are to be prepared for examination. Death is fearful to the one who is not ready. But to the one whose life has been a daily cramming for the finals, it is a welcome signal, a signal that will bring his whole life to realized fulfillment.

How true, Lord, that eternity is now. To wait for its dawning is to wait too late. "Now is the acceptable time" (2 Corinthians 6:2, ASV). Lord, continually teach me this lesson; yes, write it upon my heart.

"And now, little children, abide in Him, so that when He appears, we may have confidence and not shrink away from Him in shame at His coming" (1 John 2:28).

FEBRUARY 20
Praying from a Close Relationship

I will renew with God my covenant of prayer. Theoretically, I have always believed in prayer. Practically, my life has been strewn with pleas that were never answered.

How can I square such failure with the clear teaching of Jesus? "Ask, and it shall be given" (Matthew 7:7); "whatever you ask in My name, that will I do" (John 14:13).

Jesus encourages me to ask anything, to ask repeatedly and unashamedly, and to keep on asking until the answer comes.

But haven't we been taught to pray "If it be Thy will"? Shouldn't we defer to God's sovereign control of things and try to get on the inside track with Him before asking?

However, there are conditions to answered prayer. (1) I cannot "regard iniquity in my heart" (Psalm 66:18, KJV), that is, give iniquity place, time, and attention. (2) I cannot "ask amiss," that is, to further my lustful desires (James 4:3, KJV). (3) I cannot be "wavering" (James 1:6–7, KJV), that is, wanting something so little that it really makes no difference whether I get it or not. (4) I must "abide" in Christ (John 15:7). To abide in Him means to be drawn toward Him as a flower is drawn toward the sun.

Now I begin to see what answered prayer really means: a life of total dedication to God, a life lived in Him that is so real that I can discern His desires, His mind, His will. If I pray from the midst of that intimate relationship, my prayers will never fail. When I reach that point I will never need to ask, "If it be Thy will." The Christian who keeps asking God for the benefit of His will does not know Him in a deep, abiding way. The Christian who is constantly a delight to God will be one to whom God will reveal His mind.

"And whatever we ask we receive from Him, because we keep His commandments and do the things that are pleasing in His sight" (1 John 3:22).

FEBRUARY 21
The Sin of Clutter

The Lord has spoken crisply to me lately through Leviticus 21:18 (KJV), which says the priest shall not have "any thing superfluous." God will not tolerate any monstrosity or curiosity in His holy place. Of what use is the extra part, the additional member? A sixth toe or finger may not be diseased, but it certainly will obstruct service. Am I guilty of extra baggage or extra weights that I have been commanded to lay aside (Hebrews 12:1–2)? I must distinguish between what is possible and what is expedient. When Jesus sent out the seventy (Matthew 10), He reduced them to a basic expediency: *one* purse, *one* cloak, and *one* pair of sandals. No heavy metals, no lingering, and no nonsense. There was work to be done, and the baggage-laden disciple was simply asking to be swept out of the race.

The trouble is, my expediency is always too large. I have a distorted view of the necessary. God says, "Flee Sodom and Gomorrah," and I, like Lot's wife, keep looking back to see if I can drag my possessions with me. The Lord says, "Strip yourself for battle," and I load myself with every thingamajig in the armory because I have to be prepared for *every* eventuality. Lord, teach me like Mary to cling to the "one thing . . . needful" (Luke 10:42, KJV). Deliver me from Martha's extra baggage of worry, anxiety, and fear. Help me to say yes to Your definition of what is basic and no to my continual sin of clutter.

Jesus was the most uncluttered Person in all history. Not one sliver of extra baggage did He carry, even down to His thoughts, feelings, and emotions. His naked body on the cross was a symbol of His perfection in simplicity. Lord, let me learn of Him!

"Therefore do not be anxious for tomorrow; for tomorrow will care for itself. Each day has enough trouble of its own" (Matthew 6:34).

FEBRUARY 22
Being Topsy-turvy for God

I must be careful not to be a topsy-turvy Christian. The world will make me that if I let it. I have to walk through life with God's corrective lenses, but this means training my eyes to see properly. The Jews of Thessalonica complained that Paul and Silas had "turned the world upside down" (Acts 17:6, KJV). From whose standpoint? According to his critics, Paul's gospel seemed crazy. He was called, as was Hosea, a fool and a madman (Hosea 9:7). But, from God's standpoint, Paul and Hosea were simply putting things back in their proper place.

I have noticed, Lord, when my faith grows weak and my love grows cold how easy it is to rationalize my condition. I can see why Judas could convince himself to sell Jesus. How easy it is to support unbelief by logic! The worldly minded Israelite had no difficulty finding Egypt rather pretty and Assyria a land of charm. Demas could have found a hundred reasons for forsaking Paul. If I choose to walk the world's way, I can easily manufacture reasons for doing so without any effort.

Lord, help me to realize where "right side up" is. The lenses of the world are twisted, distorted, opaque. Teach my spiritual mind to "re-see" according to the new lens of the Holy Spirit. Let me not succumb to the world's "be sensible, be reasonable" when I know that what makes sense to the world is utter nonsense to You. "The world through *its* wisdom knew not God" (1 Corinthians 1:21, ASV, italics added). Lord, let me be a fool and mad for Your sake!

"For My thoughts are not your thoughts, neither are your ways My ways,' declares the Lord" (Isaiah 55:8).

FEBRUARY 23
Going Beyond Feeling

Lord, so often my religion stops in the emotional. We sing, "O Lord, send the power just now," and we usually mean feelings. We think if the service is especially touching, if tears flow, if we feel humbled and tender, God's power has come upon us. Not necessarily. We must go beyond feelings to life. The prophets were most emphatic that repentance show itself in justice, in equity, in helping the fatherless and the widows, and in relieving the poor. To them, a right attitude toward God meant a kind, gracious attitude toward others. The emotional service is excellent if it serves to rend our hearts instead of our garments (Joel 2:13). If we experience a humbling before God, then straightway forget what manner of men we are, our hearts have been left unrent.

Lord, so many decisions are made today based on feelings. But once the feelings are past, we tend to return to our former ways. "A hundred people came forward!" "Scores came to the altar!" Fine and well. But does that mean a hundred broken hearts? Does it mean a hundred disciples? A hundred Christian soldiers? Lord, You need followers of the Lamb and spiritual virgins, not those who merely come forward. It is easy enough to go forward, but how crucifying to go back to Mr. So-and-so and love him for Christ's sake!

Sackcloth and ashes, ripped clothes, and fatty sacrifices mean very little unless they are expressions of my inward rendered heart, where the very roots of my life are transformed and all mankind is made the better for it. I thank You, Lord, that when You give us the power of Your Spirit, it always is "in the *inner* man" (Ephesians 3:16, italics added). That is where we need it, down in the roots of our personality, where life-changing action always occurs.

"Behold, Thou dost desire truth in the innermost being, and in the hidden part Thou wilt make me know wisdom" (Psalm 51:6).

FEBRUARY 24
Holy Laughter

Lord, I promise I will learn more perfectly from You the art of holy laughter. The laughter of men is based on the incongruous—the fat man unable to blow up a balloon or the thin man able to eat a ponderous meal. But Your laughter, Lord, deals with absurdities. C. H. Spurgeon laughed at the absurdity of a tiny mouse worrying lest Joseph's granaries should run out of wheat. Sarah laughed at the absurdity of her conceiving and bearing a son in her old age (Genesis 18:12). So did Abraham (17:17).

Holy laughter is the result of a sharp, clear faith. And faith in the word of an all-powerful God makes human problems look absurd. Holy laughter is more than a sense of humor. It is a gift that results from spiritual sight. A sense of humor can be innate, worldly, and cruel. But the gift of holy laughter is the result of a sharpened spiritual vision, the ability to see the huge mountain range of God's ability high above the plain of human frailty.

Holy laughter is also a correct view of ourselves. God's commands to us are often so unusual they catch us—and others around us—by surprise. It is in the "surprise," the difference between what we think God nicely ought to do and what He actually does, that holy laughter comes. For example, read the story of Rees Howells, founder and former director of the Bible College of Wales, and his giving up one meal a day, by God's command. How could he possibly convince his mother that God asked him to reduce his meals to two a day as an act of obedience and discipleship? Her concept of God was a nice God who would never ask anyone to give up what was good for him!

Lord, I thank You for the times of holy laughter You have given me. May I never go without them, for when I do, my eye is too dim to see either You or myself with crystal clarity.

"Then our mouth was filled with laughter, and our tongue with joyful shouting; then they said among the nations, 'The Lord has done great things for them'" (Psalm 126:2).

FEBRUARY 25
Restoring What the Locust Has Eaten

God, I thank You that You are the Master of the irreversibles. I remember the devastating plague of locusts that devoured Israel's crops in Joel's day. Yet, Lord, You called that multiplied swarm "*My* great army which *I* sent among you" (Joel 2:25, italics added).

Lord, teach me the lesson of the locusts. Let me learn that You are the Lord of devastation, too. Life is full of irreversibles. The crop that the locusts devoured was a *lost* crop. The year that the locusts had eaten was a *lost* year. The months that the prodigal spent in the far country were *lost* months. I heard a man cry out in agony, "O God, I'm bringing You the ashes of my life!" His early years were *lost* years. Israel's thirty-eight years in the wilderness were *lost* years, and the generation that died there was a *lost* generation.

Lord, so many people have made *lost* decisions: the person who would not obey the missionary call, the man who married the wrong woman, the youth who followed the wrong career. Lord, have You anything to say to them?

"I will restore . . . the years that the locust hath eaten" (Joel 2:25, KJV). God is the great Restorer. But how? How can He reverse the irreversible and change the inevitable? By time!

The next year the seed was planted and the harvest reaped. In a year the Almighty wiped out every trace of the locust. When Jesus healed the impotent man He wiped out thirty-eight years of irreversible weakness. He reversed the process of leprosy in the leper, of sin in Zaccheus, of death in Lazarus. Jesus is the great "turner-around." He makes time fly backward and makes Naaman's flesh like a child's; the irreversible becomes reversed in His hands, and we eat what the locust cannot touch. Do so, Lord, in me!

"Who redeems your life from the pit; who crowns you with lovingkind-ness and compassion" (Psalm 103:4).

FEBRUARY 26
Forsaking What We Should Forsake

Teach me, Lord, how to forsake without being forsaken. I know You will never forsake me, but I am not sure I can pass the test of forsaking what I should forsake. I greatly admire the decision of Moses, who "forsook Egypt, not fearing the wrath of the king" (Hebrews 11:27, KJV). He forsook the spirit of Egypt, the wealth of Egypt, the claims of Egypt. But I am fascinated by the fact that he did all this while still *in* the land of Egypt.

I have forsaken many things that did not count for Christ's sake. I was happy to give up things that no longer had any meaning for me. It is so easy to sacrifice what you no longer desire! But Moses sacrificed Egypt for God's sake while still surrounded by its immense charm and magnetism. Lord, how hard it is to make a decision for You when surrounded by wealth, popularity, position, and power. To see God *then* is to have the eye of faith indeed; and to decide for God *then* is to forsake this world even as Christ forsook it when He denied Satan's offer of its kingdoms.

Lord, please make me a voluntary forsaker, not a forced one. Lot was forced to forsake the riches of Sodom, while Moses gladly gave up Egypt. You will separate me, Lord, from every clinging thing in Egypt; but first You ask me to do it voluntarily. You want me to love You enough and trust You enough to make it my own decision. But if not, You will save me by the skin of my teeth. That is how intense Your desire is to make me a man of God and not a mollycoddle; a saint and not a warmed-over replica of Egypt.

"But it is not so among you, but whoever wishes to become great among you shall be your servant; and whoever wishes to be first among you shall be slave of all" (Mark 10:43–44).

FEBRUARY 27
A Spiritual Virgin

Lord, am I one of Your spiritual virgins? What is a spiritual virgin? One who "follow[s] the Lamb wherever He goes" (Revelation 14:4). As in the physical sense, a spiritual virgin is one who is utterly and completely given to the one for whom he or she is intended. The spiritual virgin not only has known no other, but longs for and desires no other. He is a firstfruits and is blameless in his loyalty to his one Master.

I am aware, Lord, that spiritual virginity is a spiritual quality that You greatly desire in all Your people. It has nothing to do with salvation because, in that case, who among us could be saved? Nor does it have to do with service, for the Bible is full of men and women who did exploits in the name of their God who, nevertheless, showed the human weaknesses of sin and disobedience (David, for example).

A virgin is not a representative of a certain class of elite, but the one who manifests a quality of spiritual devotion to God that He finds enormously pleasing and delightful. Too often God has to deal with us as Hosea dealt with Gomer, his unfaithful wife. God graciously forgives our unfaithfulness, brings us back home, and restores us to His service. How comforted I am by Your mercy, O God!

Lord, I covet spiritual virginity, the quality of devotion that never flags, tires, deviates, or adulterates. My example in this is He who never faltered or hesitated but who in all things did Your will and followed Your way perfectly. He who has planted His virgin life in me will propel me in the virgin way.

"Who may ascend into the hill of the Lord? And who may stand in His holy place? He who has clean hands and a pure heart, who has not lifted up his soul to falsehood, and has not sworn deceitfully" (Psalm 24:3–4).

FEBRUARY 28
Surviving or Overcoming?

I am determined not merely to survive as a Christian, but to overcome. Too often my life has been a "hanging in there" kind of thing, when actually God has called me to be an overcomer. Do I get into one scrape after another and then say, "Thank God I got out of that one alive"? Is that all there is, getting out of things alive?

The secret of overcoming is adequate resources, and the secret of adequate resources is tapping the infinite supply of God. I have been struck with the poor widow's plight (2 Kings 4). She had a little oil, nothing more. Creditors were pressing her to sell her sons as slaves. Elisha advised her to procure all the empty jars she could lay hands on, then pour what little oil she had into them one by one until each was full. Then it happened! By some wondrous power the oil kept flowing until every jar was full.

Where did the oil come from? Where else but the same place as the loaves, the fish, the wine, the manna, and the thousand other things God sent His poverty-stricken people! God was simply supplying out of His storehouse that which was perfectly visible to Him but not to them. If only we could see God's infinite supply! I am not an overcomer because I am not a taker. God's enormous quantities are at my disposal if only I will claim them. The lack is not with God; it is with me. I can grit it out with sheer determination and scant faith, but I will never overcome that way. God, let me believe You, really believe You, for therein lies my ability to fight and overcome, not merely exist. It is "according to [Your] riches in glory" (Philippians 4:19). You measure Your supply; and according to our faith, You allow that supply to be tapped.

"And the Lord said to Abraham, 'Why did Sarah laugh, saying, "Shall I indeed bear a child, when I am so old?" Is anything too difficult for the Lord?'" (Genesis 18:13–14).

FEBRUARY 29
How Not to Be Offended at Jesus

Christ's teachings are hard to understand. Example: "Eat My flesh, drink My blood or else you will have no life in you" (John 6:53, free trans.). Did He say this purposefully? Never mind the "stumbling in the dark" Pharisees, Jesus had *disciples* who were just as spiritually insensitive and unseeing. He had to put *them* to the test. The test is always this—at what point do I refuse to accept what Jesus is saying and take offense at Him? That's the point at which I draw back and walk no more with Him.

Like it or not, Jesus will constantly make Himself an offense to me. To *take* offense is the mark of an untrue disciple, to take *no* offense the mark of a true one. The antagonist relationship is always necessary when the training of minds, souls, or lives is at stake. The classroom teacher is an antagonist, the drill sergeant is an antagonist, the developer of Olympic champions is an antagonist. Where love enters the picture the antagonism is greater because love desires the greatest growth for the loved one.

I will never have a more demanding taskmaster than Jesus Christ. The voices of the world, the flesh, and the devil are soft and wooing. They beg me to indulge myself: "Take your ease; eat, drink, and be merry." That's why the wise preacher says, "It is better to go to the house of mourning, than to go to the house of feasting" (Ecclesiastes 7:2, KJV). The house of feasting is the self-indulgent, easy, soft, no-sacrifice way of living that results in death even while the person is still alive (1 Timothy 6:6). The house of mourning is the way of life hammered and shaped into His image by ceaseless discipline, hardness, and endurance. Every Christian has a choice; I can keep my life only to lose it, or lose it for Christ's sake only to find it again. How glad I am for God's help here—He both *wills* and *works* His good purposes in me (Philippians 2:13).

"Jesus said therefore to the twelve, 'You do not want to go away also, do you?' Simon Peter answered Him, 'Lord, to whom shall we go? You have words of eternal life'" (John 6:67–68).

MARCH 1

Appeasing the Tiger

I vow to the Lord not to succumb to the principle of spiritual appeasement. I will not feed the tiger merely to satisfy him. I remember the bitter lesson King Ahaz learned in trying to play both ends against the middle. He appeased the king of Assyria by giving him expensive gifts from the Temple. Result? "He helped him not" (2 Chronicles 28:21, KJV). Poor, distressed Ahaz turned to Syria and sacrificed to its gods, "but they were the ruin of him" (v. 23, KJV). The king's mistaken hope was that in appeasing the enemy he would be satisfied and move away. The more he appeased, the worse the situation became!

Am I so self-deceived that I believe that if I give in to sin, its grip will be weaker over me? Do I really think that if I give in to Satan he will thereafter leave me alone?

I like Paul's word, "Do not give the devil an opportunity" (Ephesians 4:27). Do not give him a chance to maneuver, get a toehold or a grip on you. Do not give him the satisfaction of a look, a glance, or a listen. Look at the wreckage of those who gave him a chance—Eve, David, Judas. The price is too steep!

My carnal nature loves to appease. I shrink from pain and struggle; so it is easier to feed the tiger in order to keep him quiet. Appeasement is the habit of a slovenly life, not the habit of a soldier. There is something inwardly crumbly if I am not able to stand up to the enemy and say as Jesus said, "Get out of my sight!" Appeasement is my confession of defeat and failure, my resignation from discipleship, my surrender to the one who nailed my Redeemer to His cross. Help me to say with the apostle Paul: "Not for a moment did we yield" (Galatians 2:5, Berkeley). Each refusal will strengthen me, each resistance will make me a better soldier of Jesus Christ.

"Therefore, take up the full armor of God, that you may be able to resist in the evil day, and having done everything, to stand firm" (Ephesians 6:13).

MARCH 2
The Art of Noninterference

I must learn not to practice the art of interference. God has absolutely no use for me as a midwife. My function in the Kingdom is not to help with the birth, but with the process of growing after birth. Too often I have aborted God's dealing with a person by saying, "I wouldn't do that!" or "I would go in that direction!"

Peter was the great interferer. When Jesus announced His plan to submit to crucifixion, Peter jumped in immediately and tried to scotch the idea. "Get behind Me" was Jesus' stern reply (Matthew 16:23). God will not have our hands meddling with His will. Still Peter did not learn. At the seaside after the resurrection, he was more concerned with John's future than his own, and again Jesus had to correct him, "What is that to you? You follow Me!" (John 21:22).

It is very difficult for me to learn the difference between when *God* uses me and when I use *myself*. The problem is not one of motive, but discernment. I am so dull of eye and calloused of heart that I cannot see the delicate movements of God in the hearts of others. I want to rush them into the Kingdom; I want to push them to commitment; I want to solve all their problems in a trice. I blame people for their troubles by saying, in effect, "If you had only listened to me!"

When the Israelites received their daily portion of manna, some of them, instead of eating it naturally, cooked it with fancy recipes and the taste was that of "oil" (Numbers 11:8). How many lives have I made oily simply by meddling? I must always remember to be God's tool, not God's hand. Lord, let me always be Your ready helper, and let me always be "at hand" to You. Let me have the joy of being a "*chosen vessel*" for You (Acts 9:15, KJV).

"No man can by any means redeem his brother, or give to God a ransom for him—for the redemption of his soul is costly, and he should cease trying forever" (Psalm 49:7–8).

MARCH 3
Tuned in to God's Signals

Teach me, Lord, that my use of the Bible itself can be a great stumbling block to me. The Pharisees were great students of the Old Testament; humanly speaking, they knew it as well as Jesus Himself. But what a difference! They were hung up on clouded meanings, empty traditions, and picky interpretations, whereas He spoke with "authority" (Matthew 7:29).

The fault was not in their hearing. They were constantly bombarded with the Word, from infancy to old age. It was read, preached, and externalized in every facet of their lives. Yet they were whitened graves "full of dead men's bones" (Matthew 23:27). God save me from a fate like that!

Save me also, Father, from their fatal error: they did not mix the Word "with faith" (Hebrews 4:2, KJV). To hear the Word of God is not enough, though certainly necessary. I must mix what I hear with faith, I must believe it to be truth, and finally I must obey what it tells me to do.

The universe is full of radio signals. But only when I turn on my radio and pick up the frequency do I receive a message. God's Word is full of continually emitted signals intended for me personally, but only as I am tuned in does the message ever penetrate my being. God is saying something to me right now from His Word about that personal need or problem, but I keep cloying the message by getting hung up on Greek words, theological meanings, archaeological evidence, and historical data. Sometimes I feel that God wants to shake me, as Moody used to shake his audiences by saying: "Listen! I've got a message for you and I want you to hear it!"

Lord, You are the God of the *now*, and Your Word is Your message of the *now*. I will not tune You out, Lord; I will tune myself and the world out, and I will listen to Your personal message to me right now.

"It is the Spirit who gives life; the flesh profits nothing; the words that I have spoken to you are spirit and are life" (John 6:63).

MARCH 4
Godliness Is Not Geographical

I promise God right now that I will not let my relationship to Him be determined by *place*. Godliness is not produced by topography.

How vividly Jesus made this point to the woman at the well (John 4). She was emphatic about Mount Gerizim, "the place where men ought to worship" (4:20). Jesus replied that it did not matter where she worshiped; it was the *how* that she had to be correct about. The *how* of worship is in spirit, that is, in being properly tuned to God spiritually.

I am impressed with Jeremiah's parable of the ripe and spoiled figs (Jeremiah 24). The good figs were the Jews who had been taken captive to Babylon, while the rotten figs were the Jews who remained in the Holy Land.

The parable ends forever the sin of place. Babylon was supposed to be the evil place, Judah the good. But that was not true of the figs, for the rotten ones were in the good place; the good ones in the rotten place.

How this speaks to my heart just now! Babylon with all its evils did not corrupt the captive Jews. Why? Because the right kind of geography was inside them, not outside. Their hearts were right though their surroundings were evil. It was exactly the reverse with the Judean Jews, whose hearts were wrong though their surroundings were right.

How often I have blamed my friends, my family, my job, or my environment for hindering my progress with God. False! The blame lies in my own negligent heart. The battle is won or lost within myself. Babylon can become my purest heaven, or Judea my deepest hell, depending upon the state of my heart. God, I thank You that Jesus was a "tender plant" in a dry desert (Isaiah 53:2, KJV). You want to make me the opposite of my surroundings, a touch of heavenly beauty in a barren land.

"God is spirit, and those who worship Him must worship in spirit and truth" (John 4:24).

MARCH 5
Personal Sin

I can never be a true disciple of Jesus Christ until I adequately despise sin. It is not enough for me to abandon sin; I must loathe it. God refers to sin in terms of beastliness, the stubborn horse, the wily snake, the mud-loving pig. That is not accidental. The beast does what is natural to it; its behavior is instinctive, and it is not redeemable. The beastliness of sin represents sin in its farthest distance from God, not merely that which is *different* from God, but that which is *opposite*.

My true feeling about sin is never reflected about sin in general; it is always about sin in *me*. God never redeems abstractions or principles; He redeems people. Until I can loathe the sin that *I* commit, the "darling sin" as George Whitefield once called it, I will never understand God's attitude toward my sin and His undying determination to redeem me from it.

My true attitude toward a specific sin seldom is formed before I commit it; that occurs afterward. It is difficult to see sin in its true light when it approaches me to tempt me. Then sin may often appear as "good" to the taste, "a delight to the eyes," and "desirable to make one wise" (Genesis 3:6). But once it has done its work, I see its viciousness, I feel defiled, I mourn my actions, and I turn to God in pitiful humiliation for His cleansing power.

To be a true disciple of Christ I must see the beastliness of sin before it works its devastation upon me. I must hate it everlastingly. I must never lose my grip on the fact that it was my very own sin that drove Jesus to tears, to loud outcries, to moaning and groaning, and to the bloody nails. When I feel this way about my sin, I will understand Isaiah's "Woe is me" (Isaiah 6:5) and what it means to be cleansed with a coal from the altar.

"Search me, O God, and know my heart; try me and know my anxious thoughts; and see if there be any hurtful way in me, and lead me in the everlasting way" (Psalm 139:23–24).

MARCH 6

Needed—An Intercessor

I must remember that I have no claim upon You, Lord, that is based upon myself. Not even my redeemed self. When Aaron entered the tabernacle to minister for his people, he wore a turban to which were attached the words "Holy to Jehovah" (Exodus 28:36–39, ASV). As long as the high priest wore that miter, all the gifts of the people were accepted by God. It was in the priest, not in the giver, that the acceptance lay.

I offer to God my many gifts—prayer, money, strength, family, time, talents, and so forth. But not one of them is acceptable to God apart from Jesus Christ my High Priest. None of my gifts is free from self, greed, pride, or uncleanness. I can offer little if anything that does not smell of the world and its influence. I need someone to perfect my gift to God, to take it right from my hands, and make it His very own, without any spot or blemish, so that God is perfectly delighted with it. I cannot offer anything to Him directly from myself and have it accepted. Even when I have done my very best, says Jesus, I am still counted among His "unprofitable servants" (Luke 17:10, KJV). This statement forces me to recognize that no matter how pure and willing my motive, the clinging tendrils of earthiness still bind me. Even my best misses the mark.

My only approach is through my wounded High Priest. My claim to acceptance lies first in His Calvary sacrifice and second in His never failing love. Need I worry, then? Never! "He ever liveth to make intercession for [us]" (Hebrews 7:25, KJV). This means more than His endless existence; it means my endless favor with God and my endless assurance that everything fleshly has been strained out of my relationship to Him. Hallelujah!

"For we do not have a high priest who cannot sympathize with our weaknesses, but one who has been tempted in all things as we are, yet without sin" (Hebrews 4:15).

MARCH 7
The Exceeding Life

I must remember that God has called me, not to a "succeeding" life, but to an "exceeding" life. Success is something entirely out of my hands, but excess is a matter to which I must give diligent attention. Unless my righteousness shall "exceed the righteousness of the scribes and Pharisees," said Jesus, I will not "enter" (Matthew 5:20, KJV).

My Master did not come to earth to match earth's best, but to produce heaven's better. He does not call disciples to equal the flower of man, but to produce the glories of God. What value is my discipleship if Socrates faces death with better hope than I? What good is Christ to me if Marcus Aurelius shows better resignment to his circumstances than I? In what way am I better spiritually than my unsaved neighbor if he manifests a more tranquil, gracious spirit than I?

Jesus Christ is in the business of producing superlatives. The saint, says F. J. Huegel, missionary to Mexico, is the *"fairest* flower." The two sins of Israel, basically, were forsaking God and not glorifying Him enough. There were multitudes of Israelites who were not idolaters, but the same could have been said of many non-Israelites. The sin of Laodicea was that which made it so attractive to the world—balance, sense, moderation—the very thing that makes Jesus nauseated.

I must exceed. I must be an overflowing lake, not merely an infilled one. I must be so righteous that I sting, rebuke, and shame the world as Noah did. Unless I feel the jealousy or antagonism of the world, I am a poor disciple of Jesus Christ. I must make the world either despise or desperately long for the righteousness of Jesus Christ working within me. I can do this through Him who is "made unto us . . . righteousness" (1 Corinthians 1:30, KJV).

"Have you considered My servant Job? For there is no one like him on the earth, a blameless and upright man, fearing God and turning away from evil" (Job 1:8).

MARCH 8
A Loan to God

I must learn heaven's method of bookkeeping. God will not receive a gift from anyone; He will be no man's debtor. Hannah could not give Samuel as a gift to God, so she "lent him to the Lord" (1 Samuel 1:28, KJV). For this loan God returned her investment at 500 percent interest: "The Lord visited Hannah . . . and [she] bore three sons and two daughters" (2:21, ASV). Challenge any bank to match that!

God, teach me that if I would preserve my capital (and who wouldn't?) I must loan it entirely to You. If I invest myself in myself or this world, I will not only lose my interest but also the capital itself. D. L. Moody, keen businessman that he was, took as his life verse: "The world passeth away, and the lust [desires] thereof: but he that doeth the will of God abideth for ever" (1 John 2:17, KJV). He left the selling of shoes to sell Jesus Christ, and now in heaven the fantastic rate of interest keeps pouring in.

If I am wise I will copy Hannah and Moody. I will total my assets today and invest them in one bank—heaven—and with one banker—He who has promised never to leave, fail, or forsake me.

> "Lend me thy boat," the Master kindly said
> To Simon, wearied with unfruitful toil.
> He lent it gladly, asking but the smile
> Of Him who had not where to lay His head.
> Oh humble toiler, when He calls thy name,
> Lend Him thine all. The Master ne'er forgets
> Discouraged fishermen or empty nets!
> *Author Unknown*

"And the one on whom seed was sown on the good soil, this is the man who hears the word and understands it; who indeed bears fruit, and brings forth, some a hundredfold" (Matthew 13:23).

MARCH 9
The Uncomplicated Relationship

L ord, I have often been guilty of "fussiness" in my relationship to You. I have not been "like a weaned child [who] rests against his mother" (Psalm 131:2) with You. I have fretted because I didn't have my daily devotional instead of being content with being devoted. I have worried because I have not prayed enough instead of making my life itself a prayer. Too often my deep inward relationship to You is disturbed because I feel I must constantly prove myself to You.

This is not the rest You promised, Lord, nor will it ever be until I learn that a child does not need to earn its mother's love, or live in the constant fear of losing it. The child finds contentment in the simple relationship itself. You are concerned with my being, not my doing. You are not as impressed with my regular church attendance as You are with my heart being a continual altar. You want me to be a light, not strive to shine; to be a disciple, not act like one.

How uncomplicated was Jesus' relationship to You. It was easy, natural. He could make the most striking claim ("I am the light of the world," John 8:12) as naturally as we eat bread and butter. There was no pumped-up striving, no anxious grasping. He *was*—that is all there is to it!

Lord, if I am fussy with You, how fussy I will be toward others! My holiness will become prickliness, and others will avoid me like a plague. If my spirituality offends others, it is a sign that I am too self-conscious of it. I should be the last person in the world to know that I am a blessing to others. I must be as Moses, who "did not know that the skin of his face shone because of his speaking with [God]" (Exodus 34:29). Give me that holy indifference to the effects of godliness, which is in itself godliness.

"Surely I have composed and quieted my soul; like a weaned child rests against his mother, my soul is like a weaned child within me" (Psalm 131:2).

MARCH 10
Serving God with Our Bodies

As Your disciple, Lord, I must come to terms with my body. When Jesus saved me, He did not do it in units; He did it wholly. My hand is as much redeemed as my soul, and my brain just as much covered by the blood of Christ as my heart.

When Aaron was consecrated as high priest, the sacrificial blood was placed on his right ear, right thumb, and right big toe (Exodus 29:20). Were You being picky, Lord? No, I see it now. The lesson is obvious: Aaron's body, just as much as his heart, had to be priestly. That is why the sin of the golden calf was so odious and reprehensible to God. Later the body that God had appointed to service and consecrated by blood callously fashioned a golden idol for the people to worship (Exodus 32:1–6)!

God, do not let me repeat Aaron's sin! Do not let me use what Jesus so painfully purchased to do that which Jesus personally despises. I am owned, I am His possession. I have no right to throw my gold into the fire and make myself an idol. I dare not defile my body that way.

I see now why Paul said, "I beat my body" (1 Corinthians 9:27, NIV). As a disciple, I must pummel my body into submission rather than let it violate my calling. How often I must do it! My enemies are the world, the flesh, the devil, *and my body.* How often my spirit wants to soar into the heavenlies and conquer with Christ but is dragged down and hindered by my glands, my nerve impulses.

Yet, Lord, I rejoice in that happy word of Paul: "The Spirit . . . will . . . give life to your mortal bodies" (Romans 8:11, NIV). The Spirit is sent from Jesus to minister to the body as well as the soul, to quicken it when it flags, to revive it when it slumps, and to manifest Christ's complete redemption over me. Lord, let my body fly the flag of His victory!

"May the God of peace Himself sanctify you entirely; and may your spirit and soul and body be preserved complete, without blame at the coming of our Lord Jesus Christ" (1 Thessalonians 5:23).

MARCH 11
Standing Clean Before God

Lord, I will learn the full meaning of my standing before You. I have gloried in my standing in Christ—justified, accepted in the Beloved. This has been a delicious truth and warming to my heart. But, Lord, You have been talking to me about another kind of standing—standing in my own name.

My standing in Christ means that my sins are forgiven, and this without any work or self-effort of mine. But I also am obliged to stand before You in responsibility, in immediacy, in accountability. Elijah said the Lord was the One "before whom I stand" (1 Kings 17:1). These words chill me, Lord. They warn me that standing in Christ is not the same as standing before You as a servant. His standing settles the problem of my sin; my standing deals with the matter of discipleship. I cannot possibly excuse myself from the second standing if I claim the first.

How must I stand before You? *Blameless!* You said to Abraham, "I am God Almighty; walk before Me, and be blameless" (Genesis 17:1). This is Your ideal for me, Lord. You desire my standing before You to be unblameworthy, that is, characterized only by pure motives. My standing is acceptable to You only if I have "clean hands and a pure heart" (Psalm 24:4).

I see what this means to me, Lord. You will not tolerate Your children resting in the finished work of Christ in such a way that their lives become sloppy and disgraceful. No, You call us to accountability for the way we live, for the way we use our time, talents, and energy. We are to face the enemy, not fresh from a slugabed's nap, but fresh from the glistening presence of a holy God. Thank You, Lord, that You encourage us in this: "Then will I restore you, and you shall stand before Me" (Jeremiah 15:19, Berkeley). The standing is essential, and so is the restoring of God, which makes it possible.

"What then shall we say to these things? If God is for us, who is against us? He who did not spare His own Son, but delivered Him up for us all, how will He not also with Him freely give us all things?" (Romans 8:31–32).

MARCH 12
Developing a Hardness

Lord, to be an exemplary disciple of Jesus Christ I must learn to develop a hardness. I notice that Jesus Himself was a mixture of tenderness and hardness, and unless I develop the same mixture I will either drift off into maudlin sentimentality or else become excruciatingly rigid.

Jesus never became hard toward His Father's will, but always toward those things or people who might prevent Him from doing that will. "He resolutely set His face to go to Jerusalem" (Luke 9:51). If I decide to follow Jesus I will be pulled in many directions, all for my good and to save me from myself. The disciple who does not deliberately develop a hardness will find himself too weak to resist the siren calls.

Jesus also developed a hardness toward people, even His closest friends, whenever they appeared to block His path in doing God's will. I think of statements like "Get behind Me" (Matthew 16:23); "What is that to you?" (John 21:22); "Woman, what do I have to do with you?" (John 2:4); "If I do not wash you, you have no part with Me" (John 13:8); and others like them and notice how stern Jesus sometimes sounded.

I must always be soft, Lord, toward human need but incorrigibly hard against human shortsightedness. Who is shortsighted but he who in the name of God prevents me from doing the will of God? That is why I must always love my friends and family, but always keep a sharp eye on the one who would self-indulgently make my softness become downright sin. Where does the strength come from to follow Him so closely? "Our sufficiency is of God," Paul said (2 Corinthians 3:5, KJV). That was the sufficiency that enabled Paul to set aside his beloved obstacles and say, "I am ready not only to be jailed . . . but also to die for . . . the Lord Jesus" (Acts 21:13, TLB).

"No soldier in active service entangles himself in the affairs of everyday life, so that he may please the one who enlisted him as a soldier" (2 Timothy 2:4).

MARCH 13
A Cheap View of Heaven

Forgive me, Lord, for holding a cheap view of heaven. I have rejoiced indeed that Jesus died to make a place for me there; but Your Word keeps hammering into my head the difference between having a right to heaven and being made suitable for it.

Isn't that what Paul means: "Christ . . . loved the church and gave Himself up for her"—that is the right—"that He might present to Himself the church in all her glory, having no spot or wrinkle or any such thing" (Ephesians 5:25–27)—that is the fitness.

It is one thing to arrive in heaven by the skin of my teeth, but how much better to arrive there applauded! The right is what Jesus Christ has done *for* me; the fitness is what He has done *in* me. Simple faith in Him (how easy it is!) assures me of a place in heaven; but only ruggedly following Him (how difficult!) assures me of an abundant "entrance" (2 Peter 1:11).

I confess, Lord, that I have been one of those who have cheapened Your grace. I have led many to believe that the ease of accepting Christ as Savior also applies to the lived-out Christian life. God's grace is not softness, as witnessed by Calvary's wounds. God's grace is simply permission, not qualification. It merely opens the door to God's great school of training and discipline; it does not promise to carry us to the skies on flowery beds of ease.

Thank You, God, for Your grace! Without it we earthlings would be endlessly, hopelessly lost. But, Lord, may we never throw Your grace to the pigs by assuming that the ticket to enter is the graduation diploma!

"For this reason, they are before the throne of God; and they serve Him day and night in His temple; and He who sits on the throne shall spread His tabernacle over them" (Revelation 7:15).

MARCH 14
God's Hedge Around Us

The great gospel message is that in Christ Jesus I am free. Thank You, Lord, for this truth. But it is just as true that in Christ Jesus I am bound, hobbled, hedged, and limited. My freedom is really only my freedom to change hobbles and to realize that Satan, my former hobbler, meant only viciousness for me while Christ, my new hobbler, intends only eternal welfare and good for me.

You said about Israel, "I will hedge up her way with thorns, and I will build a wall against her so that she cannot find her paths" (Hosea 2:6). This was the wall of confinement. Whenever we rebel against You and grow surly, as Israel did, a confining hedge will always be placed around us. Despite its confinement, that hedge was an expression of Your love, Lord. It shows the extent to which You will go to protect Your children from sinning and, therefore, from reaping a sad harvest.

Job had a confining hedge also. Satan said, "Hast Thou not made a hedge about him?" (Job 1:10). Thank You for this hedge, Lord. It is a hedge of protection around an obedient child of Yours to keep out the external enemy.

Lord, You build a hedge around every one of Your children. I may, if I will, break through the hedge and run pell-mell after my own selfish desires. But if I do, the consequences will be mine also. If I stay within the hedge, the consequences are Yours.

Thank You for Your hedges, Lord, whether illness, poverty, disappointment, sorrow, alienation, or whatever. I find my freedom when I realize that the hedge is not a confinement of my love for You, or Yours for me. It does not hinder my obedience to You, but contrariwise, makes me free to be abandoned to all the glories of a God-planned life.

"O satisfy us in the morning with Thy lovingkindness, that we may sing for joy and be glad all our days" (Psalm 90:14).

MARCH 15
Tempting God

I must be careful, Lord, never to tempt You. I am commanded never to "tempt the Lord thy God" (Matthew 4:7, KJV). Your anger was constantly aroused against the Israelites because they tempted You with their murmurings and complainings.

I must distinguish between proving You and tempting You. You invite me, Lord, to prove You (Malachi 3:10), and You glory in demonstrating Your power to Your children. When Gideon tested You in the matter of the fleece, You willingly accommodated him (Judges 6).

I must learn the difference between the two. To prove God is to take His Word and act upon it, put it into action. To tempt God is to go beyond His Word and overtest Him. Whenever I go beyond the Word of God I always desecrate the character of God, which is something God will never tolerate. That is why He becomes angry at being tempted.

Tempting God occurs in many ways: being impatient with Him, quarreling with His directions, comparing *unfavorably* His treatment of me with the world's treatment of me, complaining about my lot that He gives me, making greater demands on Him than He intends to fulfill, and refusing to submit to the authority He has placed over me.

God loves to have His Word obeyed and put to the test, but He resents having His character and name defamed. Lord, members of the wilderness generation left their bones in the desert because they decided Your word was not good enough for them. Lord, let me never treat You as not good enough for me. Let me never revile You because I consider You less than You promised You would be! Let me shout with Joshua: "Not one thing hath failed of all the good things which the Lord . . . [promised]" (Joshua 23:14, KJV).

"'I love Thee, O Lord, my strength.' The Lord is my rock and my fortress and my deliverer, my God, my rock, in whom I take refuge" (Psalm 18:1–2).

MARCH 16
Holding Spiritual Wonder

I always go stale, Lord, whenever I lose my sense of spiritual wonder. Spiritual wonder comes from knowing that spiritual realities such as God and heaven are not far-off things, but things near at hand.

When the two disciples recognized Jesus after walking with Him on the Emmaus road (Luke 24:13–32), they were only seeing what had been there all the time. God gave them, momentarily, a glimpse into the spiritual world that existed continually around them.

How much of heaven do I miss, Lord, simply because my eyes are held down by discouragement, doubt, boredom, or stark unbelief? A desert, biologists say, may seem empty; but to the one who has eyes to see, it actually teems with life. So with the heavenlies. We need the prayer Elisha prayed for his servant, "Lord . . . open his eyes that he may see" (2 Kings 6:17). When he "looked spiritually," the boy saw the resplendent forces of God on the surrounding hills.

Lord, I see the secret now. It is looking at things *spiritually*. To look logically, carnally, suspiciously, or naturally is to hold our eyes down and thus miss Jesus and a heart-moving experience.

Also, I must look *expectantly*. God's great heroes have always lived in two worlds. They saw wonder and transmitted that wonder to others because they lived in sight of the heavenly scene.

Lord, I find myself caught in a vicious circle: I lose my wonder because my faith is too puny; then my faith grows weaker because there is not enough wonder on which to feed. At that point I must deliberately untie myself from every carnal bandage and ask the Holy Spirit to anoint my eyes again with spiritual sight. When that happened to the Emmaus disciples, they saw Jesus!

"I have heard of Thee by the hearing of the ear; but now my eye sees Thee; therefore I retract, and I repent in dust and ashes" (Job 42:5–6).

MARCH 17

Ministeps in Prayer

L ord, I need to learn persistence in prayer. Many things I do not receive, as James says, because I "do not ask" (James 4:2). But just as often, Lord, I receive not because I ask "amiss" (v. 3, KJV). One of the "amiss" things I do is to pray without persistence.

I am impressed with Abraham's praying for Lot (Genesis 18). When he reached a certain point in his praying, "the Lord . . . left communing with Abraham" (v. 33, KJV). The cup of prayer was full. There was no need to ask further. Heaven had acquiesced to the prayer, and all that was needed then was time to make the answer effective on earth.

The cup of prayer fills whenever I pray intensely and abundantly. Thus, in prayer quantity as well as quality is very important. I see now, Lord, why You said, "If *two* of you shall . . . ask" (Matthew 18:19, KJV, italics added). Prayer is often accentuated when two pray, and much more when twenty-two or a hundred and two pray. When the cup fills and heaven acquiesces to the prayer, we immediately have assurance in our hearts. That explains, Lord, why I have had "rest" in prayer long before the prayer was answered.

But persistence is hard to manage, Lord. My enemy here is impatience, which quickly leads to discouragement. I need the broad view, the eternal scheme of things. Teach me that my ministeps in prayer are vastly important to the answer, and that instant answers are not always heaven's ways of doing things. I am advised to stop fretting impatiently and to "wait for the Lord" (Psalm 37:9). It is those who wait on God, the ones who adjust their schedules to His, who "will inherit the land" (v. 9b).

"Be anxious for nothing, but in everything by prayer and supplication with thanksgiving let your requests be made known to God" (Philippians 4:6).

MARCH 18
The Dwarfed Disciple

God wants no "dwarfed" men serving Him (Leviticus 21:20). Lord, am I a dwarf? Smallness of stature is not what God has in mind. Look at Zaccheus, whose frame was small but whose heart was really giant-sized (Luke 19:1–10).

God does not want men representing Him who are dwarfs in heart and mind. Look at the opposite in God: He gives liberally (James 1:5); His mind is of great understanding (Romans 11:33–34); His plans and purposes include the whole world (John 3:16); He loves everlastingly (Jeremiah 31:3). It is no wonder that God rejects disciples who are narrow, petty, childish.

Smallness in a Christian is the result of largeness in the ego. He sees himself as all-important. He has not learned the law of detachment; he feels that he himself is as necessary to God's work as the flow of God's power.

That is not all. If I am dwarfish toward others, it is because first I am dwarfish toward God. I can never be stingy, prejudiced, and opinionated if I have opened my being to the One whose life is a Niagara of large-hearted outflow. Paul's word strikes me forcibly here, "Grow up . . . toward . . . Christ" (Ephesians 4:15, Berkeley). The end of my dwarfishness is the stature of Christ, and I am to be making continual progress in that direction. The essence of dwarfishness is: that is not what the person is *supposed* to be. To be small at childhood is natural, but at maturity?

If I am a dwarf it is because something has gone wrong with my spiritual growth mechanism. It is not the will of God that I remain in a state of perpetual babyhood. Lord, help me to grow up—and on toward Jesus Christ! For He is not only my way—He is my destiny.

"But grow in the grace and knowledge of our Lord and Savior Jesus Christ. To Him be the glory, both now and to the day of eternity. Amen" (2 Peter 3:18).

MARCH 19
Arguing with God

Lord, I must put argument in its proper place. The only place I am allowed to argue is with You, not with men. Even with You, Lord, my privilege of argument is limited.

Moses argued with God about the call to go to Egypt (Exodus 3–4). The argument was not to convince God, but to convince Moses. Argument is allowed only until I am convinced. When Moses continued to argue even after God had answered his questions and doubts, God became angry with him. The issue of the argument is always decided by God, and the decision is made before I even open my mouth. But God allows me to argue the issue with Him because He wants to confirm me in the action, not leave me indecisive or confused.

But I must never argue with men. If I give men a message from God and they do not agree with it, I must not argue with them but, rather, leave the issue in the hands of God. He must do the convincing, not I. If I take that prerogative out of God's hands, I only frustrate His work.

I am allowed to counsel with my Christian colleagues in order to determine the mind of God (Acts 15), but that is different from argument. Argument says, "You will see it my way," but counsel asks, "What is God telling us to do?" A true disciple counsels but never argues.

Lord, give me grace to overcome my natural tendency to argue, which is carnal, and grace to be Your mouthpiece, not Your lawyer. Give me the grace to display Him who is my "Wonderful Counselor" (Isaiah 9:6, NIV), for He is the source of all wisdom and knowledge and the sweet Persuader of the soul.

"The Lord God has given Me the tongue of disciples, that I may know how to sustain the weary one with a word" (Isaiah 50:4).

MARCH 20
Interpreters of God

L ord, I see Your *acts*, but may I have the privilege of knowing Your *ways*? "He made known His ways to Moses, His acts to the sons of Israel" (Psalm 103:7).

I thank You, Lord, for Your dealings with Abraham. "Shall I hide from Abraham what I am about to do?" (Genesis 18:17). You took him behind the scenes and showed him not only *what* but *why*. To take a human being behind the scenes is always a sign of maturity in the school of discipleship. All believers can see what God has done *after* the fact; but deep disciples see those actions *before* the fact. However, the greatest disciples are those who see why God is doing what He is doing before the fact.

What the world sadly needs is interpreters of God, not merely prophets. Being infinite, God is so often misunderstood. This misunderstanding alienates men from God. The acts of God must be explained to men, and God is always seeking persons like Abraham and Moses to understand His mind and then translate for men.

What a perfect Interpreter Jesus was! He was interpretation *in the flesh*. To the extent that I let God's message be manifest in my flesh, to that extent I become the best interpreter of God's ways! What a privilege God extends to us, to become His interpreter to men! Imagine being a "letter of Christ . . . written . . . with the Spirit" to be read by all men (2 Corinthians 3:3)!

"No man has seen God at any time; the only begotten God, who is in the bosom of the Father, He has explained Him" (John 1:18).

MARCH 21
The Right of Rejection

I have always been taught that Jesus Christ is the Receiver of men. I believe that teaching with all my heart. But unless I see the same Jesus as the Rejecter of men, I will never fully understand His dealings with us.

Salvation is not a one-way but a two-way street. I must commit myself to Jesus Christ, but He must also commit Himself to me. Some early followers of the Lord "believed" in Him, but He did not believe in them (John 2:23–25). He did not commit Himself to them, because He knew their hearts and saw their insincerity.

Since Jesus had the right of rejection, so do all His disciples. I must be as distinguishing as my Lord and refuse to commit myself to triflers, tarriers, and in-betweeners. I must search for the lost sheep who are anxious to be found and the prodigal son who is willing to come home.

I must be rigid in this. Even fleshly ties did not cause Jesus to soften or weaken His spiritual standard. His "mother" and His "brothers" were those who do "the will of My Father" (Matthew 12:48–50). This underscores an absolute standard in Jesus Christ: the spiritual takes precedence over every other relationship! He never turned away a truly needy, seeking person. But He scorned the religious showman.

I must beware of the frothy person whose religious commitment only takes care of his purse, his stomach, and his senses. These people abound. For them I must exercise the right of rejection and not believe in them, even as my Lord did not nineteen hundred years ago. Yet I must never cut myself off from those whom the Lord has accepted, those who "[work] righteousness," that is, do the right thing toward Him (Acts 10:35, KJV).

"For Thy lovingkindness is before my eyes, and I have walked in Thy truth. I do not sit with deceitful men, nor will I go with pretenders" (Psalm 26:3–4).

MARCH 22
Spiritual Success Is Imitation

I will not take God's right of selection out of His hands. Often I have said, "That person would make a good Christian," or "This one would make a good pastor or missionary." But God cannot afford to accept my selection of candidates for His work. My tendency is always to *engineer* God's program instead of being engineered by it.

My responsibility is to sow the seed, not make it grow. That means I must be "indifferent" to (that is, not overwhelmed or depressed by) outcomes, especially disappointing ones. Jesus was rejected by the rich young ruler, whom He loved; yet He accepted that rejection as a matter of course (Mark 10:17–23).

In our success-oriented culture, I must be doubly sure that I am *not* successful in the ordinary sense. Spiritual success is neither selection nor prediction. Spiritual success is *imitation*: "My Father worketh hitherto, and I work" (John 5:17, KJV). That means following the pattern the Father has created for me.

The great danger in my spiritual life is to take the pattern out of God's hands and reshape it according to my tastes, likes, and dislikes. A true disciple must never be afflicted with the "if only" disease. He cannot succumb to the "might have been's." He gladly accepts the word, "Elect according to the foreknowledge of God the Father" (1 Peter 1:2, KJV), not according to *me* or any other human being. That means duty first, then rest. "Who is the man who fears the Lord?" asks David (Psalm 25:12). If I reply, "I do," then the promise is assured, "He will instruct him in the way He should choose." Selah, ponder that!

"For He says to Moses, 'I will have mercy on whom I have mercy, and I will have compassion on whom I have compassion'" (Romans 9:15).

MARCH 23
God Uses Trivia!

I must always remember that God is not only holy, He is meticulous. David expressed this when he said, "As for God, his way is perfect" (Psalm 18:30, NIV). Then he followed with the necessary corollary, "God . . . makes *my* way perfect" (v. 32, NIV, italics added).

When God looks at me, He determines my *perfection*. I am not speaking of moral perfection here; that is another matter. God determines me for a specific role (of which I may not be aware) in His Kingdom, and He relentlessly moves me forward until He reaches the place where I am perfectly placed for Him. Since I may not know where that place is, I may be in utter darkness as to what He is about. My life may appear to be a series of meaningless circles or zigs and zags, as if only the wind were in control. Never mind! God slowly draws us to His goal, His zenith, where the perfection will be just as complete here as up there.

When I finally reach my goal and look back, I will be amazed to discover what inconsequential, minute, and extraneous things God used to bring me on my way. The things that irritated me no end, that caused tedious delays, that provoked me to temper and irritability, were the very things that became my best teachers. The Bible shows that God used such things as a king's indigestion, a captain's deep sleep, a baby's hungry cry, a barefaced lie, a dream, and a shepherd's stick to bring about amazing events. Who am I to deny God any trivial accident, turn of events, or occurrence in my life today? The very trivia of my life are being used by God to bring me to perfection!

Before such a God I can only bow with David and say, "God!—perfect is His way [with me]!" (Psalm 18:30, Berkeley).

"What does the Lord your God require from you, but to fear the Lord your God, to walk in all His ways and love Him . . . ?" (Deuteronomy 10:12).

MARCH 24
Loved but Not Spoiled

Because I am so pitifully weak, God devises a discipline of embarrassments for me. His embarrassments are painful and irritating. His discipline is severe and hard. He never coddles us. I heard a Christian once say, "I am one of God's spoiled children." Never! There is no such child in God's family. On the contrary, God has such a charming list of humiliations for us that not one of us will dare to say he is spoiled.

Loved? Yes, infinitely so. Cared for? Most certainly, with never a slight. Protected and preserved? Without a doubt, for such He has promised. But spoiled, pampered, babied? Absolutely not! God would rather have no children than undisciplined, selfish, egotistical ones. It is for this reason His humiliations are necessary. They take the raw saint and fashion him into a disciplined soldier of grace. They take the swelling of pride and deflate it into substance and solidness. They take the erring, cowardly, and fearful and fashion them into specimens of splendid sainthood. God is in the business of making me into a saint, and His arsenal of embarrassments is wonderfully supplied for the process.

The apostle Peter said, "Don't be surprised when afflictions touch you" (1 Peter 4:12, author's trans.). Lord, may Your humiliations never catch me by surprise, for such is the way of a God whose ways are past finding out. But may I always be surprised at the outpoured love that You shower upon a humiliated child of Yours, for Your humiliations always lead to Your honors: "I will rescue him [from distress], and honor him [the natural result]" (Psalm 91:15).

"But the Lord is faithful, and He will strengthen and protect you from the evil one" (2 Thessalonians 3:3).

MARCH 25
The Subtle Power of Sin

I must realize that the closer I walk with God, the more subtle sin will become. The natural man does not hate sin as *sin*; he only hates the mess he has gotten himself into. But the disciple soon discovers that sin has great undoing power, the power not only to neutralize the present but also to cancel the past.

Israel made a calf of gold and said, "This is your god, O Israel, who brought you up from the land of Egypt" (Exodus 32:4). This was a direct contradiction to what Israel said earlier, "*Thou* hast led the people whom Thou hast redeemed" (Exodus 15:13).

Sin is always contradiction. It is the great no to every manifestation of God's truth and power. Even more, it destroys the *present* benefit that past blessings have brought us. The great strength occasioned by the song of Moses was wiped out by the creation of the calf.

God answered prayer for me yesterday, and I found that it still nourished me today—until I made my calf of gold. Yesterday's blessing is dissolved by today's idolatry.

The subtle power of sin is that it prevents me from relying on my spiritual savings account. Sin not only defeats me but it also strips me of my armor.

What is my defense against the insidious thing? Only my bedrock relationship with God. That is one thing sin cannot change, remove, or dissolve. God has vowed my salvation, not on the basis of what *I* experience, but on what *His Son* experienced for me. While sin can eliminate a day's or a year's growth in my soul, it cannot eliminate the thing that makes that growth possible—the vibrant, pulsating life of God.

"For the law of the Spirit of life in Christ Jesus has set you free from the law of sin and of death" (Romans 8:2).

MARCH 26
Spiritual Begging

I will remember that faith is, as Dr. Gresham Machen, professor of apologetics at Westminster Seminary, used to say, "The beggar attitude." God is in the business of making beggars out of all His disciples. The natural man bristles at this. He wants to be self-sufficient, capable, unneedy.

According to the world's standard, the church at Laodicea had arrived. It was rich, increased with goods, and had need of nothing (Revelation 3:17). Yet Jesus said it was the worst of all His churches, fit to be thrown out.

I love to be self-sufficient! I loathe depending upon someone else! Yet God continually whisks away my resources until I crawl beggarlike to His door and ask for help. This is because I stubbornly refuse to be beggarlike in *spirit*.

The Bible is full of beggar-spirited people: Abel, the Syrophoenician woman, the publican, and others. They received the blessing while the self-sufficient ones went away empty. Jesus said I must become a child. Is there ever a greater beggar than a child? Beggary is a child's nature and never a blush about it. That is the way God wants me to be. It is when I beg that God is able to put His (not *my*) resources into my hands; and, after all, nothing works like God's power.

The spiritual beggar has a keen eye of faith, a proper system of values, and a successful method of prayer. He knows that when all the niceties are strained out of his coming to God, the whole matter boils down to "his need and God's supply." That is why beggars are direct, simple, and expectant. What a beggar George Mueller was! Lord, may heaven's doors be open toward me like that!

"Now faith is the assurance of things hoped for, the conviction of things not seen" (Hebrews 11:1).

MARCH 27
God's Likes and Dislikes

If I am to be a fruitful disciple I must respect God's *likes* and *dislikes*. The Bible is full of the things God likes and the things He dislikes. If I am to keep irritation out of our relationship, I must respect the fences of God.

I do this in human relationships such as marriage, friendship, and church service. The only difference is that human relationships are often petty and selfish, whereas God's fences are always pure.

God hates many things—a proud look, a lying tongue, murderous hands, a wicked heart, mischievous feet, lies, troublemakers (Proverbs 6:17–19). But He particularly despises an empty sacrifice (Isaiah 1:14). If I offer that sacrifice with all the correctness of the Law, yet without the heart affection to accompany it, it creates only irritation in God's heart.

The difficulty with the empty sacrifice is that I may never know when I am offering it. Mental mistakes are far more obvious than emotional mistakes. I cannot teach wrong doctrine very long before being found out, but who can examine the heart?

So my sacrifices—praise, prayer, gifts, service—must be constantly scrutinized by me, because I may be ever so correct in form yet ever so lacking in devotion. Do I say, "I love You, Lord," and yet wince at the hypocrisy You see in my heart? Lord, may I ever please You with "the sacrifices of righteousness" (Psalm 51:19, KJV), which is the sacrifice after Your own heart.

"And do not neglect doing good and sharing; for with such sacrifices God is pleased" (Hebrews 13:16).

MARCH 28

God's Joy Versus Sin's Weariness

L ord, I must be very careful not to be sin conscious lest I become weak and exhausted. The burden of the Lord may be a conviction of my sin and is therefore necessary; but as soon as I am conscious of my sin, I must rid myself of it by confession (Psalm 32:5; 1 John 1:9). And once confessed, I must have nothing more to do with it.

Nehemiah had the correct solution for a sin-conscious people: eat and drink, share with others, and praise God, "for the joy of the Lord is your strength" (Nehemiah 8:10).

Conviction of sin, while necessary, is weakening and must be turned into confession and praise in order to save my sanity. The inward look is depressing and discouraging, and I must avoid, at all costs, people who are continually turning me inward. Many people are turned from Christ because they see morbidity in Christians who have not gotten beyond sin's conviction to sin's confession.

I must never treat sin lightly; neither must I give it so much time, attention, and place in me that I am actually enslaved by it. Many Christians seem to enjoy looking within and relish seeing themselves corrupt and sinful. I must never give sin any more of my time than it takes to let it do a redemptive work in me—to drive me to my God and His cleansing, and then to praise, strength, and growth! For God wants me alive and well, not caught in the octopus arms of sin. "Blessed is he whose transgression is forgiven, whose sin is covered!" (Psalm 32:1).

"Who is a God like Thee, who pardons iniquity and passes over the rebellious act of the remnant of His possession? He does not retain His anger forever, because He delights in unchanging love" (Micah 7:18).

MARCH 29

Mind Your Own Business

Nothing will cause me as much trouble in my Christian life as the sin of a wandering eye. If my eye wanders it will not be long before my heart follows it. Paul said to Archippus, "Take heed to the ministry which you have received in the Lord, that you may fulfill it" (Colossians 4:17). Archippus had become afflicted with a wandering eye, and that led to a cold heart and a slack hand.

One of the old Puritans used to write on the flyleaf of his books: "Mind Thine Own Business!" God has given me a work to do, and I am to focus on it until it is done or He will remove me from it. If I glance with the eye of *ambition* on other things I might do, which seem more interesting and profitable, I am preparing myself for a stern admonition from God. Above all, I must avoid the wandering eye of *jealousy*: "See how much he's reaping, and look at how little I've got!" To be jealous means "God is not treating me fairly," and nothing displeases the Lord more than an accusation like that!

Jesus said of the Pharisees, "They *have* their reward" (Matthew 6:2, italics added). Yes, they do. I may pick the standards of my own success if I choose, and the rewards will be immediate and instant. But they will not be God's rewards. How much better to hear Him say, "*Faithful* servant" (Matthew 25:21, KJV, italics added). Faithfulness rules out wealth, fame, achievement, and notoriety. But it does not rule out the highest compliment of all: "You paid attention to the job I gave you, and you did it!" Faithfulness is a characteristic of Christ (Isaiah 11:5), and it will characterize those of us in whom His Spirit rests.

"I am God Almighty; walk before Me, and be blameless" (Genesis 17:1).

MARCH 30
Developing in Solitude

I must always remember that the best kind of disciple is developed in solitude. I must not succumb to the idea that my salvation lies in the group. The very concept of the Body of Christ in the New Testament reflects the peculiarity, individuality, and therefore the aloneness of every individual member. Of course there is common life, but merely having common life is not the same thing as discipleship.

The heroes of the Bible were essentially lonely people. Those who know God deeply do not learn the deep things of Him from others. That is why deeply spiritual people have always been treated as "strange." Paul was accused of being out of his mind (Acts 26:24). Jesus was grossly misunderstood, even by His closest friends. It is easy to understand why disciples are "stoned, . . . sawn asunder, . . . tempted, . . . slain with the sword" (Hebrews 11:37, KJV), even by "religious" people!

I find disturbing signs around me that tell me the group is my hope, my health, and even my destiny. The group is god. But, Lord, the more I trust the group, the less I trust You. Quite the opposite, the group is really my stumbling block, my hindrance to the kind of personalized experiences with You that are necessary to the creation of strong discipleship.

Lord, it takes immense courage to enter discipleship training. But where the burden of the Lord is upon me, I will be able to count the cost and go on. I will lose a great deal earthwise, but what transcendent blessings I will gain heavenwise! There is no greater compliment than "of whom the world [is] not worthy" (Hebrews 11:38).

"Now the Lord said to Moses, 'Come up to Me on the mountain and remain there'" (Exodus 24:12).

MARCH 31
Turning Evil into Honey

My *reaction* when I am confronted by evil must be more than negative; it must be positive. I must seize evil and turn it into an actual triumph. Jesus did more than ignore Satan; He defeated him at the cross. Joseph's brothers meant to do him "evil," but God turned it into "good" (Genesis 50:20).

How do I do that? Isn't it God's prerogative to operate on evil, "defang" it, and transform it into an opportunity for good? Absolutely! That is God's continual relationship to evil. Calvary is once for all, official. Yet the *principle* of Calvary is always with us, because God and evil are antagonistic; even more, evil is a necessary matrix out of which redemption comes.

If I am a true disciple of Jesus Christ, then I will manifest Calvary's principle of compelling evil to yield a victory to me. That means illness can be a pulpit to preach God's patience, strength, and glory. That means a complete reversal of my former attitude toward evil—fear of it. That means I welcome evil that occurs in my life as an opportunity for God's grace to transform it into positive steps of progress in my growth. Thus, I am transformed from a worried, harried, fearful disciple into a citizen of heaven who reflects the serenity of the country to which he belongs.

I will be a living example of the riddle of Samson: "Out of the eater came something to eat, and out of the strong came something sweet" (Judges 14:14). As with Samson, I must do more than put the lion to death; I must compel it to yield its honey, by which I am made the stronger. That is my goal: to make evil become honey!

"'Let us tear their fetters apart, and cast away their cords from us!' He who sits in the heavens laughs, the Lord scoffs at them" (Psalm 2:3–4).

APRIL 1

Overasking in Prayer

I must be careful in my prayers never to *overask* anything of the Lord. The mother of James and John asked Jesus that her sons might sit in the two most important places in His Kingdom: at His right hand and the left (Matthew 20:20–21). Jesus' reply was sharp, "You do not know what you are asking!" (v. 22). Salome had overstepped her bounds; she had overasked!

I always know when I have overasked because it means asking for more than the Lord has explicitly promised. Jesus had promised each of His disciples a throne (Matthew 19:28), but this was not enough for James and John; they wanted the throne on each side of Jesus. That was too much and Jesus had to reprimand them.

To overask means to yield to the ever subtle voice of self, which is willing to spiritualize anything just so it can have its way. It means to want that little bit extra (just a teeny bit!) that self craves, and all in the guise of dedication to God's service. God promises, "I will supply your needs," and we plead, "And a few comforts too?" God says, "I will make you a blessing," and we beg, "And well known along with it?"

The one who overasks wants to "commercialize" on God. He is like a beggar who ups his demand when he sees the large number of coins in the giver's hand. He is like Lot, who was not satisfied merely to be rescued from Sodom but wanted to pick the site of safety after the deliverance (Genesis 19:20).

To all profiteers in prayer, Jesus has only one word: "You do not know what you ask." No, indeed, we do not. For if I overask I am opening myself to a Pandora's box of things beyond my good—and even my safety. I am much better off when I receive what Jesus has promised, and not an atom more!

"Not that I speak from want; for I have learned to be content in what-ever circumstances I am" (Philippians 4:11).

APRIL 2

Conquering Pain

Today I am in pain and I must ask God to teach me what it means. The most painful thing about pain is its alienation, just as a sore thumb feels alienated from the body. That is why Jesus, at the deepest point of His suffering on the cross, cried out about being "forsaken" (Matthew 27:46).

There are levels of suffering just as there are levels of glory. The ordinary man suffers simply because he is a son of Adam. He suffers *internally*, he bears the pain in his body because he is alive. No other person need be involved. The next level of suffering is substitutional—pain borne for others, like a mother burdened with the care of her child, or a soldier injured in war. This kind of pain exists because others exist. The third kind of pain includes the second one, but goes beyond it. It is *adopted* pain. This was the kind Jesus suffered for us.

Jesus never became sick internally; He took what belonged to others and made it His own. It was inevitable that Jesus, in becoming man and with our redemption in mind, should have a direct confrontation with pain. It is also noteworthy that Jesus did not adopt our pains to remove them but to purify them. That is why His followers still suffer, still go through the fire, in what is called "the fellowship of His sufferings" (Philippians 3:10). In sharing our sufferings with Jesus, we also share in what He did with suffering—turn it into a stepping-stone to glory.

I must never deny pain, for that would be a denial of the cross of Christ. Nor must I fight pain, for that would be an improper use of it. Jesus adopted it and conquered it and so must I. But I can never conquer it alone. I can do it only through Christ, who gives me the right to enjoy what He so gloriously accomplished.

"For momentary, light affliction is producing for us an eternal weight of glory far beyond all comparison" (2 Corinthians 4:17).

APRIL 3
Contemplating Evil Action

I will never become a strong disciple of Jesus Christ until I properly understand my *relationship* to evil. Evil does not become evil to *me* until *I* allow it to become so. A cancer is strictly a fibrous mass in my body until I become afraid; then it becomes evil to me. Jesus said of Satan, "The prince of this world cometh, and hath nothing in me" (John 14:30, KJV). The evil one attacked Jesus time and again, but he never won any ground. That sets the pattern for me: I must not let evil invade me, violate me, spoil me. Even more, I must not even consider doing evil, for love "thinketh [takes into account] no evil" (1 Corinthians 13:5, KJV). Just as contemplating temptation is the beginning of sin, so contemplating evil action is the beginning of defeat.

That means I must not let evil dwell in my mind, my thoughts. That is where "the renewing of [the] mind" (Romans 12:2) must come in. A renewed mind is God's mind, and God will never allow evil to upset Him. Thinking godly, however, is not an action of self-effort. It is really effortless, like the flow of the Niagara Falls. I must simply allow Christ to flow through every impulse of my being; then my mind will be automatically, continually renewed.

Lord, I must never be naive and pretend evil does not exist. I must always recognize its existence but never its authority. The moment I bow to its yoke I start my slide downward. Whenever I turn from evil I can always depend upon Your support, for "the eyes of the Lord are [always] toward the righteous, and His ears are open to their cry" (Psalm 34:15).

"And after you have suffered for a little while, the God of all grace, who called you to His eternal glory in Christ, will Himself perfect, confirm, strengthen and establish you" (1 Peter 5:10).

APRIL 4
Faith Needs an Opportunity

I will remember that faith, like muscle, must be exercised in order to grow strong. In other words, there must be the occasion, or provocation, of faith. Most of the time my natural inclination is to *escape* this provocation. But I must put on the right kind of glasses and see provocation, not as a disaster, but as an opportunity for God to work.

Miracles occur when there is a tremendous voltage between *need* and *supply*. That is like the positive and negative particles that cause a thunderstorm. If I am to see God work dramatically, I must bring an acute need face-to-face with God's supercharged supply. The need is always there as long as sin and man exist, but the missing element is the intensified power of supply. That is where God needs a conductor, a man of faith, like Moses, Elijah, or the Lord Jesus. Wherever they went they were natural "lightning rods" that drew the power from God.

I also must remember that faith decays from lack of stimulus. Quite often I have "little" faith simply because I have had little opportunity to exercise it. Faith grows by being challenged. If my life is so-so and average, I do not need to pray for faith but for more problems, difficulties, and challenges. That means the courage to dare, to launch out, to expose myself to the pains, hurts, and heartaches of this world.

A person without faith is admitting he has no concern for others, for we cannot long spiritually for others without becoming aware of deep, sore, bleeding wounds. By means of our faith those wounds can be healed, and God is waiting for believers! How I long to be like Abraham, who was "strong in faith, giving glory to God" (Romans 4:20). That is it—to be strong enough so that the result is always *glory.*

"By faith Moses . . . refused to be called the son of Pharaoh's daughter; choosing rather to endure ill-treatment with the people of God, than to enjoy the passing pleasures of sin" (Hebrews 11:24–25).

APRIL 5

Loving Our Loved Ones Properly

As a disciple of Jesus Christ I must come to terms with my family, my loved ones. My natural tendency is to become dependent upon them—upon my wife for physical comfort, my children for companionship. If I do this, I am going against everything that characterizes the discipled man. The key word is *dependence*. God has graciously given me a wife and children, but they must not be my dependence.

I must relate to my loved ones as Abraham related to his son Isaac. On Moriah, Abraham was willing to sacrifice his dearest possession. So I must consign my loved ones to the altar, I must sacrifice them, I must give them up. I must cut clean the lines of dependency forever.

To be dependent means to be vulnerable to tragedy. I have seen many of God's children devastated because they built their lives on their loved ones, and then God called the loved ones home! I must always live, in a sense, as if God *had already* called my loved ones home. I must always place the shadow of the cross over their fair faces.

This does not mean *loving* my dear ones less, or *enjoying* them less. It simply means I cannot love them without putting Jesus between us. And it reserves the right for Him as the third party to control the relationship.

I think that is what Jesus meant when He said that unless I hated my loved ones, I could not be His disciple (Luke 14:26). If I consign my dear ones to Moriah it seems like hatred, but it really isn't; rather, it is the deepest kind of love, both to my Savior and my dearest earthly treasures. That is the inseparable kind of love Paul refers to in Romans 8, and it is born in a Calvary relationship with those who are very close and very precious to me.

"'Simon, son of John, do you love Me more than these?' He said to Him, 'Yes, Lord; You know that I love You.' He said to him, 'Tend My lambs'" *(John 21:15).*

APRIL 6
Eating and Drinking with God

One of the sure signs that a disciple is reaching a mature relationship with God is in the matter of *relaxation*. "They saw God, and did eat and drink" (Exodus 24:11, KJV). People who claim that God must always be approached with holy fear do not really know God.

If I am awkward in the presence of God, I do not know Him too well. He wants me to become familiar enough with Him to "eat and drink" in His presence. He wants to call me His "friend," as He called Abraham, Moses, and the twelve disciples. Familiarity is not a sign of flippancy, nor does it always breed contempt. Does God say of me as He said of Abraham, "I *know* him" (Genesis 18:19, KJV, italics added)? God knows everyone, but does He know me as an intimate friend in whom He confides?

Jesus elevated His disciples from "servants" to "friends" (John 15:15, KJV). To be a servant of Jesus is a high calling indeed; but to be a friend means to be in on His plans, thoughts, feelings, and purposes. How amazing that many Christians never know at a given moment how Jesus *feels*. They know His *general* purposes from the Word, but they do not know His heart and mind concerning a particular situation. Elisha *knew* when God was going to take his leader, Elijah, from him into heaven (2 Kings 2:3), because he was more than a servant; Elisha was a friend of God.

To be relaxed in God's presence means that there is no fence between us. Trust and love have replaced fear and timidity. Awe has given way to acceptance. It is no light matter to have arrived here, and God is very careful about whom He admits to this intimacy. May God count me worthy! What an honor to be "comfortable" with God!

"Whom have I in heaven but Thee? And besides Thee, I desire nothing on earth. My flesh and my heart may fail, but God is the strength of my heart and my portion forever" (Psalm 73:25–26).

APRIL 7

Being a Ready Christian

There is a sense in which a disciple is never ready for combat, no matter how hard he trains. After Jesus told Peter that Satan was going to "sift you like wheat," the apostle replied, "Lord, with You I am ready to go both to prison and to death!" (Luke 22:33). Poor Peter! He stubbed his toes on the words "I am ready."

And so will we, unless we realize that we are never quite ready for Satan, sin, and evil. Peter's readiness was pride and ignorance. If he really had been ready, there would have been no need for Christ's intercession for him (v. 32).

Quite often after we have come away from a fresh victory over temptation we say, "There! I've got Satan on the run now!" We feel confident, elated. That is the danger point because it weakens our resolve to be nothing and to trust Christ supremely. To be ready means: "I've got the victory; it's nailed down for good." This attitude is a surprising underselling of Satan. The only One who is ever ready for Satan is our Champion, Jesus Christ. We cannot give up one moment's trust in Him without endangering ourselves.

The only kind of readiness the Bible commends me for is that of Paul: "I am . . . ready to be offered" (2 Timothy 4:6, KJV). As a disciple, I must be ready to pour out my life and my all for Jesus Christ my Lord. I must be ready to pour myself out in a libation of love and service for others. In matters such as these, I must be instantly ready, like a soldier on call day and night. Being "battle ready" means I must put on God's armor, not mine; but being "service ready" means I must tolerate no hindrance to a complete pouring out of my all to Him who poured out His all for me. "Now thanks be unto God, which always causeth us to triumph in Christ" (2 Corinthians 2:14, KJV).

"Therefore I am well content with weaknesses, with insults, with distresses, with persecutions, with difficulties, for Christ's sake; for when I am weak, then I am strong" (2 Corinthians 12:10).

APRIL 8
A More Than Adequate Christ

Lord, I will remember that I must grow in my knowledge of Jesus. To know Him is more than the first contact with Him as Savior. John the Baptist said, "I knew him not" (John 1:33, KJV). Didn't John recognize his relative? But John was speaking spiritually. Before the Holy Spirit revealed to him who Jesus really was, John did not *know* Him (v. 33b).

There are only two ways I can know Jesus: by the Word and the Spirit. History, art, and literature will teach me absolutely nothing about Him. He is the only person who walked this earth who must be spiritually discerned if He is to be known at all. The moment I shut my eyes to the Word and my ears to the Spirit, I cease learning about Jesus. Even worse, the knowledge that I once gained about Him begins to seep away from me. This explains why disciples who once were "on fire" for Jesus gradually grew cool and finally left their plows.

Knowing Jesus is a daily thing. Many Christians by their actions, lives, and fruit constantly say, "I know Him not." It is pitiful to see believers walk though life pretending to know Him. The only knowledge of Jesus they have is that of the initial saving contact. Thank God, this knowledge is enough for sinners, but it is never enough for disciples.

I must never offer the world a Jesus whom I know is necessary. I must offer it a Jesus whom I know well enough to describe as "altogether lovely" (Song of Solomon 5:16, KJV).

"Now as they observed the confidence of Peter and John, and understood that they were uneducated and untrained men, they were marveling, and began to recognize them as having been with Jesus" (Acts 4:13).

APRIL 9
Feeling the Sensitivity of Christ

A disciple must always realize that he lives in a world of cost. When God became flesh, He penetrated time and space in Jesus Christ to redeem fallen man. But God could not do this without cost.

So with me. For Christ to be "formed" in me (Galatians 4:19), I must be willing to bear the cost. Dietrich Bonhoeffer says that the image of Christ is formed in us only when we *suffer* for Him. That is debatable, but at least it is true that for God to become man in Christ meant suffering: rejection, loneliness, and finally death.

When Christ comes into my life He brings His intensified feelings with Him. That is why a Christian is more sensitive than an unsaved person to evil and wrong. Further, the more Christ has of me, the more intense those feelings inside me become, for, after all, Jesus Christ was the most evil-sensitive person who ever walked the earth. I cannot walk very far with Him without weeping over the lostness of man, the insanity of evil, and the intolerable suffering that evil brings upon human beings.

I notice one obvious thing about Satan: he is absolutely lacking in feeling. If he possessed any feeling at all, he would no longer be Satan. He is the opposite of God, who is total feeling. Whenever evil prevails in men, they, like their infernal master, become "past feeling" also.

A mark of true discipleship is utter sensitivity to evil and utter compassion for those bound in its grip. That is the cost all disciples of Jesus Christ have to pay. That is why Jesus said, "In the world you have tribulation" (John 16:33). Tribulation? That troubles and scares me, Lord. Then I hear You speak again, "But take courage; I have overcome the world."

"The Lord redeems the soul of His servants; and none of those who take refuge in Him will be condemned" (Psalm 34:22).

APRIL 10
How God Overcomes

As a disciple I must choose my weapons of warfare, but they must not be "carnal" (2 Corinthians 10:4, KJV). Violence, treachery, and deceit are expressions of the natural man and never the spiritual. They are the products of a life controlled by sin.

My weaponry is to be spiritual, that is, God's way of fighting a war. God does not destroy evil in a sudden stroke, although He could. To be *that* impatient with evil is not godly; there could be no salvation for anyone on that basis. To strike, to crush, to annihilate—those are the ways of Satan, not God. God overcomes by being overcome; Christ conquers by being crucified. Love wins by surrendering, yielding, submitting. It takes the sting out of evil by dying for it, thus giving birth to feeling, which is the first step in the process of our conversion.

My first step to victory in the holy war is to give up the natural way. The spiritual way is the way of love, which never cuts, wounds, or grieves, and yet it always wins (1 Corinthians 13:8). It is impossible for me to express the spirit of love naturally; I can only express it when Jesus Christ expresses it through me. Thus, it is absolutely true that Christian victory is not a thing but a Person.

The only way I can deal with the world of pain is to suffer that pain inwardly. If the suffering Servant lives in me, He will make me a sufferer also. You cannot bring God's love up against human need without suffering a cross; and God wants to see that cross in me in order that the redemption life of His Son might flow to a badly torn, hurting world. For in His death is our life, and in His life is our victory (2 Corinthians 4:10).

"The love of God has been poured out within our hearts through the Holy Spirit who was given to us" (Romans 5:5).

APRIL 11
Walking the Invisible Way

The true disciple lives in the upper realm where he "sees" invisible things constantly. It is the *temporal* realm that causes anxiety: that feared enemy, that inching cancer, that empty pocketbook. But once I see the wealth of the invisible world, the temporal sphere fades into insignificance.

Everything visible is subject to decay—I must not forget that. Bodies grow old, houses fall into ruin, the earth erodes, and the sun (like all stars) is subject to death. But everything invisible is beyond decay. Angels do not grow old, the human spirit does not die, and God Himself is beyond change and decay. Paul said that three things abide—faith, hope, love—all characteristics of the invisible world. The rich fool of Jesus' parable was the man who forgot that part of him—his spirit—was eternal, and so he spent all his time comforting his body (Luke 12:20). There is no greater foolishness.

True worldliness is really lack of vision. The worldling says, "What I see is all there is." So he uses his time, strength, and will in cultivating the physical and the tangible. Result? "The world is passing away" (1 John 2:17) and so is the man of the world.

I must follow the footsteps of those who went the "invisible" way: Abraham, who looked for an invisible city (Hebrews 11:8–10); Elisha, who saw invisible armies (2 Kings 6:17); and Moses, who followed an invisible God (Hebrews 11:27). Only as I immerse myself in the invisible world do I abide; and only as I obey invisible laws do I live.

"But as it is, they desire a better country, that is a heavenly one. Therefore God is not ashamed to be called their God; for He has prepared a city for them" (Hebrews 11:16).

APRIL 12
The Road Between

The most difficult part of my pilgrim life will not be when I begin, or when I end, but on the road between the two. The beginning is usually accompanied by a wave of exultant joy, like Columbus beginning his voyage. The end, though weary, is attended by the joys of accomplishment. But the road between has neither; therefore, I must be certain not to give up.

Most of the warnings of the Bible are addressed to me in that vulnerable stage. "They that wait upon the Lord shall renew their strength" (Isaiah 40:31, KJV); "Let us run with patience the race . . . before us" (Hebrews 12:1, KJV); "Press toward the mark" (Philippians 3:14, KJV); "Lo, I am with you always, even to the end" (Matthew 28:20). Paul feared being a "castaway," not at the beginning or at the end of his career, but in the red-hot fight of the road between (1 Corinthians 9:27, KJV). And Jesus had a strong word for the disciple who "put his hand to the plough" and turned back (Luke 9:62, KJV).

The difficulty of the middle part of the road is the absence of a cheering section. When I made my initial decision to follow Christ, what cheers came from loved ones and friends! When I shall come within sight of the celestial city, what a rousing welcome awaits me from those who went before me! But very few, if any, stand in the heat and dust of the road between to cheer me on. My comforts diminish, my friends are busy with their own journeys, and even God seems to have withdrawn a little. I must live trusting the naked Word of God without "feelable" assurance. I must endure "as seeing him who is invisible" (Hebrews 11:27, KJV). It is a hard, hard life; yet the same God who called me will surely stand by me until He rings me on to the final stage of the journey, and to the welcome shouts of the heavenly Zion. Hallelujah!

"Do not fear, for I am with you; do not anxiously look about you, for I am your God. I will strengthen you, surely I will help you, surely I will uphold you with My righteous right hand" (Isaiah 41:10).

APRIL 13
Process Salvation

I must imbue my mind with the fact that salvation is a process. True, it has a starting point; therefore, I can say, "I am saved, or I have been saved." But since it is also a process, I must say, I am "in the process of being saved" (1 Corinthians 1:18, Williams). The same *process* works conversely in the unsaved; they are "being lost" or "are on the way to destruction" (2 Thessalonians 2:10, Williams).

Once I get over the hump of believing everything is settled, then I can begin to grow. Many evangelicals are notoriously shallow Christians because they cannot get past the "everything is done" aspect of their salvation. So they tend to stagnate instead of growing.

I am impressed with Jeremiah's lesson at the potter's house. "The vessel . . . was marred . . . so he made it again" (Jeremiah 18:4, KJV). God is continuously "making us again," that is, correcting, shaping, and improving us until little by little the wonderful life of His Son, Jesus Christ, is seen and felt through us. The comforting thing about process salvation is what I do with my failures—I let the Master Potter mold them into something redemptive. Thus, failures need not drive me to despair but, rather, to hope, because salvation means that God is saving me daily from my weaknesses and sins.

My salvation is a daily miracle, and my expectation from God must be daily too. I can tell you what God *did* for me; but even more, I can relate what He is doing for me *now*. The process of salvation means that heaven will not be populated with newborn babies but mature saints, and their praise will be the praise of *experience*. The excitement of the Christian life is watching God slowly but surely transform me from a marred vessel into a vessel of honor, meet for the Master's use.

"But speaking the truth in love, we are to grow up in all aspects into Him, who is the head, even Christ" (Ephesians 4:15).

APRIL 14
The Government on His Shoulder

I must settle once and for all where my *responsibility* rests. I am a notorious worrier, wanting to control every facet of my life, and fearful of anything that is not under my control. Now God challenges me, "Who's going to run your life?" If it is I, then I must bear the responsibility; if God, He must bear the responsibility.

My Bible tells me, "The government shall be upon his shoulder" (Isaiah 9:6, KJV). It also tells me that when Jesus found me He placed me on His shoulders (Luke 15:5). There is no question here as to who bears the responsibility for me. Peter says, "Throw all your anxiety onto Him, for His concern is about you" (1 Peter 5:7, Berkeley).

I cannot have two masters; therefore, I must make a choice. If I choose God as my Master, I must relinquish all responsibility to myself. This means I cannot be perplexed about God's will for my life, for if it is His responsibility, then *He* must inform *me*, not I Him. All anxieties should cease for, if they do not, then I have assumed charge once again. If the government is really on His shoulder, then all questions should cease. For God will make clear to me at the right time what I need to know and what I need to do. Also, restlessness should cease, for restlessness means I am not in control, I am not on top of things. Being "on top of things" is now God's business and not mine. Therefore I rest.

My sole responsibility is not responsibility but *response*. I merely look to the "hand" and the "eyes" of my Master (Psalm 123:2) and respond to His wishes. I obey with alacrity and that is my triumph and my joy! Then I hear myself saying with the psalmist, "I delight to do Thy will, O my God" (Psalm 40:8).

"I urge you therefore, brethren, by the mercies of God, to present your bodies a living and holy sacrifice, acceptable to God, which is . . . good and acceptable and perfect" (Romans 12:1–2).

APRIL 15
When Christ Becomes Incarnational

I must avoid all classes of theology except the one Jesus espoused—incarnational theology. Jesus did not write a textbook on theology; He lived it. "The Word became flesh, and dwelt among us" (John 1:14). But I notice one thing about Christ's incarnation: it was unto death. Likewise, my commitment to Christ must be unto death, otherwise it is an insincere commitment.

The sufferings of Jesus were the manifestation of His love for us. And since He suffered infinitely, His love is infinite. So God does not measure my life by activity, but by suffering, for it is in suffering that my love to Him is shown. I think the formula goes something like this: I cannot suffer for Him unless I love; I cannot show love for Him unless I feel; and I cannot feel (properly, that is) unless Christ is implanted and growing in me. When Christ comes to live in me, He brings with Him that which is natural to God—sympathy, grace, kindness, charity, love, and mercy. No one who is fully possessed by Christ can avoid showing these qualities any more than a rose can avoid showing color.

God measures my life by whether or not I lay down my life for the brothers (1 John 3:16). But this involves a prior decision: Shall I live or shall I die? This was precisely the decision Jesus answered long before He became man. The moment He assumed human flesh, the die was cast; there was no turning back. So when Christ becomes incarnational in me, I am naturally propelled in the direction of a laid-down life. I become servantlike in ministry and I stoop to wash the dusty feet of others. I cannot call Him Master and be otherwise. But what a joy to know that "as He is, so also are we in this world" (1 John 4:17).

"This is pure and undefiled religion in the sight of our God and Father, to visit orphans and widows in their distress, and to keep oneself unstained by the world" (James 1:27).

APRIL 16
Praise in the Midst of Emptiness

God wants to develop me into a "yet" Christian, and I must respond to this. A "yet" Christian is one who, like Habakkuk, faces a bleak, dismal future and says, "Yet I will rejoice in the Lord, I will joy in the God of my salvation" (Habakkuk 3:18, KJV). Because of the near invasion of Babylon, Habakkuk could see that shortly the fig trees would not blossom, the vines would not grow fruit, the olive would fail, the fields would produce no crops, and no herds would be found in the stalls. In other words, hopelessness. What was the prophet's response to all this? "Yet I will rejoice."

It is easy to praise in the midst of plenty, but praise in the midst of poverty is true sainthood. It is all very well to sing "Hallelujah" with a full stomach, but can I sing it into an empty flour barrel? I am nice and loyal to God if He helps me; but am I still loyal if He does not? Like Peter, I am full of boast in the upper room, but what about when I am near the courtyard fire?

I am afraid that much of my religion is the "excrescence" type—the result of a comfortable stomach, the substance of my leisure moments. Too often it is my afterthought, my extra curriculum, my suburban status symbol. When God sends a Babylon to decimate me, I have a hard time saying, "Yet I will rejoice." I fear I am a soldier for the parade, not the battle. I love the bands, the flags, the cheering; but gunfire makes me nervous!

I need to learn what Habakkuk learned: "The just shall live by his faith" (Habakkuk 2:4, KJV). If I can only master that all-important lesson, I will not have to worry about my "yet's." I will have enough of them for time—and for eternity! Thank You, Lord, that You are "long suffering toward us" (2 Peter 3:9, NSRB) and because of that patience You are preparing me to become a "yet" Christian.

"The Lord is good, a stronghold in the day of trouble, and He knows those who take refuge in Him" (Nahum 1:7).

APRIL 17
God Chooses Our Portion

Lord, too often I have given you a Scrooge image. My puny faith and large problems have sometimes made me wonder if behind a frowning providence You hide a *frowning* face. I look at the massive forces that surround me—illness, worry, accident, death—and I suffer from a dreadful inferiority. I am often cowed, harassed, and compressed into a thin, weak existence.

Lord, show me the portion You have for me. It is the portion that You have selected for me, and it is measured out daily. That portion assures me that what I receive today comes from Your hands and, whether painful or sweet, is intended for my eternal good. I cannot lose what You have promised. Not one single atom will be denied me. You measure out my portion carefully and fairly. If I gladly accept it, You will cause Your bounteous blessings to pour into me and through me to others.

Sometimes, Lord, I have botched things up by grabbing my own portion. How patient You are, Lord. If I insist on seizing my own portion by selfish strength, You will not compete with me. You will let me have my way until I learn the bitter lesson; all "seized" portions lead to ultimate bitterness. Your portion may be bitter, Lord, but it always leads to ultimate sweetness.

Let me always allow You to choose my portion; otherwise, exhaustion and failure will follow. And when You choose, what glory! Like Israel, I am free to choose what has been chosen for me and, in choosing, will "live" (Deuteronomy 30:19).

"For He will give His angels charge concerning you, to guard you in all your ways. They will bear you up in their hands, lest you strike your foot against a stone" (Psalm 91:11–12).

APRIL 18

A Servant in Name or Act?

L ord, I must ask myself often, "Am I a servant in word or in deed?" I am reminded of Jacob, who addressed himself before his brother, Esau, as "your servant" (Genesis 32:18). But that was a servantship of fear; therefore, it was in name only. I must be careful not to *call* myself a servant, but to *be* a servant. It was only after the Jabbok experience, when Jacob wrestled with God, that he became a true servant (Genesis 33:5). Lord, let me never fail to have a Jabbok experience; otherwise my servantship becomes hollow.

Uriah Heep called himself "Your humble Servant," but he was anything but. I must be careful not to give out titles about myself, but rather to give out the content of the titles. A preacher's son once said, "When I grow up I'm going to become a preacher so I can tell people what to do!" He wanted the *office* of servant without the *function*. But many Christians—I am included—are just as childish! We love to be *thought* humble, servantlike, and helpful without having to go through the discipline of becoming like that.

There is only one way to become a servant, or slave, as the Bible describes it: by relinquishing. A slave has no rights, owns no property, is completely controlled by his master. The moment I pretend to be someone or lay claim to something, I cease to be a servant. Even my claim to salvation is through Another. I cannot become an acceptable servant until I have experienced the self-denial of Philippians 2:5–8, and I cannot experience that until I am willing to follow the One who denied Himself everything in order to give us everything. The aftermath of servantship is honor and glory (Philippians 2:9–11; 2 Timothy 2:12), and God longs to see me through to the finish.

"But that with all boldness, Christ shall even now, as always, be exalted in my body, whether by life or by death. For to me, to live is Christ, and to die is gain" (Philippians 1:20–21).

APRIL 19
The Bottom Line of Safety

As a disciple I must understand how the principle of *protection* works. Protection, to the natural man, is anything that works—guns, bribes, or whatever. To the spiritual man, protection is a Person.

The great illustration of divine protection is the Passover. "When I see the blood I will pass [hover] over you" (Exodus 12:13). God did not skip over the house with blood; He covered it with Himself. The same idea occurs in Isaiah 31:5 (ASV), "As birds hovering, so will Jehovah of hosts protect Jerusalem." In the day when the Assyrians threatened Jerusalem, God put Himself between His people and their enemies. When any of God's people are so threatened, God Himself becomes the buffer.

A missionary from China testified that when the Communists threatened to brainwash her, the Lord Himself intervened between her and her captors. They seemed unable to get at her to break her down; the wall of God's presence was in between. As a bird hovers over the nest to protect her young, so the Lord personally hovered over His servant to protect her. It is literally true that nothing can harm us without passing through our Father.

Since my protection is the personal presence of God, I must be careful not to trust in "horses" and "chariots" (Isaiah 31:1), for in them is "woe." Even to be anxious about protection is in itself a sign that I do not believe God. The Bible does not say, "Fear not, you have a great insurance policy," but "Fear not, for I am with you" (Isaiah 41:10, TLB). The bottom line of my safety is the presence of God, and His presence is so close that He squeezes Himself between me and my peril. Anything less than Himself spells disaster! He delivered Israel from the pursuing Egyptians, by coming "between" them (Exodus 14:20); and that is the way He delivers us.

"He will cover you with His pinions, and under His wings you may seek refuge; His faithfulness is a shield and bulwark" (Psalm 91:4).

APRIL 20
Counterfeit Discipleship

I must understand what it means to be a counterfeit Christian. The Bible reveals many—Judas, Demas, Diotrephes—and so does human experience. I have known a number of "saints" who no longer walk with God. This is enough to chill me with fear, then drive me to my knees in self-examination.

Who is counterfeit? Only the *end* will really tell. But since I cannot afford to wait for the end, I must know now.

As I study the Bible's counterfeits, I seem to see one outstanding characteristic: accepting unconcern. Nowhere do I find Judas examining his relationship to Jesus, scrutinizing his feelings to see if they stand up to the light. I see him move along with a numb indifference to everything spiritual. Like a chameleon, the counterfeit takes on the color of his surroundings without asking, "Am I still a chameleon?"

A counterfeit really *cannot* ask questions about his relationship with God. It is the mixture of light and darkness that produces shadows; total darkness creates no shadows. That is why I am challenged by Paul: "Take heed lest [ye] fall" (1 Corinthians 10:12). If I take heed, it is a good sign I am not a counterfeit. If I "watch," "take heed," and "examine myself," then I am doing what the counterfeit *cannot* do, which makes the difference.

My continual concern about my relationship to Christ is a sure sign that I belong to Him; to be unconcerned is to be fatally wrong. When Christ offered me rest, He did not mean, "Take Me for granted." A soldier on inspection does not need to ask, "Am I still in the army?" only, "Am I pleasing my commander?" The counterfeit never asks that! Above all, I rest in His supreme knowledge, "The Lord knows those who are His" (2 Timothy 2:19).

"That the name of our Lord Jesus may be glorified in you, and you in Him, according to the grace of our God and the Lord Jesus Christ" (2 Thessalonians 1:12).

APRIL 21

A Reservoir of Faith

I will never know how much I owe to someone else's faith. God does not always grant me blessings on the strength of *my* faith. Sometimes my faith is very weak; yet blessings come just the same. I can only explain this in terms of Galatians 2:20, "I live by the faith of the Son of God" (KJV). Is it possible that Jesus believes for me, as well as dies for me and lives for me?

I am not sure I know the answer to this mystery. I do know that a paralyzed man was forgiven his sins because four of his friends believed for him. "When Jesus saw *their* faith, he said unto the sick of the palsy, Son, thy sins be forgiven thee" (Mark 2:5, KJV, italics added). Isn't this also implied in Paul's word to the Philippian jailer: "Believe in the Lord Jesus, and you shall be saved, you and your household" (Acts 16:31)? This is a strange activity of faith. It overflows the possessor and infills the surrounding needy ones until it blesses them also.

I think the message to me is: Be a reservoir of faith, not a well. A reservoir fills up and then overflows and continually blesses its surroundings. A well demands work and coaxing.

I must not lament the lack of faith in my family, my church, my neighborhood. *I must believe for them!* God will bless them, not because of their lack, but because of my fullness. This does not mean that God will bless them unconditionally (without faith, who can please Him?). It simply means that my faith triggers God's action. Once God begins to act, tiny slivers of growth begin to appear where before there was nothing but barrenness. Thank You, Lord, for the "gift of God," which is faith (Ephesians 2:8), the gift whereby not only I, but dear ones around me, are blessed with a spread table.

"In hope against hope he believed, in order that he might become a father of many nations, according to that which had been spoken, 'So shall your descendants be'" (Romans 4:18).

APRIL 22
Going Back to Lystra

God will never allow His disciples to "get around" scrapes; they must go "through" them. Nor will He allow us to get beyond a defeat unless we have sucked the victory out of it.

Paul and Barnabas "returned to Lystra" (Acts 14:21), the very place where a few days (or weeks) earlier they were stoned (v. 19). After such rough treatment, the natural man would have avoided Lystra as he would a plague! But not the spiritual man. God will not have him bypass Lystra without learning its lesson and winning a victory.

The reason I am not making progress in my discipleship right now may be because there is a Lystra in my life and I will not go back and turn it into a victory. Jesus did this with Jerusalem; the very place where He was crucified was the place where He harvested three thousand believers in a single day! I must conquer my Lystra or I will never grow an inch toward maturity.

God will allow (has even *planned*) many "Lystras" in my life, and I will bear the scars of such encounters for the rest of my life. But God will not allow Lystra to be a blot on any record. That heated quarrel, that unchecked appetite, that strained relationship must be refaced, and the damage must be undone by contrition, repentance, and forgiveness. I may have to return many times until God is satisfied that the defeat has eventually become victory. It takes immense courage to face the pain and shame again, but out of the matrix of that pain is born a mature disciple. God, encourage me to face my Lystra again, despite the threat of a second stoning! I cannot do it alone, but Jesus, my great "returner," will go with me! Did He not say, "My presence shall go with you"? And did He not promise, "I will give you rest" (Exodus 33:14)?

"If we confess our sins, He is faithful and righteous to forgive us our sins and to cleanse us from all unrighteousness" (1 John 1:9).

APRIL 23
The Ministry of Drastic Choices

As a human being I crave acceptance, but as a disciple of Jesus Christ I must expect to be misunderstood and at times rejected. When Jesus was growing up, He was "in favor with God and men" (Luke 2:52). But after His baptism and filling with the Spirit, Jesus was no longer in favor with His neighbors, His kinfolk. When they heard Him preach they were filled with anger, threw Him out of the city, and wanted to throw Him off the cliff (Luke 4:28–29). Why such a sudden reversal?

The world does not like to be disturbed. It loves its traditions, habits, and folkways. Jesus, filled with the Spirit and on a mission, disturbed their peace. He was no longer the placid carpenter, the quiet but trusted neighbor. His Father had called Him to preach, to teach, to heal, and ultimately to die, and this new ministry called for drastic choices, clean commitments, and bold actions of faith.

Like his Master, the disciple cannot worry about being rejected, or even being *understood*. The life of self-sacrificing discipleship is so at variance with the world's craving for comfort that never shall the twain meet. If I am too popular or too highly acclaimed, I had better check my message! "Give them what they want" is deplorable advice to a modern prophet. The messenger of God must be ready to fellowship with his Master, the angels, and a few faithful ones who have grasped what he is saying, and forget the masses. I love the "good shepherd" title that Jesus gave Himself (John 10:11), especially when I realize that it was said for the benefit of one who had been excommunicated from the synagogue for Christ's sake (9:34). To all whom the world has rejected for His sake, Jesus Christ is the "door" to green pastures and abundant living.

"Then I heard the voice of the Lord, saying, 'Whom shall I send, and who will go for Us?' Then I said, 'Here am I. Send me!'" (Isaiah 6:8).

APRIL 24
God the Stretcher

My greatest problem as a disciple is thinking naturally. I am bent that way from birth, and all my education reinforces it. But, Lord, how ceaselessly You try to teach me to think spiritually!

How many loaves of bread does it take to feed a hundred men? Twenty, of course (2 Kings 4:42–44). How many loaves of bread does it take to feed five thousand men plus others? Five, of course (John 6:9). But the answer does not lie in the amount of bread but in the amount of stretching it takes to get the crowd fed. God is the great stretcher who takes our meager gifts and makes them reach the maximum. That is why when I was a student and my income was meager, my needs were met. Now that I am older and my income is much larger, my needs are still being met. If I gather too much I have no surplus, and if I gather little I still suffer no lack (Exodus 16:18). This is because God operates on spiritual laws, not mathematical, and He tries to get me to think on those same higher laws.

I look at the scarcity; God looks at the oversufficiency. I look at the usual, the customary, while God looks at the miraculous. If I sit down and count the cost, I will never reach the correct figure. If I wait until the moment is ripe, it never will be! If I expand only to the limits of the known, I will fail. God wants me to "launch out into the deep," where I am abandoned to the laws of the spiritual. He wants me free enough from the restraints of the natural to enable Him to deal with me from His vantage point, the reservoir of the spiritual where there is never a lack or a shortfall. This is the God who challenges (and comforts) me with that easiest of all questions: "Is any thing too difficult for the Lord?" (Genesis 18:14).

"Now to Him who is able to do exceeding abundantly beyond all that we ask or think, according to the power that works within us" (Ephesians 3:20).

APRIL 25
Suffering the Point of the Sword

Lord, I realize that to be a follower of Jesus Christ I must feel the point of the sword. The prophecy of Simeon to Mary, "A sword will pierce even your own soul" (Luke 2:35), is true of anyone who is willing to let Christ be formed in him.

The pain of following You, Lord, is not merely rejection by the world or even by my loved ones. It is the rejection of *self*. The other kinds of pain—those caused by men—are easily borne because You are my comfort and Companion. But the pain of self-rejection is one that has no antidote. The very cure for that pain, Jesus Christ, is the One who allows the pain in the first place. Therefore, there is nothing to do but bear the growth of Jesus in me.

The pain of the sword point is a lifelong experience, since self is always with me and will fight bitterly every attempt to put it to death. My nature sometimes cries out strongly for expression, whether lust or revenge or greed, and this expression runs up against the sword point of Jesus. The pain of Jesus is the pain of an alternative: I cannot have Jesus and my sinful desires growing in line at the same time!

The only consolation I have in this painful battle is the same one Mary had—bringing Jesus to birth is worth it! To see Him "formed" in me and thus visible to someone else is worth all the anguish. To see Him loved, worshiped, and accepted by others, as Mary eventually did, is my ultimate delight and joy. "Faithful is He who calls you, and He also will bring it to pass" (1 Thessalonians 5:24) is the word for me today, as I quaver at such a high vocation as letting Christ be formed in me.

"For to you it has been granted for Christ's sake, not only to believe in Him, but also to suffer for His sake" (Philippians 1:29).

APRIL 26
The Cross Versus Natural Talent

Lord, I will remember that my service for You must not be hindered by self-effort, "lest the cross of Christ should be made of none effect" (1 Corinthians 1:17, KJV). It is so easy to think I am doing You a service, when in reality I am feeding my own ego. Paul did not use rhetorical devices when preaching the gospel, lest his natural talents and abilities get in the way. The moment I become inclined toward my natural instincts, that moment I rob the cross of its persuasive power.

The cross is a power all by itself. "And I, if I be lifted up . . . will draw all men to Myself" (John 12:32). God does not need me for what I am in myself; He only needs me as a channel to send His power through me. My greatest problem as a servant of Christ is to keep the *me* from getting in His way. What God has promised to bless is not *me* per se, but the free-flowing message of the cross through me. God is obligated to honor His Son, not me, and He *only* honors me when I in turn honor His Son.

Lord, I must understand that You called me, not because there is some intrinsic or subtle value in me, but only because You desire to reveal Your Son in and through me. I may indeed draw people by means of a pleasing personality or speaking gifts, but that does not mean I am accomplishing Your purposes through me.

Lord, may I be willing to follow the biblical formula: I must die if I would live; I must be a submissive "Moses' rod" if I would lead people from slavery to freedom. This is my great consolation: not what *I* did for Christ, but what *He* was pleased to do through me! "The grace of our Lord was poured out on me abundantly, along with the faith and love that are in Christ Jesus" (1 Timothy 1:14, NIV).

"But may it never be that I should boast, except in the cross of our Lord Jesus Christ, through which the world has been crucified to me, and I to the world" (Galatians 6:14).

APRIL 27
The Subtlety of Temptation

I find, Lord, the longer I am a disciple the more different temptation becomes. In my natural state, temptation was a problem only if there was a chance I would get caught. In my spiritual state, it becomes a problem because it upsets the delicate balance between assumed spirituality and real spirituality.

Temptation, for every disciple, has two hazards: *time*, that is, making a shortcut; and *method*, that is, substituting a different way for God's way. Every temptation, therefore, forces me to reexamine my spiritual foundations and to choose whether I will wait for God's time or seize my own time. In this way God uses temptation to make me "learn obedience" even as Jesus learned obedience.

The farther we walk with God, the more subtle temptation becomes. It is like approaching a bright light; the closer we get, the sharper the shadows are. The temptation of Jesus in Gethsemane was far more subtle than the temptations He suffered in the wilderness. Each new level of commitment for us opens up a whole new range of possible deviations from that commitment. That is why David Brainerd groaned as much over his weaknesses before his death as when he first began to follow the Lord.

When I am tempted I am consoled by Jesus, who is "touched with the feeling" of my infirmity (Hebrews 4:15, KJV). He cannot remove my temptation, nor can He be tempted for me, but He understands the battle I am in, and He cheers me on to victory. He also prays for me (Luke 22:32). He never lets me go, no matter how often I fail, because He has put His life in me and has determined that His life must not fail. "Because he himself suffered when he was tempted, he is able to help those who are being tempted" (Hebrews 2:18, NIV).

"God is faithful, who will not allow you to be tempted beyond what you are able, but with the temptation will provide the way of escape also, that you may be able to endure it" (1 Corinthians 10:13).

APRIL 28
Unblemished Service

In reading Your Word today, Lord, I noticed a curious thing: what is demanded of the priest (Leviticus 21:16–24) is also demanded of the sacrifice (Leviticus 22:17–25). In fact, the wording in both cases is almost the same!

This speaks forcibly to me. I cannot divorce myself from my service to You. I cannot have one standard for myself and another, different standard for my service. I must not perform beautifully as a teacher, speaker, or musician and then live personally on a shoddy basis. What is true of one must be true of the other.

My service to God must be unblemished (Leviticus 22:20), which means all sins confessed. It also must be whole, entire, unmutilated (see vv. 22, 24), which means I cannot be halfhearted about it. And it must be nonalien (v. 25), which means I cannot offer someone else's service and call it mine. If I offered myself to God blemished, broken, and alien, I would never be saved! My service, therefore, cannot be offered God on any plane that is lower than when I offered Him my soul for salvation.

I find myself shocked when I compare a person's performance with what I see in his life. His performing artistry woos and impresses me; yet when I look closely at him, I see brokenness, blemish, and mutilation. That distresses and puzzles me, Lord! What causes me even more anguish is this question: Do others find the same inconsistency in me? One thing is sure: God demands *consistency*; and if I, or any disciple, come up lacking, I must relentlessly root out the disparities until both life and service are one.

Am I sufficient for these things? Never! But "our sufficiency is God-given. And He has qualified us to be ministers of a new covenant" (2 Corinthians 3:5–6, Berkeley). Thank God for His sufficiency!

"But we have this treasure in earthen vessels, that the surpassing greatness of the power may be of God and not from ourselves" (2 Corinthians 4:7).

APRIL 29
Christ the Inside Savior

If I am to be a worthy disciple of Jesus Christ, I must come to terms with my inside. Jesus Christ is not out there; He is in me, as far as my discipleship is concerned. This means that no matter how I love books, revere people, and admire nature, in the last analysis I must confront the Christ who resides within. Too often I have lined up my life according to the outer lights instead of with Christ, the inner light, and this has only led to confusion.

Since Christ is within me, I must adopt two stances. First, I must listen to Him, and that involves a degree of turning inward, which my friends may often misunderstand. Second, I must allow Him expression, which is more than "following Jesus" or "walking in His steps." As the Spirit "clothed" Himself with Gideon, so I must let Jesus Christ clothe Himself with me. This is what Paul meant in 2 Corinthians 4:10, "that the life of Jesus also may be manifested in our body."

It is in me, not out there, that need and supply meet. Despite the beauty of the figure, Jesus does not walk beside me, for an "outside" Savior cannot meet the needs generated in my inmost being. That is why Paul says he did not know Christ "according to the flesh" anymore (2 Corinthians 5:16). The only Christ Paul knew was one inside him, a supreme Lord and Master, and not an outside figure whom he was trying to follow. Jesus Christ meets my need of guidance by propelling me from within.

With an inside Christ, I can rest; I will never lose my Guide. His presence is no farther than my heartbeat, His power no farther than my thought. "How precious also are Thy thoughts to me, O God! . . . When I awake, I am still with Thee," for You will "lead me in the everlasting way" (Psalm 139:17–18, 24).

"But if the Spirit of Him who raised Jesus from the dead dwells in you, He who raised Christ Jesus from the dead will also give life to your mortal bodies through His Spirit who indwells you" (Romans 8:11).

APRIL 30
Thinking Spiritually

Lord, I must distinguish between common sense and Spirit sense. The natural man lives by common sense, which means doing the expedient thing. But I must live by Spirit sense, which means doing the holy thing.

When I first became a Christian, I found a lot of variance between the expedient thing and the holy thing. I found myself stretching the truth (for the Lord's sake), telling social lies (not to hurt anyone's feelings), and doing other things that made common sense, but the Spirit within me was grieved. Gradually I came to see that the Spirit was not interested in saving my skin or making me attractive to others; He was interested in making me attractive to God the Father.

That meant the old mind-set had to go. The conniving, wheedling, and looking for an advantage had to give way to thinking spiritually, that is, thinking heavenly, what heaven desires of and demands of its citizens. That meant a crisis of will, for God does not make us mature men and women against our wills. As in all crises with God, a death took place and a new life of resurrection began in the power of the Holy Spirit. His thoughts then became paramount and, to a certain extent, automatic. His life became the natural life, and Spirit-thinking became the new common sense.

Augustine is reported to have said, "Love God and do as you please." The mature Christian will not have to ask, What shall I do? or, What shall I say? He does the commonsense thing. Only major decisions now need to be crisis decisions; the others are simply the result of a flowing relationship with Him who makes the best sense of all, eternal sense. "Let this mind be in you, which was also in Christ Jesus" (Philippians 2:5, KJV). With His right mind in me, His right behavior will necessarily follow.

"Be renewed in the spirit of your mind, and put on the new self, which in the likeness of God has been created in righteousness and holiness of the truth" (Ephesians 4:23–24).

MAY 1
Spiritual Childishness

I must be careful not to be impatient with God, for impatience is childishness, and childishness is an obstacle to God's working in me. Moses was childish when he cried, "You have not rescued your people at all" (Exodus 5:23, NIV). He thought God should have delivered His people from Egypt *immediately*, and since God did not respond that way, Moses impatiently exploded against God.

Childishness destroys the very character of God. It says, "God promised but He has not done it." It reckons that God's actions must be compressed into *my* time schedule and must be done in *my* way. It is the frustration of a baby who cannot control his parents, who cannot cope with an adult world. Childishness is essentially trying to bring God down to earth and forcing Him to obey earthly laws instead of the laws of heaven. It is like a child who would render his parents infants instead of becoming mature as they are.

Am I a sulking Christian? Do I flare up like Moses, pout like King Saul, or sulk like Jonah? Do I get peeved at God because I cannot control Him, put a handle on Him?

The remedy for childishness is not time, for many people are still childish in later years. The remedy is a good look at ourselves, for nothing stops the pouting better than a good look in the mirror! That is why I must use my Bible constantly, not only for what it tells me about God, but what it tells me about myself! The Bible, like my mirror, is my truest friend. It tells me what I *need* to know.

James tells me that if I look properly at my spiritual mirror and correct the pouty look, I will be "blessed" in what I do (James 1:25). That is the maturity I want, Lord, to be blessed in what I do.

"If then you have been raised up with Christ, keep seeking the things above, where Christ is, seated at the right hand of God" (Colossians 3:1).

MAY 2
Flubs, Flaws, and Brittleness

I must not be disheartened when I flub in my spiritual life. A lot of my flubs are not sins, just mistakes, and mistakes are the marks of immaturity and greenness. An infant makes endless mistakes, but his parents do not give up on him—they realize he is just an infant. They know that he will outgrow a lot of his childishness.

As a disciple of Jesus Christ I must believe in progressive satisfaction. When God begins a work, the result thereof must be His satisfaction. His creation was very good. He viewed the work of His Son on Calvary and was satisfied. So I believe He is progressively satisfied with His work in His children, especially His growing children. This does not mean that our condition at a given moment is perfect morally, but it means that, like a potter, He is satisfied with our progress.

This also means that I must forget comparison with others. Comparison means we are at the same point, on the same level. But no two children of God are ever at precisely the same point or on the same level. I must not, therefore, compare myself to David Brainerd, Henry Martyn, or Jim Elliot. I must only ask God if *He* is satisfied with my progress at a given moment. If He is, all is well, even though flaws and specks appear in my makeup.

The basic thing God looks for in me is not the absence of flaws but the presence of moldable clay. He can easily work out the flaws, but He cannot do a thing with clay that is hard, brittle, and crumbly. Brittleness means I have been hurt somewhere along the line and have not gotten over it.

Lord, I want to be the *best* clay, soft and conformable to Your image! You ask, "Can I not . . . deal with you as this potter does?" (Jeremiah 18:6). Yes, Lord, You can—abundantly, perfectly, eternally.

"My little children, I am writing these things to you that you may not sin. And if anyone sins, we have an Advocate with the Father, Jesus Christ the righteous" (1 John 2:1).

MAY 3
Behaving Like God

God will not accept any of my excuses for not *acting godly*. My paltry excuses—"I am only dust," "in me dwelleth no good thing," "He knoweth my frame"—are often only crutches to get me out of one scrape and ready for another. God wants me to stop acting like dust and flesh and start acting like Him.

How can I act like God? There are many ways, but here is one: "No one has beheld God at any time; if we love one another, God abides in us, and His love is perfected in us" (1 John 4:12). This verse sweeps away all my crutches! I act like God when I am filled with love toward others. This verse says that I can have the unspeakable privilege of behaving like God, of showing others what God is like. That is not the privilege of angels or super saints, but of common clay like myself.

The greatest need of our day is for God to become visible. He is visible to a certain extent in nature, but nature never conveys God's love. And unless God's *love* is conveyed, His fullness is not conveyed. That is where you and I come in; we may show others a mini-glimpse of God's love.

My excuses are further destroyed when John says, "He has given us of His [own] Spirit" (1 John 4:13). That ends our camouflage! There is no use saying, "But I'm not a loving person, I'm not made that way!" We *are* made that way by the Holy Spirit who is in us by faith. He sheds "the love of God . . . abroad in our hearts" (Romans 5:5, KJV).

Lord, the world desperately needs a good look at You. Help them to get a glimpse of the lovely person You are by looking at me. And help me no longer to hide behind the mask of "it can't be done," for "I can do all things through Christ, who strengtheneth me" (Philippians 4:13, NSRB).

"And this is His commandment, that we believe in the name of His Son Jesus Christ, and love one another, just as He commanded us" (1 John 3:23).

MAY 4
Taking the Fear Out of Change

As a disciple of Jesus Christ I must learn the discipline of *change*. My preconceived ideas of God's direction will be upset frequently because I am only God's servant, not His counselor. When the cross came into view, Jesus did not become frustrated, but said, "Even so, Father: for so it seemed good in thy sight" (Matthew 11:26, KJV).

Jesus submitted willingly because He knew the *intent* of the Father. That is the key: to be assured of God's intent. We may forget the details as long as we accept the Person who is inaugurating the changes. To haggle over details, to fuss over delays, and to sulk when God seemingly changes His tactics is really an unconscious defamation of God's character.

So often God will tell me, as He did the disciples, "It is not for you to know" (Acts 1:7). The basic difference between a natural and a spiritual man is that the natural man demands to *know*, while the spiritual man is content to *obey*. That is why God does not make *knowledge* the condition of anything. He does not say, "O ye of little *knowledge*," but, "O ye of little *faith*" (Matthew 6:30, KJV, italics added). Knowledge comes either with, or just after, the happening.

So much of our lives is lived in the dark. It is in the "nevertheless afterward" that we finally understand what God has been up to all the while. Many Christians make themselves ill by trying to fathom God. Peace comes by letting the attitude of Jesus come through: "Yes, Father, for this was your good [will]" (Luke 10:21, NIV). I can adapt to change if only I will adapt to the One who changes. The nub of it is right there, in my relationship with Him. In the hands of a changeless God, I need fear no change.

"Every good thing bestowed and every perfect gift is from above, coming down from the Father of lights, with whom there is no variation, or shifting shadow" (James 1:17).

MAY 5

The Gift of a New Life

My discipleship under Jesus Christ means I witness for Him, but I must be careful to be a biblical witness. Much witnessing around us today is nothing more than egotism in spiritual dress. John the Baptist is the biblical example of a true witness. "He was . . . sent to bear witness of that Light" (John 1:8, KJV). The ministry of witnessing for Jesus Christ is not expressed as a verb but as a noun. We do not "witness." We *are* witnesses.

Many Christians are confused by the modern emphasis on "gifts." The confusion lies in the fact that every Christian is supposed to have gifts, and the gifts are indications of something extra special.

The only gift *every* Christian has is a new life from God, the life of Jesus Christ. Since Jesus Himself was a Witness (Revelation 1:5), witnessing will be the normal result wherever He is. Witnessing is basically a state of *being* rather than a function of *vocalizing*.

John was not occupied with seeking and finding his gifts, but simply pointing to Jesus Christ as the Lamb of God. His ministry was to make men Christ-dependent, not John-dependent. The preoccupation with gifts can make us little gods in our own little kingdoms, the very opposite of what a witness is supposed to be. Because John was Christ-centered, his life was its own advertising campaign, encouraging others to follow Jesus.

No wonder Jesus said of him, "Among those born of women there has not risen anyone greater" (Matthew 11:11, NIV). Yet in the same breath Jesus said the "least" of us could be as least as great as John. Lord, may others take notice of me for this one reason: that I have "been with Jesus" (Acts 4:13).

"Prove yourselves to be blameless and innocent, children of God above reproach in the midst of a crooked and perverse generation, among whom you appear as lights in the world" (Philippians 2:15).

MAY 6

Just Say the Word

By Your grace, Lord, I will not be a propped-up disciple. Such a disciple always says, "I will not believe, *except*." Like Thomas and Gideon, he must see tangible signs that God is with him and he will not budge without them.

Signs are so comforting, and I need them at times, but Your desire, Lord, is to make us sign-less Christians who simply take You at Your Word. How often I have prayed, "Lord, lead me, and show me a sign that I am headed in the right direction." There is nothing wrong with signs *after* the fact; but it is asking for signs before the fact that shows I am shaky in my trust.

I must emulate the centurion of Capernaum who asked Jesus to heal his sick servant (Matthew 8:5-13). He said, "Just say the word, and my servant will be healed" (v. 8, NIV). In other words, "Not even Your physical presence is necessary; Your word is enough." How often have I taken the naked Word of God as sufficient, and not asked for props, signs, or even His manifest presence? No wonder Jesus said, "I have not found anyone in Israel with such great faith" (v. 10, NIV).

Too often I am like Abraham, whose trust had a sliver of doubt in it. "What [sign] wilt thou give me, seeing I [am] childless?" (Genesis 15:2, ASV). He wanted to believe God, but the flesh kept getting in the way. So God accommodated him (as He often does us) and gave him "the stars" (v. 5) as a sign. It was *then* that Abraham "believed in the Lord" (v. 6). But how much better to have said what the centurion said later, "Just say the word!"

Lord, make me a "Just say the word" disciple, and let me not need to be propped up even by such wonderful things as Your stars! Let me say with Mary: "Be it done to me according to your word" (Luke 1:38).

"Forever, O Lord, Thy word is settled in heaven. Thy faithfulness continues throughout all generations" (Psalm 119:89–90).

MAY 7
Convenient Discipleship

Lord, I must come to terms with the "ifs" of endurance. I thank You, Father, that You are infinitely able to *secure* my salvation, but You do not encourage tasters, sippers, and triers-out. I must therefore wrestle with that weighty word of Paul: "If we endure, we shall also reign with Him; if we deny Him, He also will deny us" (2 Timothy 2:12).

To deny Christ means to pretend I do not know Him in situations in which knowing Him would be an embarrassment. I can deny Christ in business, in social circles, in my family, and even in my church. Denying Him means my discipleship is a convenience, and when it ceases to be convenient to me I simply throw it off like a coat.

If I make a practice of denying Christ, surely I will pay a penalty. The time will certainly come when, in desperation, I ask for help and God will find it "convenient" not to hear me (Isaiah 59:1–2). If I maintain the right to choose when I should or should not behave like a disciple, it means there is something drastically wrong with my commitment. The word *choose* drops from a true disciple's vocabulary once he has surrendered himself to his Lord.

I cannot be a part-time disciple. There is no such thing as trial discipleship. God will not accept my discipleship if I deliberately snub His Son for worldly gain and for the praise of men. However, even though I may fail, stumble, and fall, God will graciously forgive and set me going again. He will heal my faithlessness and love me freely, for His anger is turned away (Hosea 14:4).

"And He summoned the multitude with His disciples, and said to them, 'If anyone wishes to come after Me, let him deny himself, and take up his cross, and follow Me'" (Mark 8:34).

MAY 8
The Hard Sayings of Christ

Lord, may I never be one of those who becomes offended at a "hard saying" of Yours (John 6:60, KJV). Many of Your sayings are indeed hard, but may I never murmur against them, or ever decide to follow You no longer (John 6:61, 66).

You disturb me often, Lord, both by Your sayings and by Your actions in my life. But a Christ who never disturbed me, who never corrected me, who never disciplined me would be a Christ unworthy of my trust. I praise You for the many times You comforted and consoled me and nursed my wounded feelings back to health. But I thank You also for the times You refused to comfort me and told me to stop whining and get on with the job.

Most of the time when You give me a "hard saying" I am on the brink of a startling discovery about You or about myself. It is often a prologue to a wonderful thrust forward. It is like lightning on a black night, which suddenly reveals the landscape and shows me what I never knew was there.

Hard sayings are always dividers; they divide the true disciples from the spurious, they divide truths from falsehoods, and they divide the right feelings from the wrong ones. A hard saying is a purifier that strips away all the crusty accumulations and leaves me clean.

Hard sayings are painful, Lord, and they hurt. But how much better to have a hard saying from Jesus, who loves me infinitely, than a smooth saying from Satan, who only wants to twist and bend me away! Lord, give me sense to appreciate, yes *love*, Your hard sayings and so take a giant stride to glory. "I will never forget thy precepts; for with them thou hast given me life" (Psalm 119:93, NSRB).

"The Lord's lovingkindnesses indeed never cease, for His compassions never fail. They are new every morning; great is Thy faithfulness" *(Lamentations 3:22–23).*

MAY 9

The Anger of God

I must keep my thinking straight about God's anger. I have been taught that since Christ died for my sins, thus satisfying God's *judicial* anger, He will never become angry with me as His child. That is wrong. For God not to become angry with me when I show perverseness would be a dereliction of His fatherhood. If I have never felt His parental anger, then I have never sinned. Who of us can say that?

My comfort is not to *deny* God's anger but to understand it. For one thing, God's anger with His children is *momentary*, "Nor will He keep His anger forever" (Psalm 103:9). God's judicial wrath against unrepentant sinners is abiding and eternal (John 3:36), but His parental anger against me is swift and transitory. The moment its cleansing work is done, it abates and finally ceases.

Also, God's anger against His people is slow in rising. He is "slow to anger" (Psalm 103:8). Only after repeated warnings and grievings does the Lord finally show "burning anger" toward us (Psalm 85:3). His is not the cold, deadly wrath of the state executing justice upon a criminal; it is the tried patience of a father who longingly wants his son to walk the right way. God's anger, therefore, is veiled love. It is the cry of a God who can be hurt by His people.

God is always in control of His anger. As a Father He relents as the occasion demands; and despite His occasional chastening, how much sweeter *that* rod than the everlasting burnings. Lord, may I always respect Your anger, and may I always speedily end what brought it to birth against me! Let me enjoy the turning away of Your anger and the fresh outpouring of Your love when my faithlessness is healed (Hosea 14:4).

"Incline Thine ear, O Lord, and answer me; for I am afflicted and needy. Do preserve my soul, for I am a godly man; O Thou my God, save Thy servant who trusts in Thee" (Psalm 86:1–2).

MAY 10
The Ministry of Life or Death

Lord, teach me that being Your disciple is a life-or-death matter. Jesus said, "The words that I have spoken to you are spirit and are life" (John 6:63). He did not say, "My words are *living*"; He said, "My words are *life*." This means that wherever the Word is released, there is life. Whenever the Word enters a human being, that person begins to show (spiritual) life. That means that I must constantly be in a condition in which the Word can flow uninterruptedly through me. The moment I block the flow by disobedience, pride, or perverseness, that moment life stops.

It is difficult for me, as an evangelical believer, to imagine that I can be the bearer of spiritual death. But it is true. The kind of spiritual death I am thinking of here is not the death of my salvation but the death of my godly influence. Outwardly, the Pharisees obeyed every rite and tradition; but because the Word had stopped flowing through them, they were inwardly like tombs (Matthew 23:27). And so I may conform to every orthodox doctrine and yet, because I refuse to let the Word continually flow through me, I may be harboring inward putrefaction and decay.

At any given moment I am the minister of life or death. It all depends upon my relationship to Jesus' words. This explains why Achan was destroyed after he stole the "devoted" thing (Joshua 7, ASV). God could not allow a man who had disobeyed His word to minister death to the entire camp.

I am sobered by my responsibility. Yet I rejoice because I can indeed be the channel of life to my surroundings. I can be God's oasis to a barren environment. Lord, let me be a contagion of Your life! May I be like Ezekiel's river, which brought greenness to a parched and barren land (Ezekiel 47:12).

"For we are a fragrance of Christ to God among those who are being saved and among those who are perishing; to the one an aroma from death to death, to the other an aroma from life to life" (2 Corinthians 2:15–16).

MAY 11
God Buffers His People

Lord, I thank You that You are my "buffer." The Lord is my buffer; I shall not feel pain. How often have I been reminded of that beautiful thing You did for Your people when the Egyptians pursued them: You placed Your defending angel between pursuer and pursued (Exodus 14:19–20). Thank You, Lord, for the many times Your angel has stood between me and a grievous hurt, a smarting pain, and an otherwise crushing blow.

God will not unload on us more than we can bear (1 Corinthians 10:13). That means He trusts our own spiritual strength to deal with the pain *up to a certain point.* But when He sees that the load is greater than our ability to handle it, He personally intervenes and takes the pain on Himself. I see now, Lord, what Isaiah meant when he said: "In all their affliction He was afflicted, and the angel of His presence saved them" (Isaiah 63:9). God is the great absorber of our excess suffering; that is why we are "able to bear it."

I once heard an older believer, ill in the hospital, say: "I can't understand it! Me, of all people, in utter peace!" She had expected to feel *pain*; instead, she felt the evidence of His presence. How often do we rejoice that God saves us from our sins! But it is just as true that He saves us from our sufferings by interposing Himself between them and us.

We worship a scarred God. But may I never forget, Lord, that the scars were inflicted because You loved me enough to step in between, to become my buffer, to take upon Yourself that which was rightly mine. Your love overwhelms me, God! No wonder Paul said it "surpasses knowledge" (Ephesians 3:19) and Isaac Watts described it as "so amazing, so divine."

"Return to your rest, O my soul, for the Lord has dealt bountifully with you. For Thou hast rescued my soul from death, my eyes from tears, my feet from stumbling. I shall walk before the Lord in the land of the living" (Psalm 116: 7–9).

MAY 12
Spiritual Shame

I must live so as never to be "ashamed before him" (1 John 2:28, KJV). Certainly this refers to His second coming and our assembling before Him. But it also refers to the kind of life we should live *before* He comes.

To be ashamed before Him means I have forced Him to view my sin. Paul makes this clear: "Shall I . . . take the members of Christ to make them members of a prostitute?" (1 Corinthians 6:15, Berkeley). A preacher's son trampled his father's marigolds, but his father caught him in the act. The boy cried, "Don't look at me!" He was ashamed because his father was forced to see his disobedience.

Shame is the realization of a contrast. The greater the contrast, the greater the sense of shame. If I have a sense of discomfort in the presence of the Lord, it is always because of some sin. "Dead" people have no such discomfort; but spiritually alive people can become acutely pained by the presence of even the smallest sin. To be ashamed before Him, therefore, is a mark of spiritual life, even as the pin pricking of the doctor hurts because the patient is alive.

To be ashamed before Him means that Christ is really with me, but something has happened in our relationship. I must try, by His help, to live in an unclouded relationship with Him so that I will never feel shame. It is the life that never has to cry out to Him, "Don't look at me," the life in which God and His disciple walk together because they are perfectly "agreed" (Amos 3:3, KJV).

"Against Thee, Thee only, I have sinned, and done what is evil in Thy sight, so that Thou art justified when Thou dost speak, and blameless when Thou dost judge" (Psalm 51:4).

MAY 13
Who Is on the Cross?

Imust be careful not to let my service for Christ become an extension of myself. Do I enjoy preaching because I am the center of attention for an hour? Do I enjoy teaching because I hold the class in my power for a brief span? Do I enjoy winning souls because the results bolster my ego?

I can see how subtle the flesh really is. It does not mind being dressed in religious clothing as long as it does not have to die. The heart of the matter is: Who is on the cross and who is on the throne? The great historical switch has taken place: Christ *was* on the cross and is now on the throne; self *was* on the throne and must now be impaled upon the cross. If I ever switch the two and reverse history, I am in trouble!

Self's great, eternal ambition is to escape its cross and sneak back on the throne. Often I have looked at the cross where self hung and said, "There, crucified once and for all!" Yet, a second look reveals an empty cross and an escaped self, very much alive and demanding recognition.

Crucifying self is not negation. Negation says, "You are dead." But true Christian living says, "You are dead to self, but alive to Christ" (see Galatians 2:20). Even more, Christianity says that *before* I can become alive to Christ, not afterward, I must die. It is not the *person* who dies, only the tendency to deify the person. Jesus did not consider "equality with God a thing to be grasped" (Philippians 2:6). If Jesus, who was God, refused to grasp His deity, how much more must I, a sinner, refuse to deify myself? The answer is not a once-for-all crucifixion, but a daily thing. The sweetest song a disciple can sing is Galatians 2:20, "I have been crucified with Christ; . . . but Christ lives in me." After death comes life, and after crucifixion, victory.

"Knowing this, that our old self was crucified with Him, that our body of sin might be done away with, that we should no longer be slaves to sin" (Romans 6:6).

MAY 14
Taking and Giving Offense

As a disciple of Jesus Christ I must learn never to *give* or *take* offense. Jesus said that the world constantly offends us, but we as His followers must never offend (Matthew 18:7–9). He was so strict about the matter that He said even an eye, a foot, or a hand must be cut off rather than offend someone else. He meant this: get rid of anything that causes offense to someone else, no matter how painful to yourself.

Yet, as a discerning disciple, I must expect offenses to come my way. I must be wise as a serpent (in expecting offenses) yet harmless as a dove (in giving them). It is only natural that somewhere along the way I will offend others. The gospel itself is offensive to many, and if I preach it faithfully I will most certainly put some people out. But that is not the offensiveness Jesus is talking about. He is talking about the offense that comes *from an evil mind.* He is thinking about the offense that comes *from an evil intention.* We cannot make everybody love us; but we can, like Daniel, force those who dislike us to say, "It's because of his God."

Taking offense is a different matter. By God's grace I must *never* take offense, as Jesus Himself did not. Regardless of how evil the intention, how vile the source of the offense, I must never attribute to a person's action a malicious cause, but rather turn my case over to God and say, "Lord, You judge in the matter." Thus, vengeance is safely given to Him.

The offenseless life is a rugged discipline for the follower of Jesus Christ. Yet the same Jesus who exemplified it perfectly on earth will not fail to continue that good work in me. The One who said I am to be as harmless as a dove (Matthew 10:16) will not ask me to do the impossible; He will energize me for it.

"And while being reviled, He did not revile in return; while suffering, He uttered no threats, but kept entrusting Himself to Him who judges righteously" (1 Peter 2:23).

MAY 15
Purified Desires

Lord, I am convinced that You want me (and all Your disciples) to be as carefree as possible. The life of discipleship is a life of gradual disencumberment, whereas the life of the worldly minded is one of gradual encumbering. The true disciple does what Paul's captain did—unloads the cargo. But the earthly minded man keeps adding cargo as long as he lives.

The self-centered life naturally multiplies its cares because it multiplies its desires. One pleasure must give way to two, and one piece of worldly goods must eventually produce many. The result of all that self-gratification is not peace of mind but increased anxiety. Jesus called that anxiety "the cares of this world" (Matthew 13:22, KJV). Cares are produced by desires, and desires are born in the naturally selfish heart of man.

As a disciple of Jesus Christ, I must strike at the heart of worldliness. It does not lie in things, but in the *desire* for things. I must not crucify my desires; I must direct them. Only desires that are manifestly displeasing to God must be crucified, but all other desires must be purified by the washing process of prayer (Mark 11:24).

Desires that have been purified lead to a holy carefreeness. When God answers my desires, He does so without adding sorrow (Proverbs 10:22); but when I seek my own self-gratification, I sow the seeds of bitterness. The world is full of boredom and ennui because those are the fruits of a self-centered existence. When I find my gratification in self-denial for Christ's sake, I find myself marvelously stimulated with the excitement of an eternal adventure. Self-denial is practical immortality to be realized now and to be enjoyed forever! If I seek first the Kingdom of Heaven and all its right ways, all things will be mine (Matthew 6:33).

"Humble yourselves, therefore, under the mighty hand of God, that He may exalt you at the proper time, casting all your anxiety upon Him, because He cares for you" (1 Peter 5:6–7).

MAY 16
Justify or Judge?

One of the abilities God is helping me to develop is the ability to humble myself. God told King Josiah, "Because . . . you humbled yourself before the Lord . . . I truly have heard you." As a result, he would not witness God's judgment on his people (2 Kings 22:19–20). The key word is "yourself." When I became a believer, God placed in my hands the right to judge myself. If I fail to exercise that right, He will do it for me. Judging myself is simply reviewing my relationship to God. Most of the time that review will reveal something lacking or wanting. It is at that point that I must humble myself by admitting I am lacking and then asking God's forgiveness.

If I judge myself, I am forgiven but not *chastened* (1 Corinthians 11:31–32, KJV). But if I neglect to judge myself and then the Lord must step in to do it for me, it means that He must add His "chastening," which means feeling His rod of correction. When I was a young believer I used to say, "Accept Christ and God will never judge you." Now I know that is wrong. Really, it is, "Accept Christ and you will come under daily judgment!" Not the judgment of God's wrath upon my sins, but the judgment of God's Spirit upon the quality of my life.

The world knows nothing of judging itself, only justifying itself. That is a key difference between a disciple and a worldling. I can always gauge my spiritual life by asking a simple question: Am I justifying myself or judging myself? The justifier reveals that something has gone wrong underneath; the carnal nature is again in control. But the one who judges reveals that the Holy Spirit of God is alive and well in his heart. It is at that point that "the Lord of peace himself [will] give [him] peace at *all* times and in *every* way" (2 Thessalonians 3:16, NIV, italics added).

"For the sorrow that is according to the will of God produces a repentance without regret, leading to salvation; but the sorrow of the world produces death" (2 Corinthians 7:10).

MAY 17
How to Handle Quarrels

Lord, I must not practice the manly art of self-defense. I must take Jesus as my example in this. When He was reviled, He did not revile in return, but rather committed Himself to His heavenly Father (1 Peter 2:23). I must not answer all my critics. For one thing, they are too many and to satisfy them would take all my time. For another thing, my critics may unwittingly be my best friends. Like a mirror, they show me my faults and shortcomings that my blinded eyes could not see otherwise.

I respond to my critics with either thankfulness or silence. Thankfulness to them for being "kind" enough to point out areas in which I may improve; and silence if the criticism is malicious and mischievous. By silence I mean silence toward *them*, not silence toward God. Criticism should drive me to prayer and to the placing of the critic in God's hands. I pray that if the criticism is fair I will accept it; if not, that God will defend me.

I must be careful not to line up support when under attack. It is so easy to take sides, to collect friends, and to make the criticism develop into an issue where battle lines are drawn. To do that is to refuse to admit I need correction, to refuse the benefits of criticism. Further, it creates an endless cycle of petty charges and counter-charges that only cater to pride and ostentation. Among believers there may be differences of opinion, but no quarrel is ever necessary. Whenever a quarrel, a rift, or a schism develops in the body, someone has forgotten to say, "Forgive me!"

Jesus is my example as the perfect handler of criticism because He went to the cross with a pure conscience. And so I am counseled to "keep a good conscience [as Jesus did] so that in the thing in which [I am] slandered, those who revile [my] good behavior in Christ may be put to shame" (1 Peter 3:16).

"An arrogant man stirs up strife, but he who trusts in the Lord will prosper" (Proverbs 28:25).

MAY 18
We Are Debtors

I must always remember, Lord, that my talent is my liability. When I invest money in a savings bank, that money is not the bank's *asset* but its *liability*—it is owed to me. So it is with any talent God gives me; it does not belong to me but to the people for whom God intended it.

Worldly people tend to be deceived about that. If God blesses their businesses, they take the credit; if God gives them good health, they attribute it to taking good care of themselves; if God gives them obedient, responsive children, it is because they as parents set a good example. Thus, even their goodness is corrupted by self-deceit.

Paul has a word here: "Who makes you different from anyone else? What do you have that you did not receive [from God]?" (1 Corinthians 4:7, NIV). These are pertinent questions that I am obligated to answer. If God has bestowed anything special upon me, I must first acknowledge that it came from Him, and then use it as it was intended—to bless and lift up others. The only "asset" I have is the *obligation* of God, His promise to save me for His eternal glory. Any natural gifts or endowments I may have are my obligation, under God, to others.

Paul says, "I am debtor" (Romans 1:14, KJV), which puts it concisely. All Paul was he "owed" to others, and he did not take his talent and bury it in the ground. The only way my gifts can live, thrive, and prosper is by using them for others. Kept for myself, they—and I—will die. The deadness that we find so stifling in the world is not the deadness of inactivity, but the deadness of accumulation—"I must look out for number one." On the contrary, Jesus says, "Give, and it will be given to you; good measure, pressed down, shaken together, running over" (Luke 6:38).

"For not one of us lives for himself, and not one dies for himself; for if we live, we live for the Lord, or if we die, we die for the Lord; therefore whether we live or die, we are the Lord's" (Romans 14:7–8).

MAY 19
The Lord's Ways Are Right

I will accept, Lord, the way of uncertainty in this life. I must expect that not all Your secrets will be revealed this side of heaven, because what is a heaven for? I believe the theme of heaven will be "the Lamb redeemed us with His blood" (cf. Revelation 5:9); and "all the Lord's ways are *right*" (cf. Psalm 107:7).

God leads me not in a comfortable way but in a right way. The Lord's right way means putting me through experiences that most clearly produce His Son's image in me. Since God is leading me to realize an internal, not external, goal, many of my experiences will make no sense in this life. It is not essential that they make sense; it is only essential that God appoints them for me. Therefore, I must walk like a blind man, trusting the hand (and heart) of my heavenly Father.

I must also remember to be thankful for *all* experiences, since they all "work together for good," that is, the good of being conformed to the image of Jesus Christ (Romans 8:28–29). Since that is the highest good any human being can attain, it will be worth all the pain and trouble.

Since every person is different, he must reach his highest good in a different way from anyone else. That is why I cannot "footprint" anyone else's experiences. What God has devised for me suits my personality and makeup perfectly. When I arrive in heaven He wants to be able to say, "I have taught thee in the way of wisdom; I have led thee in right paths" (Proverbs 4:11, KJV).

If I could only see the finished product, as God *now* sees it, I would spend the rest of my days in unceasing, overwhelming praise. I would sing, "The steps of a good man are ordered by the Lord" (Psalm 37:23, KJV). Lord, let me begin and continue that song by faith!

"The steps of a man are established by the Lord; and He delights in his way. When he falls, he shall not be hurled headlong; because the Lord is the One who holds his hand" (Psalm 37:23–24).

MAY 20
Doing What We Cannot Do

I must realize, Lord, that discipleship for You is not only doing what I *can*, but what I *cannot*. When Jesus said to the paralyzed man at Bethesda, "Arise, take up your pallet, and walk" (John 5:8), He was asking the impossible, humanly speaking. If my Christian life is to be measured by what I *can* do, I am left with a purely human religion. If, on the other hand, Jesus Christ is who He says He is, then He will often command me to do the impossible for His sake as well as mine.

It is amazing, Lord, how I believe strongly in a supernatural God, and yet just as strongly try to live a natural life. You commanded Abraham to offer Isaac on Moriah, a thing he *could not* do because it violated Your promise to him (Genesis 22). Yet Abraham believed that what *could not* be done also *could* be done, even if it took a miracle to do it. Abraham's expectancy was in a miracle-working God. This is where I so often fail. I believe in a miracle-working God *in the Bible*; but for me? I believe that God works miracles in Argentina, but it is hard to believe He works them in my own home.

Discipleship, if it means anything, means something just beyond my reach. If it is simply *my* idea, *my* talent, *my* energy, and *my* versatility, then I can quietly dismiss Jesus Christ and go on my way without Him. So God forces me to do the impossible, not once but often, for in no other way is He ever going to express His Son in me. Soon now I may hear Him say, "Get up, take your bed, and walk!" Or, "Get to Moriah and offer your Isaac." When I hear those words I will know a miracle is in the making, for I could not obey them apart from Him who is "able to do exceeding abundantly" above all I could ask or think (Ephesians 3:20).

"And they were utterly astonished, saying, 'He has done all things well; He makes even the deaf to hear, and the dumb to speak'" (Mark 7:37).

MAY 21
When Jesus Acts Strangely

I must accept the fact that there will be times when Jesus Christ will act "strangely" toward me. When the Syrophoenician woman came asking Jesus to cure her daughter, Jesus put a distance between Himself and the woman. He did three things: He refused to answer her; He said He came to help others; and He said (of all things!) that children's food should not be given to dogs (Matthew 15:21–28). After those "strange" responses, I should think the woman would have left in a huff. But she did not and Jesus knew she would not, since He was only testing her faith. Once that faith had been tested, it was given full permission: "You have great faith! Your request is granted" (v. 28, NIV).

When Jesus acts strangely toward me, it is for my education. He wants my faith to be purified by obstacles until it reaches the point where it can ask the limit. I can always tell when I have passed the test, for then Jesus says, "Let it be done as you desire."

Sometimes when I pray, things grow worse instead of better because Jesus is beginning His "obstacle" ministry in order to strain selfishness out of my prayer. He wants my faith battle-ready, and the only way He can accomplish that is to put Himself where He seems to be out of my reach momentarily. That is why troubles pile up when I feel *most godly*, not when I have sinned. The combination of piled-up troubles and an "absent" Savior tends to discourage me, but it is exactly there that I must be doggedly persistent, like the Syrophoenician woman, until Jesus finally turns and says, "Your faith is *great!*" The brief moment of His forsaking will pass, and with great mercies He will return and gather me and vindicate me (Isaiah 54:7, 17).

"I will say to God my rock, 'Why hast Thou forgotten me? Why do I go mourning because of the oppression of the enemy?'" (Psalm 42:9).

MAY 22
Identifying with Others

In order to be an effective servant of Jesus Christ I must learn the meaning of identification with others. Aaron the high priest wore the names of Israel's tribes on his shoulders and breast, a beautiful symbol of the identification of the priest with the people (Exodus 28). In the most absolute sense possible, Jesus, our High Priest, "became us" (Hebrews 7:26, KJV), not merely in becoming man, but in becoming our sin-bearer (2 Corinthians 5:21).

Identification with others is more than bearing one another's burdens; it is stepping into the other person's shoes. Since we cannot do this literally, it must be done vicariously and spiritually. It means feeling the hurt, the pain, and the sin as if they were our own. Paul felt in his heart the very lostness of his Jewish brothers (Romans 9:1–3).

We cannot adequately pray for others until we identify with them to the point where the thing we pray for becomes ours. When Rees Howells, founder of the Bible College of Wales, prayed for a tubercular woman, God said to him, "Will you become tubercular for her sake?" Of course God did not perform the transaction, but His servant had to be *willing*, thus showing his true identification.

The burden of identification is the true burden of the Lord. Nothing is as exhausting and depleting. That is where the battle occurs and the wrestling takes place. The greatest victories God can give us come out of identification with others. Holding services, preaching, and attending committee meetings are child's play in comparison. Jesus will bear the scars of identification with us forever. And so will I, if I follow Him in that direction. Yet in that direction lies His—and my—greatest glory. "God is not unjust; he will not forget your work and the love you have shown him as you have helped his people" (Hebrews 6:10, NIV).

"He made Him who knew no sin to be sin on our behalf, that we might become the righteousness of God in Him" (2 Corinthians 5:21).

MAY 23
Bearing the Cross

Lord, I will not make a fetish about bearing my cross. The purpose of the cross is to release me from myself in order to become useful to the world. But if I am constantly occupied with my cross, I am of no use to myself or anyone else. Oswald Chambers once said, "Self-sacrifice may be a disease." I cannot afford to make my cross an object of adoration; I must make it an instrument of crucifixion. My cross is anything that competes with the claims of Christ on me. My cross becomes my cross only when I am confronted with an alternative, when Christ says, "Leave all that would compete with Me, and follow Me."

I cannot manufacture my cross, for that is the worst kind of hypocrisy. It is either there or not. Simply denying myself a tiny pleasure, then being proud about it, is certainly not the cross Jesus Christ was talking about.

The cross is continual. I cannot die to self once and for all. I must "die daily" as Paul did (1 Corinthians 15:31). Today the point of crucifixion may be one thing, tomorrow something else. As long as I live, and as long as my flesh craves preeminence, I will be confronted by the continual alternative: my will or Christ's. Thus I am never free from the pain of being scarred by my cross. Now I see why Paul said, "I fill up . . . what is still lacking in regard to Christ's afflictions, for the sake of . . . the church" (Colossians 1:24, NIV). The pain of my cross is Christ's pain that He endured for others; only as I suffer the pain of dying to self can I live (as Christ did) for others. That is the "glory" life Paul exultantly proclaimed: "God forbid that I should glory, except in the cross of our Lord Jesus Christ, by whom the world is crucified unto me, and I unto the world" (Galatians 6:14, NSRB).

"Therefore Jesus also, that He might sanctify the people through His own blood, suffered outside the gate. Hence, let us go out to Him outside the camp, bearing His reproach" (Hebrews 13:12–13).

MAY 24
Guidance from Behind

I must get used to the idea that God is not always in front of me, leading the way. He has promised to always guide me, but sometimes He guides me from *behind*. "Your ears will hear a word behind you, 'This is the way, walk in it'" (Isaiah 30:21). Strange guidance, indeed, from behind!

In Argentina I watched a shepherd girl lead her flock of sheep. How did she do it? Sometimes in front, sometimes on the side, and sometimes from behind. The psalmist says, "He *leadeth* me" (Psalm 23:2, KJV, italics added); that is guidance from the front. But verse 3 says, "He *driveth* me in the paths" (author's trans.). That is guidance from behind.

Guidance from behind means one of two things: either there is trouble ahead and I need to be forced through it; or my resolve is getting weak and God has to use a little muscle persuasion to get me moving along the road.

God has led me more with "behind guidance" than with "before guidance." When God is in front He is easily seen and I slack my trust a little. But when He is behind I have got to rely on His commands without seeing Him; therefore, I am more vulnerable to failure and mistake unless my faith is strong. My very vulnerability is the school in which God teaches my faith to be strong.

If I am trusting God, He will never let me make a wrong move. But all the same, He will allow me to suffer the anxiety of a *possible* wrong move, just to keep my faith in fighting trim. That anxiety is painful, but not half as painful as reaping the results of a *real* wrong move. God carefully monitors my anxiety level and will not allow it to overflow. "I will tell the next generation that this God is my God, He will be my guide, even unto death" (Psalm 48:13–14, author's trans.).

"And I will lead the blind by a way they do not know, in paths they do not know I will guide them. I will make darkness into light before them and rugged places into plains" (Isaiah 42:16).

MAY 25
The Masters God Puts over Us

It is quite possible that God will farm me out to other masters for my own spiritual education. The Jews of Jeremiah's day were told, "Serve the king of Babylon, and live!" (Jeremiah 27:17). God decided to farm out the Jews to Nebuchadnezzar for seventy years until their idolatry was purged. So the king of Babylon was their new "temporary master," and they were to cooperate with him and "live."

It surprises me that good King Hezekiah, godly as he was, did not cure the Jews of idolatry, but bad King Nebuchadnezzar, pagan as he was, did! The lesson for me is, my touchy neighbor may do me more good than my godly pastor. My atheistic foreman at the factory may purge me from my impatience faster and better than my Bible class teacher. This I know—God will not quibble over instruments. If He could use Babylon to purge the Jews, He can certainly use an unlikely agent to purge me.

This explains why my circumstances are filled with specially chosen people. Regardless of their relationship to God, God has a special relationship to them. They are His tools for the fine work of chiseling character in His disciples. That means that I must change my attitude toward the "unspiritual" and "worldly minded" people who make up my environment. Without them I can never become what God intends for me to be. So I am going to start praising God for them. I will no longer tell God what instruments He is going to use to shape me. And I will thank Him for the instruments He has already chosen. I can rejoice that God's agencies are for my sake, "so that the grace that is reaching more and more people may cause thanksgiving to overflow to the glory of God" (2 Corinthians 4:15, NIV).

"And I will give you the treasures of darkness, and hidden wealth of secret places, in order that you may know that it is I, the Lord, the God of Israel, who calls you by your name" (Isaiah 45:3).

MAY 26
The North Side of God

I will make no progress in my discipleship if I limit God to one side. He has two sides. One shows His infinite kindness and patience, the other His firmness and resolution, which the Puritans called "the stormy north side of Jesus Christ." Most of the teaching about God I have heard refers to His grace, love, and kindness. I am seriously deficient in learning that He has a north side as well.

Jeremiah saw these two sides of God. In chapter 18 he saw God mend the broken clay jar and put it back to usefulness. In chapter 19 he saw God break another jar to pieces (19:10) as an illustration of what He would do to His people in the future (vv. 10–15). I must learn this somber message.

Too many people feel that God's patience is limitless, His love is inured to pain, His discipline is soft and delayed, and, anyway, Calvary "covers it all." Such a distorted view of God leads us into all kinds of looseness, laxness, and sloppiness in discipleship. But God is no such pushover. If I do not yield to His love, I must yield before His pressure.

Am I so hard of heart that it takes a blow to wake me up? Must I be slave-driven in order to appreciate the loveliness of His person? Or am I so tuned in to Him that the slightest movement of His finger will make me yield? Am I clay in His hands, soft and responsive, or a mass of hard, brittle parts?

God reserves His stormy north side for the callously indifferent, but He is never unfeeling toward those who cry for mercy and help. What kind of a God is He? "He delighteth in mercy." What will He do for us who come suppliant and contrite? "He will turn again, he will have compassion upon us" (Micah 7:18–19, KJV). Such a God is our God forever.

"And we proclaim Him, admonishing every man and teaching every man with all wisdom, that we may present every man complete in Christ" (Colossians 1:28).

MAY 27
The Workable Idea

I must adopt a workable standard in my dealings with others. The standard must be *biblical* and it must be *workable*. A departure from either will spell failure.

The standard is simple: absolute conformity to an ideal; and on the other hand, wholehearted compassion for the one who fails the ideal. I believe both elements of this standard are biblical and workable. I believe both elements are essentially biblical, that is, God uses this standard in His dealings with us.

I must never discard the ideal. If I do, there is no point whatever in going on with this discipleship business. If I say to myself (and others), "Trust Christ as Savior, but sin all you please," I have obviously tied myself up in a deadly contradiction. On the other hand, if I say, "Trust Christ as Savior, but never sin again," I have placed upon myself a burden that is too much for flesh and blood to bear. So I live on the razor's edge of an exciting adventure—reaching for the purest ideal while encouraging myself not to give up if I slip and stumble en route.

This relieves me of tension with my fellow Christian workers. Failure to reach the ideal is not disaster, provided, of course, there is proper recognition of the fault and proper contrition regarding it. But upward we go in our next try, always aiming where God wants us to be, always trusting His power to get us there. The flesh may momentarily stall us, but by God's grace it will not permanently restrain us. Believers are born to victory, and His inward driving power will always propel us higher. For we "have put on the new self who is being renewed to a true knowledge according to the image of the One who created him" (Colossians 3:10).

"Wretched man that I am! Who will set me free from the body of this death? Thanks be to God through Jesus Christ our Lord!" (Romans 7:24–25).

MAY 28
Our Bodies as Channels

As a disciple I must rightly understand the use of my body in my service for Jesus Christ. First, I must consider my body to be a channel, not a receptacle. There are two great spheres in the world: the sphere of vast human need and the sphere of God's infinite supply. The connection between the two is my body. So often we pray, "Lord, bless us," or, "Lord, have compassion on us," or, "Lord, revive us." Such prayers indicate God's reluctance. The Bible teaches us He is just the opposite; He longs to pour out His richest mercies upon us. The trouble is not with the *source*, but with the *channel*. How many bodies are available for His kindnesses?

Second, I need to realize that people are far less indifferent to God than I think they are. They deeply long for the reality that only God is able to give them. Too often they are turned away from God because He is misrepresented to them by His children. They see our preoccupation with our comforts and ease, our emphasis on material possessions, our ambition for place and prominence, and *of course* they become indifferent!

The meeting place for a seeking God and an indifferent world is through my body. If I yield my body to Him, He will use it as a message-sender to the unsaved. I will not need to pray for God to come in from the outside, so to speak, for He will be inside working through me. My pleas for power, compassion, and strength will be unnecessary; these will be mine already through Him who now possesses me.

My attitude toward my body should always be: I thank God for you, I will never pamper you, I will let Him who owns you possess you, and I will let others see Him in you. For my body is "a temple of the Holy Spirit" and I am not my own. So I will "glorify God in [my] body" (1 Corinthians 6:19–20).

"Sacrifice and meal offering Thou hast not desired; my ears Thou hast opened; burnt offering and sin offering Thou hast not required" (Psalm 40:6).

MAY 29
Blaming God for Failures

Sometimes I have experienced the very opposite of what I thought God would do. As a result, I have had bitter sessions with Him, and blamed Him for failing to fulfill my expectations. I said with Jeremiah, "Thou hast deceived me and I was deceived" (Jeremiah 20:7). Jeremiah preached God's word, but the results were not what he expected. His hearers beat him and threw him into jail. That is when he turned on God and blamed Him for the outcome.

The world blames God daily. There is not a trouble or a catastrophe that God is not blamed for. It is characteristic of the natural man to shift the blame to someone else; it is uncharacteristic of the disciple to do so. Therefore, we must ask why.

Blaming God is, first, the result of *confused expectations*. Jeremiah expected certain things to happen; God allowed different things to happen. He had programmed God too tightly, too rigidly; and when his program did not materialize, he grew tense and bitter. Second, it is the result of becoming *too personally involved* in the results. This is dedication out of control. Results are always in God's hands, and we must not feel personally responsible for them; otherwise, the tension will make us burst out against God.

Blaming God is the sign of an overheated disciple. Zeal for the Lord's work has consumed him. His sensitivities have been strained finer than they ought. It is time to back off, cool down, and get disengaged. Only One could be that zealous for His Father's house and not get strained. The rest of us, the common clay, need the quieting admonition, "Be still, and know that I am God" (Psalm 46:10, KJV).

"But as for me, I would seek God, and I would place my cause before God; who does great and unsearchable things, wonders without number" (Job 5:8–9).

MAY 30
Seeking Recognition

Lord, my discipleship means that I have surrendered the right to be successful. God's word to every disciple is, "Seekest thou great things for thyself? seek them not" (Jeremiah 45:5, KJV). If I strive to be great in God's work, I will never make it. Greatness is God's handiwork, not mine or man's.

I must let the world come to me; I must not run after it. The world *will* come to me if I have something to offer it, even as it came to Jesus. The world is surprisingly sharp when it comes to values; it knows whom to seek out for the things it desperately needs. I must not envy the martyr or long for a "famous" suffering. It takes greater courage to endure the daily irritation and drudgery of a situation where nothing heroic for Christ seems to happen. Suffering for Christ's sake has its own exhilaration, but where is the exhilaration of the daily trivia of a barren task?

Seeking recognition and attention is characteristic of the worldling, not the disciple of Jesus Christ. Of course, some of God's servants do receive attention and renown, but the true servant will ignore such honor and strive to call attention to his Lord and Master. He will treat such fame not as an asset but as a hindrance, so much "refuse" (Philippians 3:8, NSRB) unless it enables him to glorify his God.

To serve God unnoticed takes sublime dedication. God is not looking for great men, but for men who will allow Him to manifest Himself greatly in them. My chief end is to glorify God (not myself), and to enjoy Him (not a dazzling name) forever. May I never glory in my wisdom or strength, but in this: that I understand and know Him who is my God (cf. Jeremiah 9:23–24).

"But we have renounced the things hidden because of shame, not walking in craftiness or adulterating the word of God, but by the manifestation of truth commending ourselves to every man's conscience in the sight of God" (2 Corinthians 4:2).

MAY 31
The True Persuader

As a disciple I must never try to persuade people to follow Christ. My responsibility is to tell the good news of Jesus Christ; the rest is up to God. Jesus never tried to persuade people. He said, "Follow Me" (Matthew 9:9; John 1:43), in an almost matter-of-fact way, and He let the facts of His life and ministry speak for themselves. Preaching the gospel is not buttonholing people, but simply telling the facts of Christ's person.

I will find myself in deep trouble if I pressure people into a commitment. That probably explains why so many "converts" fall away in such a short time. People can be easily persuaded to do anything (emotional beings that we are!).

The great Persuader is the Holy Spirit, who operates under the authority of the Father and persuades concerning the Son. The Spirit may use mental and/or emotional persuasion, but last of all He reaches the will, and it is there that the real power is applied. When He reaches the will, the Spirit first weakens the will to resist Christ, then He strengthens the determination to accept Him. All of this is done apart from the preacher, the evangelist, or the personal worker. In that last final step, in the inner sanctum of the soul, there are only two persons left.

A proper understanding of spiritual persuasion will immediately cause me to reject the Madison Avenue approach to soul-winning, or any other human approach to persuasion. I cannot persuade; only God can. My sole responsibility is to witness, to tell the facts about Jesus Christ, who said, "Go home to your people and report to them what great things the Lord has done for you, and how He had mercy on you" (Mark 5:19).

"But by His doing you are in Christ Jesus, who became to us wisdom from God, and righteousness and sanctification, and redemption" (1 Corinthians 1:30).

JUNE 1
Typing Jesus Christ

I will subscribe to discipleship by *typing*. Jesus Christ has no other kind of disciple than the one made by a pattern. Disciples are made by "observing" (keeping, practicing) what He commanded us, not merely by learning His commands. Teaching doctrine is important, but the teacher of the doctrine is of immense importance. Jesus set the pattern for all disciples when He said, "Follow Me." Later, Paul continued the same pattern by saying, "Imitate me" (cf. Philippians 3:17, Phillips). Every Christian has the responsibility of becoming a type or pattern by which others may mold their lives.

The work of the Holy Spirit in us is to shape us according to the pattern He has received—Jesus Christ Himself. The goal of the Spirit is not to make us encyclopedias of doctrine, but living types of the Son of God. Even more, the Spirit seeks to make us living types of Jesus for the ones who are watching us daily. So we are types *of* Someone else *for* someone else.

Discipleship is not the result of a formula, or a seminar, or an educational institution, but the work of a Person (or person) on another person. What we *are* lives in perpetual memory; what we *say* withers away like the chaff. We never have to strive, sweat, or labor to make disciples; we automatically make them or drive them away by whether or not Jesus is being formed in us by the Spirit. In a sense we do not *make* disciples; they are being made or unmade constantly by simply watching us.

My responsibility is not to "gather a following" or say, "I'm going to disciple you," but simply to let the Spirit fill me; making disciples will then be the most natural result possible. The highest joy a witness can feel is when people say to him: "Let us go with you, for we have heard that God is with you" (Zechariah 8:23).

"For whom He foreknew, He also predestined to become conformed to the image of His Son, that He might be the first-born among many brethren" (Romans 8:29).

JUNE 2
The Desires of Our Hearts

Is it wrong for a disciple to long for the "desires of [his] heart"? This is what God promises those who "delight" in Him (Psalm 37:4). I believe that when a man delights in God, the Lord opens his spiritual eyes to "visions" and "dreams" that would be unheard of in his natural state (Joel 2:28). Those desires are not implanted by the Almighty for disappointment. Arthur Hewitt, a Congregational minister in New England, said, "A man cannot do God's will and avoid his own heart's desire." The only time a disciple cannot realize his heart's desires is when he seeks them by his own efforts.

God has plans for every one of His children that are far beyond the stretch of their imagination. They are plans of "welfare" and hope, not "calamity" (Jeremiah 29:11). A man's desires come from within the man himself, while God's desires for a man come from without. They are implanted in him by a new relationship with God, but in such a way as to assure the believer that his desires are indeed his own.

God will never allow my divinely planted dreams to be thwarted. That is why Abraham went back down Moriah's hill with Isaac, why Nehemiah found favor with the king, and why Simeon and Anna were allowed to live so long. I must strongly resist the notion that it is wrong to have dreams, wrong to let my heart desire. A man without divinely implanted longings does not know much about the Spirit of God. The impediments—sickness, suffering, imprisonment, death—no more affect my desires than a feather can affect Gibraltar! Who can say no when God says yes, and who can deny a dream when God has determined that it will be realized? "'For I know the plans that I have for you,' declares the Lord, 'plans for welfare and not for calamity to give you a future and a hope'" (Jeremiah 29:11).

"And it will come about after this that I will pour out My Spirit on all mankind; and your sons and daughters will prophesy, your old men will dream dreams, your young men will see visions" (Joel 2:28).

JUNE 3
The Seed of Revival

L ord, teach me to understand the meaning of revival. I have often prayed for revival, hoping to be the revivalist and therefore the center. At other times I have longed for revival because it meant crowds, interest, and excitement. How wrong were those ideas! Revival is anything but pleasant; it is a searching, searing time when God's holiness burns hotly against our sins. It is knowing that God is a "consuming fire" (Hebrews 12:29); knowing God's "terror" (2 Corinthians 5:11, KJV); and crying out, "Woe is me" (Isaiah 6:5).

Revival has one chief aim—the removal of sin and the purifying of the believer. We read of revivals and wholesale conversions, but these are the results of revival. Revival itself concerns two parties, God and His people. The message of revival is: What are you doing about your piled-up sins? Revival is a sign that, because of His thinning patience, God has moved His people to confession. But it also means something else: God loves us so much that He is anxious to put us back into a right relationship with Himself. In revival, God says, "I love you, so get rid of your sins."

The seed of revival is the grief of the Holy Spirit; the confession of the people is the Spirit's grief vented. Only when the Spirit is "ungrieved" can blessing come. It is at that point that God's people can take a mighty leap forward. Unless I have a contented Holy Spirit within me, I need revival. Revival is God's surgery for people who have grown dull of hearing.

The psalmist's deep cry encourages us: "Will you not revive us again, that your people may rejoice in you?" (Psalm 85:6, NIV). It is a welcome day when revival comes, for then we are restored and delivered (vv. 4, 7).

"Wilt Thou not Thyself revive us again, that Thy people may rejoice in Thee? Show us Thy lovingkindness, O Lord, and grant us Thy salvation" (Psalm 85:6–7).

JUNE 4
Satan's Plan of Salvation

Lord, I must ever be aware of the wiles of Satan. I sometimes forget that *he* has a "plan of salvation" also. He is great at promising "deliverance" (Hebrews 11:35, KJV). In fact, his deliverance mimics the great deliverance that You promise Your children. In being tempted by Satan, Jesus was promised deliverance from the cross (Matthew 4:9). Many martyrs were promised deliverance from their pains by a simple recantation. All Satan requires for his deliverances is exactly that which God requires: commitment to him.

I must always remember that Satan wants *me* alive and well on planet earth. What despot, however evil, wants his subjects distressed and unhappy? The usual caricature—that Satan wants us destroyed, mutilated, or distorted—is not true. He wants us to fulfill ourselves and be the happy subjects he wants us to be—but in *his* way. That is why it is very difficult to convince unsaved worldlings that they are *not* having a good time. The fact is, they are! Further, it is difficult to get worldlings to exchange their immediate happiness, which Satan gives, for an eventual happiness, which God promises.

The difference between God's deliverance and Satan's hinges on a crucial point: Do I live for myself, or for others? Satan says, "Serve me, and I will give you everything you want." God says, "Serve Me, and I will give you only what is good." Satan's philosophy will eventually kill me, for the end of a self-serving soul is death. God's philosophy will make me eternally alive, for the person who gives his life for others will live forever. Never will God leave me naked before my enemy as long as my face is turned toward Him, and never will He recant His oath that no power of any kind will ever be able to pry me away from Him (Romans 8:35–39).

"What I have forgiven, if I have forgiven anything, I did it for your sakes in the presence of Christ, in order that no advantage be taken of us by Satan; for we are not ignorant of his schemes" (2 Corinthians 2:10–11).

JUNE 5
The Hurts of Jesus

I will accept the fact, Lord, that life with You is a series of "hurtings." Animals suffer pain, but only human beings can become morally and spiritually better because of their pain. Unless I suffer grief, I am not likely to grow into a mature disciple of Jesus Christ. One of the greatest disappointments You can suffer, Lord, is to see me battle my griefs and yet not become better. You have said, "I kill, and I make alive; I wound, and I heal" (Deuteronomy 32:39, KJV). It is to my sorrow that I do not become healed or come alive when God allows me to feel pain. Jesus wounded Simon Peter with a look that drove him to tears; he wept "bitterly" (Luke 22:62). Oswald Chambers says, "To be hurt by Jesus is the most exquisite hurt conceivable." The hurts of Jesus, if I accept them properly, are the healings of tomorrow. I need His hurtings to cauterize the shallow and superficial in my life. If I walk very long with Him, life will be a series of cuttings, woundings, and grievings. Two personalities cannot walk together without woundings and healings.

Say what I will, life will deal me hurts one way or another. But I can choose. I can say to the world, "Hurt me," and it will. But the hurt of the world is a "survival of the fittest" hurt in which there is no mercy and no redemption. The world does not care if I die; it only cares that I get out of the way if I cannot compete. But Jesus deals with losers, outcasts, beggars. He has a place for them in His eternal plan. He hurts them in order to polish and shape them, to sting them into an awakened condition, to remind them that dust can have a destiny, and that human frailty can be covered with eternal glory.

Thank You, Lord, for making paupers into princes and raising the needy to sit upon thrones (Psalm 113:7–9).

"Be gracious to me, O God, be gracious to me, for my soul takes refuge in Thee; and in the shadow of Thy wings I will take refuge, until destruction passes by" (Psalm 57:1).

JUNE 6
The Unpredictability of God

Lord, I will accept the discipline of uncertainty. There are times in our pilgrimage in which we simply do not know what to do. I remember Hudson Taylor's words, "Nothing is settled yet," and realize that they are the words of every disciple, and are spoken often. I have learned, Lord, that You create a delicate balance of certainty/uncertainty in every servant of Yours, because such is the way of bringing about obedience. Even Jesus had to learn "obedience from the things which He suffered" (Hebrews 5:8).

God never leaves us in doubt about the certainty of *salvation*, but He certainly leaves us in doubt about *tomorrow*. It is the unpredictability of God that makes us trust Him utterly. Also, it is the unpredictability of God that makes the Christian life an exciting adventure. When I make God predictable, I make myself frustrated. I have noticed other Christians who also make the same mistake. Whenever their God does not do the predictable thing for them, they either give up walking with Him, thus in effect calling Him a liar, or they continue to walk with Him, but sullenly and bitterly.

To stand uncertainly at a crossroads does not mean God has abandoned me. In those times He watches me with an extremely watchful eye, and He waits until patience and trust are perfected in me. Then He gives the signal to move. Until I receive the signal clearly, I must stand where I am at all costs. If God brings me *to* a crossroads, it is His business to get me *beyond* it. I can rejoice in a God who is never mistaken, never late, and never nonplused. Only He can "declare . . . the things that are coming and the events that are going to take place" (Isaiah 44:7). Therefore, He has told me, "Do not tremble and do not be afraid" (v. 8). This God is our God forever!

"O our God, wilt Thou not judge them? For we are powerless before this great multitude who are coming against us; nor do we know what to do, but our eyes are on Thee" (2 Chronicles 20:12).

JUNE 7
Discouragement

I must be ever alert to the feeling of *discouragement*, which is a sin. Discouragement says, "I refuse to accept God's plan for my life." Discouragement always comes when our expectations are confused. Discouragement is the result of not letting God alone. It is a tragedy that I accept Jesus as my "Lord" and then grow discouraged because He frustrates my expectations. If Jesus is my Lord, then Romans 8:28 must always be my textbook. It is impossible to have one without the other.

I must reckon with the causes of discouragement and see them in their proper perspective. Am I criticized by others? Let me rejoice! Do I not realize that God uses diamonds to sharpen diamonds? Let me remember that it was criticism that started Joseph on his way to Pharaoh's throne; and God will let criticism put me on a throne also, if I let Him.

Am I suffering lack of success? Don't I realize that success is the result of God's careful timing, not mine? And don't I realize that if I am faithful where God put me, success is inevitable?

Am I discouraged because the way is hard and painful? If so, I must realize that God is preparing plowed ground to yield fruit a hundredfold. God will never give me a hard way without a "nevertheless afterward" (Hebrews 12:11, KJV). When I am in difficulty I must pray, "Lord, give me patience to wait for Your 'afterward.'"

Am I harassed by Satan, and are his whisperings getting to me? I must remember his history: everyone who ever listened to him suffered horrible defeat. I will honor God by my trust; I will please Him, affirming: "All things [do] work together for good" (Romans 8:28, KJV). I believe that God will "go before [me] and will level the mountains; . . . [and] give [me] the treasures of darkness" (Isaiah 45:2–3, NIV).

"In my distress I called upon the Lord, and cried to my God for help; He heard my voice out of His temple, and my cry for help before Him came into His ears" (Psalm 18:6).

JUNE 8
The Healthy Pain of Discipleship

The chief lesson I must learn about the life of discipleship is that it is a life of pain. Too often my message has been, "Accept Christ and have a life of peace and joy." Of course peace and joy follow, but not without pain, and that is where so many Christians grow discouraged and faint.

The pain that comes to us in following Christ is the pain of *change*. It is the change from living naturally to living spiritually. It comes, as Blaise Pascal says, from the ungodliness that is still left in us. The greater our resistance to this change, the greater our pain will be. The reason heaven will have "no . . . more pain" (Revelation 21:4, KJV) is that every will has been brought into complete harmony with God's will; thus, the tension of wills, which is the source of pain, will be gone.

Many Christians make themselves unhappy because they resist the pain that in itself indicates victory. We live miserably because the natural man loves comfort and ease, and we have an erroneous view of the kind of work we expect Jesus Christ to do in us. He came to make us victorious, not comfortable, and victory means the gradual displacing of our natural life with His triumphant spiritual life. The difference between a Christian wallowing in self-ease and one who is triumphant is *pain*.

The comforting thing about the pain of discipleship is that it is a healthy pain. It is not the pain of breakdown and death, but the pain of healing and restoration. It builds and fashions me into the man God intends for me to be; it develops an incredibly strong character; and it perfects the image of God in me. "After you have suffered for a little while, the God of all grace . . . will Himself perfect, confirm, strengthen and establish you" (1 Peter 5:10). Thank God for the school of pain! May God make me a worthy graduate!

"Turn to me and be gracious to me, for I am lonely and afflicted. The troubles of my heart are enlarged; bring me out of my distresses" (Psalm 25:16–17).

JUNE 9
Praying in Christ's Name

I must realize that God gives me unlimited authority in prayer, but only when I am praying about His business. I must not get the idea that I may pray for personal ease, comfort, and material success and expect to get answers. When God puts Himself at my disposal in prayer, it is ultimately for His cause, not mine. I must not build my life *inwardly*, thinking only of my own personal needs, although God cares about these, and expect God to accommodate Himself to me. Jesus said, "Ask me for anything in my name, and I will do it" (John 14:14, NIV). But to ask anything in His name means *concerning His affairs*. I would not think of usurping my boss's authority and using my position in his business to selfishly promote my own interests. Why should I do so with the affairs of Jesus? So for protection in my service for Christ, for the supply of my needs, for strength, and for all, I am to use His authority with the Father, but only as it affects His work and purpose.

Using the name of Christ in prayer immediately brings into my hands all that Christ is with the Father. Christ always prayed to His Father for the welfare of His work on earth, but when He left He gave that privilege and responsibility to me. I am now to use His position with the Father to carry on the work He left for me to do. I must not abuse that trust! I must not make selfishly mine what is His. That privilege in prayer, if it is not to be abused, means Christ must be preeminent in me. His work must be my first concern. His glory and honor must be my meat and drink. By being totally consumed for Him, I assure myself that I will learn to pray the "prayer of a righteous man [that] can accomplish much" (James 5:16). That kind of praying is awesome in its power and effectiveness.

"If you abide in Me, and My words abide in you, ask whatever you wish, and it shall be done for you" (John 15:7).

JUNE 10
Christ Does Not Tantalize

I must not put myself at too much of a distance from Jesus Christ. As I read of His mighty works, teaching, preaching, and living, I am often tempted to say as an excuse for myself, "But He is the Son of God."

True, He is the Son of God. But if I put too much distance between Himself and me because of His unique sonship, I have missed the message of the New Testament. Christ lived His earthly life in the strength and power of the Holy Spirit (Matthew 3:16; John 3:34). He triumphed over the sins, ills, and woes of man by dependence upon the Spirit, not by reverting to His deity. He stripped from Himself every other dependency except faith. He did this to live as we have to live, that He might demonstrate that victory is possible in the very center of our human condition.

Jesus Christ is not a tantalizer; He is a Savior. The works He did, He said, we can do (John 14:12). The peace He enjoyed, we may enjoy (14:27). The joy that characterized Him and made Him radiant can make us radiant also (15:11). He is the "Author" (or Pioneer) of our faith. As such, He shows me what victory is. But He is also the "Finisher" (Perfecter) of our faith. As such, He shows me *how* to attain that victory. What Jesus Christ *was*, He is able to re-create in me; what Jesus Christ *did*, He is able to redemonstrate in me.

Let me never again deny who Jesus Christ is. I will deny it if I keep insisting He is a heavenly person instead of a person *from* heaven who invaded humanity by taking flesh upon Him. Once Jesus Christ became flesh, He forever undercut my excuse for failure. I must now accept Him for what He truly is—a Savior who begins on my level! "Thanks be to God, who always leads us in triumphal procession in Christ" (2 Corinthians 2:14, NIV).

"Therefore, He had to be made like His brethren in all things, that He might become a merciful and faithful high priest in things pertaining to God, to make propitiation for the sins of the people" (Hebrews 2:17).

JUNE 11
Using the World

I must not deny the therapeutic influence of the world. Of course I must take seriously the biblical warnings that "being the world's friend is being God's enemy" (James 4:4, Amp.). Yet the world offers me an opportunity to toughen my spiritual fiber if I use it properly.

The Israelites were to conquer Canaan "little by little" (Exodus 23:30). Victory was to be gradual so the people would not become too exalted or proud, and so they would not decimate their strength. That gives me a clue as to how I must relate to the world. I must use it as an opportunity to develop spiritual muscle, or else why all the training and discipline? Soldiers do not make themselves battle-ready only to enter a state of peace and rest! But in using the world for the proving of my battle-readiness, I must do it "little by little" in case the world proves too much for me, as it did for Israel.

Too often I am tempted to run from the world and hide. I fear its contamination and seduction. Bravo! I must never treat it with anything other than respect, for indeed it can contaminate and seduce. But Jesus confronted the world aggressively and defeated it (John 16:33). By His help I must do the same. I must dare the world to overcome the light that is in me (John 1:5); I must provoke it to look seriously at Jesus Christ and His claims (Colossians 1:28). I must always be on the offensive, never yielding to the world's charms for an hour, but always pressing the battle into its own territory. That way I shall grow stronger "little by little" until Christ is known in an alien land. The world will be my "bread," even as the Anakim were "bread" for Israel (Numbers 14:9, KJV), if only I do not "rebel" and "fear."

"For whatever is born of God overcomes the world; and this is the victory that has overcome the world—our faith" (1 John 5:4).

JUNE 12
Spiritual Heart Trouble

The stress of modern living is increasing the risk of heart trouble, but heart trouble has always been a risk for a disciple of Jesus Christ. My heart is my citadel and I must keep it strong if I hope to triumph.

I must not "err in [my] heart" (cf. Psalm 95:10). It is bad enough to err in my ways or in my mind, but if I err in my heart I will begin to sow the seeds of ultimate defeat. To err in the heart is to be unpersuaded, unconvinced by God's Word (Hebrews 3:8–10). It means that God speaks in vain and His words carry no weight; He might as well have remained silent. If I ignore God's message, before long I will become a firm unbeliever, which in turn will lead to hardness of heart (Hebrews 4:7).

Peter erred in his *ways*; once repentant, he found restoration with his Lord. But Judas erred in his *heart*; he ignored the teachings of Jesus and developed a resistance to the forgiveness Jesus offered.

I cannot presume that because I am saved I am in no danger of developing heart trouble. The many New Testament warnings were not uttered for the empty air but to make me a disciple with a clean heart, to keep me from regarding God's words as trivia, and to make me realize every message from God is of the highest worth.

The most restless, discontented people are not the poor or the overworked; they are the hard of heart. To be strong in heart I must let God convince me, and keep convincing me as long as life flows on. The man convinced by God carries the flowers of eternity in his heart. Hezekiah once said to Isaiah, "The word of the Lord . . . is good" (Isaiah 39:8, NIV). Whenever we ascribe goodness to God's Word, it is a sign that God has convinced us and therefore our hearts are tender and pliant in His hand.

"My heart is steadfast, O God, my heart is steadfast; I will sing, yes, I will sing praises! Awake, my glory; awake, harp and lyre, I will awaken the dawn!" (Psalm 57:7–8).

JUNE 13
Spiritual Thirst

I must not get the idea that if I accept Jesus as my Savior my thirst will end. If anything, it will *increase*. Jesus Himself was thirsty, as expressed in His words to the woman of Sychar, "Give Me a drink" (John 4:7). We miss the point if we think Jesus was *only* physically thirsty. A greater thirst—love—was burning inside Him.

The two "thirst creators" of life are *love* and *sin*. The woman symbolized the eternal dissatisfaction sin creates in us. Jesus, on the other hand, symbolized the eternal restlessness of love as it seeks to bless its object.

It is not wrong to be dissatisfied, as long as the causes of that dissatisfaction are *holy*. The woman was pitiable, not because she was driven by thirst, but because of what brought her to that thirst. But Jesus was suffering the thirst that was commendable because His need was created by love.

Love makes us just as thirsty as sin does, and it drives us to seek satisfaction, as sin does. But because love fulfills itself in the welfare of others, and not for itself, it is holy and ennobling. Jesus and the woman came from opposite poles, driven by thirst, until each found the other and became satisfied.

I must take care that I am driven by the right urges, feelings, and motives. I must seek those who have become "thirsty by sin" so I can lead them to Him who can make them "satisfied by righteousness." The thirst of love always gives; the thirst of sin always takes. Lord, give *me* to drink! You have said in Your Word: "I will pour water upon him that is thirsty, and floods upon the dry ground" (Isaiah 44:3, KJV).

"Jesus stood and cried out, saying, 'If any man is thirsty, let him come to Me and drink. He who believes in Me, as the Scripture said, "From his innermost being shall flow rivers of living water"'" (John 7:37–38).

JUNE 14
The Razor Edge of Failure

One of my strong affirmations is the security of the believer. I think it is a precious truth, but I also believe in the *insecurity* of the believer. I think it is a precious truth also. How many times have I stumbled because I thought I was secure, and how many times have I been victorious because of my very insecurity? If the Israelites had one main fault, it was false security (1 Corinthians 10:1–13). Despite the fact that they passed through the Red Sea, were guided by the cloud, and had been fed manna, they lusted after "evil things" (v. 6). They had every reason *not* to fall; yet fall they did, all because their past blessings became sedatives instead of stimulants. That is a warning to me: I must not "think security," or I will fall (vv. 11–12).

The best way for me to live is on the razor edge of failure. I must be insecure enough to cling to the everlasting arms. If God blesses me as He did the Israelites, I must immediately assume that these blessings are a preparation against future problems, not guarantees of perpetual bliss. I must appreciate my blessings and use them correctly, but never grow maudlin over them.

I must get rid of my security complex. Success has a way of dimming my spiritual eye and slackening my spiritual hand. Being in Christ is no assurance whatever that I will be immune from the lashings of Satan, the tantalizings of the world, or the rigors of God's disciplinary grace. I will be safe only as I run scared, scared enough to be babylike in my total dependence upon God, for the man who makes the Lord his trust is blessed and will not go astray (Psalm 40:4).

"Now then let the fear of the Lord be upon you; be very careful what you do, for the Lord our God will have no part in unrighteousness" (2 Chronicles 19:7).

JUNE 15
Possessing the Gate of the City

I will realize and act upon the principle that every victory must lead to an occupancy. Merely to conquer a bad habit, to win over an alienated friend, or to drive doubt out of my heart is not in itself sufficient. I must follow up those triumphs with being "more than a conqueror," that is, seizing the territory so the enemy cannot recapture it.

When the Israelites conquered the Amorites, they followed up their victory by occupying their land (Numbers 21:21–32). This made any counterattack by the enemy impossible. I must nail down my victories in such a way that counterattack is impossible. Otherwise, as Jesus reminds me in His parable, the end may be worse than the beginning (Matthew 12:43–45). The only way to crucify my fleshly desires is to drive them from my mind, then let the Holy Spirit create new, fresh desires in me. The only way I can conquer hate is to replace it with love. I cannot conquer bitterness by confessing it; I must replace it with praise and thankfulness. In short, there must be no vacancy after victory! As Paul puts it, I must "withstand" (fight and overcome the enemy), after which I must "stand." Too often I have withstood, only to fail to stand afterward. It does not take the enemy long to recognize an unguarded post and seize it.

I love the word Laban gave to his sister Rebekah when she was leaving to marry Isaac: "May your descendants possess the gate of those who hate them" (Genesis 24:60). The city gate was the city's most crucial defense; once lost, the whole city was lost. That is where victory will lead me to make inoperative those things that would keep me from enjoying what Christ dearly bought for me! "The Lord your God will Himself cross over before you; He will destroy the [enemy] from before you. . . . Be strong and courageous" (Deuteronomy 31:3–6, Berkeley).

"For in the day of trouble He will conceal me in His tabernacle; in the secret place of His tent He will hide me; He will lift me up on a rock" (Psalm 27:5).

JUNE 16
Unadorned Worship

I must make my spiritual life as simple as possible. God is the most complex Being in the universe; yet when it comes to His relationship to people, He wants utter simplicity. The altar the Israelites were to build for God was to be of unhewn stones, with no tool or cutting instrument used upon it (Exodus 20:25). The message is clear. God knows man's tendency to adorn, to artify, to decorate a thing until man's talent overshadows the instrument itself. Medieval art is an example of that. God wants to make Himself so available, so disposable to man that He wants no hindrance to a hungry, seeking heart. That means no rules or conditions to keep people from God.

The Laodicean church was the model of organization and regulation, but it was dead! I can become so structured, so habitualized, so regular that my devotional life becomes a self-centered worship of rules rather than God. My life with God must be spontaneous. God reserves the right to break in, change habits, start new directions, and otherwise keep me on tiptoe expectancy. God is not finicky, but He understands human nature and He does not want us majoring in things that do not count.

I must not become upset if someone interferes with my schedule, interrupts my "quiet time," or tampers with my routine. God may be in that very interruption, calling me to Himself instead of to the scaffolding I have built around Him. I must be a Nathanael in worship as well as in life, a person without twists or deviousness, but open-hearted and direct in my communion with my God. The "blessed" ones of the Beatitudes (Matthew 5:1–11) are those with qualities of utter simplicity and transparency; they carry away enormous bundles of the blessings of God.

"And what does the Lord require of you but to do justice, to love kindness, and to walk humbly with your God?" (Micah 6:8).

JUNE 17
Learning to Forbear

Next to the problem of self, the greatest problem I will have as a disciple is my relationship to others. When that relationship is pure, there is no greater joy; when sour, no greater heartache. But what do I do when a friend becomes a "holy irritant"? I use the formula of the apostle Paul, "Forbearing one another in love" (Ephesians 4:2, KJV). Someone has said, "There are two pets every Christian family should have: bear and forbear."

To forbear means I will accept others as they are without rejection. I have been guilty of two sins in my interpersonal relationships: I tend to pick my friends, hoping to avoid trouble; and when I cannot pick them, I try to reform and reshape them, hoping to avoid trouble. Both are impossible ways of relating to others. I must realize that when I surround myself with "similar prophets," people who see things as I do, who are quick to agree and slow to disagree, I am not doing them and myself any justice. To develop properly as a disciple, I need a "troubler," someone who tells it like it is, regardless. That is what Elijah was to Ahab (1 Kings 18:17). Though Ahab did not know it, Elijah was his best friend. Unfortunately, Ahab did not forbear Elijah, so he failed.

My critic, my irritant, my troubler will do wonders for my heart if only I will learn to forbear. I must grant him the right to exist and say his piece so I can learn from him and even be molded by him. God deals with me in strange ways, none stranger than my troubler. He may be God's velvet glove to smooth away the crustiness of my heart. The crowning truth of my relationship to my troubler—regardless of what he may say or do to me—is "God meant it for good" (Genesis 50:20).

"And be kind to one another, tender-hearted, forgiving each other, just as God in Christ also has forgiven you" (Ephesians 4:32).

JUNE 18
Growth in Understanding

Jesus has certain expectations of all His disciples. He expects us to make progress in our understanding of spiritual things. He asked Nicodemus, "Are you the teacher of Israel, and [yet you] do not understand these things?" (John 3:10). The Pharisee did not understand the simple, elemental things of the gospel, the "earthly things" (v. 12) that should have been clear to him from the Old Testament.

Jesus asked the disciples who missed the meaning of His lessons, "Do you *still* not understand? Don't you remember the five loaves for the five thousand?" (Matthew 16:9, NIV, italics added). The disciples were still puzzling over "earthly things" when they should have gone on to "heavenly things," that is, deeper truths of the Lord.

I must not spend my time relearning the obvious or searching agonizingly for a truth that is "nigh [me], even in [my] mouth" (Romans 10:8, KJV). To go over a lesson again and again, after the Lord has made it clear, is to provoke Him. Nicodemus dealt with the truth almost daily; yet he could not see it. That is inexcusable. What is more inexcusable is for me to learn the simple, basic steps of the faith but never get beyond them to the "heavenly things."

I have wondered at the paucity of the church and its tiny impact on the world in general, even though there are far more of us today than ever. Can it be that we are still infants, learning our ABC's, never getting beyond kindergarten? Do we hear Jesus saying, "Do you *still* not understand?" Are we still battling the enemy with infantile weapons? The urging of God is overwhelming: "Let us leave the elementary teachings [ABC's] about Christ and go on to maturity" (Hebrews 6:1, NIV). That is the will of God for us—maturity!

"And your ears will hear a word behind you, 'This is the way, walk in it,' whenever you turn to the right or to the left" (Isaiah 30:21).

JUNE 19
Developing a Spirit of Meekness

Since the Bible puts a premium on meekness, I must cultivate it. Meekness is not weakness, as many have pointed out; but, in the words of a Christian brother, "Meekness is 'I accept God's dealings with me without bitterness.'" Meekness says God is always right, I must always accept what He sends me, and I must always do it with gladness of heart.

Bitterness is always the opposite of meekness; its constant cry is, "It isn't fair!" That is what Naomi said after returning from Moab, where she lost her husband and two sons: "Do not call me Naomi [Pleasant]; call me Mara [Bitterness], for the Almighty has dealt very bitterly with me" (Ruth 1:20). God had become her adversary; He "witnessed against" her and "afflicted" her (v. 21). "*I* went out full, but the *Lord* has brought me back empty" (v. 21, italics added). It is easy to see that poor Naomi was unloading the full responsibility of her forlorn condition on the Lord, and "it wasn't *fair!*"

Naomi's story was put in the Bible because she mirrors every one of us. How many times have I turned sour against God because He "witnessed" or testified against me instead of for me, and "afflicted" me instead of blessing me! The real tragedy is the cheap, short-sighted view we have of God. Yet how many of us nurture this "distorted God" concept subconsciously until it colors all our attitudes and directs all our actions!

Meekness says what Mary said, "Here I am. . . . Let it be with me as you say" (Luke 1:38, Berkeley). Meekness shouts, "God is good, God cannot do wrong, God will treat me *fairly!*" The great example of meekness is Jesus Christ, and what a God He revealed! Lord, drive out every root of bitterness in me and name me on Your list of meek saints!

"He will not cry out or raise His voice, nor make His voice heard in the street. A bruised reed He will not break, and a dimly burning wick He will not extinguish" (Isaiah 42:2–3).

JUNE 20
The Principle of No Advantage

In my ministry to others I will follow the principle of *no advantage*. It is characteristic of the natural man to serve those who are in a position to return the service, whether in business, politics, or, unfortunately, even in Christian service. Too often I have been guilty of this despicable practice. By God's grace, no more!

Paul thanked the Philippians for supporting him and ministering to him in spite of his "bonds," his prison chains (Philippians 1:3–7, KJV). Those good-hearted Philippians were using the principle of no advantage. In return, Paul could only thank them and promise to pray for them. Yet, that was enough! Paul must have remembered when Ananias visited him after his conversion and called him "Brother Saul" (Acts 9:17). No advantage for Ananias there; in fact, danger! Barnabas did the same thing for Saul when he befriended him before the leaders at Jerusalem (Acts 9:27). Two friends in his time of need—Ananias and Barnabas—helped a shunned convert because of their love for Christ.

Whom do I befriend? Whom do I help? Whom do I minister to? Do I seek the renowned, the wealthy, the prominent and serve them in the fond hope that someday they will accept me, recognize me, honor me? I can be just as guilty of "Hollywoodism" in the church as outside of it. I can be just as carnal in exalting "stars" of the Christian church as I can in honoring "stars" of the world. The object of my ministry is the brother in need, whoever he is, the man "fallen among thieves," the one who cannot pay me back. Let Jesus be my example. He did not seek that which is *mine*; He sought *me* (2 Corinthians 12:14), and thus set the pattern for all His servants.

"But I say to you, love your enemies, and pray for those who persecute you in order that you may be sons of your Father who is in heaven; for He causes His sun to rise on the evil and the good" (Matthew 5:44–45).

JUNE 21
Holy Dissatisfaction

I will practice the art of *holy dissatisfaction*. God deals only in holy, not unholy, dissatisfaction. This means dissatisfaction in spirit, not in the flesh. Jesus referred to this as being "poor in spirit," and the result of this poverty is to receive the "kingdom of heaven" (Matthew 5:3).

The Bible is full of dissatisfied holy people. I am sure Abraham left Ur because of the emptiness of the worship of the moon goddess Ishtar. David built his kingdom on men who were tired of Saul's spiritual arrogance; his collection of men "in distress . . . in debt, and . . . discontented" (1 Samuel 22:2) was the raw material for his empire. The disciples of John the Baptist, and later Jesus' disciples, were men who were tired of this world's politics of greed and selfishness; they longed to see God's Kingdom in operation on this earth. No matter where I look in church history, I see a trail of dissatisfied men and women who longed for higher, better things. They sought and found a spiritual ideal, and left a spiritual empire behind them.

Holy dissatisfaction always begins with God and ends with God. I can be easily dissatisfied about things—politics, money, the world situation—but that is usually selfish, and it leads nowhere. But holy dissatisfaction begins within me, in my spirit; it sees poverty there, and then it begins the quest for satisfaction that must lead to God. I will never be much of a disciple unless I have felt this kind of dissatisfaction; the greater the dissatisfaction, the stronger my discipleship. I need to keep asking myself, Are you satisfied? If I answer yes, there is a sense in which I have become my own obstacle to a flourishing discipleship for Jesus Christ. On the other hand, when I "mourn" I have His comforts, and when I "hunger and thirst" I have His filling (Matthew 5:4, 6).

"Do not let your heart envy sinners, but live in the fear of the Lord always. Surely there is a future, and your hope will not be cut off" *(Proverbs 23:17–18).*

JUNE 22
Harnessing Our Emotions

As a disciple of Jesus Christ I must come to terms with my emotions. The usual image of a saint is one who has disintegrated his emotions, but it is better to visualize him as one who has harnessed his emotions. The Bible tells us to crucify the "flesh," not the emotions (Galatians 5:24). On the other hand, unless emotions are controlled, they may run from sensuality to depression.

The biblical sequence is clear: my emotions are to be controlled by my disposition of "mind," and my disposition must be controlled by my will. When Paul said, "Let this mind be in you" (Philippians 2:5, KJV), he was not speaking of Jesus' brain, but His way of thinking, His disposition. If Christ is alive in me, it follows that His way of thinking is alive in me; therefore, all I need to do is to turn my will over to Him, and consequently His disposition begins to appear in my life.

If allowed to run free, my emotions can lead me into danger. That is because emotions do not make moral choices. I can fall in love with a sinner as well as a saint; I can fear God as well as Satan. Unless my emotions are disciplined and prevented from going too far, I can expect a pack of troubles. A true disciple is—not emotionless, nor is he unemotional; he simply has learned when to let his emotions run and how far.

If I do not rule my emotions, they will rule me. Whenever fear, love, hate, prejudice, or any other emotion dominates me, I become a neurotic. My victory lies in forcibly denying my emotions any preeminence by an act of the will. I must keep putting the reins of my life into the hands of Jesus Christ so that I may "will one will" with Him at all times. Total surrender to Christ is total control of my life, including the emotional side of me, which so much needs His mastery (Romans 12:1–2).

"But the fruit of the Spirit is love, joy, peace, patience, kindness, goodness, faithfulness, gentleness, self-control; against such things there is no law" (Galatians 5:22–23).

JUNE 23
The Surprise Visits of God

I must expect occasional surprise visits from God. Jesus made a surprise visit once to the Jews of the Temple when He dropped in and "looked round about upon all things" (Mark 11:11, KJV). That was a surprise visit of inspection. I should expect many such visits in my lifetime. A surprise visit from God is a time of special, unique awareness of His presence. It may be for simple fellowship, to correct a wrong tendency within, to commend a right tendency, or to convey a message.

The Bible is full of God's surprise visits. He sought out Abraham to reveal to him the coming destruction of Sodom and Gomorrah (Genesis 18:1). Jesus suddenly appeared to the two disciples going to Emmaus and convinced them of His resurrection (Luke 24). He appeared to Zechariah, Mary, Paul, Ananias, and others. Outside the Bible, God has appeared to many, including Charles Finney, whose doubts He challenged, and A. J. Gordon, whose ministry He challenged.

I cannot read Christ's letters to the seven churches of Asia Minor (Revelation 2–3) without feeling that He was their constant Visitor. He repeats the phrase "I know . . . I will come" throughout. This reveals a Jesus who is personally aware of His people at all times.

To be visited by God, that is, to be made more acutely aware of His presence, adds to the excitement of being His disciple. To be visited means my life is enriched, invigorated, and refreshed. It means another strand in the rope that binds me closer to God. The visit may occur anywhere—in the solitude of my study, in a worship service, or walking a busy street. It catches me by surprise, may last a moment or hours, and leaves me one notch nearer heaven. In times like these I seem to hear Him say, "Thou shalt be called Hephzibah . . . for the Lord delighteth in thee" (Isaiah 62:4, KJV).

"And it came about that while they were conversing and discussing, Jesus Himself approached, and began traveling with them" (Luke 24:15).

JUNE 24
Attacking the Citadel's Strong Part

It is true that Satan attacks us at our weakest point. But it is even *more* true that he attacks us at our strongest point. How did he cause Peter to fall? By striking him where the disciple thought he was strong—his ability to command leadership, to do the heroic, to be a "star." "I will lay down my life for You" (John 13:37). But as with Samson, his strength was his weakness, and Satan knew it. Peter not only had *depths* of which he was unaware, there were also *heights*; and it was on the heights that Satan caught him.

Have I not felt the same thing? In the place where I felt strong and bulwarked, Satan tripped me up. Where I felt secure, he stripped me naked.

I think of Job. Satan trapped him in his *integrity*, his strongest spiritual asset. Perhaps Job thought too highly of his integrity, perhaps it became his pride; and where pride entered, he developed a blind spot.

I think of Jesus. It was in His very sonship that Satan tried to dislodge Him. "If [since] You are the Son of God, command that these stones" (Matthew 4:3). Satan knew Jesus was God's Son; acting on that knowledge, he tried to shrewdly twist Jesus' strongest element into something devious. He attacked the strongest part of the citadel.

I must not think of Satan as only a wily serpent who sneaks around nibbling at my exposed weak parts. I must see him as a frontal foe who hammers hard at my very strengths. That means I must be careful to let my strengths simply be my *strengths*, but never my boasts. I am assured that because Christ is in me, I can be just as frontal with Satan as he is with me: "Resist the devil and he will flee from you" (James 4:7). Then my strengths can remain my strengths through the victorious One.

"You will tread upon the lion and cobra, the young lion and the serpent you will trample down" (Psalm 91:13).

JUNE 25
The Blessing That Precedes Us

G od has a special kind of blessing for some of His choice disciples. It is a blessing that *goes in advance* of the disciple as he pursues his pilgrim way. God said to the Israelite: I will send my fear before thee . . . to whom thou shalt come" (Exodus 23:27, KJV). If I obey God fully, He will not only be *with* me, He will be *before* me; and in going before me, He will prepare and condition the hearts of the people whom I shall meet.

One of the unique features of the ministry of Jesus was the way people were prepared to meet Him. "It was noised that He was in the house" (Mark 2:1, KJV). Because of His complete obedience to the Father, Jesus became perfume in His hands, which He spread all over Palestine. Listening to Jesus teach became a matter of comparing His fame to His performance. But since He was so obedient, His fame and performance were one and the same.

My goal as a disciple should be to achieve the kind of obedience that sends God before me. Often I have heard people say of another, "His very presence was a blessing to us!" This was possible because God went before that person and overcame opposition and melted the hearts of the people to receive him. If I look for victory *on the spot*, I may be disappointed. Victory comes like a garden grows; first sow the seed, then reap the harvest. By walking closely to my heavenly Father I am now sowing the seeds of a victory to be harvested later. Not only do I benefit, but that victory may be far beyond the bounds of my present location. Peter's perfume reached as far as Joppa (Acts 10) and Paul's floated across the Aegean Sea (Acts 16:9).

May God make me that kind of disciple! There will be people in my future who will need the touch of God. By walking the disciple's path now, I am preparing for our future meeting, at which time they will become my triumph for Christ.

"For I have come to have much joy and comfort in your love, because the hearts of the saints have been refreshed through you, brother" (Philemon 7).

JUNE 26
Slightly Soiled, Greatly Reduced

I must ever be watchful of the quality of service I render God. The priests of Malachi's day were content to lay stale, moldy bread on the altar of God (Malachi 1:7). I must remember that as the sacrifice is, so is my heart. I must never afford God the privilege of the "second best." It is always easy to judge my service to God by asking: Is it more or less than what I would do for myself?

To be an exemplary servant I must emulate Paul's attitude: "I do not seek what is yours, but you" (2 Corinthians 12:14). The moment I let my eye waver from the man to his possessions, I am in danger of choosing second best. Gehazi's action warns—and frightens—me here. He loved Naaman's possessions more than Naaman himself (2 Kings 5:20–27).

Is my love to God a "firstfruits"? Is it an offering of the "firstborn"? The famous sermon of Dr. Charles Koller, former president of Northern Baptist Seminary, entitled "Slightly Soiled, Greatly Reduced in Price," is sensible advice for the retailer in business, but it should never characterize my service to Jesus Christ. Yet how often have I dealt with God in second-rate goods! That will earn me the title "contemptible" (Malachi 2:9, KJV).

I must learn that the condition of whatever I offer God is indicative of how much I value Him. Is He moldy and sickly to me? If so, that is how I will return His service. I am encouraged by God's word to Abraham: "You . . . have not withheld your son, your only son [from Me]" (Genesis 22:16). God wants from me an offering that by its nature shows Him how much I love Him. If He is my all in all, then I will put no price on my offerings, as He did not when He gave His Son for me and, in doing so, showed me the best sacrifice forever.

"Teach me Thy way, O Lord; I will walk in Thy truth; unite my heart to fear Thy name. I will give thanks to Thee, O Lord my God, with all my heart, and will glorify Thy name forever" (Psalm 86:11–12).

JUNE 27
The Breakings of God

I must distinguish between God's threshold for sinners and His threshold for disciples. For sinners, God keeps a very low threshold, so low that any person may enter the house of salvation. But disciples have a high threshold to Christian service, so high that none but the qualified may enter. For example, no man could serve as a priest in God's house who had a broken hand or foot (Leviticus 21:19). That was a reminder to Aaron and all his sons that lameness in walk and slackness in service would not be tolerated by the Most High.

Yet, isn't it necessary to be broken in order to serve God? Didn't God make Jacob lame and change him from Jacob to Israel, a prince of God (Genesis 32:24–32)? Wasn't the body of God's Son broken at Calvary to provide salvation for all who believe?

I think the difference is this: the disorders of the "natural" man, such as a lustful eye or an irascible temper, must never be allowed in our service for God. But God's "brokenness" is essential. A man broken by God is an obedient man. Further, he is a vulnerable man, vulnerable to feeling the hurts, pains, and griefs of the people he must serve. God breaks a person, not to let goodness *out*, but to let goodness *in*. Something enters him that flavors his whole being, tenderizes his heart, and makes him able to empathize with others.

I think of Isaiah's broken heart (Isaiah 6) with the resulting cleansing and commissioning. A great servant began a great service with a great breaking! If I am to know success in the service of my Lord, I must know what it means to be broken by His hand. My bread must be broken and my grapes must be crushed if I am to feed a multitude for my God.

"Then I said, 'Behold, I come; in the scroll of the book it is written of me; I delight to do Thy will, O my God; Thy Law is within my heart'" (Psalm 40:7–8).

JUNE 28

Living at Headquarters

As a disciple I must be rightly connected at all times with my headquarters. Where is it? Paul gives me the location: "Seek those things which are above. . . . Set your affection on things above" (Colossians 3:1–2, KJV). Heaven is the nerve center of everything that controls my life, or the life of the church, or even the life of the world. Just as a soldier "lives" in the mind of his commanding officer, so I must live in the mind of Jesus Christ. Phrases like "independent operation," "unilateral action," and "self-devised plan" never occur in the vocabulary of the military man. He waits for the signal from the proper authority, then he moves.

My failure in many areas of my discipleship stems from misinterpreting the signals from my command post. Sometimes I have read my own desires into the command and acted as if the command were mine. Sometimes I simply could not hear the signal because it was drowned out by the interference of the world. There is only one cure for failure: stay closely tuned to your command post! I must not be distracted by earthly activities, rumors, or fears. I even must not let frontline action dictate my next move.

If I live in my headquarters, that is, keep my mind in heaven and what is going on there, it will make a vast difference in my behavior on earth. I wonder how many "important" things on earth are really important in heaven? How many things that I consider essential are really peripheral? Does heaven worry about the things that vex and worry me? Are they top priority with God? If I could only visit my command post and visibly see what is top drawer to my Commander, I think I would come back with a complete reversal of my priorities. This I must do, for I am a man "under authority," the authority of my Commander in Chief, Jesus Christ.

"Therefore it says, 'When He ascended on high, He led captive a host of captives, and He gave gifts to men'" (Ephesians 4:8).

JUNE 29
No Private Closets

God's desire for His children is that they be wholly set apart for Him. "Every cooking pot in Jerusalem . . . will be holy to the Lord" (Zechariah 14:21). God must not be confined to Sundays, quiet times, or deeper life conferences. He is the God of the every day, the kitchen as well as the sanctuary, the golf course as well as the altar. Similarly, in my life there can be no private closets to which the Lord has no access. If I make a separation between my God and my business, I am making a sorry mistake.

I must not repeat Saul's mistake of keeping part of God's property for myself (1 Samuel 15:9). The sanctification must be whole, complete, even down to the "pots and pans" of the kitchen. I cannot say, "Lord, save my soul, but leave my mind and heart alone." I cannot *offer* Him my spirit but retain the full right to use my body as I wish. I cannot seat Jesus in the parlor of my life but shut Him out of my study, my family room, or my bedroom.

Paul prayed for the Thessalonian believers: "May your spirit and soul and body be preserved complete" (1 Thessalonians 5:23). That is all of us, complete and entire! F. B. Meyer kept the key of one closet in his life that was off limits to God. Not until he surrendered the key did he have peace, and not until the closet was cleansed did he have power.

God wants to become very personal with me. He wants to socialize with me, "eating and drinking" with me, as Jesus did with the people. He wants to make every area of my life "awesome," as He made Bethel for Jacob (Genesis 28:17). He wants to be the Master of my thoughts as well as my emotions, instincts, and even my subconscious. When He becomes all that, my life will become radiant with His abounding presence.

"'Yet even now,' declares the Lord, 'Return to Me with all your heart, and with fasting, weeping, and mourning'" (Joel 2:12).

JUNE 30
God's Normal Person

The more I strive to become a true disciple of Jesus Christ, the more opposed the world will be toward me. The world will use terms like *fanatic* or *religious nut* if I seek to become one of God's "normal" men. Jesus Christ was God's greatest expression of the normal; yet the world would not have anything to do with Him because they claimed He was "beside himself" (Mark 3:21, KJV). Alexander Whyte says, "Either He was beside Himself, or they [His critics] were." There is no middle ground, for the mind of Jesus and the mind of the world are exact opposites. To Jesus, God His Father was the center of His life, the Determiner of every thought and act. To the world, God is a pleasant glaze, a pretty covering, a fragrant perfume, but never the heart and soul of its life and action.

Is it normal to enjoy God and seek a close relationship with Him? The world would say, "OK, but be reasonable." It becomes uneasy in the presence of a person who spends a great deal of time with God. Is it normal to resist the desires of the flesh and be dead to the attractions of the world? The world says no and looks with fishy eyes at the man who disagrees. He is "different."

The world is never anti-God; it is little-God. It wants me to have just enough of God to make me "nice," but never enough to make me expose its heart. Worldly people worship "the God who doesn't interfere." The Bible gives me a choice: Am I to be God's normal man, or the world's? Whatever I choose, I am bound to please and bound to offend. The eternal question is: Who is worth the pleasing? Moses did not take long to answer: "Choose life in order that you may live" (Deuteronomy 30:19).

"For if we are beside ourselves, it is for God; if we are of sound mind, it is for you. For the love of Christ controls us" (2 Corinthians 5:13–14).

JULY 1

The Advantage of Going Backward

As a younger Christian I had a friend who advised me, "Never look back, always look forward!" That was good advice then, but now I wonder. Should we *never* look back? We should always look back in regard to our roots. When Paul said, "Forgetting those things which are behind" (Philippians 3:13, KJV), he meant his shortcomings. The man who never looks back is a man off course.

When God told Jacob, "Go up to Bethel" (Genesis 35:1), He meant, "Go back to the place where I first visited you" (cf. 28:16–22). Jacob and his family were in acute danger and their only safety was to return to the place where God was their Defender. To Jacob, Bethel was the place of the first vow. I need to visit again and again the place where God and I met, and where we first made our eternal commitments to each other. This personal reviving is my defense against whatever Canaanites might destroy me.

Jeremiah reminded the Jews that if they wanted "rest for [their] souls" they would have to "ask for the *old* paths" (Jeremiah 6:16, KJV, italics added). Spiritual progress is never found by cutting ourselves off from our spiritual roots. There is, indeed, a hazard in looking back, as Jesus pointed out (Luke 9:62); but there is also a hazard in keeping our eyes forever fixed forward.

The return to our roots is for the recapturing of our first love to God. The decline of religion always begins in taking God for granted. The call "Come back to Bethel" is the heart cry of a God who knows that love can grow cold, faith can shrivel, and vows can be broken. The one who returns is the one who finds rest, strength, and deliverance (Isaiah 30:15). God waits for the sign of my returning face and, seeing it, promises to be "gracious" (v. 18).

"But I have this against you, that you have left your first love. Remember therefore from where you have fallen, and repent and do the deeds you did at first" (Revelation 2:4–5).

JULY 2
Openness with God

I must never forget that God's knowledge of me is *complete*. "Thou . . . art . . . acquainted with all my ways" (Psalm 139:3). This means that God knows my subconscious as well as my conscious life. He knew me in the womb (vv. 15–16), which means He knew my genes, my hereditary traits, and all the unborn capabilities for good and evil. In the hands of an evil being, such knowledge would easily be my undoing. But in the hands of a God of infinite love, such knowledge is my safety and my salvation.

God will accept me as I am, warts and all, provided I do not try to pretend. Pretension is the mark of social custom, the device whereby human beings are able to tolerate one another. To be barely, rigidly open with each other would be to turn the human race into a vast asylum. But God, who knows us completely, never uses that knowledge to take advantage of us. Nevertheless, God expects me to be as honest with Him as I am capable of being. This means that I must be honest with myself. If I am self-deceived, I can never be open and honest with God.

Despite God's complete knowledge of me, He can do nothing for me until I release my will to Him. "Try me and know my . . . thoughts" (Psalm 139:23) is a plea. Once released to help, God will use His complete knowledge of me to guide me in "the everlasting way" (v. 24). This means controlling my subconscious, where areas exist of which I know nothing, and using it for profit instead of for loss. When Jesus said to Simon, "Thou art Simon . . . thou shalt be . . . Cephas" (John 1:42, KJV), He was beginning to change a man from a mass of raw instincts into a refined copy of Himself. Jesus knew what He had to start with. He knows it with me. But He also knows the end to which He intends to bring me, polished and glorified.

"And there is no creature hidden from His sight, but all things are open and laid bare to the eyes of Him with whom we have to do" (Hebrews 4:13).

JULY 3
God the Great Prosaic

I believe that God is the great romantic. But I also believe that He is the great prosaic. If I exclude God from the minutiae and trivia of my life, I am doing myself—and Him—a great disservice. One psalmist says a sparrow found a house for herself and her young inside the underpinnings of God's altar (Psalm 84:3). While mighty transactions were going on *upon* the altar, God was making provision for a tiny fledgling *underneath*.

This speaks to my heart. One of my chief sins is to make God so majestic and infinite that He cannot be prosaic. I have romanticized His work so much that I have come to feel that the humdrum detail of the daily round is an intrusion, as trifling of His presence and power. I have looked upon daily chores as something alien to God's ways of doing things, instead of realizing that irksome detail is just as ablaze with God's glory as the burning bush.

God notices when sparrows fall, He dresses flowers, He counts the hairs of my head, He measures my height (Luke 12:6, 7, 25, 27). God not only works with trivia and delights in it, but I might almost say God majors in trivia. He devised the massive detail of the universe and tends it. He also is the Architect of the trivia of my life—my mood swings, my cycles, my interruptions, my friend's impromptu request, and a thousand other things that drain my strength and energy. God is concerned about *one* lost sheep, *one* lost coin, and *one* wayward son. When they are found, He rejoices!

Like a loving parent, God is interested in the cuts and scratches that infest my daily life. What concerns me, concerns Him (1 Peter 5:7). He loves to do what humans detest—to be "bothered." It is no bother to Him when I pour my heart's trivia out to Him, for He "careth" for me.

"Thou dost scrutinize my path and my lying down, and art intimately acquainted with all my ways" (Psalm 139:3).

JULY 4
God's Wet Nurses

It is said that God has no grandchildren, and that is true; but He has a lot of wet nurses! When God called Aaron to assist Moses in delivering the children of Israel, He said to Moses, "You shall be as God to him" (Exodus 4:16). Aaron was too immature for the great responsibility, so Moses was to be his spiritual guide and stay.

Most of the time we have to see God *in* someone before we see God Himself. Timothy's faith was a hand-me-down, one that he had seen operate in his grandmother, Lois, and his mother, Eunice, and now it was operating in him (2 Timothy 1:5). I do not mean that Timothy did not have to exercise personal faith; I mean that he expressed his personal faith in God when he saw that faith working in others. In shepherding Timothy, Lois and Eunice were like God to him; they were God's wet nurses.

Roughly speaking, God's flock can be divided into two groups: the wet nurses and the wet nursed. God's concern is to get as many qualified wet nurses as possible, because those who need nursing are always around and always plentiful. It took God eighty years to make an assistant out of Moses; that is how highly He prizes the role. Andrew shepherded Peter, but it did not take Simon long to become a shepherd himself, so eagerly did he follow Jesus.

I cannot appoint myself a guardian, only God can do that. But I can pledge to follow the Lord "wholly," as Caleb did, and put myself under His discipline with such rigor that He will count me approved. One thing is certain: no one ever follows the Lord without someone else watching, and often the watchers step into line and begin following too. The disciple's great joy is that of John: "I have no greater joy than this, to hear of my children walking in the truth" (3 John 4).

"But I have prayed for you, that your faith may not fail; and you, when once you have turned again, strengthen your brothers" (Luke 22:32).

JULY 5
A Sorrow Like His

There are times when a disciple of Jesus Christ experiences indescribable sorrow, like Jeremiah's. "Look and see if there is any sorrow like my sorrow" (Lamentations 1:12, margin). This is not the sorrow of bereavement or failure, but a sorrow that touches at the heart of the atonement of Christ, a sorrow like *His*. It is a sorrow directly related to sin; in fact, it is produced by sin.

Jeremiah was not responsible for Jerusalem's sins (and punishment); yet he felt the anguish of those sins, just as Jesus felt anguish for our sins on Calvary. The terrible anguish is a sign that God is at work, for the conflict between sin and holiness always results in bitter pain. Conviction of sin is really "sorrow" for sin, the sorrow that wrongness produces in the human heart. Every disciple will experience this sorrow, not once but many times, sometimes for his own sin, sometimes for the sins of others. Whenever this sorrow comes, it always means revival, whether that revival is personal and local or whether it engulfs a church or a community.

As a disciple, I must recognize the difference between sin's sorrow and other kinds of sorrow. A feeling of inward heaviness may not be indigestion or alienation or lack of success, but the prompting of the Spirit concerning an undetected sin in my life or in the life of my worshiping community. As with Jeremiah, I may be called upon to feel the pain of the sins of others, as if I were the cause, in order to be a proper intercessor for them. That is the redemptive power of sorrow, and it is always a prelude to the coming blessing of God. Those are the birth pangs of a new day, a new blessing, or a new tide from God. "As soon as Zion travailed, she also brought forth her sons" (Isaiah 66:8).

"The Lord is righteous; for I have rebelled against His command; hear now, all peoples, and behold my pain" (Lamentations 1:18).

JULY 6
Fulfillment or Fulfilling

I must at all costs avoid the deadly delusion of self-fulfillment. I am hounded on all sides to be the person I was meant to be, to realize my full potential, and to explore the capabilities of the possible me. Even Christians have succumbed to this idea, and now I am told that in Christ I shall be able to fulfill myself as God intended, in contrast to being self-fulfilled by the world.

The error in all this is that the Bible nowhere talks of *self*-fulfillment. The only fullness the Bible knows about is the fullness of Christ. He is the fullness of God (Colossians 1:19; 2:9); He is the fullness of the church (Ephesians 1:22–23); and He is the fullness of everyone who draws fullness from Him.

Self-fulfillment is only another form of pride, and hardly different from the ignominious sin of Lucifer (Isaiah 14:12). We progressive moderns, however, have so covered the term with attractive clothing that it no longer appears as sin, but as an inherent right of the personality. Self-fulfillment is expressing my full self, achieving my glory, and carving out my niche in life. Its ultimate goal is the coronation of self. Further, it is a fatal contradiction. How can everyone fulfill himself? The total exaltation of everybody would result in racial mania. The fulfillment of all my desires usually means the denial of someone else's.

As a disciple, I must not talk of *fulfillment*; I must talk of *fulfilling*. When I received Christ, I received His fullness. As I live out His fullness, I flesh out His presence on this earth, I make full His manifestation to men (Ephesians 4:13). Instead of fulfilling myself, I fulfill Christ; I make Him the "Man above all," the rightfully crowned King, "that *in all things he might have the preeminence*" (Colossians 1:18, KJV, italics added).

"For in Him all the fulness of Deity dwells in bodily form, and in Him you have been made complete, and He is the head over all rule and authority" (Colossians 2:9–10).

JULY 7
The Spirit of Readiness

God never treats our sanctification lightly, but He always puts it to the test. He will come between ourselves and that which we love until we can hold what we love with light hands. "Take now your son, your only son, whom you love, Isaac" (Genesis 22:2). God will demand our Isaac as often as it is necessary to reduce him to something *expendable*. God never tests us on what we *hate*, but what we love can easily turn us aside from doing His will.

I must never forget the *object* of my sanctification. It is *them*. "For their sakes I sanctify Myself," said Jesus (John 17:19). When I made my decision to trust Christ for salvation, that was for *my* sake. But God never stops working on us until we are ready for the second decision: Are we willing to sanctify ourselves for *their* sakes? The moment we say yes, that moment God begins to perfect our sanctification by weaning us away from every selfish desire in it. God knows that unfulfilled sanctification leads to backsliding, and untested sanctification leads to carnality.

Sanctification always needs the spirit of readiness. Our lamps must be constantly trimmed and burning (Matthew 25:1–13). By being ready I am preparing the way of the Lord (Isaiah 40:3), who longs to intervene redemptively in every human situation. My ready sanctification, for their sakes, acts like a well-grounded conductor ready to receive the lightning of God's power and transmit it to human need. Sanctification is never an inward, subjective thing and never asks, "Am I getting holier every day?" It becomes an outward thing, concerned with the spiritual welfare of others, and asks, "How can I bring the power and love of my heavenly Father to them?" The sanctification of Jesus was God's greatest love letter to the world. I am well sanctified when I become a fair copy of that love letter.

"For even the Son of Man did not come to be served, but to serve, and to give His life a ransom for many" (Mark 10:45).

JULY 8

Service Is No Self-Centered Spectacular

I must always maintain a high view of Christian service. Most modern Christian views of service are shallow and sometimes shoddy. Godly service is described by Isaiah as something total, "If you *pour yourself out* for the hungry" (58:10, author's trans.). A lot of Christian service misses the ideal.

Most of our Christian service today revolves around two things: first, our gifts and talents, and second, our education. Young people are constantly reminded to use the gifts the Lord has given them and by all means "get a good education." Worthy suggestions! But if that is all there is to Christian service, we have missed the weightiest. It takes no effort to use our gifts; in fact, it is an effort not to. Nor is it much sweat to pass on the fruits of our education, to "notebook" our way through to success.

Service is pouring out our soul. How much is contained in the very words! Jesus did not come parading His gifts, showing off His talents, putting on a self-centered spectacular. Certainly He had no education to trumpet. But His was the model service of a soul turned inside out, the sharing of what He was inwardly. He was the perfect embodiment of the Old Testament sacrifice, an offering *to* God *for* others. Service is offering to God all we are, to be used for others as God directs. It is out of this total sacrifice that the materials are taken for meeting those needs, as God applies them.

The "pouring out of the soul" is the equivalent of "laying down our lives for the brothers" (see 1 John 3:16). Not until I am ready to do that am I capable of rendering effective service, or capable of following Him who was the embodiment of the perfect Servant. Thank God for His example and even more, for the grace He gives us to become poured-out souls for Him.

"But even if I am being poured out as a drink offering upon the sacrifice and service of your faith, I rejoice and share my joy with you all" (Philippians 2:17).

JULY 9
Amusement Versus Pleasure

I must not despise pleasure as if it were an evil in itself. But I must be sure I follow pleasure as the Bible defines it, not as the world defines it. Pleasure, to the world, is amusement, entertainment. It can run the gamut from a Beethoven concerto to a pornographic display. Biblical pleasure, on the other hand, is the satisfaction of contributing to someone's growth.

Jesus Christ experienced pleasure. "For the joy set before Him [He] endured the cross" (Hebrews 12:2). Jesus' pleasure was not the result of something done to or for Him, but something done to or for others. Amusement is self-destructive because it ends in itself, it has no future. But godly pleasure is eternal because the good it creates runs on endlessly, like the ripples of a pond when a pebble is tossed in. Amusement dulls the harsh realities of life temporarily, but pleasure keeps a person in tune continually.

The key to Bible pleasure is that "Christ did not please Himself" (Romans 15:1–3). Yet, in the wonderful formula of God, Christ's passion to please others resulted in seeing "the travail of his soul" and being "satisfied" (Isaiah 53:11, KJV). If I seek a self-ministry, trying to satisfy myself first and foremost, I will eventually wither. To continue "having devotions" and "keeping myself in tune with God" just for my own sake is running the risk of failure. But to keep myself strong in my relationship to God for the sake of others is the only way to keep myself continually strong in Him. Even the most dedicated Christians can wind up as castaways if they forget that ministering to others is the only sure way to minister to themselves. I please my heavenly Father when He sees in me the same quality of self-sacrifice He saw in Jesus, which enabled Him to say, "This is My beloved Son, in whom I am well-pleased" (Matthew 3:17).

"And He died for all, that they who live should no longer live for themselves, but for Him who died and rose again on their behalf" (2 Corinthians 5:15).

JULY 10
The God-Intoxicated Person

The closer I live to God, the more sensitive I will be to the needs of people. Is there any greater sensitivity to human need than "God so loved the world"? The tragedy is that often we become harder toward people as we walk with God. If so, something is terribly amiss. It was after John had walked with Jesus for two years that he wanted to rain fire upon the heads of the Samaritans (Luke 9:51–56). I must not think that merely being in company with Jesus is going to make me tender-hearted toward mankind.

The Old Testament priest, when ending his official duties, was to put on the common clothing of the people (Ezekiel 42:14). So my service to God must make me people-prone; otherwise it is empty service. I must come from the sanctuary on the people's level. Jesus came from His Father dressed in human flesh, and that sets the pattern for me.

Walking with God can make me intolerant, demanding, and holier-than-thou. This means there is something in my makeup that has not caught the mind of God. Something in my heart has not softened to His touch. I have received enough of Him to stimulate me, but not to intoxicate me. God-intoxicated men are marvelously warm and alive to human needs. John, the "son of thunder," later became the "apostle of love," but only after God had so possessed him that he breathed love from every pore. I must be more than merely "touched by God." I must be like Paul: "We were gentle among you, even as a nurse [with] her children" (1 Thessalonians 2:7, KJV). He was a "consumed" disciple whose heart beat as tenderly as the One by whom he was consumed. Only in this way do I begin to approach the servant ministry of Jesus Christ.

"But we proved to be gentle among you, as a nursing mother tenderly cares for her own children" (1 Thessalonians 2:7).

JULY 11
Becoming Weary of God

I must be aware of two kinds of weariness in my life as a disciple. The first is the weariness of giving out faster than I take in. That is the weariness of overcommitment; it is the fatigue of being overexercised in my service to God for others. The second kind of weariness is more subtle; it is the weariness of God Himself. Micah refers to this when he points his finger at the Israelites: "My people . . . how have I wearied you?" (6:3).

As a disciple, I will discover that my life will be a series of emptyings and fillings. As I empty myself in service, I must refill myself by drawing upon God's infinite resources. If I fail to refill, I will become drained and exhaustion will occur. One of the chief reasons I fail to refill is because I have become tired of God. In other words, I have lost my desire to be filled by God.

It is inconceivable that I can exhaust a transcendent God. Therefore, weariness can only be a symptom that something has gone wrong with my pipeline to heaven. Either it is stopped up with something or it is broken or I simply do not exert myself to turn on the spiggot. The latter occurs whenever I have discovered an interest that, for the moment at least, transcends my interest in God. Weariness with God usually begins with a wandering eye. That leads to a wandering heart, and soon I am off chasing a will-o'-the-wisp that seems momentarily delightful. It is in that stage of things that I become weary of God; He has lost His color, His richness, and His appeal to my heart. I am clearly on dangerous ground, and that is why God makes His strongest appeals to rekindle my appetite for Him. He asks me to deliberately surrender the trinkets for the gold; He begs me to give up the hewn fountains and get back to the flowing river of life (see Jeremiah 2:13).

"For My people have committed two evils: they have forsaken Me, the fountain of living waters, to hew for themselves cisterns, broken cisterns, that can hold no water" (Jeremiah 2:13).

JULY 12
The Discipline of Decision Making

The process that brought me to Jesus in the first place goes on long after I have trusted Him as Savior. The difference is not in the nature of the decision, but in the nature of the thing sacrificed. When I yielded to the saviorship of Christ, I sacrificed my sins; now in my Christian walk I must keep sacrificing those things that keep me from being my best for Him. The "pearl of great price" makes this clear. The merchant sold his good things in order to obtain the best thing (Matthew 13:45–46).

I must learn to do business in my Christian life, to "exchange" things as Jesus did. "*In exchange* for the joy lying around Him, He endured the cross" (Hebrews 12:2, author's trans.). Jesus saw what was infinitely good and surrendered it for something infinitely better. Daily I will be confronted with a "good" that must be exchanged for a "better"; otherwise I invite spiritual stagnation. The discipline of decision making does not end the moment I accept Christ as my Savior. It is in this process of making decisions that God weans me more and more from what I am to what I was meant to be.

To be able to use that which is better I need insight and willpower. Insight tells me the difference between the "common" and the "holy" (Ezekiel 22:26); willpower commits me to it. Thus, my Christian life will always be a series of crises, both major and minor, that will seem very much like the crisis that brought me to Christ. I must forever accept the fact that both birth and growth are traumatic; yet the trauma leads to a burgeoning spiritual life that is positively thrilling! The "things . . . that God has prepared for those who love Him" (1 Corinthians 2:9) are for *this* life, not only the life to come, and they make the Christian adventure richer than any sight or sound experienced by the natural man.

"And Elijah came near to all the people and said, 'How long will you hesitate between two opinions? If the Lord is God, follow Him; but if Baal, follow him'" (1 Kings 18:21).

JULY 13
Molded by Circumstances

A s a disciple of Christ I must not feel ultimately responsible for myself at any time. That is clearly brought out in the hearing of Jesus before Pilate. "Don't You know," said Pilate, "that I have power to crucify You and power to release You?" (John 19:10, author's trans.). That was a fatal deduction on the procurator's part. The power was not in *him*, but in God (John 19:11). It is true that Pilate did exercise crucifying authority against Jesus. But he was only the instrument, not the source of that authority.

I am absolved from the responsibility of my destiny. What happens to me is not the whim of sickness, accident, my employer, my loved one, or a chain of circumstances. In this I am not guaranteed comfort (the cross of Jesus was not exactly comfort), but I am guaranteed certainty, security, and the exact fulfillment of God's will in me as a person.

Since I am molded by, but not ordained by, my circumstances, there will be times when the engineers of such circumstances will be covered with confusion. Can you imagine Sennacherib's face when he was told that he had lost 185,000 elite soldiers in one night (Isaiah 37:36)? Can you imagine the horror of Herod's court when they were told their monarch had been eaten by worms (Acts 12:23)? Those are reminders that God is alive and well!

I need not fear the hands of men as long as I am in the hands of God. In a certain sense, Pilate was only incidental in the life of Christ. That is how I must relate to my "Pilates"; they are necessary ingredients in God's pattern for me, but I am not a victim of their wills, attitudes, or decisions any more than Christ was a victim of Pontius Pilate. "You are from God, little children, and have overcome them; because greater is He who is in you than he who is in the world" (1 John 4:4).

"Humble yourselves in the presence of the Lord, and He will exalt you" *(James 4:10).*

JULY 14
Wanting Something More

One of Satan's subtlest temptations is to make me believe that God is holding out on me. That was his approach to Adam and Eve. I must understand that simply being a Christian does not end the attack. I am bombarded with all kinds of suggestions that there is "something more" to Christianity than what I have already received. Satan always whispers, "Christ is not enough; you need something additional."

Yet the Bible clearly tells me, "Ye are complete in him" (Colossians 2:10, KJV). There is absolutely nothing, and no one, that God can give me in addition to Jesus Christ. Whatever I need is to be found in Him and Him alone. If Christ is not enough, nothing is enough, and I am doomed to eternal restlessness in that case. But the trouble is not with the Godward side of things. The trouble is with me. If Christ is not enough, it is because I have shut the door of faith to what He can do in me. If Christ is not satisfying me, it is because there is a piece of grit somewhere in my spiritual machinery that is grinding things down to a halt. If I am in the "something more" condition of faith, I am on dangerous ground. I am open to any tempting suggestion by Satan. I begin to experiment with things, hoping to find the "something more" that is not in Jesus Christ.

Wanting "something more" is a telltale sign that the pipe is clogged. There is an abundance in Christ that we have scarcely dreamed of, much less experienced. If I do not experience Him in that fullness, I must make more room for Him, for God cannot give me any more of Christ than He has given; He can only ask for something more of me. "As you received Christ Jesus as Lord, continue to live in him, rooted and built up in him, strengthened in the faith . . . overflowing with thanksgiving" (Colossians 2:6–7, NIV).

"For of His fulness we have all received, and grace upon grace" (John 1:16).

JULY 15
Stiffening the Will

As a Christian, I invite a great deal of trouble when I choose to live in my *emotions*. God wants all His children to live in the *will*. The emotions are to my spirit what desserts are to my body—tasty but not substantive. The will is the "steak and potatoes" of the Christian life. Many times I will be confronted by a spiritual dilemma that can be solved only by an act of will. The Bible does not say, "Do you feel you should do this?" It says, "Stop sinning!" (see 1 John 2:1). If I consult my emotions I will never beat a path to righteousness, for, frankly, sin is very pleasing to the emotions.

One of the psalmists was delivered from a serious illness. In gratitude to God, he resolved to surrender his life to the Lord as long as he lived (Psalm 116:2). How did he implement this surrender? By an act of the will. The psalm describes five "I wills" that I would like to call (homiletically speaking) the "I wills" of dedication (vv. 2, 9, 13, 17, 18). No doubt this man had come through a soul-shaking emotional experience; yet he grounded his new direction on the right foundation—his will.

Many of the emotional problems that confront us today can be cured, not by counseling or preaching, but by the sheer act of decision. Because we do not decide morally, we stand under the reprimand of the Word of God for *living selfishly*. We have become emotional babies and cripples because we do not stiffen our spines and simply do what God has clearly commanded us to do! Of course, emotional illness must be recognized for what it is, and it must receive tender, loving care; but spiritual malaise due to spinelessness has only one prescription: *I will do His will!* "If you become willing and obedient, you shall eat the good of the land" (Isaiah 1:19, Berkeley).

"Pay close attention to yourself and to your teaching; persevere in these things; for as you do this you will insure salvation both for yourself and for those who hear you" (1 Timothy 4:16).

JULY 16
Investing in What Will Endure

The disciple of Jesus Christ must eventually come to terms with the world. By "coming to terms" I do not mean compromise; I mean a way of dealing with it. First I must recognize what the world is; and then I must learn how to conquer it. What the world *is* can best be described by defining what it is *not*; it is "not from the Father" (1 John 2:16). The world's basic motives, instincts, and attitudes do not originate from God. The world's *behavior*, therefore, cannot be of God. If I have been born again into God's family, I should not be surprised to find that this world is "no friend to grace."

As to conquering the world I must remember that "the world and its desires pass away" (1 John 2:17, NIV). That nondurability is characteristic of the world. Many aspects of the world are sinful and temporary, but many other aspects are good and temporary. The only way I can conquer the world is to invest myself in something that will endure.

The "eternal life" of the Bible is more than endless existence; it is qualitative existence as well. To have eternal life is to "know . . . God" (John 17:3). But to know God in the Bible sense is to be personally acquainted with His qualities such as love, mercy, and righteousness. Those are the qualities that have no limits, no ends. To say that I own three houses means that one day I shall have to leave them; but to say I am filled with the love of God means that I have something that will last forever. The Bible always urges me on to possess that which I cannot leave or lose. The biblical "fool" is always the man who sacrifices the "far off" for the near at hand. The opposite is shining victory. "To him who overcomes [the world], I will grant to eat of the tree of life, which is in [the midst of] the Paradise of God" (Revelation 2:7).

"For by these He has granted to us His precious and magnificent promises, in order that by them you might become partakers of the divine nature, having escaped the corruption that is in the world by lust" (2 Peter 1:4).

JULY 17
A Christian Must Be Believable

L ord, as a disciple of Yours I must not only *believe*, but *be believable*. There is no use whatever pointing to the grace of God unless that grace has been operating in me. A businessman once said to his employees: "My reputation is in your hands." So the Lord's reputation is in our hands.

I now see why Jesus said that hard-to-understand word about sins being "forgiven" and sins being "retained" (John 20:23). There is a sense in which the destiny of others rests upon the followers of Jesus Christ; not in the absolute sense, but the functional sense. It is in that sense, I believe, that Paul meant: "Be . . . followers of me, even as I also am of Christ" (1 Corinthians 11:1, KJV). It is only to the extent that I am a believable follower of Christ that I will be able to persuade others to follow Him also.

My influencing others to follow Christ must begin with my *believing them*. That is, I must convince them that I believe that they are the proper objects of God's love and Christ's redemptive sacrifice; that they are in themselves of infinite worth and value to God; that God will guarantee every effort to save them, if only they will turn to Him.

When you come right down to it, a disciple is only as fruitful for his Lord as his credibility is to the people who listen to him. Peter found Jesus because of Andrew, Paul because of Stephen, and so forth. They had to be convinced by men first. They were *believed in*; therefore, they *believed*.

I cannot believe in men, and therefore cannot persuade them, unless they see in me the innocent love that is characteristic of the Spirit-filled disciple. Thus, I am believable only to the extent that God's love appears unmistakably in me. That must be my goal. "Brothers, we instructed you how to live in order to please God . . . do this" (1 Thessalonians 4:1, NIV).

"Therefore, since we receive a kingdom which cannot be shaken, let us show gratitude, by which we may offer to God an acceptable service with reverence and awe" (Hebrews 12:28).

JULY 18
Letting the Spiritual Instinct Take Over

A Christian has an instinctive push toward righteousness because of his new nature. Just as his old nature drives him to temptation and wrong, so his new nature moves him toward goodness. I think evangelical Christians tend to give the old nature too much attention and room; they seem to expect to sin and fall, and keep on doing so. But we should also expect to succeed and be victorious over sin because that is the bent of the new man.

God's seed is in us (1 John 3:9). Seed means growth and expression, and God's expression is always holy. I am sure many believers stumble and fall, and yet "better things" that "accompany salvation" (Hebrews 6:9) are expected of us. The beautiful and yearned-for "fruit of the Spirit" (Galatians 5:22) is set in exact contrast to the "fruit of the flesh"; yet, both are instinctive and, if given a chance, will abound in us. Which fruit will it be? Paul says that God "began a good work" in us and He will keep bringing it to maturity in us until the day of Christ (Philippians 1:6). There is a determinism in the new man that is difficult to deny!

As any gardener knows, fresh seeds dropped into the ground must be given a chance. Weeds must be removed, the ground must be prepared, and sufficient moisture and sun must be applied. Do that for the new man, the Bible cries out, and see what will happen! The fruits of the new nature, says Peter, are many and attractive (2 Peter 1:1–9). But we have to make them "abound," that is, allow them to *multiply* in us (v. 8, KJV). If we let them *shrivel* or "lack" (v. 9) we are blind and forgetful.

In short, I have all the equipment I need for a triumphant, godly, fruitful life. That is God's part. My part is to make room for it, clear the rubbish away, and let spiritual instinct take over from there.

"For if these qualities are yours and are increasing, they render you neither useless nor unfruitful in the true knowledge of our Lord Jesus Christ" (2 Peter 1:8).

JULY 19
Beginning Where God Begins

As a disciple I must realize that to end well, I must begin well. In the words of Jesus, I must "count the cost" before I begin.

But how do I begin? Jesus said, "You are to be perfect, as your heavenly Father is perfect" (Matthew 5:48). What kind of a beginning enables me to reach *that* goal? I would very much like to earn the Lord's praise, "Well done . . . good and faithful servant" (Matthew 25:21, KJV). How do I earn it?

The more I see of the goals and expectations God has for me and the more I see of my own inadequate resources, the more tempted I am to sit down in despair—except for one thing. My beginnings must be God's beginnings. My contribution to that beginning may be only a tiny flicker of faith and will, but God's contribution is an enormous gust of power that carries me on to the finish. The Bible says Abraham "believed in the Lord; and he [the Lord] counted it to him for righteousness" (Genesis 15:6, KJV). Abraham's tiny, flickering faith plus God's power resulted in righteousness.

How often I see that in the Bible! A man with a paralyzed body looks helplessly to Jesus, generates faith, will, and intention, and soon he is on his way home carrying his pallet on his back (John 5:8–9). What a beginning, God's power pulsating in response to a man's feeble but sincere willingness! I see now that the demands, expectations, and accomplishments that the Bible makes and desires of me are realistically possible. I see also that God does not tease us by offering a paradise that is hopelessly out of reach. The impossible Sermon on the Mount, the impossible fruit of the Spirit, and the impossible love character of 1 Corinthians 13 are all gloriously possible—if I begin with God. "That you may know . . . his incomparably great power for us who believe" (Ephesians 1:18–19, NIV).

"And without faith it is impossible to please Him, for he who comes to God must believe that He is, and that He is a rewarder of those who seek Him" (Hebrews 11:6).

JULY 20
Walking with God Alone

There is a sense in which the call of God will come to me alone. God does not call a group; He calls individuals to form a group. But the call itself is unmistakably personal. I must respond personally; I cannot send a substitute.

God called Abraham "alone" (Isaiah 51:2, KJV). The lonely call led to lonely experiences: the night walk under the stars, with the promise of universal blessing (Genesis 13:14–18); the lonely altar of prayer for Lot (18:22); and finally the lonely walk to Mount Moriah to sacrifice Isaac (22:5). Yet all of that loneliness was to lead to making him the one in whom "all the families of the earth" (12:3) were to be blessed.

That seems to be a law of the spiritual world as well as the natural: I begin with God alone, I end with many. As George Matheson says, "The brook becomes a sea." Jesus Christ went to the cross alone, was buried alone, and arose alone. Yet His loneliness was the seed that enabled Him to return with a great army of followers. His generation will continue to widen until it finally engulfs the whole earth.

> Let Him lead thee blindfold onwards,
> Love needs not to know;
> Children whom the Father leadeth
> Ask not where they go,
> Though the path be all unknown
> Over moors and mountains lone.
> *Gerhard Tersteegen*

"From this one man, and he as good as dead, came descendants as numerous as the stars in the sky and as countless as the sand on the seashore" (Hebrews 11:12, NIV).

"Jesus therefore perceiving that they were intending to come and take Him by force, to make Him king, withdrew again to the mountain by Himself alone" (John 6:15).

JULY 21
God's Break-Ins

I will not walk as a disciple very long before realizing that God is a God of break-ins. Look how He broke into Abraham's life: "The God of glory appeared to . . . Abraham" (Acts 7:2). The patriarch's normal, average, everyday life was broken into. Whenever God does that it always means a new direction for things, such as the time He broke into the life of Paul.

The *appearances* of God, whether visible or inward, are always along the line of an interruption or change. Often the change is not understood by us. "He went out, not knowing where he was going" (Hebrews 11:8). Abraham did not understand that God was going to make him a universal man, a true "father of the faithful." So it must come to me as a disciple. God must reserve for Himself the right of the initiative, the right to break into my life without question or explanation. That shattering phone call, that disturbing letter, that unquenchable vision may indeed be the first stage of God's interruption in my life. I must be ready, never doubtful.

Since God does the initiating, He must be responsible for the consequences. Nowhere does God ever start something and then say, "All right, the rest is up to you!" The consequences of God's actions are just as ordained as the origination of those actions. For me that is a warning—do not tamper with consequences that God has already appointed for me. But that also is my comfort; I need not worry about something that is out of my hands.

My response must always be to keep a sharp eye on God and obey His Word implicitly. Then He will surprise me with delights! "Be ready by morning, and come up . . . and present yourself . . . to Me on the top of the mountain. . . . And the Lord descended in the cloud and stood there with him" (Exodus 34:2–5).

"For this very night an angel of the God to whom I belong and whom I serve stood before me, saying, 'Do not be afraid, Paul'" (Acts 27:23–24).

JULY 22
Social Approval Is Conditional

To be a disciple of Jesus Christ does not mean I must be a social outcast. Christ does not negate my natural human proclivities; He enhances them. Social approval is necessary for emotional health, and Jesus Christ is not aiming for my dismemberment from the human family. The basic issue is: social approval at what price?

In a parable, Jesus said, in effect, "Aim low and you will be promoted, and then you will have the respect of others" (cf. Luke 14:10). Social respect is not off limits for the disciple, but it is conditional. It is based upon the lowly-mindedness of Christ. Infinite trouble follows the natural man's grab for place. He seeks the high, lofty position, regardless of the price he pays or the people he destroys getting there. I must never submit to a drive or propensity like that. Jesus did not come seeking social approval; but because He came in a lowly minded manner, social approval became His reward. By avoiding social approval directly, Jesus did the very thing that brings it most surely.

Social approval is necessary to my well-being. But social approval is not limited to earthly beings. A great "cloud of witnesses" (Hebrews 12:1) is eagerly interested in all that happens to me and is, in a sense, the "cheering section" for all saints. If I do *well*, that is, do Christ's thing, I will earn their rousing approval. Thus, the pilgrim way is replete with soul-stirring encouragements. If my way seems lonely and isolated, it is only for a while. "But God, who comforts the depressed [downhearted], comforted us by the coming of Titus; and not only by his coming, but also by the comfort with which he was comforted in you" (2 Corinthians 7:6–7).

"Now may our Lord Jesus Christ Himself and God our Father, who has loved us and given us eternal comfort and good hope by grace, comfort and strengthen your hearts in every good work and word" (2 Thessalonians 2:16–17).

JULY 23
The Coming Examination Day

I must realize, Lord, that the only record of my life that exists is the one I write myself. I see now what the judgment seat of Christ is—only a playback. It is there we receive "the *things* done in [this] body [our earthly life]," not simply the reward of those things (2 Corinthians 5:10, KJV).

I will meet my actions again, like a rerun movie. But this time I will see them from God's standpoint, how they were recorded in *His* eye and ear. There can be no addition to, or subtraction from, what I *was* and *did*.

The books of God (Malachi 3:16) are nothing more than His retrieval system. Lord, Your eye and ear remember everything! My "examination day" will be only my rereading day, and You will show me the daily pages written with my own life. There is a sense in which heaven and hell are now, right here. Not in the sense of fulfillment, but in the sense of possibility. My destiny is not decided later, in eternity, but now while I live on this earth. The destiny is only the echo of my present decision.

Also, not only destiny itself, but the *quality* of that destiny is decided here, whether stubble or precious stones (1 Corinthians 3:12).

Lord, what a responsibility! Only one walk through life and yet an eternity depending on it! How glad I am for my gracious Forerunner, who first removed my sins by His Calvary work and who promises to walk in me and beside me to help me. He wants to help me write the story of my life, which one day will cause Him to smile. After all, Jesus is in the business of producing "approved" saints! He wants to be able to say to me, "Well done . . . faithful servant: . . . enter . . . the joy of thy lord" (Matthew 25:21, KJV).

"You therefore, beloved, knowing this beforehand, be on your guard lest, being carried away by the error of unprincipled men, you fall from your own steadfastness" (2 Peter 3:17).

JULY 24
Presenting Our Credentials

As Your disciple, Lord, I must be aware of the rights and privileges of *ministry*. The holy vessels of the tabernacle were dedicated with blood because they were a "ministry" (Hebrews 9:21). Just as there can be no remission of sins without blood, neither can there be a ministry without blood. No man has the right to speak (or do anything else) for God unless he has been touched by blood, that is, unless he has been given the right to speak on the basis of Christ's death on Calvary.

Whenever God deals with men He always does so through the rights Jesus Christ won at Calvary. Just as an ambassador must present his credentials, so every person who serves God must show that he has been touched with the blood of Calvary. Apart from that, he has no right to serve. Do I have my credentials, or am I a false prophet?

But there is another side to the coin. Simply having the right to speak does not mean I accept the *privilege*. Many have been to Calvary and have been given the right, but have rejected the privilege. The Body of Christ is full of underprivileged members; underprivileged because of their own selfishness, fear, or indifference. It takes both blood and oil to become a servant of God. The blood stands for the call; the oil stands for the power. Both are necessary for effective, fruitful service.

The high priest applied the blood and the oil *continually*. So must I continually review my call and enduement. The vessels of my ministry for Him must come daily under His eye. Only then do I "present my credentials." "But we have this treasure in earthen vessels, that the excellency of the power may be of God, and not of us" (2 Corinthians 4:7, KJV).

"Restore to me the joy of Thy salvation, and sustain me with a willing spirit. Then I will teach transgressors Thy ways, and sinners will be converted to Thee" (Psalm 51:12–13).

JULY 25
Being "in Mission"

A disciple of Christ must learn to distinguish between his *mission* and his *call*. His mission is that of every Christian—spreading the good news of Jesus Christ everywhere; but his call is God's appointment to a specific place at a specific time. The mission is general and fundamental, the call is specific and personal. My main responsibility in life is to be *in mission* for Jesus Christ; my main response in life is to fill that personal niche that God calls me to.

I may look at missionary work and say, "I'm not called to be a missionary." Wrong! Every Christian is to be a missionary, that is, to be "in mission." My particular function in mission may differ from someone else's; but regardless of the function to which God calls us, we are all missionaries!

Sometimes I have heard wrong advice being handed out: "Don't become a missionary unless God calls you to it." Rather it should be: "You are a missionary because God has ordained all His children to be such." But when it comes to my function in mission, then I should not intrude upon God, but wait until He tells me where and when to serve. That means that I can be a businessman or a doctor, teacher, carpenter, or whatever, and be in mission.

The basic issue in mission is not whether I am a foreign missionary, a home missionary, or a layman. It is whether or not I am willing to accept God's mission as my mission. I must realize that it is where God is acting today. If I claim to know, love, and obey God, I cannot help being "in mission." "The preaching of Jesus Christ . . . now is manifested, and . . . according to the commandment of the eternal God, has been made known to all the nations, leading to obedience of faith" (Romans 16:25–26).

"And He said to them, 'Go into all the world and preach the gospel to all creation'" (Mark 16:15).

JULY 26
Battle for the Body

Lord, I must develop a proper theology of the body. We Christians are prone to think of our bodies as "houses of the soul" and, to an extent, we are right. But our bodies are also "battlefields of destiny." The parable of the dispossessed spirit makes this clear (Matthew 12:43–45). The aim (I might say "passion") of Satan is to possess our bodies as vehicles for carrying out his purposes in this world. So intense is this desire that he calls our bodies "my house" (v. 44).

But God also has designs upon my body. He needs my flesh and bones for carrying out His purposes in this world (Romans 12:1–2). He needs to indwell me just as much as Satan does, otherwise His program will fail. So an intense struggle goes on ceaselessly over the possession of our bodies. Even when Satan is thrown out of us, nevertheless he seeks to reenter; and, if necessary, he brings reinforcements to get the job done (Matthew 12:44–45).

There is no middle ground in this battle for my body. Either God or Satan is in control at any given moment. The control by one displaces the control by the other. The kingdom of one is enhanced or retarded by the control he has over our bodies. In a sense our bodies are little "Mount Calvarys" where the conflict still rages, not to decide who is victor, but whether His victory is going to be maintained in us.

Like it or not, I am in the midst of battle. I cannot excuse myself from it. I must enter it by an act of my will; Jesus Christ is the Savior of my body (Ephesians 5:23). That Savior is able to "sanctify [me] entirely . . . spirit and soul and body [and keep me] preserved complete, without blame at [His] coming. . . . Faithful is He who calls you, and He also will bring it to pass" (1 Thessalonians 5:23–24).

"Or do you not know that your body is a temple of the Holy Spirit who is in you, whom you have from God, and that you are not your own?"
(1 Corinthians 6:19).

JULY 27
Bountiful Giving

There are levels to Christian giving and, as a disciple, I must give on a disciple's level. The minimum level of giving is the tithe (Matthew 23:23). This is the obligatory gift, the amount I owe God, and the refusal to return this to God is *theft* (Malachi 3:8).

The second level of giving is the "offering" (Exodus 25:2, KJV). The offering is in addition to the tithe and designed for a special purpose. It can be a simple thank offering to the Lord or a generous gift or whatever.

The third and highest level of giving is giving "bountifully" (2 Corinthians 9:6). Rees Howells called this "princely giving." It is the kind of giving Jesus called the disciples' attention to when they watched the widow give her mite; it was "all her living" (Mark 12:44, KJV). This kind of giving recognizes a fundamental principle in our relationship to God, the principle of the "new tenant." Once we commit ourselves totally to God, the new tenant takes over and thereafter He dictates policy, even down to the way we are to spend our money. Or really, His money. We do not use our money unless we first have given Him a requisition.

Bountiful giving is always connected with ministry. It is the material expression of God's overflowing love through us to others. It is the substance that tangibly reminds people that God is alive and He cares. As a disciple I must put my bank account as well as my talents in God's hands. Once in His hands, I must let Him draw as much as He wants; then I stand back and watch Him refill richly what He has taken away. You "will glorify God . . . for the liberality of your contribution . . . to all . . . because of the surpassing grace of God in you" (2 Corinthians 9:13–14).

"As it is written, 'He who gathered much did not have too much, and he who gathered little had no lack'" (2 Corinthians 8:15).

JULY 28
Ministry to Others

How do I make the necessary distinction between ministry to myself and ministry to others? The Bible certainly makes clear that the threshing ox has a right to eat the grain it has threshed (1 Corinthians 9:9), and the priests ate the leftovers of the bread and sacrifices. But here is an important point I must remember: I am allowed to partake only in the exercise of my service to others. Nowhere does the Bible say I can sit down, take it easy, and still expect to eat the fruits of the service.

As I look again at Jesus' statement about the vine and the branches (John 15), I am struck by the fact that the branch did not partake of the *fruit*; it partook of the *vine itself*. The branch exists for ministry, to pass on the life of the vine until fruit forms at its tips, so that the needy who are around about may be satisfied. The branch's satisfaction comes from the vine, yes, the very root of the vine.

I must be careful not to use God for myself. The life of discipleship is just the opposite: God using me for Himself. I must beware of asking God for something that ends with me, such as health, money, or success. I must never lose my vision of God as Master, whose right it is to command me for His purposes; or treat Him as my servant, who must satisfy my every whim. My life must be a branch that simply transmits the fruit of the vine to the eater. The more fruit I channel and the more the needy are satisfied, the greater is God's glory (John 15:8)

Then I will be like Joseph, who was "a fruitful bough, a fruitful bough by a spring; its branches [ran] over a wall" (Genesis 49:22). His "blessings are greater than the blessings of the ancient mountains, than the bounty of the age-old hills" (v. 26, NIV).

"You did not choose Me, but I chose you, and appointed you, that you should go and bear fruit, and that your fruit should remain" (John 15:16).

JULY 29
Looking at Death

A Christian's relationship to death changes when he accepts Christ as his Savior. In the mind of the natural man, death reigns (Romans 5:14); but in the mind of the committed believer, death fades into the shadows and he becomes occupied with "life and immortality," which have sprung up inside him because of the gospel (2 Timothy 1:10). To be sure, death does not cease to be a fact, but it ceases to be a pertinent fact. Just as Christ, after He died, found that death had no more power over Him (Romans 6:9), so the believer, who is in Christ, finds death unimpressive and weak.

The Greeks used to say, "A man can't look at death or the sun very long." True enough, but the believer does not look at death at all (or does not *need* to). He is now the possessor of eternal life, which is more than immortality. Immortality is endless personal relationship with God, the attribute of only those who know God through Jesus Christ. Thus, I am not to be occupied with dying, but with living; that is, with an increasing knowledge of God that builds my life with richness that will blossom forever.

A believer in Christ already has the seeds of eternity in his heart; therefore, there is no need to consider death, which, after all, is only a momentary hesitation in his eager strides to glory.

"We look not at the things which are seen, but at the things which are not seen; for the things which are seen are temporal, but the things which are not seen are eternal" (2 Corinthians 4:18). A person who has spent a lifetime saying no to self and yes to Christ will find very little that death can do to him. Death's final no has long been satisfied, and Christ's final yes will be a welcome, joyous leap into eternity.

"Jesus said to her, 'I am the resurrection and the life; he who believes in Me shall live even if he dies, and everyone who lives and believes in Me shall never die. Do you believe this?'" (John 11:25–26).

JULY 30
God's Claim and Our Rights

I will not walk very far with God without facing the matter of *claims*. I need to understand three such claims: God's claim on me; my claim on God; and the world's claim on me.

A claim is a legally incontrovertible right, and the first one I must always take care of is God's claim on me. He has a right to me because He created me; I am His by manufacture. He also has a right to me because He redeemed me (Isaiah 43:1); I am His by redemption from slavery (1 Corinthians 6:19–20). Now it is true that the whole world belongs to God; but to the extent that I am aware that I am His property, to that extent I am responsible for yielding His claim to Him. God will never give me rest on this matter until I do so.

The claim of God is not merely theoretical; it is practical, very much so. Think of it for a moment. If I am wholly God's and acknowledge it, then He has the right to tap any particular part of me or my possessions at any given moment! Is there a poor person down the street whom God wants to help? He may tap my bank account for the purpose, for my dollars belong to Him. Is there a tribe of naked savages that has not yet heard of Jesus Christ? God may commandeer my body and fly me to the jungle to tell them the good news in their own dialect. After all, my tongue belongs to Him.

The moment I acknowledge God's claim on me, I am, in a practical sense, a surrendered person with no rights of my own. I am at the disposal of every need, being subject, of course, to the Lord's direction. Never again will I exist in isolation. The world, as John Wesley said, will indeed become my parish. "He died for all, that they who live should no longer live for themselves, but for Him who died and rose again on their behalf" (2 Corinthians 5:15).

"Know that the Lord Himself is God; it is He who has made us, and not we ourselves; we are His people and the sheep of His pasture" (Psalm 100:3).

JULY 31
Tapping God's Resources

The second claim that I must realize is *my claim on God*. My claim on Him is a legal right that God cannot refuse, the right to utilize and tap God's resources when my own resources have run their limit. For example, there is no sense asking God for strength to get to church on Sunday mornings when my own two good legs will easily carry me there. But if I were *paralyzed* and it was God's will that I go, then I would have the right to tap God's power to get me there. On this point God could not rightfully refuse, and His power in this situation would be the same as if it were my own.

The method by which I stake my claim upon God is by means of His promises. The promises of God, by the way, are not for everybody, and I will get myself into a lot of mischief by claiming them at random. There is no point in citing Philippians 4:19 as a claim upon God for money if I have thousands of dollars of my own in the bank. I may present my claim only when I am in the center of God's will and when I have run out of resources. Then I may come before God with His promise, claiming what is rightfully mine. His promise is a far better check than any bank draft; His power has far greater healing properties than any medicine.

I think of Moses, who tapped God's power to open the Red Sea; of Elisha, who tapped God's oil reserves for the impoverished widow; of Daniel, who tapped God's wisdom for the solving of mysteries, and I realize that these men were bold enough to stake their claims upon God, and they won. May God give me equal grace and make me equally victorious! "His divine power has granted to us everything pertaining to life and godliness . . . by these He has granted to us His precious and magnificent promises" (2 Peter 1:3–4).

"For as many as may be the promises of God, in Him they are yes; wherefore also by Him is our Amen to the glory of God through us" (2 Corinthians 1:20).

AUGUST 1
The World's Claim on Us

The third claim that I will confront as a disciple is *the world's claim on me*. This is the claim Paul had in mind when he said, "I am debtor" (Romans 1:14, KJV). The basis of that claim is the inherent right every person has in the finished work of Calvary. If Christ died for "the whole world" (1 John 2:2), then the right to be saved cannot be denied anyone who truly wants it. This means that my function in this world is essentially a missionary one.

But even more, the world has the right to *find God* in me. One purpose of Christ's incarnation, among others, was to show the world what God was like in the flesh. Seeing God in Christ was more than a privilege; it was a right. For if God loves the world and seeks to redeem it, then the world has a right to partake of that redemption as it was conveyed to them by the human agency of Christ.

Since Christ is no longer in the world physically, He must convey Himself to the world through His followers, you and me. That means my unsaved friends have the right through me to partake of God's love, or any of His other qualities, such as truth and mercy. It is as if God invited them to a party—in me—and I cannot rightly turn them away. I cannot choose to do things for myself if it means denying someone else the right to come to the banquet. I must treat the outsider as if *I* were outside; how would I feel if, hungry and thirsty, I were denied access to the God who is my basic right?

Lord, help me to be sensitive to the claims of others, who were born to be claimed by the measureless love of God in Christ. May I say with Paul, "The love of Christ controls us . . . and He . . . gave us the ministry of reconciliation . . . we beg you on behalf of Christ, be reconciled to God" (2 Corinthians 5:14–20).

"But you shall receive power when the Holy Spirit has come upon you; and you shall be My witnesses both in Jerusalem, and in all Judea and Samaria, and even to the remotest part of the earth" (Acts 1:8).

AUGUST 2
God Is Looking for Intercessors

One of the richer purposes God has for me as a Christian is that I become an intercessor. An intercessor is someone for whose sake others are blessed. You and I are forgiven our sins "for Christ's sake" (Ephesians 4:32, KJV). Every spiritual blessing God bestows upon men is due to Christ's intercession for us (Ephesians 1:3).

Jesus Christ is the perfect Intercessor whose life and character earned Him the right to plead with God for others. But the privilege of interceding for others is also given to Christ's followers. Moses interceded time and again for his people Israel, and for his sake Israel was both spared and blessed as a nation (Exodus 32:11–15).

The outstanding quality God requires of all intercessors is not sinlessness (otherwise no one could qualify) but utter selflessness. Moses was willing to be blotted out in order that Israel might be spared destruction (Exodus 32:32). Paul was willing to be "cursed" in order that Israel might be saved (Romans 9:3, KJV). Am I that kind of an intercessor?

Intercession need not be an earthshaking ministry but a simple one, such as between family members. Lot was blessed for Abraham's sake (Genesis 19:29), and Jacob's family was exalted for Joseph's sake (Genesis 47:6). Am I that disciple for whose sake others around me are favored by God?

God is looking for intercessors (Isaiah 59:16) and is delighted when He finds a person to bless others. God wants me to have an intercessor's heart, one that feels keenly the pain and sin of others. Then, for my sake, He will bless them! My attitude should always be that of Samuel, "Far be it from me that I should sin against the Lord by ceasing to pray for you; but I will instruct you in the good and right way" (1 Samuel 12:23).

"Brethren, my heart's desire and my prayer to God for them is for their salvation" (Romans 10:1).

AUGUST 3
The Interceding Disciple

I can never become one of God's intercessors without remembering that Jesus Christ "made intercession for the transgressors" (Isaiah 53:12, KJV). That statement means more than the fact that Jesus prayed for His crucifiers or makes atonement for us. It means He created the office or function of intercession. He made intercession *possible*. Had He not come as the great interceding Savior, no one could ever have interceded for anyone else.

For me to become an intercessor, then, means that I am fulfilling a function that Jesus Christ created, that I am doing it *for His sake* and *in His wake*. It also means that I have gained a certain level in my relationship to God in which I have gained a certain authority in intercession. Norman P. Grubb calls this "the grace of faith." That is not a single answer to prayer, but a whole series of answers based upon my definite standing with God as an intercessor. For example, Moses reached such intimacy with God that he talked with God "face to face" (Exodus 33:11). As a result of this extremely high privilege, Moses was able to use his authority as an intercessor to save Israel from certain extinction because of their sin in the matter of the golden calf (Exodus 32:10). Had Moses not been *there*, in the high, holy position of Israel's intercessor, the nation would have been obliterated.

I think of others who have been there, and I have been challenged! What about Isaiah, Jeremiah, Ezekiel, Hosea, Paul, Luther, Wesley, and countless others for whose sake people were given the gift of life? Lord, I want to be an *interceding* disciple, capable of sparing from death and bringing to life those for whom Jesus Christ died! I cannot appoint myself to this ministry (even Jesus did not do that, Hebrews 5:5), but I can live devoted to Him so that He may not pass me by when next He needs an intercessor.

"For there is one God, and one mediator also between God and men, the man Christ Jesus" (1 Timothy 2:5).

AUGUST 4
God Sees the End Product

Despite my sins, God is able to deal with me because He sees me complete in Christ (Colossians 2:10). That is not only a theological position, but also a means of my relating to all my brothers and sisters in Christ. I often fail in my interpersonal relationships because I see people as they are, not as they are *in Christ*. Paul's ambition for everyone was to "present every man perfect [mature, full grown] in Christ" (Colossians 1:28, KJV). In preaching the gospel, Paul had to see his hearers as already completed in Jesus Christ.

I have heard Christians say, "I don't know why God puts up with me, I'm so weak and erring." Indeed we are. But God puts up with us because He sees the end product as actually realized. The difference between what we are and what we shall be is the process of working out the ideal, which, in God's eyes, has already been achieved. God is patient with us because He sees us perfected, and you cannot become impatient with perfection.

So it is with my brother and me. The reason I am impatient with him is because I see his raw, ragged faults, not "the measure of the stature of the fullness of the Christ" in him (Ephesians 4:13, Amp.). The moment I see him "perfect in Christ," that moment I will lose my irritation, discouragement, and exasperation with him. To be troubled by my fellow Christian is really not *his* fault, it's mine, because of a shortsightedness concerning Christ's finished redemption. I deny, for my brother, the Calvary work of Jesus Christ. I must keep in mind that heartwarming word of John, "It has not appeared as yet what we shall be. We know that, when He appears, we shall be like Him, because we shall see Him just as He is" (1 John 3:2). Thank God for foreseen perfection—for my brother and for me!

"And He said to them, 'Why is it that you were looking for Me? Did you not know that I had to be in My Father's house?' And they did not understand the statement which He had made to them" (Luke 2:49–50).

AUGUST 5
The Community Action of Sin

Just as there is community action in righteousness (I am forgiven my sins "for Christ's sake," Ephesians 4:32, KJV), so there is community action in sin. Achan's sin resulted in the death of many of his fellow countrymen (Joshua 7:5). For that reason Achan was discovered with his sin, which was stealing what belonged to God, and his whole family was destroyed (7:24–25). His family suffered judgment with him as a symbol that no one sins unto himself any more than he dies unto himself.

Community sin begins with Adam; I am a sinner because he was. But if I were the only sinner in the world, others would still suffer because of me. In fact, the more godly my acquaintances and fellow Christians are, the more they will suffer because of my sin. Since I am not a solitary Christian but a member of a body, when I sin I infect the body and the cells nearest to me suffer the worst. The Bible warns me against having a "root of bitterness" in me by which "many [are] defiled" (Hebrews 12:15). Paul warns that sin, like leaven, permeates the whole dough (1 Corinthians 5:6).

So sensitive is my example to my fellow believers that even the "appearance" of sin (1 Thessalonians 5:22, KJV) must be avoided for their sakes. As far as possible, I must live free from ambiguity. Above all, I must never repeat the behavior of Jeroboam, who "made Israel to sin" (1 Kings 14:16). The tragedy of Jeroboam was that he never realized the community action of sin. He sinned and a nation sinned with him.

I am encouraged by the "keeping" power of God, "The Lord is your keeper" (Psalm 121:5). If He is my Keeper, He will protect me from *all* harm, the harm *to* others as well as the harm *from* others.

"And if one member suffers, all the members suffer with it; if one member is honored, all the members rejoice with it. Now you are Christ's body, and individually members of it" (1 Corinthians 12:26–27).

AUGUST 6
God's Testimony of Salvation

When it comes to witnessing, God has two desires: He wants us to witness concerning Him, and He wants to witness concerning us. So witnessing is a two-edged sword that cuts both heavenward and earthward. I have heard a great deal about our witnessing for God, but I have heard little or nothing about God witnessing for us.

What is witnessing? Affirming what is a fact. When I witness to Jesus Christ, I am simply confirming that He is what He claims to be, the Son of God and the Savior of men. On the other hand, when Jesus Christ witnesses to us, He affirms either one or two things about us. The first is illustrated by Abel, who offered his gift by faith, and "obtained witness that he was righteous" (Hebrews 11:4, KJV). When Abel offered his sacrifice, God immediately witnessed to the whole universe that Abel was now "righteous." This was affirming the fact that Abel was declared righteous (justified) in the record book of heaven.

The same thing happens to every one of us who "offers the gift of faith," that is, accepts the sacrifice of Calvary as his own. How do we know? We know by God's witness of us; He affirms the fact that we are now in Christ, and testifies on our behalf before the whole universe. Thus, the assurance of salvation does not rest upon our feelings, which rise and fall with body rhythms, health, circumstances, and even the weather; but upon God's word of testimony that I, upon the expression of my faith in Jesus Christ, am declared righteous in the heavenly account book.

Thank God for a sure word of testimony! And thank God that the Judge Himself has already taken the witness stand and has vindicated me! "There is therefore now no condemnation for those who are in Christ Jesus" (Romans 8:1).

"Everyone therefore who shall confess Me before men, I will also confess him before My Father who is in heaven" (Matthew 10:32).

AUGUST 7
God's Pleasure in Us

The other aspect of God's testimony of us concerns our *manner of life*. Enoch is our example. "Before his translation [into heaven] he had this testimony, that he pleased God" (Hebrews 11:5, KJV). What kind of a life did Enoch live that made God testify on his behalf? Twice the Bible records the statement, "Enoch walked with God" (Genesis 5:22, 24). This walking with God by faith is a behavior that so pleases God that He testifies to it, makes public acknowledgment of it, and affirms it as a fact before men.

It is one thing to receive God's testimony of my salvation, and it is an easy thing to obtain. But to receive God's testimony of my *life* is only earned by walking in obedience to His Word. No one can walk carelessly, selfishly, or indulgently and expect God to say, "I am pleased with you." God does not own a diploma mill. He does not hand out plaudits carelessly. Remember, God's testimony is the affirmation of a fact.

God's pleasure in us is a reflexive thing. When God is pleased with us, it is because He testifies to something in us to which He responds, something with which He agrees, something that arouses His interest. I think God is pleased when He sees His own image and likeness reflected in us. It is like a father who sees himself in his son, or a teacher who sees himself in his pupil. When I walk with God by faith I am really affirming that God is the greatest Being in the universe, and God is pleased because I have chosen the highest goal any human can choose—God Himself.

Is God pleased with me or does He still find in me the speckles of doubt and unbelief? How I long for the testimony, "He pleased God!" My great destiny is to be "conformed to the image of His Son" (Romans 8:29), and my great privilege is that here and now that process can begin.

"That you may walk in a manner worthy of the Lord, to please Him in all respects, bearing fruit in every good work and increasing in the knowledge of God" (Colossians 1:10).

AUGUST 8
The Fortress Personality

In my ministry for Jesus Christ I must expect to be pulled toward two extremes, the extremes of overprotectiveness and overgenerosity. The first is the "fortress complex" in which I wrap myself up in isolation and forbid anyone to come near. The second carries Paul's "all things to all men" to such an extreme that I become "nothing to everybody."

Job claimed that he had not "eaten [his] morsel alone" (Job 31:17), which means he had not refused to open his life and possessions to others. The fortress person is motivated by either fear or selfishness, and Job was possessed by neither of these. Neither should I, as I face a restless world of unsatisfied people. God does not have a fortress personality; neither does Jesus Christ. Where His Spirit rules freely in a human heart, there will be no icy containment, no frigid refusal to open the door to lame feet.

On the other hand, I must not be so open, so free, and so unprincipled that I become a spiritual smorgasbord. If I am blown with every wind of doctrine and idea, it will not be long before I will not have *any* doctrine, and this will, in effect, end my ministry.

To be a fortress person means I lose my ministry; to be a smorgasbord person means I lose my identity. I cannot afford to lose either!

What is the answer? How do I avoid either pitiful extreme? I believe it is following the example of Jesus Christ, who was absolutely open toward ministering to people in need, but absolutely closed toward doing anything other than the will of His Father. Once I set my heart on doing only His will, I will not have to worry about consequences. Augustine said it sublimely: "In His will is our peace."

"Go, eat of the fat, drink of the sweet, and send portions to him who has nothing prepared; for this day is holy to our Lord. Do not be grieved, for the joy of the Lord is your strength" (Nehemiah 8:10).

AUGUST 9
Congruent Disciples

I must always remember that God is not looking merely for men, but for congruent men; not merely disciples, but congruent disciples. For example, when God wanted to show men what He was like, He sent Jesus Christ into the world dressed in human flesh. Jesus Christ was congruent to the personality of God. Isn't that what He said to Philip? "He who has seen Me has seen the Father" (John 14:9).

Congruency is God's method of using a life to explain a principle or a truth. Nowhere in the Bible is there a textbook on faith. But the Bible presents Abel, Enoch, Noah, and Abraham to show what faith is by the way they lived. Hebrews 11 could easily be called "the congruency of faith." When God wanted to show us what His love was like, He made it congruent in the death of His Son on Calvary.

We who are Christians are expected to show the world the congruency of the gospel. Paul urges, "Conduct yourselves in a manner worthy of the gospel of Christ" (Philippians 1:27, NIV). The gospel is simply a collection of words, terms, and phrases, all of which are difficult to understand unless they are made clear by someone's life. Looking at us, the unsaved community should be able immediately to see a connection between what we are and what the gospel is declaring.

Even more, we Christians are expected to show each other the congruency of many of God's wonderful truths. Truths that are difficult to understand, such as intercession, identification, and crucifixion, become wonderfully clear when they are made congruent in us. My life should be, as was Paul's, a "pattern" of the way God works with men. How exciting to be God's chosen pedagogue! God help me to be a congruent Christian!

"That you may walk in a manner worthy of the God who calls you into His own kingdom and glory" (1 Thessalonians 2:12).

AUGUST 10
Paying the Vow of Life

I must realize that it is often easy to vow a vow, make a promise, to God, but it is not always easy to pay that vow. One man, near death, made a promise to God based on the condition that God would heal him. God did, so the psalmist said, "I shall pay my vows to the Lord . . . in the presence of all His people" (Psalm 116:14).

The greatest vow I can make is to promise my life to God. He treats that vow with the utmost seriousness, and He soon tests me to see how serious *I* am. If I promise to "go with Him through the garden," it will not be very long before God leads me into Gethsemane, and there my promise must stand, or else I am a humbug. My ambitions for a crucified life are quickly thrown into the crucible, and I soon find out whether I am dead to the world or still harbor a spark of life.

After reading Isaiah 20, I feel amazed at how willing Isaiah was to be nothing in order to obey the word of God. For three years the prophet lived, "naked and barefoot" because God wanted to show the ultimate nakedness of Egypt through his behavior. I can only thank God that He has never asked me to walk "naked and barefoot" among my people. Would I be *that* dead to pride, criticism, and social pressure?

The cross of Christ was the ultimate of disgrace, of revulsion. Yet in that place of horrible dehumanization He paid to His Father His vow, which He had made in the past ages of eternity. Do I grumble because I have to pay a pledge or invest my time each week in the welfare of others? May I say honestly with Paul, thank God I can "glory . . . in the cross of . . . Christ" (Galatians 6:14, KJV). For it is in the cross that I find strength to pay all my vows to Him who vowed to suffer the cross for me.

"Make vows to the Lord your God and fulfill them; let all who are around Him bring gifts to Him who is to be feared" (Psalm 76:11).

AUGUST 11
Loving Others Redemptively

God commands me to love others. However, He does not mean I should love them naturally, but *redemptively*. Redemptive love is the way God loves us, expressed convincingly in the life of Hosea, the prophet. His wife left him and went to live with another man, and Hosea had the humiliating experience of having to buy her back from her adultery (Hosea 3:1–3). Think of buying back what is already yours! Yet that is what God did for us.

Redemptive love knows no shame; it is concerned with the loved one, not its own feelings. Jesus did not cry out in self-pity, "Poor Me," when He was hanging on the cross. Hosea did not stint when he doled out the shekels for his wife. He took her sin and disgrace as his own and for her sake he paid her debts willingly and brought her safely back home.

Redemptive love binds and makes permanent. Gomer never again left her husband. How could she, after love like that? I am a weak brother indeed if after looking at Calvary and being brought home to God's house, I still steal away and consort with the world. Redemptive love is the most powerful binding force in the world.

I cannot copy God's redemptive love, no matter how hard I try. I cannot determine to love others. Even loving my wife, Paul says, must be "as Christ . . . loved the church" (Ephesians 5:25). The moment I fall back to the natural, even in natural relationships, I begin to run out of my supply. My only hope is to *receive* and *express* the redemptive love of God. That love is spread abroad in my heart by the Holy Spirit, and even the most natural of my relationships must come under that spiritual, redemptive love. "Beloved, if God so loved us, we also ought to love one another. . . . We love because He first loved us" (1 John 4:11, 19).

"And we have come to know and have believed the love which God has for us. God is love, and the one who abides in love abides in God, and God abides in him" (1 John 4:16).

AUGUST 12
Creating a Spiritual Legacy

I must remember that God is not only interested in my life, but also in my "afterlife." I do not mean my life in heaven, but my life's continuing influence on this earth. The status God wants me to attain is that of Abel, who "being dead yet speaketh" (Hebrews 11:4, KJV).

There are many ways to "live after," but one of them is through my children and grandchildren. The Bible says it is possible for me to lay up an inheritance for my children and grandchildren (Psalm 103:17–18). That inheritance is spiritual, one that assures them the "mercy" and "righteousness" of the Lord for along time to come.

The natural man also wants to provide for his children, but he usually does it through financial means. How many rich people leave "mercy" and "righteousness" to their descendants? And which is more important, dollars or mercy and righteousness?

But how do I leave such a spiritual inheritance? That is where *I* come in. God is willing to establish an estate for me if I fear Him, keep His covenant, and obey His commandments (Psalm 103:17–18). In short, if I live a God-fearing, God-honoring life now, the results of that life will accrue under God's trusteeship for the benefit of my children and grandchildren. That does not mean they will be unconditionally converted, but it does mean they always will feel the influence of God's mercy and righteousness.

What better provision can I make for my children? What better way, long after my sun has set, to continue speaking for God? That was the promise to Caleb: "Surely the land on which your foot has trodden shall be an inheritance to you and to your children forever, because you have followed the Lord [your] God fully" (Joshua 14:9).

"A good man leaves an inheritance to his children's children, and the wealth of the sinner is stored up for the righteous" (Proverbs 13:22).

AUGUST 13
Denying Our Humanity

The test of a true disciple of Jesus Christ is how willing he is to deny his humanity for the Lord's sake. To know God personally is not to deny one's humanity, but to fulfill it. Yet there are times when God calls upon me to set aside that which is basically human in order to fulfill His will.

Ezekiel is a good example of that. God took his wife, "the delight" of his eyes, in sudden death; yet Ezekiel was not to weep or mourn or eat the bread of mourners or cover his lips (Ezekiel 24:15–18, NIV). God forbade the expression of sorrow. What heartlessness! What callousness! Surely God is not that kind of a taskmaster.

That kind of denial of our humanity happens every day. Missionaries leave their loved ones to go abroad for Christ; they even leave their children in another country to be educated while they deny themselves parental love and joy. Where would the church of Jesus Christ be without the parahumans, the ones who leave all for His sake? There are times when God must ask us to give Him our simple human desires and instincts, which are not wrong in themselves, for the sake of His work. The point is: Am I willing to be parahuman for Christ?

The greatest sermons ever preached for You, Lord, are not the verbal kind given from a pulpit, but the kind in which the Word becomes flesh in daily experience. Only You could have given Ezekiel grace *not to weep*. It is that kind of grace that makes us not *less* than human, but *more* than human. Lord, I absolutely do not have that kind of grace in myself; but thank You, Lord, that You give "grace in exchange for grace" (John 1:16, author's trans.).

"Seek the Lord and His strength; seek His face continually. Remember His wonders which He has done, His marvels, and the judgments uttered by His mouth" (Psalm 105:4–5).

AUGUST 14

God's Perfect Love

Lord, it is Your will that I learn the way of *perfect love.* Human love, refreshing as it is, cannot begin to be compared with God's perfect love. That kind of love is described in 1 Corinthians 13; it is demonstrated in the life and death of Jesus Christ. Human love is bargain hunting—I will love you if you love me; but divine love is philanthropy—I will love you regardless of cost or return.

I must not love my fellow human beings less than Jesus Christ loved me. Just as He loved the very ones who drove the nails into His hands, so I must love my fellow worker who stabs me in the back, my neighbor who spreads lies and scandals about me, or a member of my family who returns my love with surly disobedience and rebellion. Perfect love cannot be insulted! People criticize this kind of love by saying, "Yes, but they'll take advantage of you!" Is that the worst thing possible, to be taken advantage of? All men and women who have dared to follow Christ have been taken advantage of, even as their Lord and Master was before them. Is that a crime?

But let me also consider this: When people take advantage of me, God fills in the gap. If they give me the worst room in the hotel, God will fill that room with His glory. If they give me the worst of companions to put up with, God will transform that companion into His image. In short, when I obey God and let His perfect love fill my heart, He takes the responsibility of making His will *more profitable* than the will of the world.

Perfect love is not a formula; it is a Person. As I allow the Holy Spirit to fill me, perfect love will become my rule, not my exception. I will "walk in love, just as Christ also loved [me], and gave Himself up for us, an offering and a sacrifice to God as a fragrant aroma" (Ephesians 5:2).

"If anyone serves Me, let him follow Me; and where I am, there shall My servant also be; if anyone serves Me, the Father will honor him" (John 12:26).

AUGUST 15
Riding the Bandwagon for Jesus

I must recognize the danger in following Jesus Christ. That danger is best described in the behavior of the multitudes who followed Christ on His "triumphal entry" and shouted, "Hosanna . . . Blessed is he who comes in the name of the Lord!" (Matthew 21:9, NIV). When the multitudes reached Jerusalem, they were quickly chilled by the angry Pharisees, and later they dispersed in coldness and defeat.

It is so easy to follow a "bandwagon" for Jesus. He is often popular and widely acclaimed, and then I am strongly tempted to cash in on His popularity. Many of our programs, our crusades, and our missions have a dash of Jesus about them, but they also can be ego trips or publicity splashes that promote me as a spiritual leader, a notable "man of God." Jesus did not call me to be a leader; He called me to be a servant. The servantship concept is not to be understood as a proud butler, rigid and starched, but rather a doormat for everyone to walk on. It is not in my victories that spiritual power is generated, but in my defeats; as Paul says, "When I am weak [helpless], then I am strong [dynamite]" (2 Corinthians 12:10).

The tragedy of the "Hosanna shouters" was that their discipleship was too weak, too shaky. The Pharisees easily scared them and, even worse, cowed them into shouting, "Crucify, crucify," just a few days later. Weak discipleship can easily degenerate into deluded opposition to the Christ we once followed.

Lord, may I never use You as my pole vault to success, and may I never shout "Hosanna" unless I can shout it at the foot of the cross. Thank You, Lord, that You are "able to keep [me] from falling" onto dry-rot discipleship, and finally to present me to the Father "with exceeding joy" (Jude 24, KJV).

"What shall I do with you, O Ephraim? What shall I do with you, O Judah? For your loyalty is like a morning cloud, and like the dew which goes away early" (Hosea 6:4).

AUGUST 16
Making the World Green

What is the chief result of a disciple's life? The very same result that characterized the life of Christ—He made things live. The Nile is called the "breadbasket" of Egypt because it changes barren deadness into living greenness. God sends us disciples into a spiritually arid waste and expects us to leave it fertile and green. Ezekiel's river of blessing began at the altar and traveled down through brown deadness, but what a result! Everywhere the river went, everything lived (Ezekiel 47:9).

Have you ever noticed the sharp contrast of Hebrews 11? Against a bleak background of death, those men and women of faith created life. Look at Abraham: "From this one man, and he as good as dead, came descendants as numerous as the stars in the sky" (Hebrews 11:12, NIV). The deadness of Abraham's body was the beginning of a miracle—by faith. That is how Jesus lived. He constantly touched "dead" people, spiritually as well as physically, and made them live.

Greenness is the test of a disciple. Is my path strewn with people whom I have touched into life? Worldly men can coerce others into conformity, but the man of God can ignite them into spontaneous, living obedience. But only—how important!—if the disciple himself is in direct touch with Him who is life. Do the signs of life follow me—healed wounds, enlightened minds, neutralized self, reborn souls, purified relationships, contained evil, and an atmosphere charged with the glory of God?

Lord, my purpose in life is to make the "land live," but only as You, the Prince of life, live out Your life in me! Thank You for that heartening promise, "I will put My Spirit within you, and you will come to life" (Ezekiel 37:14). Then, Lord, make the land around me live also.

"And he will be like a tree firmly planted by streams of water, which yields its fruit in its season, and its leaf does not wither; and in whatever he does, he prospers" (Psalm 1:3).

AUGUST 17
God's Deep, Abiding Call

As a disciple of Jesus Christ my goal is to glorify God, my function is to witness for Him, and the specific area in which I am to witness must be at the *call of God*. Isaiah was specifically called and directed (Isaiah 6:8–9). So must I be, whether as an overseas missionary, a local pastor, or a layman occupying a niche in secular work. The call can be for *one* family, and that may be my lifelong ministry for God. Many people say, "The need is the call." But the need is not the call; the call is a directive from God that I am to work in a chosen area. I may have to pass up many needs on the way to ministering to the need to which God has called me. If the need were the call, I would be utterly and continually distracted.

Many people reply, "I feel no call to a particular work." Can it be that God has gone out of business? Is redemption complete? The reason I do not feel a call is because I am not listening carefully enough; I am too distracted by the sounds of life outside me. God calls every one of His children to be His ambassador to *someone*. Even the most isolated, incapacitated, restricted servant of God has an audience somewhere. To deny that God can use us in limited circumstances is gross hardness.

The call of God cuts directly across our comforts, our plans, and our security. Can you imagine Jesus planning for retirement? There is no retirement for soldiers thrust into the front lines to rescue souls from the grip of sin. "Here am I, send me" is the response of those touched by Calvary's fire, not those looking for a comfortable religion. "I thank Christ Jesus our Lord, who has given me strength, that he considered me faithful, appointing me to his service" (1 Timothy 1:12, NIV).

"For if I preach the gospel, I have nothing to boast of, for I am under compulsion; for woe is me if I do not preach the gospel" (1 Corinthians 9:16).

AUGUST 18
The Need Is Not the Call

When I respond to God's call, "Who will go for Us?" (Isaiah 6:8), I must be certain that I am not motivated by sentiment. The human heart is tender and can easily be touched by visions of starving thousands, or multitudes begging for the gospel. Except for those whom the Spirit has touched, people do not beg for the gospel; they beg to be left alone.

If sentiment is my reason for yielding to God's call, it will not be long before my humanitarian impulses change to doubt, criticism, and finally despair. My human impulses may be sympathetic, but they are not redemptive; and the world's encompassment by sin is far too strong for my puny sympathy. I need more than emotional involvement to push back the kingdom of Satan; I need the invincible power of God. Jesus Christ was motivated by two overwhelming things: sacrificial, redemptive love, and the call of God, which required His obedience. Unless the same two forces are active in me, my response to God's call will be a short-lived failure.

Nor must I respond to God's call by *manipulation*. If I respond to my pastor's call or my missionary's call or my friend's call, I am simply asking to be put at the mercy of their resources. But if I respond to God's call, I am placing myself at the mercy of His resources. How can I tell whether it is God or others issuing the call? By *time*. If God is calling, the call will grow stronger each passing day.

There is only one way to be ready for God's call: to be touched by a coal from the altar (Isaiah 6:6–7). My response is to come to the altar; God's response is to purge me and issue me the call. The result will be a never ending procession of sons being brought to glory (Hebrews 2:10).

"And how shall they preach unless they are sent? Just as it is written, 'How beautiful are the feet of those who bring glad tidings of good things!'" (Romans 10:15).

AUGUST 19
Choosing the Dependent Life

My life, Lord, must be a copy of Your Son's life on this earth. I am not necessarily to copy His acts—raising the dead, feeding the five thousand—but I am to copy *Him*. "As He is, so also are we in this world" (1 John 4:17). Just as Jesus went through a certain pattern, so I am to duplicate that pattern in my life.

The pattern is one of *dependence*. "By myself I can do nothing" (John 5:30, NIV). Those are not the words of a helpless Christian, but the strong Son of God. He deliberately chose to live a life of utter dependence upon His heavenly Father. He taught only what the Father allowed Him to teach; He revealed as truths only what the Father permitted; He walked only where the Father directed. No life has ever been lived on this earth in such utter dependence upon the Father as the life of Jesus. In that sense I am to copy Him. "Without me ye can do nothing" (John 15:5, KJV). To accept Christ as Savior and Master is to become a dependent.

What would have happened if Jesus Christ had become independent of His heavenly Father? What happens when I become independent of Him? The result is complete confusion and utter misery. Just as Jesus was necessary to the Father's plan of salvation for mankind, so are we necessary to the ongoing of that salvation today. A breakdown of obedience means a breakdown of the instrument of salvation to others.

What a responsibility that is, and yet what a joy! Who else in the world offers us an opportunity to connect to an eternal scheme, in which what we do now has consequences that will never die? Jesus Christ calls us to follow "in His steps" (1 Peter 2:21), that is, to live the life He lived on this earth. What an honor!

"And He who sent Me is with Me; He has not left Me alone, for I always do the things that are pleasing to Him" (John 8:29).

AUGUST 20

Accomplishing in the Spirit's Power

The second area in patterning my life after Jesus Christ is in my relationship to the Holy Spirit. What was Christ's relationship to the Spirit? Again, one of utter dependence. Nowhere do we read that Jesus performed any miracles or uttered marvelous teachings *before* His baptism and filling by the Spirit. But at His baptism, at about thirty years of age, God filled Him with His Spirit "without measure" (John 3:34). From that point on Jesus was a dynamo of power, healing, teaching, and snatching people from death and from demon possession. Even His ability to die for us on Calvary was accomplished through the Holy Spirit (Hebrews 9:14).

That simple dependence upon the Holy Spirit was necessary on Jesus' part for the accomplishing of God's will through Him. It is also necessary on *my* part if I am to accomplish God's will through me. God does not build His work on my personality, gifts, or abilities; He builds it on the Holy Spirit in me, with or without my abilities.

The world calls Jesus Christ a "religious genius," which is nonsense. Jesus Christ, the Son of God, chose to let the Holy Spirit work completely through Him, and the "genius" aspect of Christ's life is simply the Holy Spirit doing the will of the Father through the obedient Son.

Victorious Christian living is not my "fulfilling myself"; rather, it is letting the Holy Spirit fulfill Himself in me. If Jesus Christ, the perfect Son of God, felt it necessary to surrender completely to the Holy Spirit, then certainly I, ingrained as I am by sin, must feel the same way.

But, thank God, it is possible! Being Spirit-filled is not a privilege of the Son that cannot be shared. "Be filled with the Spirit" (Ephesians 5:18) is my privilege too!

"The Spirit of the Lord God is upon me, because the Lord has anointed me to bring good news to the afflicted; He has sent me to bind up the brokenhearted, to proclaim liberty to captives, and freedom to prisoners" (Isaiah 61:1).

AUGUST 21
Following the Mission of Christ

A third area in which I am to pattern my life after Christ is in the area of *mission*. This is stated explicitly in Christ's word to His disciples after the resurrection: "As the Father has sent me, I am sending you" (John 20:21, NIV). Throughout His earthly life Jesus Christ considered Himself an Emissary sent by the Father (John 17:3). He came to witness for His heavenly Father, to represent His heavenly Father to men. He came to convey to men a steady stream of truth from His Father. The love that He showed was the Father's love unveiled in human flesh. He declared the Father (John 1:18).

In the same sense, but on a lesser scale, I am to witness to Jesus Christ. My function in life is to tell the good news concerning Him, to reveal His personality in me, to share His death and resurrection with others in order that they also might share the salvation that is available. But I cannot do that in my own strength, by my own will, or as a result of my own abilities and talents. I must be authorized and empowered by Another, even as Jesus Christ was by His Father.

John 17 is the great "transference" chapter. There Jesus Christ was going back to the Father, and He transmitted His work to His disciples (and to us). I cannot read verses 11–19 without sensing the thrill of continuity; I am part of an ongoing mission. Jesus Christ started the missionary explosion, and all His disciples are expected to keep it going. All heaven's authority and power are behind me as I go, whether that mission field is my immediate environment or a remote country of earth (Matthew 28:18–20). Like my Master, Jesus Christ, I am a *sent one* also!

"As Thou didst send Me into the world, I also have sent them into the world" (John 17:18).

AUGUST 22
Suffering with Christ

The fourth area in which my life is a pattern of Jesus Christ is in the area of *suffering*. "Christ . . . suffered for you, leaving you an example for you to follow in His steps" (1 Peter 2:21). Just as Jesus Christ suffered for me, so am I to suffer for Him and for others. That suffering is not the kind that human beings *normally* undergo; it is suffering "for Christ's sake" and is related to my being His disciple and sent one. It is suffering "unjustly," as Peter states it (1 Peter 2:19), as a lamb suffers without giving offense to others.

Jesus Christ did not suffer because He was an evildoer, or because He wanted political power, or because He abused His body, or because He was mischievous. He suffered because the light that He brought is always in conflict with darkness. Whenever anyone seeks to do God's will and live righteously, he will always suffer, because that is the nature of the relationship between good and evil. To the extent that I pursue the will of Christ and represent Him on this earth, I will suffer for it.

There is an exhilaration that comes to those who suffer after the pattern of Christ. Christ found "joy" in His cross (Hebrews 12:2); Paul rejoiced because he could be sacrificed on the altar for his Lord (Philippians 2:17); the early Christians rejoiced that they were counted worthy to suffer for His sake (Acts 5:41). That joy is the overflow of God's joy in heaven at the success of His work in the world.

Have I suffered for Christ? If He is my model and pattern, it will not be long before I feel the nails and the thorns, for that is the calling of those whom God calls His "beloved children" (Ephesians 5:1–2).

"And keep a good conscience so that in the thing in which you are slandered, those who revile your good behavior in Christ may be put to shame" (1 Peter 3:16).

AUGUST 23
Living in an Imperfect World

If I am serious about being a disciple for You, Lord, I will experience the tension of living in an imperfect world. The Sermon on the Mount is beautiful sentiment to the natural man; but according to his views, it is hopelessly impossible. The reason is, the natural man fights his way through life with carnal weapons, and justifies his methods by saying, "You've got to fight fire with fire, otherwise you're done for!"

But as Your disciple, Lord, I cannot accept that way of life. In an imperfect world I must employ spiritual principles, not carnal. For the natural man, to be carnal is life; but for me it is death. Paul says, "Slaves, obey your earthly masters" (Ephesians 6:5, NIV). There is no condition or compromise here. I am to be obedient always, regardless of whether I serve a perfect master. The Bible never says, "Be perfect *if,* or be perfect *except.*" God knows how imperfect, selfish, and cruel the world is; yet He says to me, "Never mind *them*; do as I say."

The great temptation to a disciple is to become *accommodating.* So he tends to lower his behavioral standards to become acceptable to the world. It takes great courage to be a "sore thumb" for Jesus Christ, and that is what I will be if I insist on treating the world according to Christ's standard. But there is no other way God can work redemptively in the natural man; he must see the *alternative* to the meaningless life he lives. Jesus Christ has set His disciples among unbelievers as the true examples of a life of truth and virtue, which is what the natural man longs for inwardly. I am to be "perfect" for his sake, as well as for God's eternal glory. When we live that kind of life, we "become [in behavior] sons of [our] heavenly Father" (Matthew 5:45, Berkeley), for that is the way our Father lives.

"To this present hour we are both hungry and thirsty, and are poorly clothed, and are roughly treated, and are homeless; and we toil, working with our own hands; when we are reviled, we bless; when we are persecuted, we endure" (1 Corinthians 4:11–12).

AUGUST 24
The Price of Power

I will never be an overcoming disciple for the Lord unless I realize what failure is. Failure, I have been taught, is when I do not pray, read my Bible, or witness daily. But those things are not failure, despite their importance; they are the *symptoms* of failure. Christian failure goes right to the bedrock of my relationship with God and can be summed up in one word: *sovereignty.*

Sovereignty is God's right to ask "unconditional surrender" of me. That was Job's problem. Many have taught that the theme of the book of Job is, "Why do the righteous suffer?" In the light of God's sovereignty, that is a meaningless question. The basic conflict between Job and God was that of ultimate control. Did God have the *right* to inflict suffering on Job, or inflict anything else, for that matter? It is beautiful to watch how Job finally comes to understand why God has led him through the dark maze; and, once he understands that God wants sovereign control, Job gladly yields it to Him (Job 40:1–5; 42:1–6).

The human failures of the Bible, such as King Saul and Judas, stubbed their toes, not on dedication, commitment, or zeal, but on sovereignty. They wanted God and His power desperately, but not at the price of unconditional surrender. Unless I am careful, it will be easy for me to repeat their mistake. Christianity is not my using God, but God using me; not my wrangling the best deal for time and eternity, but God making a beautiful vessel out of a lump of clay. Flower pot or water jar, what is the difference as long as God decides which and supplies the power to make it possible! My response to this glorious truth must be that of Eli: "It is the Lord; let Him do what seems good to Him" (1 Samuel 3:18).

"Or does not the potter have a right over the clay, to make from the same lump one vessel for honorable use, and another for common use?" (Romans 9:21).

AUGUST 25
Compromise: A Spiritual Nonessential

I must be careful, Lord, about understanding the place of compromise in my life. Compromise makes politics the art of the possible, but in my relationship to Jesus Christ it becomes the flaw of the impossible.

Compromise is always a sign of a previous accommodation. When Lot chose to live in Sodom rather than the highlands of Canaan, he made an accommodation based upon a driving desire to be rich and influential. As a result, he compromised. Compromise was his method of making his accommodation acceptable to himself; it was never acceptable to God.

The technique of compromise is to "tone down" the Word of God, to take its absoluteness, its stringency out of the way. King Saul took the command of God—"Strike Amalek and utterly destroy all that he has"—and reduced it by saying, "The people spared the best of the sheep and oxen, to sacrifice to the Lord" (1 Samuel 15:3–15). Despite that gross insult to God's word, Saul said, "I have carried out the command of the Lord" (v. 13). Thus, compromise enabled Saul to give the *appearance* of obedience while still allowing him to obtain his selfish goals.

Compromise means I have not come to grips with spiritual essentials; I still have "bleating sheep" around, and I still have an uncrucified "old man" lurking inside me. Compromise is a sign of a spiritual dichotomy; there is not a clean, sharp commitment inside.

The compromising person sooner or later stumbles over his own tangled cords, as David did concerning Uriah (2 Samuel 12:5–9). To avoid that, Lord, let me do the one thing needful, as Mary did, and offer You my *all*. If I do, it will become a sweet aroma to You and the memory of it will stretch into the expanses of eternity (Matthew 26:12–13).

"Do not love the world, nor the things in the world. If anyone loves the world, the love of the Father is not in him" (1 John 2:15).

AUGUST 26
Displayed by God

Whether I like it or not (and I like it!), I am in "show business." The Lord said to Satan, "Have you considered My servant Job? For there is no one like him on the earth" (Job 1:8). Disciples are for display, saints are for spectacle. God the Master Artist does not ply His talents to a raw sinner for nothing; He wants His chief enemy, Satan, to observe and understand what happens to a man when he becomes pliable in God's hands—the very opposite of what Satan was when he sinned.

But God must display me; I cannot display myself. The chief end of His masterpiece in me is not only for the eternal ages (Ephesians 2:7–10), but for now in the midst of this "crooked and perverse generation" (Philippians 2:15). The bumper sticker "Please be patient, God isn't finished with me yet" is true, but only *partly* true. There are elements of a finished product within me, and God wants those elements displayed for others to see.

Remember Daniel? The den of lions was not for Daniel's benefit, but for the king's. "Daniel . . . has your God . . . been able to deliver you from the lions?" (Daniel 6:20). Looking into the den, the pagan king Darius saw a servant of God displaying the victory over the lions that his faith had made possible. He was astonished and impressed, so much so that he issued a decree: "the God of Daniel . . . is the living God . . . [who] delivers and rescues and performs signs and wonders" (6:25–27). Daniel was an actor in a living drama, and the result was applause to Almighty God.

Have you seen my servant _____ ? Dare I put my name here as one whom the Lord can display? I see now what Paul meant when he called himself God's exhibition and God's "spectacle" to the world (1 Corinthians 4:9). What a glory to be a chosen showpiece of God!

"For we are His workmanship, created in Christ Jesus for good works, which God prepared beforehand, that we should walk in them" (Ephesians 2:10).

AUGUST 27
God's Delayed Explanations

A disciple of Jesus Christ must learn to understand God's silences. One of the features of the book of Job was God's silence toward him, though He was not silent to Satan, and though Job's friends were not silent to him. With all that speech making, God did not enter into dialogue with Job until the end of the book (chap. 38), and even then He did not explain why He led him through the valley of humiliation.

In Job's case, his knowledge of God's will was *delayed* and *indirect*. That is the way God usually deals with us. Even Jesus was not given full and perfect knowledge of the Father's plans (Matthew 24:36). God's usual method of pedagogy is to let circumstances tell us the tale. That is why Job had no conception of God's plan until he looked back on his path, very much as Bunyan's Pilgrim, who saw every reason for his zigzag route *afterward*. Jesus said to His disciples, "What I am doing you do not now understand, but you shall understand afterward" (John 13:7, author's trans.).

When God is silent toward me, it means I am walking in ignorance. That means I must trust Him implicitly, otherwise I will lose my way. The life of faith would end completely if God explained His every move to us. The natural man lives by reason, so he demands an explanation for everything. But the spiritual man lives by faith and he reserves God's right to be silent, because he has implicit faith in God's honesty and integrity.

"Someday we'll understand" goes the hymn, and it is true. But the someday need not be in heaven. "Afterward" for the disciples was Pentecost. "Afterward" for you and me may be tomorrow, or the next startling event in our lives. "But He knows the way I take; when He has tried me [through dark, unseeing paths], I shall come forth as gold" (Job 23:10).

"For now we see in a mirror dimly, but then face to face; now I know in part, but then I shall know fully just as I also have been fully known" (1 Corinthians 13:12).

AUGUST 28
The Lord as Our Keeper

I thank You, Lord, that the person who obeys You lives a charmed life. A charmed life for a disciple means a protected life. So complete is that protection that my life is safe even in the hands of the enemy. "He who . . . surrenders to the Chaldeans [the enemy] . . . shall have his life as a prize of war" (Jeremiah 21:9, Berkeley). God's protection means that my life is off limits to everyone but Him.

God delivered Job into Satan's hands, but with this proviso: "Spare his life" (Job 2:6, Berkeley). The protecting hedge of God's person came between Job and Satan so the evil one could not destroy him. In a sense this is functional immortality. The obedient disciple lives under the shadow of life, not death, regardless of his circumstances or dangers. Nothing can *touch* him, much less *take* him! Only when God determines that his earthly course is finished does he then cross over into the shadow of death, and even there, "Thou art with me" (Psalm 23:4).

In another sense, my life is the inner citadel of my being, the real me, and God's protection extends there also. "He shall preserve thy soul" (Psalm 121:7, KJV). That kind of protection is eternal; even death does not touch it. The disciple's body may be attacked, his mind and heart may suffer distress, but God will throw in every reinforcement He has to keep the citadel from falling. That is because the Lord is my Keeper, the One responsible to His own Word to deliver my soul safely forever.

The keeping power of God means I can live free from apprehension, though I must never live free from responsibility. When fear threatens my tranquillity, I say, "When I am afraid, I will put my trust in Thee" (Psalm 56:3).

"Indeed, the very hairs of your head are all numbered. Do not fear; you are of more value than many sparrows" (Luke 12:7).

AUGUST 29

Following the Lines of Authority

Lord, I must be careful about my relationship to Your anointed ones. The anointed ones are those set above me in authority, to whom I am most directly responsible, and who therefore interpret Your will for me in given circumstances (Hebrews 13:17). You are particular about the lines of authority—husbands-fathers in the home; pastors and elders in the church; kings, prophets, and others; as well as the ranks of heavenly orders. Even Satan, though fallen, still has the "respect" of the lower angels (Jude 9).

David had several chances to kill Saul, his rival; yet he refused to do so because Saul was "the Lord's anointed" (1 Samuel 24:1–7). Instead, David consigned Saul into the Lord's hand for judgment (1 Samuel 26:10–11). That showed David's sensitivity to the line of authority for the nation of Israel. Out of his love for God and his respect for God's will, David would not act on his own and seize power in the land.

To respect the anointed ones is not only an efficient way for God's Kingdom to operate, but also a sign of trust and dependency upon God. Just because God has put someone immediately over me does not mean that I am relieved from the responsibility of trusting Him. In fact, it is the very opposite. I must trust Him *more*, because now His will for me must be strained through an extra individual; therefore, the possibilities of error are greater.

Just as David had to trust in God to work *through* Saul, not without him, so I must trust God to work through my superior, whether he is sensitive or insensitive to God's will. He is in God's hands, and I must learn to trust and praise because of that. I say with David, "In God I have put my trust; I will not fear what flesh can do unto me" (Psalm 56:4, KJV).

"He permitted no man to oppress them, and He reproved kings for their sakes: 'Do not touch My anointed ones, and do My prophets no harm'" (Psalm 105:14–15).

AUGUST 30
Loving an Enemy

David gives me an example of how to love my enemies. He called the man who persistently tried to kill him "beloved and lovely" (2 Samuel 1:23, Berkeley). My enemy is not an irritating neighbor, a bitter-tongued boss, or a person of different skin color and speech. My enemy is, as David's was, anyone who stands in the way of doing God's will. As long as Saul was alive, David could not mount the throne of Israel. Saul's death, therefore, was David's life. Yet not once would David make any effort of his own to remove the obstacle to his kingship.

To love an enemy is the ultimate end in the negation of ambition and desire. To love an enemy is to accept his hindrance as part of God's purpose, to be serene toward him, and to realize that his hindrance, like that of Judas, is only leading to ultimate victory.

The natural man fights his enemy. He tries to remove him as an obstacle by doing him physical harm, even death. War is the full-scale display of the natural man determined to have his way. The shallowness of that way of acting is that for every enemy I destroy, ten more arise. The only way I can "conquer" my enemy is to love him. That does not mean that I "like" him; it simply means that I have good will toward him, that I place him in God's hands for disposition, and that I yearn for his ultimate spiritual blessing in Christ.

The disciple of Jesus Christ is the only person who can afford to have enemies, because he knows how to treat them. Doing the will of Christ means I will never lack enemies, but I will never lack the support of Him of whom 1 Corinthians 13 is a perfect description. As I trust Him who is perfect love, He will work out that perfect love through me.

"Never take your own revenge, beloved, but leave room for the wrath of God, for it is written, 'Vengeance is Mine, I will repay,' says the Lord" (Romans 12:19).

AUGUST 31
The Atmosphere of Unbelief

Lord, I must be aware of the negative power of unbelief and, even more, of the negative power of the *atmosphere* of unbelief. "He did not do many miracles there because of their unbelief" (Matthew 13:58). The state of my spiritual health affects others, and it even affects You, Lord. How often a meeting has been destroyed by a negative, critical attitude on the part of one of the members; and how often has the power of God been expressed simply because *one person* was in tune with the Spirit.

Lord, I often pray for the preacher, but now I realize that the congregation must be prayed for just as zealously. The crowd needs an anointing to be channels of the Lord's power, lest an evil spirit of doubt, distrust, bitterness, or criticism choke out the Lord's presence. If I leave the gathering unblessed, it is because I came in that way and was unwilling to change during the meeting. I can see easily how King Saul's dark moods affected the course of the nation.

In any gathering of Your people, Lord, I must be *of* them, or soon I will be *away from* them (1 John 2:19). I must be in tune with You, but I must also be in tune with those around me. For if I am not in tune with them, it will affect their being in tune with You. We often blame the preacher for a lukewarm sermon when it is really the people's lukewarmness that inhibits the Spirit's moving. Lord, teach me my responsibility in the gathering of Your people; I must be my fervent best when I walk in to worship You. Otherwise I am a destroyer of unborn blessings. I thank You, Lord, that Jesus Christ was "anointed" by the Spirit (Isaiah 61:1) to do many things, one of which was to keep me from my negative moods; He gives me "beauty for ashes" (v. 3b, KJV) and "oil of gladness instead of mourning" (v. 3c).

"But as for me, I shall walk in my integrity; redeem me, and be gracious to me. My foot stands on a level place; in the congregations I shall bless the Lord" (Psalm 26:11–12).

SEPTEMBER 1

The Problem of Rights

Jesus Christ is calling men and women today as He did two thousand years ago. He issues three kinds of calls: the general call, the discipleship call, and the special call.

His general call is voiced in "Come to Me, all who are weary and heavy-laden, and I will give you rest" (Matthew 11:28). That call has to do with the *burden of sin*, and it is issued to everyone. Once a person responds to this call and receives Jesus Christ as his sin-bearer, the problem of sin and its responsibility is forever settled.

The discipleship call is expressed in Jesus' words to the fishermen beside the Sea of Galilee, "Follow Me, and I will make you fishers of men" (Matthew 4:19). That call has to do with the *ownership of rights*, and it is addressed only to those who have responded to the first call. Next to the problem of sin, the problem of rights will be my most grievous. Here the battle may be fiercer and the struggle longer. Nevertheless, Jesus Christ insists that all Christians enroll as quickly as possible as His disciples. Sometimes the enrollment takes place simultaneously with conversion, sometimes it takes months or years longer, depending upon my understanding of Christ's claims and the tenacity of my will. To be a disciple means that I resign from the right to own myself, I surrender my personal sovereignty to Jesus Christ. From then on, He is my Commander and I am under His orders.

How difficult this decision is! Jesus Christ taught thousands and healed hundreds; yet, how many became *His disciples*? How many Christians are there today who are disciples? God help me to say, "Count *me!*" Help me to say with that loving servant who received the piercing of the ear, "I love my master . . . I will not go out free" (Exodus 21:2–5, KJV).

"Therefore, we are ambassadors for Christ, as though God were entreating through us; we beg you on behalf of Christ, be reconciled to God" (2 Corinthians 5:20).

SEPTEMBER 2

Handpicked by Jesus

The third kind of call Jesus Christ issues today is the special one. The first call included all people, the second included all Christians, but the third one is issued only to those who are especially handpicked by Jesus Christ for certain tasks. Those tasks may include full-time ministry such as pastoral or missionary work, but they need not. They may be just as brief and direct as the call of Ananias, "The Lord Jesus . . . has sent me" (Acts 9:17). For what? "That you [Saul of Tarsus] may regain your sight, and be filled with the Holy Spirit" (v. 17). Once his necessary ministry was finished, Ananias quietly disappeared.

The special call deals with the *direction and use of life*. Jesus Himself is a perfect example of that call. He said of the Father, "He *personally* sent Me" (John 7:29, Berkeley, italics added). Whereas the first two calls are general, this one is highly specialized in that both task and choice are decided in heaven, not on earth, and the chosen one is given to understand that he is wanted. Paul was tapped on the shoulder this way (Acts 9:15), and so was Simon Peter (John 21:19). So have many thousands of others. A high honor indeed!

The Bible warns me against handpicking myself. The "rebellion of Korah" (Jude 11) was born in an attempt to oust Moses and assume his place of leadership. That provoked God because Korah was attempting to do what only God should do: handpick people for certain tasks. I must be careful not to push people into full-time service; only God can push.

Where am I in God's "calling program" today? Have I found rest in believing, have I resigned my rights and become His disciple? If I have, I will hear Him say, "Have I not commanded you? Be strong . . . for the Lord your God is with you wherever you go" (Joshua 1:9).

"I thank Christ Jesus our Lord, who has strengthened me, because He considered me faithful, putting me into service" (1 Timothy 1:12).

SEPTEMBER 3
The Heart of Temptation

I have learned, Lord, that Satan's aim in tempting me is to destroy my will. That is clearly revealed in his tempting Jesus, my pattern. Once Jesus had accepted the Father's will at His baptism, that will was immediately put to the test in the wilderness (Matthew 4:1–11). Each of the three temptations was carefully contrived to weaken Christ's grip on the will of His heavenly Father. Once that grip is loosed, it is only a matter of time before the entire defense breaks down in sin.

Jesus was hungry and tired when Satan met Him in the desert. The needs of the body are often used as the opening wedge for an attack on the will, whether the need is for food, rest, relaxing, or whatever. I make a mistake, however, if I think that Satan will be satisfied merely to trip me up on a physical need; he is after my will. The way I handle my body is only the symptom of my basic will commitment. Satan does not try to capture symptoms; he is after the thing that creates the symptoms.

The answer to Satan's approach through the body is a reaffirmation of my will. "Thou shalt worship the Lord thy God, and him only shalt thou serve" (Matthew 4:10, KJV). There is decisiveness, finality! I can only be victorious over Satan and his allurements when I nail the peg of commitment further into the soil. I am strengthened by the response of Nehemiah, when asked to compromise with the enemy, "I am doing a great work and I cannot come down" (Nehemiah 6:3). Four times the temptation came, and four times Nehemiah reaffirmed his grip on God's will for him. So I must meet Satan head-on, not in the peripheries, and send him packing by determining once again to do God's will and stick to it, regardless. That is victory for Jesus, Nehemiah, countless others, and myself!

"Be of sober spirit, be on the alert. Your adversary, the devil, prowls about like a roaring lion, seeking someone to devour" (1 Peter 5:8).

SEPTEMBER 4

The Ego Under Temptation

Once Jesus had publicly determined to do His Father's will, Satan was after Him relentlessly. The deceiver failed to shake the Lord's grip on His commitment through the needs of the *body*, so he tried another tack. He attacked the needs of the *ego*. After Jesus' astonishing ministry of teaching, healing, and miracle-working, the multitudes wanted to make Him king (John 6:15). Here it was—the kingdom, the goal of the Father—handed to Him on a silver platter!

But Jesus recognized the snake behind it and turned down the offer. He was strong enough to resist the appeal of popularity, the gratification of the ego. Nothing turns the head so quickly, or softens the will as much, as the appeal and clamor of the crowd. Jesus did not allow Satan to feed His ego, which would have led to catastrophe; rather, He submerged His ego in the Father's will, which led to triumph.

That is how I must walk. My ego is more fragile than my body. If the deceiver cannot break my will by tempting my body, he will try to break it by tempting my ego. King David was deceived both ways: first through the sexual needs of the body, which resulted in adultery with Bathsheba (2 Samuel 11); and then through the cravings of pride, which resulted in taking a census of the people (2 Samuel 24). What sad, painful outcomes from both!

Jesus defeated the ego temptation by slipping away quietly and communing with His Father, where He strengthened His resolve. So must I, again and again, as often as the deceiver baits me, for my will is strengthened only as I carefully cultivate it in the presence of my heavenly Father. To "pray at all times in the Spirit" (Ephesians 6:18) is the way to "put on the full armor of God" and thus be able "to stand firm against the schemes of the devil" (v. 11).

"And they overcame him because of the blood of the Lamb and because of the word of their testimony, and they did not love their life even to death" (Revelation 12:11).

SEPTEMBER 5

Mental Temptation

The third way in which Satan tried to break Christ's determination to serve His Father was by means of the *mind*. Having failed to dislodge the Son by appealing to His bodily and ego needs, he then determined to loosen the foundations of His rationality. That occurred in Gethsemane. There Jesus was faced with the full foresight of the cross and all He would have to bear. What He would have to endure, Jesus saw, was a contradiction; He who knew no sin would have to become sin (2 Corinthians 5:21). The pressure of having to become what He hated was an almost intolerable burden for the Son of Man.

He exhibited all the symptoms of the pressure: groaning, tears, sweat, and inward agony. His mind was storm-tossed, swept between two contradictory principles. Three times He had to press in close to the Father in prayer, seeking help, and all the while Satan hoped His mind would snap, leaving Him broken and helpless. But again, Jesus went back to His determination to do His Father's will, regardless of how contradictory it appeared. "Nevertheless not my will, but thine, be done" (Luke 22:42, KJV). Victory came, then peace, when His will held firm before the storm.

Satan knows very well how I can be destroyed through the shaking of my mind. Being called "crazy" was one of the criticisms Paul had to face (Acts 26:24; 2 Corinthians 5:13). The protection of the mind does not come by trying to reason things out, but by being willing to stay oneself on God and letting Him unravel the problems as He chooses. "Thy will be done" (Matthew 26:42) is more than a formal prayer; it is mental therapy that the deceiver cannot undo. If I keep my will intact, God will give me the spirit of "power . . . love, and . . . a sound mind" (2 Timothy 1:7, KJV).

"For such men are false apostles, deceitful workers, disguising themselves as apostles of Christ. And no wonder, for even Satan disguises himself as an angel of light" (2 Corinthians 11:13–14).

SEPTEMBER 6
Temptation of the Emotions

The final test of Jesus Christ's commitment to His Father's will took place on Calvary. "Come down from the cross" (Matthew 27:40) was a challenge uttered by chief priests, soldiers, and people; but behind it was the deceiver himself. Having failed to entice Jesus through His body, ego, and mind, Satan tried to break His will by means of His *emotions*.

The emotional strain of the cross was staggering. The chief ingredient was *abandonment*. The abandonment of Jesus was complete—people, disciples, and even (though only for a brief time) His Father. At the point when His emotions were at their strained peak, Satan whispered to Him, "Everyone's against You; what's the use? You've taken enough; end all this business by a quick stroke of power and come down from that throne of pain. Why should You suffer anymore?"

That was the most deceitful of all Satan's tactics, for then he was in the role of sympathizer, reliever, and deliverer. How often Satan's temptations come in the guise of *deliverance!* How quickly he can break our will by leading us to *self-pity*. But Jesus saw through the trickery; He realized He could not spare Himself and still save others. He refused to abandon His commitment; He would not renege on His Father's will, and so He triumphed.

I must realize that I am always vulnerable emotionally to Satan. Yet my victory is not to shore up my emotions but to shore up my will. Emotions will fluctuate; but if my commitment to God is firm, they will stay in balance.

Lord, help me not to be distracted by my fluctuating emotional curve. The apostle Peter encourages me: "Through Him you have confidence in God . . . so that your faith and hope might rest in God" (1 Peter 1:21, author's trans.).

"For though we walk in the flesh, we do not war according to the flesh, for the weapons of our warfare are not of the flesh, but divinely powerful for the destruction of fortresses" (2 Corinthians 10:3–4).

SEPTEMBER 7
Won by Love, Not Force

Jesus Christ stakes His claim upon me from three standpoints: the *natural*, the *legal*, and the *personal*. He claims me naturally, simply because He created me: "It is He who has made us, and not we ourselves" (Psalm 100:3). We do not belong to ourselves. The earth and all its furnishings belong to the Lord, including those "that dwell therein" (Psalm 24:1, KJV).

But He also claims me because He redeemed me, thus adding a a legal right to a natural one. "You are not your own . . . you have been bought with a price" (1 Corinthians 6:19–20). The right of redemption settles forever any subversion of Christ's natural rights over me because of Satan. I am His twice; and if the first right is not enough, the second right certainly is.

Despite His two strong claims upon me, Jesus Christ still applies the personal appeal: "I beg you . . . brothers, in view of God's mercies, that you present your bodies" (Romans 12:1, Berkeley). That amazes me, Lord! A God who owns me twice still begs for my love, loyalty, and service. He pleads for my submission, not on the basis of His rights, but based on His sufferings.

God is all-wise. He knows that the batterings of force only harden and stiffen, while the appeals to mercy and love break down the hardest of wills and create the most lasting of commitments. "Just as I am, thy love unknown has broken every barrier down." So it does. And so throughout the Bible those tender, loving appeals ring out from a God who could easily blast His way to success. Thank You, Lord, for respecting me enough to win me by love and not by force! You speak wooingly to me: "You are precious in My sight . . . and I love you" (Isaiah 43:4).

"But now, thus says the Lord, your creator, O Jacob, and He who formed you, O Israel, 'Do not fear, for I have redeemed you; I have called you by name; you are Mine!'" (Isaiah 43:1).

SEPTEMBER 8
The Proper Measure of My Devotion

The mark of a disciple is in saying, "Thy will be done," but the mark of a mature disciple is in saying, "Thy will I love." I cannot congratulate myself that I have reached the pinnacle until I can say with Paul, "That good, and acceptable, and perfect, will of God" (Romans 12:2, KJV).

The goodness of God's will lies in my seeing that God is not taking advantage of me. The beginning of all sin lies in the idea that God is not to be trusted, that He is sneaky and deceitful. I see that in the insinuation, "Yea, hath God said . . . ?" (Genesis 3:1, KJV). As long as I see God in that light, I will never be able to say His will is *good*.

The acceptability of God's will lies in the pleasure it gives me. The words of Jesus are: "I delight to do Thy will, O my God" (Psalm 40:8). Until I relish God's will and find great joy in receiving it, I cannot say it is acceptable to me. The pleasure of God's will is not variable but invariable; that is, I must find joy in it regardless of whether it means pain or pleasantness.

The perfection of God's will lies in my realizing that neither I nor anyone else could do the thing any better. When I accept God's will as perfect, I am saying, "This is God's best; there is no better way."

The will of God is the proper measurement of my devotion to Him. Do I refuse His will? Then I am acting the natural man. Do I perform His will, but do it grudgingly and complainingly? Then I am acting the carnal man. Do I receive His will with joy and take delight in doing it? Then I am acting the spiritual man.

Lord, help me take my measurement today, and delight in Your will because I can say, "Thy law is *deep* within my heart" (Psalm 40:8, Berkeley, italics added).

"O how I love Thy law! It is my meditation all the day. Thy commandments make me wiser than my enemies, for they are ever mine" (Psalm 119:97–98).

SEPTEMBER 9

Positive Living

I must avoid the popular and shallow form of Christianity that appears so prominently today. There is a kind of triumphant living trumpeted everywhere in which Jesus is simply the instigator or inciter of a flow of positive thoughts and ideas that bring me personal and material success.

That kind of Christianity says I am a bundle of both negative and positive attitudes. Simply encourage the positive and discourage the negative, and lo, I am a victorious person. The problem is, however, that kind of victory is simply the victory of the *natural man*. There is nothing redemptive, remedial, or sanctifying about it.

Before a Christian can talk about victory, he must talk about dying. As J. Gregory Mantle says, the first place the natural man has got to go is to the cross. If I want Jesus at all, I have to find Him "outside the camp"; and if I want to know His victory, I have to bear "His reproach" (Hebrews 13:13). Once I get to the cross and experience the crucifixion of the natural man's selfish greeds, desires, and attitudes, then I am in a position to rise with Christ "in newness of life" (Romans 6:4) and allow His new life to become the *positive* thing that my natural self could never be. That is more than positive thinking; it is positive living.

Jesus Christ did not die on the cross to make me a confident supersalesman, but a normal mass of clay reflecting His power, glory, and personality. That does not mean I lose my identity; rather, I confirm it. The life of Christ flowing through my personality becomes a unique miracle in God's Kingdom; I am authenticated by Christ. Thus, Jesus Christ is not only my Savior; He is the Establisher and Definer of my true self. Then it becomes sublimely and personally true that "in him we live, and move, and have our being" (Acts 17:28, KJV).

"And raised us up with Him, and seated us with Him in the heavenly places, in Christ Jesus, in order that in the ages to come He might show the surpassing riches of His grace in kindness toward us in Christ Jesus" (Ephesians 2:6–7).

SEPTEMBER 10
Overcoming the World

I am reminded, Lord, that Your Word has much to say about *overcoming*. It is one thing to be a Christian, it is another thing to be an overcoming Christian. To be an overcomer is vitally important, since Jesus mentions the need to overcome in each letter to the Asian churches (Revelation 2–3).

To be an overcomer means I have been in conflict. It is a military term. In fact, the word *overcomer* is translated "him who is victorious" in the *New English Bible* and the *Amplified Bible*. It is applied to the Christian who has emerged from battle heat and stress undiscouraged in his faith and undeterred in his determination to live obediently to his God.

Jesus is the first great Overcomer. "In the world you have tribulation, but take courage; I have overcome the world" (John 16:33). To overcome the world means to refuse to be seduced by its *popularity* and to refuse to be intimidated by its *threats* (of the cross). The world always follows the same pattern, first cajoling and then, if that does not work, crucifying. The world's desire is always to "squeeze [me] into its own mold" (Romans 12:2, Phillips). The world's will and God's will are direct opposites. If I insist on following Jesus, then I must follow Him to battle against the world's passionate desire to thwart my path to "live . . . godly in the present age" (Titus 2:12).

Lord, the Bible reminds me of many who went into the battle for You and did *not* overcome—Lot, Saul, Gehazi, Demas, Diotrephes, and others. That is enough to make me realize that victory is not guaranteed—unless I cling to Him who wonderfully overcame for my sake. Then the Lord Himself will fight for me "as when he fought in the day of battle" (Zechariah 14:3, KJV).

"'No weapon that is formed against you shall prosper; and every tongue that accuses you in judgment you will condemn. This is the heritage of the servants of the Lord, and their vindication is from Me,' declares the Lord" (Isaiah 54:17).

SEPTEMBER 11

Overcoming Satan

As a Christian I must seek to overcome not only the world but also Satan. He is a more deadly foe than the world, because the world is simply a pawn in his hand (1 John 5:19). The world will tantalize and tease me, but Satan will accuse me (Revelation 12:10). The accusations of Satan hit me in a most vulnerable spot: my sinful past. He is fully aware of the life I have lived and, like a dog with a buried bone, he continually digs up what I have long since confessed to God. Not that Satan can undo my salvation, not at all. But he functions like a moral pest whose chief delight is to unsettle the mind by simply pointing to acts and facts of which I am aware. If he can keep me sifted enough (Luke 22:31) to keep me off balance, he thus impairs my ability to serve God fruitfully.

The remedy for these pestlike attacks is "the blood of the Lamb" and the "testimony" of the efficiency of that shed blood (Revelation 12:11). Since the forgiveness of my sins lies rooted in what Christ did for me at Calvary, my only recourse is to point to *it* as often as Satan points to my *sins*. The crux of the whole matter is the Word of God: Do I believe the testimony of God concerning His Son's death on Calvary? If I do, everything is settled; but if not, then I make God a liar (1 John 5:10). It boils down to this: Who is telling a lie, God or Satan? I overcome Satan the moment I stake my faith on God's Word that my "sins are forgiven [me] for His name's sake" (1 John 2:12). If I take my stand on God's Word about Calvary, I can become very bold and throw Satan out of the accusing chamber. I must deal forthrightly with him and not give him the place, time, or allowance to do his work. If I am bothered by Satan, I must end it by a firm command! If I "resist" him, he will "flee" (James 4:7).

"And call upon Me in the day of trouble; I shall rescue you, and you will honor Me" (Psalm 50:15).

SEPTEMBER 12
Winning Honors

As a disciple I must learn what to do about *honors*. Jesus is my example. When Satan honored Him (in a left-handed sort of way) by saying, "If You are the Son of God, command that these stones become bread," Jesus replied that it was more important to live by the bread of God's Word (Matthew 4:3–4). Jesus ignored the honor by refusing its implication. He chose to remain true to His mission.

Simon Peter also honored Christ by declaring He was "the Christ, the Son of the living God" (Matthew 16:16). Jesus thanked Peter for the honor, then immediately announced that the honored Son was headed for crucifixion (v. 21).

God the Father honored Jesus by putting "all things into His hands," a token of highest exaltation (John 13:3). The Son's response was to take a towel and washbasin and proceed to wash the disciples' feet (v. 5).

Those three examples show me how to treat honors. I am never to *seek* them. Certainly I am never to *glory* in them, and I am never to allow honors to *swerve* me from doing what God has called me to do. In no way did Jesus refuse the honors given; yet in no way would He allow them to prevent Him from reaching His Calvary destination or from stooping and serving His disciples.

Jesus said, "It must needs be that offenses come" (Matthew 18:7, NSRB). It is also necessary that honors come. But in either case—offense or honor—I must never be diverted from doing the will of Him in whose hand lies my final honor. Like Jeremiah, I must not be "seeking great things" for myself (Jeremiah 45:5); and if they come unasked, I am to lay them lovingly at the feet of Him who walked the Calvary road for me.

"Thus says the Lord, your Redeemer, the Holy One of Israel; 'I am the Lord your God, who teaches you to profit, who leads you in the way you should go'" (Isaiah 48:17).

SEPTEMBER 13
The Jewel of Contentment

Lord, I will cultivate what Jeremiah Burroughs, a Puritan of the seventeenth century, called "the rare jewel of Christian contentment." Contentment is not a stupid lack of awareness or sluggish laziness, but an acceptance of my lot as God's provision for me. That is "godliness with contentment," which Paul says results in "great gain" or profit (1 Timothy 6:6, KJV). Contentment is not looking at the bright side or adding up the positives of my situation, but accepting the whole package so that I can say, "I have learned, in whatsoever state I am, therewith to be content" (Philippians 4:11, KJV).

The opposite of contentment, one that I must conquer at all times, is the spirit of murmuring, complaining, and criticizing. A potent negative example is the family of Israel on their way from Egypt to Canaan. No less than twelve times in Exodus 16 and 17 the people "murmured" or "complained" against Moses and Aaron for their lack of food or water. Their murmurings were really expressions of distrust in God, as Moses clearly said, "Your murmurings are not against us, but against the Lord" (Exodus 16:8, KJV). God's reaction to those multiplied grumblings was one of anger (Psalm 95:8–11).

But should I always be contented? Should I not strive to better myself and my family? Yes, if it is within my means and power, if it is by God's permission, and if it is not for the sake of pride and glory. Contentment is essentially a denial of my avarice and greed, and a reaffirmation of God's right to grant me simplicity or abundance as it pleases Him. Above all, I will be contented with God, my chief portion, and will so live as to reflect an appreciation of His goodness.

"So I will bless Thee as long as I live; I will lift up my hands in Thy name. My soul is satisfied as with marrow and fatness, and my mouth offers praises with joyful lips" (Psalm 63:4–5).

SEPTEMBER 14
Keeping the Glow of Victory

Every disciple of Jesus Christ must come to terms with the problem of *continuance*. As a disciple I have known moments of ecstasy and glory, but also moments of sorry failure and defeat. How do I continue victoriously instead of enjoying victory only now and then, only here and there? In the words of J. Taylor Smith, a bishop of the Anglican Church of England, how do I "abide and abound"?

Isaiah teaches me that victory does not come by looking inside myself, but rather by looking *outside*. First, I must look beyond myself to see the "hungry" and "afflicted" person nearby, and then pour out myself for him (Isaiah 58:10). Hungry and afflicted souls are around me constantly, and I am to develop a way of life toward them, a way in which I share the spiritual blessings I already have. In sharing them, God will multiply and magnify my resources beyond anything I can dream. As a result of giving my portion to others, God will make my light rise at noonday, guide me continually, satisfy my soul in drought, make me like a watered garden, and make me a repairer of broken people (Isaiah 58:10–12). If Isaiah has not described continual victory here, I do not know what continual victory is!

In short, God through Isaiah is teaching me that before I can enjoy the *fruits* of victory in my own life, I must pay attention to the *rights* of victory on behalf of others. In other words, my victory is not an in-the-closet type of thing that I can enjoy alone, but something that I enjoy only in relationship to others. If I meet their spiritual needs, I will enjoy spiritual victory on a steady, continuing basis. Lord, help me to stop currying and combing my own soul, and help me to feed others the bread of Christ that they so desperately need! Then we will enjoy victory together.

"Therefore, my beloved brethren, be steadfast, immovable, always abounding in the work of the Lord, knowing that your toil is not in vain in the Lord" (1 Corinthians 15:58).

SEPTEMBER 15
Riding the High Places of Earth

The second thing Isaiah says I must do if I am to walk in continual victory is to give attention to the rights of God. He says that if I honor the Sabbath and do not use it for my "own pleasure" (Isaiah 58:13), then certain great benefits will be mine: I will delight in the Lord, I will ride on the high places of the earth, and I will be fed with the inheritance of the Lord (v. 14).

What does that mean to me in this year of our Lord? Am I to keep the Sabbath with Old Testament exactitude, down to the merest jot and tittle? No, I do not think so. Isaiah is talking about rights, the rights of the hungry and afflicted, and now the rights of God. The hungry soul has a right to the bread of Jesus Christ; he has that right both in his birth and in the cross of our Lord. If I am to enjoy continual victory, I must respect his rights. But God has rights also. He has the right to expect of me continual obedience to His will and continual adherence to every command He gives me. The Sabbath was an expression of God's will to Israel; I am to give God His way in every expression of His will, as He makes that will clear to me from His Word.

In a sense, I must not be occupied with victory, for victory is a result of a previously met pair of conditions. If I think about victory, it will escape me like a mist. But if I think about serving others, if I think about thoroughly obeying the will of my Father, victory will be as automatic and continual as each day's sunrise.

Lord, I desire to be a watered garden and to ride on the high places of the earth; but help me to see that I cannot get them by seeking them, but by seeking to feed the afflicted soul and by seeking to do Your will.

"From my distress I called upon the Lord; the Lord answered me and set me in a large place. The Lord is for me; I will not fear; what can man do to me?" (Psalm 118:5-6).

SEPTEMBER 16
Does Jesus Want Us Alive and Well?

Lord, do I have the right to automatic healing? Is sickness always an attack of Satan, and may I expel him by means of the cross? There are some sicknesses due to sin (1 Corinthians 11:30), some sicknesses due to Satan (Job 2:7), and some sicknesses for which there is no assignable cause (John 9:3). But *all* sicknesses, if used properly, are designed to be used to the glory of God (John 11:4).

For a disciple of Jesus Christ, sickness becomes a tool in the hands of God. Job was brought to a new awareness of God through his sickness; and Paul enjoyed more of God's grace through the thorn in his flesh. My first reaction to becoming ill should always be, "Lord, what is Your message in all this?"

Faith healing is not crassly demanding that God obey me. Rather, it is asking God what His will might be. In other words, I am to pray about praying. Paul asked God three times about the matter. If God reveals to me that He desires to heal me, then faith takes over and praying ceases; or conversely, if God reveals to me that sickness is to be my portion, for deeper spiritual purposes, then obedience takes over and I stop praying.

Does Jesus want me to *always* be well? Not until He has accomplished His purposes through my sickness, for having strong, healthy bodies is not God's *first* objective for His children; godliness is (1 Timothy 4:8). The body is not without its value, of course, but I must present it to Him as a "living . . . sacrifice" (Romans 12:1), which gives Him the right to do with it as it pleases Him. If He treats my body with "weakness," He will also give me the necessary "grace" to bear it (2 Corinthians 12:9).

"Before I was afflicted I went astray, but now I keep Thy word. Thou art good and doest good; teach me Thy statutes" (Psalm 119:67–68).

SEPTEMBER 17
The Blueprint Life

A s far as possible I must live the *blueprint life*. Jesus Christ lived that kind of life. "The Son can do nothing by himself; he can do only what he sees his Father doing, because whatever the Father does the Son also does" (John 5:19, NIV). I must not misunderstand—the blueprint life is not rigid command, but expected obedience. Jesus Christ was free to live His own life, otherwise He would not have been fully human. But He chose to live a blueprint life because He loved the Father absolutely, and because only by blueprinting could He ever achieve all that the Father wanted for Him and for others through Him.

The blueprint is God's *best estimate* of what I am able to do under His guidance and by His power. So it is not a limiting instrument, but rather, a liberating one. The illusion of freedom is: "I can do it better." But the misery of freedom is: "I wish I had another chance!"

The blueprint means that the Almighty, all-wise God is my Lover, not my despot. Why else would He bother? His yearning heart devises all that is best for me; yet His fairness and justice allow me to reject His blueprint, if I insist.

Jesus Christ found immense satisfaction in this: "I have brought you glory on earth by completing the work you gave me to do" (John 17:4, NIV). Jesus never sloughed His blueprint; therefore, His work was "finished." I may slough mine many times and therefore may not finish my work as perfectly as Jesus did. But if I trust my Father and rely on His power, I will "finish" out my life far better than if I had no blueprint at all. My joy is in the psalmist's assurance: "I will instruct you and teach you in the way which you should go; I will counsel you with My eye upon you" (Psalm 32:8).

"Have I not commanded you? Be strong and courageous! Do not tremble or be dismayed, for the Lord your God is with you wherever you go" *(Joshua 1:9).*

SEPTEMBER 18
Finding Our Niche

Both my happiness and my usefulness depend upon finding my niche in God's plan, and staying in it. Everything in God's Kingdom has a niche, even the stars. "The stars in their courses fought against Sisera" (Judges 5:20, KJV). I must find my niche also. God promises me power and strength only up to my niche, never beyond. If I exceed my niche, I am on my own. Too often exhaustion comes when I have gone beyond God's plan, driven perhaps by ambition or pride.

It is not hard to find God's niche, but it is hard to stay inside its limits. We fall either above or below. Paul says, "[Love] does not seek its own [way]" (1 Corinthians 13:5). That often is my trouble, seeking more than God has promised, which leads to all sorts of problems. Or sometimes I *underachieve* God's will and that leads to slippage, which forces other people to bear more than they should. Each part of my body has a function; but if one part fails, the whole body is placed under economic constraint to compensate for the failure of one unit.

If I am to stay in my niche, I must possess two abilities: the ability to see the limits of my niche so that I do not exceed them, and the ability to be utterly obedient and submissive to the God who has made my niche for me. To listen to self or others rather than God is to form the beginning of dissatisfaction with my lot, which is the first sign of rebellion. I must remember Moses' blessing on Benjamin, "He is the beloved of the Lord and dwells . . . [*by His side*] securely" (Deuteronomy 33:12, Berkeley). That is the secret: staying by His side! To remain there as His beloved is to stay where I am placed and to want no other, for His sake.

"Whether it is pleasant or unpleasant, we will listen to the voice of the Lord our God to whom we are sending you, in order that it may go well with us when we listen to the voice of the Lord our God" (Jeremiah 42:6).

SEPTEMBER 19
Finding God's Way Delightful

One of the tests of my spiritual health is: How well do I accept God's *ways?* It is one thing to accept God's *Word,* but it is quite another thing to accept His ways. That is because His ways strike me directly and, sometimes, contrarily. Yet, however I like or dislike God's ways, "the ways of the Lord are right" (Hosea 14:9). That means He always deals with me in righteousness (or fairness, justice), not in partiality. If God's ways are not pleasing to me, it is because He is righteous and I am sinful. To the extent that I am "righteous," that is, agree with God's character, I will find His ways to be perfectly delightful. If I stumble over God's ways it is because there is an element of sin in me that has not been judged.

But I must remember that while God always deals with me *from righteousness,* it is always *through love.* "I will heal their backsliding, I will love them freely" (Hosea 14:4, KJV). Love makes it possible for a righteous God and sinful people to find a common ground of meeting. Because I know God loves me, I know I can trust His ways even though they may seem painful and irksome and foreign to my nature. Love is God's way of telling me that His ways are not meant to crush but to lift me. Without that love, life under the rule of God would be horrible slavery.

God's love does not change the *content* of His ways. They may still be bitter or heavy, but love guarantees me that however rough those ways may be, they are leading me to something better, something glorious in the days to come. So love is not only my protector; it is my hope and inspiration. How thrilled I am to be serving a God who is absolutely right in all He does, yet absolutely tender in how He does it! Let His name be praised!

"When a man's ways are pleasing to the Lord, He makes even his enemies to be at peace with him" (Proverbs 16:7).

SEPTEMBER 20
God's Multiplying Power

I must learn never to measure God's resources by mine. Someone has said, "Little is much when God is in it." One of Elisha's friends, a widow, had only one jar of oil (2 Kings 4:1–7). Instead of telling her to *conserve* it, he ordered her to do exactly the opposite: pour it out. Instead of coming to the end of her supply, she continued to pour out a multiplying stream of oil until at last she ran out of containers. Then it stopped! How God enabled that oil to multiply is beyond me, but so is much that exists in the spiritual world. This much is true: how long would the small jar have lasted if left to itself? How long would the widow have lived, left to herself? How long would any of us last spiritually, left to ourselves? I think this is where I so often fail. I pit myself against the massive needs all around me, and without the multiplying grace of God, I end up broken.

God begins with my small jar, but He does not stop there. He adds His amazing multiplying power to my words, thoughts, prayers, and service until I can hardly recognize myself in them. As with the widow's oil, Someone has taken over and the cup has become a barrel. And is this not the story of Scripture? Abraham's "dead" body— and God; Moses' shepherd crook—and God; David's sling—and God; the boy's small lunch—and God; the twelve disciples—and God. It is the "and God" that makes all the difference!

If there is any failure, it is in this: I do not give God a chance with what I have. But if I do, God becomes my great enhancer and multiplier. My anchor is God's own promise: "The smallest one will become a clan, and the least one a mighty nation. I, the Lord, will hasten it in its time" (Isaiah 60:22).

"Enlarge the place of your tent; stretch out the curtains of your dwellings, spare not; lengthen your cords, and strengthen your pegs" (Isaiah 54:2).

SEPTEMBER 21
A Negative Means of Grace

I must understand that, as a disciple of Christ, God will appoint a "troubler" for me. King Ahab said to Elijah, "Is this you, you troubler of Israel?" (1 Kings 18:17). Elijah was Ahab's troubler, his thorn in the flesh. Yet, whether he knew it or not, Elijah was Ahab's best friend.

My troubler may be anyone—my wife, my boss, my pastor, my neighbor, my child. *Who* he is is not as important as what he is. He is God's appointed messenger to teach me God's secrets, sometimes painful secrets, about my walk with Him. My troubler has a special responsibility to me, but I have a special responsibility to him also. The worst thing I can do to my troubler is to ignore him; the second worst thing is to enter into conflict with him and seek to grind him into the dust. Those are two natural reactions because my troubler is a threat to my ego and pride; nevertheless, to indulge in those kinds of responses is really to hurt myself far more.

Not all my growth in grace results from *positives*—sermons, books, leaflets, conferences. Some of it results from *negatives*—an explosive quarrel, a thorough humiliation, a sharp conviction of sin, a daily exasperation. That is where my troubler comes in. He drives me to the end of my pride, loftiness, and self-sufficiency and right into the waiting arms of my Paraclete. Instead of lashing out against my troubler out of sheer desperation, I should repeat, "My troubler, my joy; my troubler, my joy." That was David's attitude toward Shimei, the man who cursed him to his face. He said, "Let him curse, for the Lord has told him. Perhaps the Lord will . . . return good to me instead of his cursing this day" (2 Samuel 16:11–12). The Lord will repay me with good for all the Shimeis I may meet along life's road.

"I know that the Lord will maintain the cause of the afflicted, and justice for the poor. Surely the righteous will give thanks to Thy name; the upright will dwell in Thy presence" (Psalm 140:12–13).

SEPTEMBER 22
The Bible Is a Fire and Hammer

I must understand that the Bible is not only my source of comfort, but my source of *bruising*. "'Is not My word like fire?' declares the Lord, 'and like a hammer which shatters a rock?'" (Jeremiah 23:29). If I have never felt the scorching of the Bible's heat or the shattering of the Bible's blow, I am not making much progress as a disciple. The Bible is a sharp instrument; it pierces, divides, discerns, and reaches into the depths of my personality, down to the thoughts and motives of my nature (Hebrews 4:12).

I must beware the man who preaches a sugar-coated faith. Faith in God is not an Aladdin's lamp that grants my every wish. I must avoid, as I would the plague, the man who preaches "Peace, peace" continually. There are times when the Bible will not give me peace; times when to comfort and assure me would be absolutely damaging to me. How can I sin and not feel the burning fire of the Word?

The false prophet is easily discovered. He is the man who offers nothing but honey, peace, joy, security, and tranquillity. He does that, of course, because it is what the natural man craves; it provides him a ready audience, a guarantee of success. A counselor who offers me a rosy goal but never mentions the painful, torturous road to it is not my friend. Jesus Christ is my true Friend. He offers me a rewarding future, but "with persecutions" (Mark 10:29–30). He wants to deliver me safe, sound, and *holy*. That is why His Word must sometimes make me ache with soreness and weep with bitterness. He knows where it all is leading—to manhood and womanhood tinged with glory. I respond with Mary's sincere humility: "Behold, the bondslave of the Lord; be it done to me according to your word," for "my soul exalts the Lord, and my spirit has rejoiced in God my Savior" (Luke 1:38, 46–47).

"Therefore I love Thy commandments above gold, yes, above fine gold. Therefore I esteem right all Thy precepts concerning everything, I hate every false way" (Psalm 119:127–28).

SEPTEMBER 23

Nailprints in the Heart

The strength of my devotion to Jesus Christ is not measured by my speech, but by my *sufferings*. When Paul urged the Colossians on to greater zeal for God, he did not argue; he pointed. "Remember my bonds [prison chains]," he wrote to them (Colossians 4:18, KJV). If his sufferings for Christ could not convince them, nothing could. Would Paul himself not know? What started him thinking about Christ—Stephen's speech or his death (Acts 7:60–8:1)?

Paul has left us many memorials of his devotion to Christ—letters, travels, sermons, miracles—but he left nothing greater than his chains, the symbol of his sufferings for Christ's sake. The measure of a person's devotion to any cause, right or wrong, is the depth of the suffering he is willing to undergo for it. That is why Paul could say, "I bear on my body the brand-marks of Jesus" (Galatians 6:17).

What scars do I bear for Christ? Scars are not an end in themselves, but signs of an inward commitment. Nor must I seek scars of the *body*, but what are more important, scars of the *spirit*. The scars of the spirit are the sacrifices of self-dependence and self-direction that I make for Christ's sake. Whether or not I ever wear physical scars for Christ is not essential; it is absolutely essential that I wear spiritual scars for Him.

A Christian once said, "There are no nailprints in my hands." Perhaps not. But a more pertinent question is: Are there nailprints in your heart? Paul rejoiced in his scars, because then, he said, "the power of Christ may rest upon me" (2 Corinthians 12:9, KJV); he was willing to trade scars for the privilege of bearing fruit. So will everyone who follows the Lamb wherever He goes.

"In all their affliction He was afflicted, and the angel of His presence saved them; in His love and in His mercy He redeemed them; and He lifted them and carried them all the days of old" (Isaiah 63:9).

SEPTEMBER 24
The Pain God Feels

I must avoid at all costs two mistaken ideas of God, prevalent in our times: first, that God is *above pain*, and second, that God *is below manipulation*. That God is not above pain is clear in the Bible; yet the impressions I get from fellow Christians is that God is as impervious to pain as He is to sin. Wrong! The two are not synonymous. God feels pain deeply. He can be "grieved," "wearied," "sorrowed," and everything else that represents distress over disobedience in His children. And what about the pain of Calvary, the pain not only of the Son but also of the Father? It was there the blood of *God* (Acts 20:28) was shed.

God suffers pain only in contact with sin. The closer the person is to God, the sharper will be the pain in the heart of God over any sin that may appear in him. One of the "groanings" of Jesus was over the betrayal of Judas, one of the Twelve (John 13:21). He wounded Jesus far more deeply than he wounded himself, so I have the capability of wounding and hurting the One who is the universe to me. In my trifling with sin, I may not realize how deeply I stab the heart of Him who bought me at so great a price.

God is not the distant, sterile judge we often make Him out to be. If He is that to us, then we have a sadly inadequate and insufficient view of sin. If I have a permissive view of sin, then God's pain becomes a mere trifling irritation that is easily shrugged off. To see what sin is, I must see Calvary, for there God took its odious, repulsive measure for all eternity. To see what salvation from sin is, I must see my living Intercessor who is able to "sympathize with our weaknesses" and who provides a throne of grace where my sin burden is dealt with until His—and my—pain is gone (Hebrews 4:15–16, NIV).

"And when He went ashore, He saw a great multitude, and He felt compassion for them because they were like sheep without a shepherd; and He began to teach them many things" (Mark 6:34).

SEPTEMBER 25
Evangelical Humanism

The second misconception of God that I must avoid is that He is able to be manipulated. The modern manipulation of God is extremely subtle, but the heart of it lies in a kind of evangelical humanism. God is looked upon as existing to serve *my* ends; not I existing to serve God's ends. There are two biblical examples of this: Simon the magician and Micah the Ephraimite.

Simon wanted to buy the Holy Spirit with money, to add to his storehouse of magical powers. So offended was Simon Peter that he responded: "You are in the gall of bitterness and in the bondage of iniquity" (Acts 8:23). That gross usage of God was commercial in motive; Simon simply wanted to get rich by using God. The same motive drove Micah of Ephraim to set up a shrine in his home and to hire a Levite to become his priest. "Now I know that the Lord will prosper me, seeing I have a Levite as priest" (Judges 17:10–13). That manipulation of God had no reference to obedience, worship, or the glorification of God; it was the same as the worship of idols.

Perhaps my use of God is nowhere near the crude misuse of Him by those two, but the pressure to bargain or bribe is always there. Do I pray, attend church, and tithe my income in order to receive special favors, or do I do those things out of realizing who God is and for the joy of obeying the majestic, glorious God of the universe? Do I seek to please Him in order that my loved one may be healed, or is it because I love Him so much I could not do otherwise? Do I write "for my gain" or "for God's glory" underneath everything I do for Him? The difference is manipulating God or ascribing my song of praise to His worthiness. "Worthy art Thou, our Lord and our God, to receive glory and honor and power; for Thou didst create all things, and because of Thy will they existed, and were created" (Revelation 4:11).

"O Lord, Thou art my God; I will exalt Thee, I will give thanks to Thy name; for Thou hast worked wonders, plans formed long ago, with perfect faithfulness" (Isaiah 25:1).

SEPTEMBER 26
The Danger of Distraction

Lord, I must avoid at all times the danger of distraction. What do I do when the earth changes, the mountains shake, and the ocean roars and swells? (Psalm 46:2–3). I am to "be still, and know that [God is] God" (v. 10, KJV). Sometimes my little kingdom totters, my family convulses, and my mind staggers to the edge. Then I must be still and know that God is God. My refuge must always be God, my rock, my defense, and my fortress.

I must avoid running to Egypt for help. This is what Israel did when confronted by a fearsome foe (Isaiah 30:1–2). The trouble with running to Egypt is that it is a "little help," and a little help can become a wholesale disaster. It is better to trust the Lord fully and be completely delivered than to trust Egypt and be partially delivered (vv. 12–13). Egypt was an illusion, a paper tiger, a tree inwardly eaten of grubs. She looked formidable, but her looks were deceiving. She had glamour but no strength. If Israel (or I) trusts in Egypt, it will be "shame, and . . . confusion" (v. 3, KJV).

How often in my desperation have I looked to a person of wealth, of wisdom, of maturity and experience and said, "You are my deliverer," only to discover the wealth, wisdom, and maturity were cold ashes. There was no help whatever! I was driven in humiliation back to the source of my strength and wisdom, back to God Himself and the everlasting arms.

It is not a sin to *have* an Egypt (after all, I am human) but it is certainly a sin to rest my weight upon Egypt, to rely upon it, rather than upon my God. To "be still" means to "relax," but I must relax on the solid rock, not the shifting sands of an ephemeral, passing trust. I love Nahum's word on this: "The Lord is good, a stronghold in the day of trouble, and He knows those who take refuge [trust] in Him" (Nahum 1:7).

"To Thee, O Lord, I lift up my soul. O my God, in Thee I trust, do not let me be ashamed; do not let my enemies exult over me" (Psalm 25:1–2).

SEPTEMBER 27
Conquering Fear

I must learn the lessons of Gethsemane, where Jesus prayed the most significant prayer that any person can pray, "Nevertheless not my will, but thine, be done" (Luke 22:42, KJV). One of those lessons is what to do about *fear*. There is no doubt that Jesus shrank from the prospect of becoming sin for us. The "agony" and the "sweat . . . like drops of blood" were symptoms of an inward turmoil as He faced the awesome forces of the infernal on Calvary (Luke 22:44). It is no sin to be afraid. We admire a physician who fears disease, a banker who is afraid of debt, a Christian who is afraid of sin. There is no "Thou shalt not fear" commandment. It is useless to try to get people to stop being afraid. After all, is not fear a part of our preservation? Do not animals protect themselves by being afraid?

Jesus in Gethsemane showed me what to do about fear. I should not *reject* it, but *conquer* it. Fear cannot be conquered unless we engage it and enter into combat with it. Jesus felt turmoil at what He saw on Calvary, and even He asked His Father to remove the source of that fear. But when He learned that the Father was unable to remove the cross (for our salvation), Jesus promptly yielded His will to the Father's, and put His trust in His Father in the very midst of His fear. He was heard because of "his godly fear" (Hebrews 5:7, ASV) and was saved "out of death" and out of its fear.

That is my remedy for fear, one beautifully expressed by the psalmist: "When I am afraid, I will put my trust in Thee" (Psalm 56:3). The moment I feel fear, that should be the signal to trust; and once I put my trust in God, I must dismiss my fear and calmly move forward. That is what Jesus, my always perfect example and pattern, did.

"Then my enemies will turn back in the day when I call; this I know, that God is for me. . . . In God I have put my trust, I shall not be afraid" (Psalm 56:9, 11).

SEPTEMBER 28

Gethsemane Leads to Calvary

Gethsemane not only shows me how to overcome fear, but how to succeed in my Christian life. In Gethsemane, Jesus prayed a prayer, "Not My will, but Thine be done" (Luke 22:42); on Calvary, Jesus shouted in triumph, "It is [satisfactorily] finished [completed]!" (John 19:30). It was in Gethsemane that Jesus sowed the seeds of victory on Calvary. I will be faced with countless Calvarys, and the only way I can prepare for them is to go through Gethsemane.

I must be a Gethsemane disciple. Gethsemane was not an isolated experience for Jesus; He went there "as was His custom" (Luke 22:39). Spiritually, His whole life was a Gethsemane; He was constantly facing the enemy's alternatives, He was continually deciding to do the Father's will. The more selfish a person is, the less he will experience of Gethsemane. He has no crisis, no agony, and therefore no victory. Believers who live in the atmosphere of Gethsemane constantly reap victory.

Gethsemane divides disciples into three groups: those who decide to *ignore* God's will, those who decide to *consider* God's will, and those who decide to *do* God's will. Victory comes only to the one who chooses to enact God's will.

I can avoid Gethsemane if I choose to do so, but I cannot avoid Calvary. The tragedy is that if I avoid Gethsemane, I will be in poor condition indeed to face my Calvary. The glorious sequence of "Calvary, resurrection, and ascension" starts in Gethsemane. Lord, let me say honestly, "I'll go with Him through the garden!"

Then Christ will respond by saying, "To him who overcomes, I will give the right to sit with me on my throne, just as I overcame and sat down with my Father on his throne" (Revelation 3:21, NIV).

"Now the God of peace, who brought up from the dead the great Shepherd of the sheep through the blood of the eternal covenant, even Jesus our Lord, equip you in every good thing to do His will" (Hebrews 13:20–21).

SEPTEMBER 29
Faith Must Be Practical

My faith must be practical. In fact, my faith is not faith unless it is practical, for "faith without works is dead" (James 2:26).

Jeremiah shows me what practical faith is. Although the Babylonian army was at the gates of Jerusalem, laying siege to it, God told Jeremiah that the day would come when He would restore the captivity of His people and return the land to them. As proof of that restoration, God told Jeremiah to buy a field from his uncle and lay away the deed in a safe place, to be used when the Jews were once again back in their own land (Jeremiah 32:6–15). Jeremiah did so, thus showing how totally he trusted the word of God.

Biblical faith is looked upon as a spring of action, a spiritual activator, a lifted latch that allows God's blessings to come pouring down. I must not merely sing about faith, or glory in it, but I must do what my faith requires. The heroes of the Bible did not believe in belief; they accepted the consequences of commitment, and their faith was justified in the results of that commitment. I am impressed with the number of verbs contained in Hebrews 11, the faith chapter: Abel offered; Enoch walked; Noah prepared; Abraham went out; Sarah conceived; Isaac blessed; Jacob worshiped; Joseph commanded; Moses' parents hid him; Moses refused, chose, esteemed, forsook, kept, and passed over; and Rahab received. What an avalanche of doings!

I cannot avoid being judged by *works!* The judgment of God will not be on how much faith I had within, but on how much was strong enough to get out. What gets out will be to God's glory and my praise. Then, like Enoch, I will have this testimony: "that [I] pleased God" (Hebrews 11:5, KJV).

"And the Scripture was fulfilled which says, 'And Abraham believed God, and it was reckoned to him as righteousness,' and he was called the friend of God. You see that a man is justified by works, and not by faith alone" (James 2:23–24).

SEPTEMBER 30
The Religion of Surveillance

I must avoid at all costs the religion of surveillance. God put this religion in proper focus when He said to Jeremiah, "Am I a God at hand . . . and not a God afar off?" (Jeremiah 23:23, KJV). I must not have a schizophrenic faith in God. I must not fly to Him in trouble and then forget Him when all is well.

I find it is easy to be a prospering Christian when I am under surveillance. But do I still behave like a disciple when I am in a strange city in which I am unknown and God is "afar off"? How much of my Christianity is simply conformity under social or family pressure? Am I simply a chameleon, taking on the color of my surroundings without the necessary change of inner impulse?

The religion of surveillance is doomed to defeat. God asks, "Can a man hide himself in secret places and I shall not see him?" (Jeremiah 23:24, Berkeley). I must not toy with God as the Israelites did, seeking Him only in danger and *totally* ignoring His claim upon them. Israel's idolatry was a symptom of the religion of surveillance. I also will become idolatrous, in effect, by pretending God has no eyes to see or ears to hear.

My attitude must be that of the woman who was so desperate to get to Jesus that she "touched the fringe of His . . . garment" (Luke 8:43–48, margin). The difference between her and the crowds jostling Jesus was that she touched in need and in faith. The result—healing and newness! I must be characterized by a continual touching of Jesus by faith, and not by just a respectable acquaintance with Him. Surveillance keeps Jesus at bay, but the touch of faith releases His almighty power for eternal results. Faith treats God as the ever present, ever ready One, my anchor and hope for every situation.

"But sanctify Christ as Lord in your hearts, always being ready to make a defense to everyone who asks you to give an account for the hope that is in you, yet with gentleness and reverence" (1 Peter 3:15).

OCTOBER 1

Our Personal Yoke

Jesus said, "Take My yoke upon you. . . . For My yoke is easy [tolerable], and My load is light" (Matthew 11:29–30). I must learn the lessons of the yoke. First, the yoke is not the burden; the yoke enables me to *carry* my burden. My burden is the normal "cargo" that every human being must of necessity tote (Galatians 6:5). In effect, Jesus is saying, "If you will become My disciple, even the natural burdens of life will become tolerable."

Second, the yoke is *personal*. Just as the burden fits me personally, so the yoke must be suited to me. The American Indians designed yokes to be worn on their shoulders, shaped personally for each one's use. So Jesus becomes my yoke, personally suited for my particular burden. His yoke is not intended to *add* anything to my burden, but to relieve it. Often a person will say, "How can people live who do not have the Lord?" That means: "How can people carry their load without the helpful yoke of the Lord?"

Third, the yoke is *Christ's*. He calls it "My yoke." He Himself had to bend under the burden that the Father gave Him, and in doing so He learned how to use the yoke. His yoke is not a thing, but an attitude of submission, with the resulting flow of power. As Jesus bent to the Father's yoke in order to lift the burden of Calvary, so we bend to Christ's yoke in gentle submission and He enables us to lift our cross and move forward to daily victory.

Jesus says, "Learn of me" (Matthew 11:29, KJV). Yes, Lord, let me learn of You so that my burden does not grind me into the dust; let me wear Your yoke, Lord, for my ease and for my victory.

"Come to Me, all who are weary and heavy-laden, and I will give you rest. Take My yoke upon you, and learn from Me, for I am gentle and humble in heart; and you shall find rest for your souls" (Matthew 11:28–29).

OCTOBER 2
The Yoke of Christ

The yoke is not only a means of adopting Christ's triumphant way of living, but it is also a sign of ownership. Jeremiah made a yoke for himself to wear as a sign that Judah, his beloved nation, would wear the yoke of the king of Babylon (Jeremiah 27:2, 12). Since Judah had worshiped Babylon's *idols*, she then had to wear Babylon's *yoke*. I cannot avoid the consequences of submission to the wrong master. Paul says that I am the slave of either sin or righteousness (Romans 6:15–16). He also implies that whichever master I serve, I must wear his yoke (or ownership). I cannot indulge in sin without giving up some of my sovereignty to it. Just as I cannot be partially married, so I cannot be partially righteous.

The only way I can escape my yoke to sin or the world or Satan is to *break* it. Naturally I cannot break that yoke by my own power, but God says He will help me: "And now I will break his yoke from upon you, and snap your bonds asunder" (Nahum 1:13, Berkeley). Praise God for His resource of power! However, that power cannot become operative in me until I will to have it do so; in short, I must want the yoke broken so intensely that I freely invite God to smash it to pieces for me. Despite the strength of the yoke, or the length of time I have served under it, God is sufficiently mighty to redeem me from its authority and stranglehold.

Jeremiah lamented that his people had broken *God's yoke* over them (Jeremiah 2:20; 5:5). God forbid that I ever find His yoke so confining, so enslaving, and so disagreeable that I ever contemplate breaking it off me. To wear the yoke of Jesus Christ is the highest of honors, and the most lasting and satisfying of vocations.

"Fight the good fight of faith; take hold of the eternal life to which you were called, and you made the good confession in the presence of many witnesses" (1 Timothy 6:12).

OCTOBER 3
The Special Orders of God

I must remember that as a disciple of Jesus Christ I am always under "special orders." "For He gives His angels [special] orders regarding you to protect you wherever you go" (Psalm 91:11, Berkeley). Those special orders are so minute and particular that they prevent my stepping on a stone the *wrong* way (v. 12). I may argue, therefore, from the minute to the gigantic, and say that if God has given orders to protect me from *pebbles*, He most certainly will protect me from greater sources of danger.

The world constantly advises me, "Keep your head!" Good advice, indeed. But God advises me, "Keep your feet!" and He even provides the wherewithal by which I may protect them. If I make the Lord my "help" (Psalm 121:2), then I am guaranteed the promise, "He will not allow your foot to slip" (v. 3). As Oswald Chambers says, "God will tax the farthest star to fulfill His promise," and He will even use any means to keep my feet from falling.

To be under special orders is not the same as to be under "sealed" orders. The special order is someone else's responsibility for me, the sealed order is my responsibility to Christ's command. Special orders are assigned to angels or to human beings. Angels are assigned to protect me from physical harm, while the Holy Spirit is assigned to protect me from spiritual harm. Occasionally God will assign a human being to protect and comfort me, as Barnabas did with Paul.

I am surrounded by protection; I am not alone; I live under the constant "watch care" of a thousand eyes and tender hearts, all assigned the task of bringing me safely to my destination. They encamp around me and have one objective in mind—my safe deliverance (Psalm 34:7).

"And the ransomed of the Lord will return, and come with joyful shouting to Zion, with everlasting joy upon their heads. They will find gladness and joy, and sorrow and sighing will flee away" (Isaiah 35:10).

OCTOBER 4

Jesus Christ Stands for Us

Like priest, like people" is not only an aphorism, but a solid statement of biblical truth. Aaron wore the names of the tribes of Israel on his shoulders and on his breast (Exodus 28:9–30). The symbolism is beautiful and meaningful. Israel was effectively represented before God on the *strength* and *love* of the high priest.

Strength and love are the twin pillars of the present intercessory ministry of Christ for me. Just as Aaron stood for Israel in the presence of God, so Jesus Christ stands for me. All the blessings that God has poured, and is pouring, upon His Son are meant for me also. He has "blessed [me] with every spiritual blessing," not because I am I, but because I am in Christ and Christ is in me (Ephesians 1:3). It is through Christ that I am entitled to receive from the Father all I need for a victorious pilgrim journey. In that sense He is my strength, my ticket to acceptance, my right to be favored by the Most High God.

Not only am I upheld by His strength, but also by His love. How long would I tolerate a resentful High Priest, doing His duty heartlessly and without compassion? Aaron carried the names of the tribes on his breastplate as a sign that his intercession was never to be without feeling, or else it would be dead intercession. Jesus Christ intercedes for me because He loves me; and He intercedes successfully for me because He died for me. My welfare before God's throne is pursued with the intensity of a mother for her child, of a king for his son. When strength and love are coupled in the person of Jesus Christ, I am perfectly represented, perfectly spoken for. No one could plead my case any better than the One who died to give me birth.

"But now He has obtained a more excellent ministry, by as much as He is also the mediator of a better covenant, which has been enacted on better promises" (Hebrews 8:6).

OCTOBER 5
The Wheels of God's Providence

There are times in my Christian life when God will be silent, but He will never be *inactive*. I must be careful to differentiate between the two. The psalmist says, "God is . . . a very present help in trouble" (Psalm 46:1, KJV). That means that regardless of whether God is saying anything to me at a given moment, He is certainly doing a lot.

Daniel helps me to see that truth. He had prayed for his people's return from captivity, but not a word came from God in reply to that prayer. Finally, after three weeks of waiting, the answer came. The answer? God had begun to answer Daniel's prayer the moment he began to pray, but the reply was hindered by the "prince of the kingdom of Persia" (Daniel 10:13) and not until twenty-one days later was the hindrance removed and the answer delivered. The important thing is: God was working while Daniel was waiting.

Now I begin to see what another prophet, Ezekiel, saw when God showed him the vision of wheels within wheels (Ezekiel 1). The wheels of Israel had ground to a halt because of idolatry; but the wheels of God were working night and day for God's people, the faithful remnant, who were interceding for their beloved land. That speaks very forcibly to me! I cannot look at the broken wheels of my life and say, "God has forgotten; God does not care!" I can only look on the inside and see God busily at work on my behalf.

If only I can believe that now, in the midst of my doubt and confusion, God has already planned and is now executing my rescue, then I can say, "He is my very *present* help in trouble." And as with every deliverance, it is never too late in the light of His eternal plan. The *permanence* of God's delivering ministry is assured by Paul: He "delivered us . . . [He] will deliver us . . . He will yet deliver us" (2 Corinthians 1:10).

"So he shepherded them according to the integrity of his heart, and guided them with his skillful hands" (Psalm 78:72).

OCTOBER 6
God's Special Treats

I must never assume that God treats me the same way all the time. His treatment of me depends upon the purposes He has in mind, and the state of my commitment at the time. David expresses that varied kind of treatment in Psalm 23. On the one hand God "leadeth me beside the still waters" (v. 2, KJV), the picture of gentle, loving treatment. But He also "*driveth* me in the paths of righteousness" (v. 3, author's trans.). The two distinctly different words show that God uses different methods to produce the results He desires for me.

"He leadeth me." Sometimes God gives His children "treats." A spiritual treat is an unexpected token of God's love and care. It may come in the form of a letter from a friend, a gift of money, a sparkling Scripture passage that strikes home, a phone call, or sometimes just a warm, bright smile. A treat comes at just the right time (in fact, the timing is part of the treat). When a treat comes I am simply to accept it graciously and thank God for it, for such a treat often stills the troubled waters of my heart and makes them quiet.

"He driveth me." The only reason God ever uses force with us is to make us walk in right paths "for his name's sake." It is never a sign of brutality. Sometimes the coercion comes from friends, family, circumstances, the church body, or the political structure. I must not reject secondary authority, that is, the agency by which God puts on the pressure, as if it were alien and foreign. Suffering is one of the great driving agencies of God, and I must accept it as such. I am assured of this: all God's drivings are leading me to a holier life—righteousness, which in turn enables me to render greater glory to His name. So whether He treats me or drives me, I am to rejoice in a God who is greater than what I deserve or fear.

"Just as a father has compassion on his children, so the Lord has compassion on those who fear Him. For He Himself knows our frame; He is mindful that we are but dust" (Psalm 103:13–14).

OCTOBER 7
God Our Shepherd

I must remember that while *positionally* God sees me perfect in Christ, *practically* He sees me as a sheep, sometimes strong and sometimes weak, sometimes obedient and sometimes vacillating. I see that in the sheep's psalm, Psalm 23.

While God the Shepherd is portrayed as competent and capable in the psalm, the sheep is not. Often the sheep is obedient and follows closely by the Shepherd's side and so enjoys green pastures and quiet waters. But sometimes I am a disobedient sheep and so must be "driven" in the right paths. I sometimes need the rod and the staff and their discipline, which is painful at the moment, but it ultimately brings its "comfort" (v. 4). Sometimes I am fearful, especially at the approach of any cavern, cleft, or valley. While every valley has its fears, the valley of death has the greatest fear of all, and so I need the extra assurance of my Shepherd's presence, which enables me to "fear no harm" (v. 4, margin).

Sometimes I am surrounded by my enemies, but even then God arranges things so that in *their* sight I am provided a table, a provision, and an oversight by my thoughtful, concerned Shepherd. He wants to show my enemies that I made no mistake in putting my trust entirely in Him.

There also are times when my cup simply overflows. Those are times when I cry out with wonder, "Why me, Lord? Why me?" When I receive those overwhelming times of joy, it is not because I am good, but because my Shepherd is and He simply desires to share His goodness with me. In fact, He pursues me with "goodness and mercy" (v. 6, KJV) until He brings me safely into His eternal home.

What shall I say of a God who understands me so fully and provides for me so completely? "Great is the Lord, and greatly [deserves] to be praised" (Psalm 96:4).

"Thou art a gracious and compassionate God, slow to anger and abundant in lovingkindness, and one who relents concerning calamity" (Jonah 4:2).

OCTOBER 8
Jesus Came to Save People

I must be careful, Lord, not to simplify Your salvation. Too often I have dismissed salvation as merely the forgiveness of my sins, whereas it is far more extensive than that. "With long life will I satisfy him, and show him my salvation" (Psalm 91:16, NSRB). Lord, my salvation is an intensely personal thing and Your purpose for me is to show me how Your salvation has worked in my life.

My life is not only afflicted with sin, but with sin's *results*. Those results have permeated every corner of my personality, infecting my feelings, attitudes, and instincts. To be forgiven the *penalty* of my sins is primary and basic, but to be delivered from all the damage sin has done is God's purpose for me until He can bring me to the place where He can *show* me His salvation. The joy of God's salvation is that He sent His Son not only to save sinners but to "save His *people* from their sins" (Matthew 1:21, italics added).

The biblical concept of salvation is basically deliverance. The gospel that Jesus came to proclaim includes the "opening of the prison to those who are bound" (Isaiah 61:1, Berkeley). He not only breaks the chains that bind me, but also leads me out of the prison into sunlight and liberty. He delivers me from the twists and turns of my own deviousness, from surliness and selfishness, from prejudice and hate, from dismal doubt and unbelief, from oppression by Satan and my own ego, and from my inner lustings and cravings. By the time God is finished with me at the end of my life, I will recognize that He has done an amazing work in me; I will "see" His salvation. That in itself will cause me to praise His name everlastingly, and give me the joy of His salvation. Lord, in that day "my tongue shall declare Thy righteousness and Thy praise all day long" (Psalm 35:28).

"And such were some of you; but you were washed, but you were sanctified, but you were justified in the name of the Lord Jesus Christ, and in the Spirit of our God" (1 Corinthians 6:11).

OCTOBER 9
Simple Alternatives

A Christian once said to me, "The Christian life is the simplest in the world—only one Person to please and only one thing to do." True! And Moses the servant of God said so explicitly: "See, I have set before you today life and good, death and evil" (Deuteronomy 30:15, Berkeley). The alternatives are surprisingly clear-cut; yet the results are far-reaching. If I choose to obey God, the result will be "blessing" (v. 19); but if I disobey God, the result will be a "curse" (v.19).

Often I have heard people say, "The Christian life is too hard!" And on occasion I have felt that way myself. Yet Moses says, "The word is very near you, in your mouth and in your heart, *that you may observe it*" (v. 14, italics added). Too often I have been overwhelmed by the goals of the Christian life instead of being concerned about the *conditions*. If I will simply meet the conditions, the goals will take care of themselves.

The Bible knows nothing about instant success. How long did it take God to deliver the Israelites from Egypt? To construct and execute the plan of salvation? There are times when blessing seems to be immediate, when miracles seem to happen on the spot, but the conditions that brought those things about were in operation long before the finished product.

I must concern myself with the elementary: Am I willing to do God's will immediately and thoroughly, without regard for the consequences? If so, God's blessing will assuredly be mine; if not, I will be cursed with the fruits of negligence. Nothing exults the heart of God more than my willingness to follow Him: "The Lord . . . will save. He will rejoice over you with delight . . . He will be joyful over you with singing" (Zephaniah 3:17, Berkeley).

"Bless our God, O peoples, and sound His praise abroad, who keeps us in life, and does not allow our feet to slip" (Psalm 66:8–9).

OCTOBER 10
Noble and Ignoble Servantship

I must not serve God as a handy tool, but as a willing servant. God has used many people in His service, some of them because they were "handy tools" and others because they were servants in heart. God called Nebuchadnezzar "My servant" (Jeremiah 25:9), but that was only because he was a "rod of anger" whom God used to punish His idolatry-filled nation. Nebuchadnezzar's servantship to God was a dubious distinction; he was simply a handy tool whom God needed, not a dedicated servant eager to serve God.

The "handy tool" concept of service is the lowest on the scale. God takes no pride in the man who is merely available, who is simply there. He uses him for a special purpose in spite of the callousness of his heart or the wickedness of his life. "How can God use such a man?" we ask in perplexity. Well, He does, but He does so without respect for the man; He does so because He is sovereign and has the right to use any instrument He chooses.

Simply to be used by God means nothing unless my service is the kind of which God can be proud. Noah was used by God because he had "grace," that is, God found spiritual qualities in him that pleased Him. Jesus was such a delightful Servant that God introduced Him to the whole world as "My beloved Son, in whom I am well-pleased" (Matthew 3:17).

I must never hold up what God has done through me as a sign of my devotion to Him. God has used some very despicable people indeed! But I must pursue after Him until He uses me, not as a handy tool, but for the sake of His own Son whose image He finds exposed in me. My desire is that God will make me "worthy of his calling" and "fulfill every good purpose" in me to the glory of Jesus Christ (2 Thessalonians 1:11–12, NIV).

"For I have come down from heaven, not to do My own will, but the will of Him who sent Me" (John 6:38).

OCTOBER 11
Developing a Sensitivity to Sin

If I am particularly stubborn about a weakness or sin of mine, God may force me to take "the cure." The cure is described in Jeremiah 27:17: "Serve the king of Babylon, and live!" Strange message indeed from a true servant of God, as Jeremiah was. We would expect to hear, "Serve the Lord and live!" But no, the right thing was wrong; the wrong thing was right.

There are times when God allows, and even commands, me to do what He has expressly forbidden. "He that is filthy, let him be filthy still" (Revelation 22:11, NSRB). "Come to Bethel [the house of God], and *transgress*" (Amos 4:4, KJV, italics added). I am horror-struck! Is that because God is unholy? Not in the least. He urges that direction because He is holy; He simply wants me to get my fill of sin so completely that the very thought of it nauseates me. None of the prophets was able to convince Israel to leave their sins; yet seventy years in Babylon did what no prophet could do. He sent them captive into the very fountainhead of idolatry, and they came out a cleansed and purified nation after seven decades.

Must God go to such extremes with me? Must I be submerged in sin in order to see its odiousness? Lord, my prayer is, make me so sensitive to sin that its slightest presence will send me to Calvary's fountain for protection! The distinguishing feature of any true disciple of Christ is paper-thin sensitivity to sin. I notice that in reading the biographies of the saints—the slightest sin made them mourn, weep, and agonize. Lord, make me averse to sin like that, for when I am averse to sin it means the Holy Spirit is deliberately refining me in the divine image; the new heart and the right spirit are displacing the old and the wrong (Psalm 51:10).

"Therefore, since we have so great a cloud of witnesses surrounding us, let us also lay aside every encumbrance, and the sin which so easily entangles us, and let us run with endurance the race that is set before us" (Hebrews 12:1).

OCTOBER 12
God's Tear Bottle

I am comforted when I realize that God is not a vast computer, but a feeling, emotional person, a grander image of myself. He loves, hates, pities, and sympathizes. Nothing proves His large heart of sympathy more than David's words, "Put my tears in Thy bottle; are they not in Thy book?" (Psalm 56:8). God has a personal tear bottle for every one of His children; therefore, there is no sorrow He does not notice and no tear He does not record. Sometimes I weep in public and sometimes in private, but private or public, God catches my falling tears and saves them.

Why does God collect my tears and note my sorrows? I can come to only one conclusion—He is saving them for some tomorrow. There must be a day in the future when God will stop collecting my sorrows and start rewarding me for them. My suffering has a purpose. The tear bottle is the measuring bottle; notched along the sides are marks to indicate how full and complete my suffering has been.

How full is my personal tear bottle, now resting in the Lord's hands? It may never be as full as that of Jeremiah, who wondered if "any sorrow [was] like unto [his] sorrow" (Lamentations 1:12, KJV); or like that of Paul, who "gloried" in his sufferings for Christ's sake (2 Corinthians 11:18, 23); and certainly not like that of Christ, whose tear bottle was big enough to hold the tears of the whole world. Do I weep over my own sins as Job did? Have I broken my heart over the hardness of men as Ezekiel did?

One day God will give me back my tear bottle—whether full or only partly so—and then I will have the privilege of doing what the woman did: pouring it over the feet of Him who both collects and rewards my tears (Luke 7:36–38). Then He will wipe away all tears from my eyes forever (Revelation 21:4).

"The Lord your God is in your midst, a victorious warrior. He will exult over you with joy, He will be quiet in His love, He will rejoice over you with shouts of joy" (Zephaniah 3:17).

OCTOBER 13
Obeying God in the Basics

As a genuine disciple of Jesus Christ I must use the building blocks of growth in their proper order. The first, and most important, building block of all is *obedience*. I must discard the notion that faith, a very important building block, exists by itself. "Faith, if it has no works, is dead" (James 2:17). Obedience is faith acting, the tangible evidence that genuine faith exists on the inside of me. While it is difficult to say which comes first, faith or obedience, without obedience my faith will never grow.

Obedience is also essential to knowledge. My cry for understanding and enlightenment will rise no higher than my head until I put into practice what God has already taught me. It is in the *usage* of my supplies that God multiplies my supplies. If I do not obey God in the basics, He will never lead me on. God never intended for truth to be deposited in the storehouse of my mind, but to be utilized in my life as a power. I will get not one candle more than what I am already using to walk in His way in the midst of the world's darkness.

Obedience is the necessary stepping-stone to fruitfulness and power. We often complain about our lack of power and beg God to hear us and send a blessing. He will send no blessing until we obey the commands He has already given us. Charles G. Finney used to say that churches could have revival the moment they *wanted* it. God's abundant power immediately accompanies the one who obeys Him. I must bring myself back to the basics of discipleship and see that the first building block is in place. Once I begin to obey, God will begin to bless, and He will lead me on until His "grand design" is finished. "For then you will make your way prosperous, and then you will have [good] success" (Joshua 1:8).

"Work out your salvation with fear and trembling; for it is God who is at work in you, both to will and to work for His good pleasure" (Philippians 2:12–13).

OCTOBER 14
The Disconnections of God

The Christian life never moves in a straight line. Certainly it is not a straight line *upward*. Quite often it is a series of apparent contradictions that may leave me perplexed and bewildered. That is *bipolar Christianity*, the Christianity that gives me no room to presume, to relax, or to take God for granted, but that which gives me ample room to trust, to rely on, and to cling to God for support.

There are sharp bipolar experiences that sometimes leave me breathless. For example, God assures me: "I will never leave thee, nor forsake thee" (Hebrews 13:5, KJV); yet my experience quite often is, "Why hast Thou forgotten me?" (Psalm 42:9, KJV), or "Thou art the God of my strength: why dost thou cast me off?" (Psalm 43:2, KJV). I look at the people of the Bible—Joseph, for example—and see how disconnected their lives seemed to be *at the time*. It was only in the "afterward" that Joseph saw any semblance of sense in the way God had led him.

Those are all bipolar experiences! Those men, as all of us, were led from point to point in a seemingly disconnected way, as if God had abandoned His blueprint. There seemed to be no running pattern of continuity in it all. Yet that is God's eternal way with sinful people. The constant shuffling of the nest keeps us constantly clinging to Him for understanding, guidance, and support. God knows what He is doing! I must not judge Him stupid, and certainly not cruel. I must honor Him by trusting Him and please Him by gladly accepting my "disconnections." Nothing delights God's heart more than my trust in Him even when I walk in darkness and have no light. In times like those I am to stay myself upon God (Isaiah 50:10).

"No longer do I call you slaves, for the slave does not know what his master is doing; but I have called you friends, for all things that I have heard from My Father I have made known to you" (John 15:15).

OCTOBER 15
The Dispenser of Rewards

I must not have a mistaken understanding about rewards. Normally, Christians make two mistakes about them: all rewards are *spiritual*, and all rewards are *future*. Not so, in both cases. God has promised many rewards that are to be claimed in this life, and some of them are material.

When the disciples asked what their rewards would be, Jesus replied that no one who had forsaken all for Him would be overlooked. "He shall receive a hundredfold now in this time . . . and in the age to come eternal life" (Mark 10:28–30, ASV margin). Some of the material rewards to be received in this life are things such as houses and land.

That puzzles me, Lord; yet I see what You mean. You do not want me to confuse my *goals* with my *rewards*. I am not to seek houses, properties, and money as a goal; my goal must always be to do God's will, regardless of the consequences. Yet, doing God's will brings its rewards, both spiritual and material, for the present time as well as in the age to come. The Israelites were encouraged to obey God and walk in His ways in order that they would live and multiply and prosper in the land that God gave them (Deuteronomy 30:15–16). As a disciple, however, I must have a slightly different attitude. I must maintain a conscious indifference to material rewards; and, if they come, I must be humbly grateful for them and use them only for the further glory of God, not for selfish ends or aims.

Lord, let me look to You as the Dispenser of both my needs and my rewards; I am encouraged to learn that You reward those who "diligently seek" You (Hebrews 11:6, KJV). But if reward is delayed, may I still glorify You with a thankful heart and a flowing word of praise!

"Behold, I am coming quickly, and My reward is with Me, to render to every man according to what he has done" (Revelation 22:12).

OCTOBER 16
The Aim of Discipleship

A soldier trains for battle, a doctor trains for healing, but what does a disciple train for? He trains for many things but they all focus around two main expressions: he bears the *image* of God, and he speaks the *message* of God.

In order to speak the message of God the disciple must become a prophet. A prophet is not a foreteller, primarily, but a "forthteller," one who hears God speak and delivers the message to God's people. Moses is an example. The Israelites said to him, "Go near and . . . tell us whatever the Lord our God tells you" (Deuteronomy 5:27, NIV). Moses was an intimate of God, and out of that intimacy he learned God's will for the nation; his prophetship was simply telling his people what God wanted them to do and to hear.

Jesus Christ was the perfect Prophet. "This is my beloved Son [that is the intimacy]: hear him [that is the prophetship]" (Luke 9:35, KJV). I cannot expect to speak for God unless I know Him in an intimate way. I cannot speak for God merely by being a theologian; I must speak for God by being His "friend" who speaks to Him "face to face" (Deuteronomy 34:10). Thus, I may be a Sunday school teacher, a salesman, or a housewife and speak for God more authoritatively than a theologian, a pastor, or a missionary.

No one can presume to be a prophet; he must be called to it by God Himself. Yet I can "desire" the gift of prophecy (1 Corinthians 14:1) and prepare myself as fully as possible for the function by an avid pursuit of God and His person. A God-hungry person soon becomes a God-filled person, then he becomes a God-explaining person. What a joy to be a God-explaining person, one who invitingly says: "Taste and see that the Lord is *good*" (Psalm 34:8, italics added).

"But you are a chosen race, a royal priesthood, a holy nation, a people for God's own possession, that you may proclaim the excellencies of Him who has called you out of darkness into His marvelous light" (1 Peter 2:9).

OCTOBER 17
Praying for Spiritual Results

I must not give up easily on prayer, even in the bleakest and most discouraging circumstances. I must look upon a prayer as a challenge, a sort of spiritual dare that the Lord throws my way. Look at Ishmael, Abraham's son through Hagar. God said of him, "He shall be as a wild ass among men; his hand shall be against every man, and every man's hand against him" (Genesis 16:12, ASV). What a doleful future! What a challenge to prayer!

Did Abraham sit down, wring his hands, and accept an impossible situation? No. For thirteen long, wearisome years he prayed. He prayed that what God foretold as Ishmael's *natural* future would not come to pass, but that instead God would turn the natural course of events in his life and bring about one of those sweet miracles of God, a transformed Ishmael. God answered his heartfelt prayer for his first-born son. "As for Ishmael, I have *heard* you; behold, I will bless him, and will make him fruitful, and will multiply him exceedingly" (Genesis 17:20a). No longer a wild ass of a man, Ishmael was to be "blessed." No longer a thorn in everyone's side, he was to be "the father of twelve princes" and the father of a "great nation" (v. 20b).

I confess, Lord, my sin of hasty impatience and easy discouragement in prayer. How often I have given up on someone by saying, "He's too tough a case; he's beyond help." Or I have given up because results were not immediate. Forgive me, Lord, for the sin of letting natural results happen instead of changing the natural into the spiritual, changing the wild asses into princes. I look at the father heart of Abraham and say, "Lord, give me a heart like that; let my Ishmael become a prince!"

"But let him ask in faith without any doubting, for the one who doubts is like the surf of the sea driven and tossed by the wind. For let not that man expect that he will receive anything from the Lord" (James 1:6–7).

OCTOBER 18
Love's Need

I have been taught from my youth that God is the self-existing and self-sufficient One. And He is, indeed. Yet the Bible tells me "God is love" (1 John 4:16), and at once I am confronted with a profundity. If God is love then God has a need, for love must always have an object. That need is certainly fulfilled in God Himself, for God is a Trinity and each Person of the Trinity is loved by the others. And yet the Bible says God loves the world (John 3:16). He loves not only Himself; He also loves the human race, and He loves *me!*

If God loves me, He needs me, for the object of one's love is necessary to the happiness and welfare of the lover. The Lover of the souls of men needs lovers; the worshiped One needs worshipers. When Jesus said to the woman of Samaria, "Give Me a drink" (John 4:7), He was expressing not merely a physical need but an emotional one, as the sequence of the story reveals. Love was in need of love; the water of life was in need of satisfaction. How else can I explain the convulsive weeping of Jesus as He overlooked the city of Jerusalem from one of its hills and realized that they had rejected Him? It was love frustrated and tormented, love denied its rightful objects.

How often I have treated my quiet time as "Give me" time, when I am concerned with my emptiness, my weakness, my weariness, and my sinfulness. My, my, my! I fail to see that Jesus Christ also has a need. He needs my love, worship, obedience, and above all, my company. I need to sit by His side as a dear friend, sharing His heart secrets as He shares mine, rejoicing in the mutual balance of our love. Lord, let me not deny You that small cup of water, and that simple invitation, "Give Me a drink!"

"And He said to him, 'You shall love the Lord your God with all your heart, and with all your soul, and with all your mind'" (Matthew 22:37).

OCTOBER 19

Love's Purity

It is a heartwarming truth that "the Lord is my portion" (Lamentations 3:24), but it is equally true that "the Lord's portion is His people" (Deuteronomy 32:9). I have often gloried in the fact that God is my joy, my inheritance, my future. But I have often forgotten that I am His joy, His inheritance, His future. He told Moses and the Israelites to build Him a home in the desert of Sinai "that I may dwell among them" (Exodus 25:8). God loves to be in the midst of His people, sharing their joys and sorrows and receiving their love and praise.

When Jesus sat with His disciples the night before His crucifixion, He asked them to remember Him (Luke 22:19). The wistfulness of a deeply loving heart is evident in that request. Love cannot stand alienation or neglect. Jesus did not rebuke Mary for pouring expensive perfume over His feet. It was the largess of love, the gratuity of love. When we pour out such an expression to Him, He rejoices with great gladness of heart.

Jesus asked Simon Peter a pertinent question, "Lovest thou me more than these?" (John 21:15, KJV). Love cannot stand a rival. Jesus calls me to love without limit, hesitation, or condition. That is the way He is: "God *so* loved the world" (John 3:16, italics added). I must so love Him! He measures my love by His own, not in amount but in quality. He cannot stand divided, spoiled, or lukewarm love. He is pleased only by His kind of love reflected in me. Let me not hesitate or hold back by so high a standard of love, for "the Lord [will] direct [our] hearts into the love of God" (2 Thessalonians 3:5). His help is assured when my spiritual love life flags and grows thin.

"Jesus said therefore to the twelve, 'You do not want to go away also, do you?' Simon Peter answered Him, 'Lord, to whom shall we go? You have words of eternal life'" (John 6:67–68).

OCTOBER 20
What God Does with Ruined Things

I must realize that God's ways are not my ways, and that is especially true in dealing with ruined things. My first inclination, when confronted with ruin, is to say, "It's finished, it's done, that's all there is to it." But God never gives up on a ruin; in fact, He begins with ruins and works on them until He transforms them into things of beauty, "beauty for ashes" (Isaiah 61:3, KJV). Ruined things are my defeat, but to God they are opportunity.

When the earth was "without form, and void" (Genesis 1:2, KJV), God sent His Spirit and His light to bring order out of chaos and beauty out of blackness. What He did physically for the original earth He does spiritually for people. It is a truth—there are no ruined people in God's category, only opportunities for God to display His creative power. There are no hopeless aspects of my personality, only aspects that are waiting to be touched by the power-driven fingers of God.

The greatest ruin of all was Calvary, and look how God turned that horrible nightmare into the cradle of salvation for all men. Is my problem worse than Calvary? Is any problem more bleak, more foreboding than that? The disciples—like all of us—considered Calvary a hopeless smashing of all their plans and dreams. They forsook Christ, fled for their lives, and considered all their work so much debris. Yet, by the third day their evening turned to morning and a complete restoration of their ruin took place. What a God! That is how He treats ruins, whether His Son's or mine! If I let Him, He will take the shattered portions of my life and build them into a breathtaking ornament of beauty. Such a God is He!

"Fear not, for you will not be put to shame; neither feel humiliated, for you will not be disgraced; but you will forget the shame of your youth, and the reproach of your widowhood you will remember no more" (Isaiah 54:4).

OCTOBER 21
God Blesses Our Intentions

The difference between successful and unsuccessful discipleship is not in the number of talents I possess, but in how willing I am to allow God to help me in what I *cannot* do. The paralyzed man was healed because he allowed the surging power of Jesus Christ to do what he could not do (John 5:8–9). The man's yearning to be healed triggered the healing process and made him start to rise, but Christ's power added the difference between his lack of power and the complete healing.

If God were to bless me for only what I did, I would be a sorry disciple indeed. But He blesses me for what I *intend* to do, *yearn* to do for Him, except I lack the power. That is where God comes in, adding His limitless power to my limited intention, and the results are delightful.

Think of Abraham and Isaac on Mount Moriah. In obedience to God's order, Abraham fully intended to offer his son on the altar of sacrifice. But God stopped the offering before Abraham could plunge the knife into his son. Yet, amazingly, God said to Abraham, "Because you . . . have not withheld your son, your only son, indeed I will greatly bless you" (Genesis 22:16–17). Abraham *did* withhold his son; but because the yearning and intention of his heart were so set on obeying the command of God, the Lord took the intention for the deed, and rewarded Abraham accordingly.

I see now what David meant when he said God will give me "the desires of [my] heart" (Psalm 37:4). God will enable me to fulfill my spiritual desires beyond my own capability; yet He will reward me for them as if I had done them on my own. The glory of the Christian life is not "I—struggling," but "God and I—overcoming!" Such a God is ours.

"Thou hast dealt well with Thy servant, O Lord, according to Thy word. Teach me good discernment and knowledge, for I believe in Thy commandments" (Psalm 119:65–66).

OCTOBER 22
Claiming the Portion

The prodigal son (Luke 15) is God's reminder to me of what happens when I say to Him, "Hands off my life!" That unfortunate son, by taking his inheritance and clearing out, was saying to his father, "From now on I'll be my own master." He denied his father the right to direct him, which in essence was a denial of his father's love and integrity.

Every disobedient Christian is an unconscious blasphemer. The moment I strike out for the far country, that moment I have condemned the character of God before the world. The pity is that, in the long run, I do not hurt God, I only hurt myself. The father's reputation did not suffer, but the son wound up in the pigpen. If I take my life into my own hands, I will be a candidate for the pigpen also. The choice is mine: either the warmth of the Father's house, or else the cold, bleak wetness of the pigsty.

The prodigal son made another mistake: demanding his inheritance *now*, instead of waiting his father's time. By his impatience the son plucked his inheritance while it was green, unready. How often have I done that! My craving nature has cried out, "Now, Lord, now!" Then I discovered my mistake and did not enjoy my portion at all. If only I had waited!

I must learn never to snatch from God's hands His daily care, guidance, and provision for my life. I must not say, "Lord, give me what is mine," but "Lord, give me only what is Yours." The difference is peace, utter peace. Further, when I "wait" on the Lord, I shall never be "put to shame"—be disappointed with His portion (Psalm 25:3, ASV).

"They will bow down to you with their faces to the earth, and lick the dust of your feet; and you will know that I am the Lord; those who hopefully wait for Me will not be put to shame" (Isaiah 49:23).

OCTOBER 23
When God Grows Weary

Isaiah the prophet reminds me that the God who never grows weary *can and does* grow weary. A contradiction? No. God never grows *physically* "weary" (Isaiah 40:28), but He does grow *morally* "weary" (Isaiah 1:14). Nothing can exhaust the Almighty's energy, but my lame, empty sacrifice can cause Him to say: "I have had enough" (1:11); "I take no pleasure in [them]" (v. 11); "I cannot endure [them]" (v. 13); "they have become a burden to Me" (v. 14).

Strong language! But no stronger than the feelings God has toward any hypocrisy He finds in me. He cannot abide the difference between a good sacrifice (legally) and a bad heart (spiritually). Neither can He abide the imbalance between a strong, loud profession and a shoddy life. God's weariness is His annoyance, His outrage at the coldhearted and perfunctory way I present my offerings to Him. He is never weary of receiving contrite sinners, but He tires of my "motional" Christianity without love.

To weary God is a serious matter; it can mean the death of my prayer life. "Though you multiply prayers, I will not listen" (Isaiah 1:15). God will not join the game we are playing. If we trifle with Him and treat Him as an unnecessary appendage, He will break His lines of communication with us and our prayers will become so much wasted air. Thus, by playing it cool and casual, I may unconsciously abort many blessings God had planned to give me. I cannot afford to be without His blessings; therefore, I must not offer Him shoddy love or lame devotion. The kind of offering He yearns for is the "freewill" kind: "With a freewill offering I will sacrifice to Thee; I will praise Thy name, O Lord, for it is good" (Psalm 54:6, Berkeley).

"Wash yourselves, make yourselves clean; remove the evil of your deeds from My sight. Cease to do evil, learn to do good; seek justice, reprove the ruthless; defend the orphan, plead for the widow" (Isaiah 1:16–17).

OCTOBER 24
Exhibiting the Light

Every disciple is called to be an exhibitionist, in the proper usage of the word. Moses instructed Aaron, the high priest, to arrange the seven lamps of the lampstand in the tabernacle so that the light shone "outward" (Numbers 8:3, Berkeley). The purpose of the lamps was to provide the light in which the priests could carry on their work.

I am sure that is what Jesus had in mind when He said, "So let your light shine before men; that they may see your good works, and glorify your Father who is in Heaven" (Matthew 5:16, ASV). I am to exhibit the glory of God, and the only way I can do so is to let that glory be transmitted through me.

But light can be *hidden*. Jesus urged us not to put our light "under a bushel" (Matthew 5:15, KJV). My light must be exposed; it must be set free to shine in public. I must avoid a monasticism or a separationism that would keep me from the kind of contact with the world in which I confront it as light. Even my church, with its high, ornate walls and stained-glass windows, can be a smotherer of the light. The lamps must be "turned outward" so that their benefit may not be lost to those who need it most.

Light can also be *extinguished*. The natural enemy of light is not darkness, but water and wind, which may extinguish it. I must not "quench the Spirit" (1 Thessalonians 5:19), which is another way of saying that I must keep my light fed with oil; I must not let it be blown out by the winds of disobedience to God's will, and I must not douse it with opposition and rebellion.

"Turn the lamps outward." The gloom-filled world outside needs the light; therefore, it needs me. Not the doubting, hesitating, fearful me, but the Spirit-controlled, joyful, self-giving me. Then I shall become a child of God "without blemish" and shine as a light in a dark world (Philippians 2:15, ASV).

"Each man's work will become evident; for the day will show it, because it is to be revealed with fire; and the fire itself will test the quality of each man's work" (1 Corinthians 3:13).

OCTOBER 25
Being Divisive for Christ

I must remember that Jesus Christ is not only a great tension *reliever*, but also a tension *bringer*. If I expect Him to relieve all my tensions, I have a vain expectancy. Merely to know and follow Jesus will create all kinds of problems for me. Mary, His mother, received that word when she gave Him birth: "A sword will pierce even your own soul" (Luke 2:35).

Have I felt the piercing of my soul because of my commitment to Christ? Have I lost friends, seen families divided, or seen increasing bitterness among acquaintances because I determined to make Him my all? Mary must have gone through a thousand agonies once Christ was born. There must have been tension in the home. "Neither did his brethren believe in him" (John 7:5, KJV). How did Mary manage to referee between her holy Son and her other natural children? How could she stand their hatred of Him, knowing all the while who He was? When Jesus later said, "A prophet is not without honor except in his home town" (Matthew 13:57), was He referring to the daily snubs of His half brothers and sisters?

Jesus said He "did not come to bring peace, but a sword" (Matthew 10:34); He came to make mothers and daughters and fathers and sons one another's enemies (v. 35). I am a very poor disciple indeed if I cannot name one person who has been offended because I chose to follow Him. But I must be careful that it is for *His* sake that enemies are made, not for my own. When my own rights and privileges are concerned, I must be as harmless as a dove; but when His rights and privileges are concerned, I must be a militant warrior. Lord, give me wisdom to discern when I must be militant; then give me the assurance of Jeremiah: "The Lord is with me as a fear-inspiring warrior. Therefore my persecutors will stumble" (Jeremiah 20:11, Berkeley).

"If you are reviled for the name of Christ, you are blessed, because the Spirit of glory and of God rests upon you" (1 Peter 4:14).

OCTOBER 26
Losing the Power of Christ

I must distinguish between my *union* with Christ, which is secure, and my *communion* with Christ, which is extremely fragile. I must not delude myself into thinking that while my relationship to Christ is secure, so is my awareness of His presence and power. There are things I can lose.

I can lose the presence and power of Christ as easily as Mary and Joseph lost Him in the caravan returning home from Jerusalem (Luke 2:41–49). By neglecting Him I can allow the weeds to grow in our relationship, choking out the fruits of a close, sweet walk with Him. Neglect needs no overt action, no sharp disobedience, just a dulling of the finely tuned relationship we once had. Then He is gone!

Or I can lose Him as Mary Magdalene lost Him, in the mad chain of circumstances that led Him to His death on the cross. The swirling turn of events that snatched Him from her was beyond her understanding, but her loss was just as real and as painful. So God can send a series of devastating losses into my life, involving friends, loved ones, opportunities, or whatever. If I turn my attention to my losses and take my eyes off Him, I will lose Him in the flow.

I can also lose Him by my sin and indifference, and hear Him say, "Your sin and iniquities have separated . . . you and your God" (Isaiah 59:2, NSRB). Of all the reasons for losing Christ, that is the most reprehensible, because it indicates a deliberate evaluation and a choice: I want sin, not Jesus. If I choose sin, Jesus withdraws and I am left only with my immoral choice.

Thank You, God, that You will never be untouched by my tears of repentance; "a broken and a contrite heart, O God, thou wilt not despise" (Psalm 51:17). You quickly restore the "joy of thy salvation" (v. 12).

"Thou hast tried my heart; Thou hast visited me by night; Thou hast tested me and dost find nothing; I have purposed that my mouth will not transgress" (Psalm 17:3).

OCTOBER 27

Sharpening Our Awareness of Christ

There is another way in which I may lose the presence of Jesus Christ, one that is difficult to understand and accept, but nevertheless true. It is the voluntary withdrawal of Christ Himself. There are times when He seems to withdraw Himself from us without any discernible reason. Yet the reason may be suggested in the Song of Solomon, where the Shulammite bride of Solomon complains twice about the absence of her lover. "I sought him whom my soul loves . . . but did not find him; I called him, but he did not answer" (Song of Solomon 3:1, Berkeley). The bride had done nothing to offend her husband; yet he was gone and could not be found. Again she says, "My Beloved had turned away; he was gone!" (5:6, Berkeley). Again she sought him and called to him, but he did not answer.

What is the Lord saying to me here? That the love of Christ to me is discerned in both the *partings* and the *meetings*, in both His presence and His apparent absence. I can understand how His presence enhances the love relationship between us, but how can His absence do so? Perhaps we will never know all the answers, but His seeming absence sharpens our awareness of Him and crushes the tendency to take Him for granted.

Very few (actually, I believe none) of the disciples of Jesus Christ enjoy the continual, unbroken realization of His presence and power in their lives. Many times we call but He does not answer; we seek Him but He withdraws from us. The reason is not always due to sin, carelessness, or indifference, for sometimes He is hiding His face to make us yearn all the more for Him; His absence will make our love grow sharper and fonder. If I lose Him for that reason, I must simply seek Him with my whole heart until I find Him again. I must do as the Shulammite did, "seek him whom my soul loves" (Song of Solomon 3:2, Berkeley), and soon I will be able to say with her, "I found him whom my soul loves" (v. 4, Berkeley).

"O God, do not remain quiet; do not be silent and, O God, do not be still" (Psalm 83:1).

OCTOBER 28
When God Separates Us

When I first became a Christian I was taught that I must be "separate," that is, I must cut all ties with evil and worldly associations. On the strength of Paul's admonition, that is a necessary thing to do (2 Corinthians 6:14–18). But I soon discovered that God did some "separating" of His own, a separation from my own brothers and sisters in Christ. Of Joseph it was said that he was "separated from his brethren" (Deuteronomy 33:16, KJV). That separation took place when God determined that Joseph was to be the "prince" of the family, and it was effected when his brothers sold him as a slave into Egypt. The man separated by God was then separated from his family, and all for an important reason.

Joseph's separation from his family was necessary in order to make possible his rise to the Egyptian throne, which made possible the cradling and growing of the infant nation Israel. Unless Joseph had been "separated," Israel would have been destroyed by powerful enemies.

Immediately after his conversion, Paul "conferred not with flesh and blood" but went into the desert of Arabia, separated from his brothers. This was another of God's separations, and it rendered Paul unspoiled to be a fresh, open messenger to the Gentiles (Galatians 1:15–17, KJV).

I am to separate myself from evil; the responsibility is mine alone. But only God can separate me from my "brothers," a separation that is designed to create a special messenger, a special voice, to communicate His message in a given, and sometimes crucial, situation. If God separates me, I must accept it without question, knowing that separation from my brothers is a transitory phase of my ministry for God that always results in "good" (Genesis 50:20), both for my brothers and for me.

"And while they were ministering to the Lord and fasting, the Holy Spirit said, 'Set apart for Me Barnabas and Saul for the work to which I have called them'" (Acts 13:2).

OCTOBER 29
Self-Separation

God's separations, however necessary, may be painful, but never as painful as the separations I bring on myself. Moses had to run away from his brothers in Egypt because he killed an Egyptian taskmaster (Exodus 2:11–15). His was a separation of self-will, violence, and fear. If I try to do God's will in the same way, I will find myself "separated" also, but it will be a painful separation.

Lot, Abraham's nephew, suffered the same fate. Unable to control his quarreling herdsmen, Lot chose to leave Abraham and settle in the Jordan Valley "as far as Sodom" (Genesis 13:8–13). The results are well known.

Yet, despite my hasty, self-centered separations, God is still the overruling and overwhelming Master of all separations. He used the separation of Moses to prepare both him and the nation for the mighty Exodus from Egypt. And despite Lot's pitiful attempt to witness for God in a sinful environment, God delivered him out of the holocaust as a permanent witness to His faithfulness in answering prayer.

During my life of discipleship for Christ, I will have to face many separations. Some I must initiate on my own, for I must have no fellowship with the works of darkness. Others God will initiate, as He separates me from my brothers for a time and for a special purpose. And still others I will stumble into because of my impetuousness and miscalculation, resulting in pain and embarrassment, but also producing deliverance and triumph as I turn the tangled strands over to God for His solution.

How wonderful is our God, who provides an "exodus" for us from every painful, hurting separation! "Surely His salvation [deliverance] is near [at hand] to those who fear Him" (Psalm 85:9).

"And there arose such a sharp disagreement that they separated from one another, and Barnabas took Mark with him and sailed away to Cyprus" (Acts 15:39).

OCTOBER 30
Separation for the Sake of Others

My perfect example in separation is Jesus Christ, who said, "For their sakes I sanctify [separate] Myself" (John 17:19). He separated Himself from His environment in order that He might enter this world and win back to His Father the people who had been separated from Him because of sin.

The separation of Jesus was voluntary: "I sanctify Myself." The only compulsion that drove Him was that of love. He did not come as a commercializer to do it for profit, except *our* profit. He became separate in a free response to His Father's will, seeking only to behave and act within the limits and guidelines of that will. Of course, in doing His Father's will He was "separated from sinners" (Hebrews 7:26), that is, separated from their plans, purposes, and acts. But He was not separated from the *society* of sinners. He was separated from *human nature* in its fallenness, but He was never separated from human beings.

The separation of Jesus was positive in its purpose, "that they . . . may be sanctified [separated] in truth" (John 17:19, ASV). He did not consider separation as an end in itself. The objective was to return an alienated race back to its fountainhead, back to its proper beginnings. Thus the pain of separation was all His, but the blessing of it was all ours.

God will call me to separation often, because He has people to reach and to reconcile. May I be as self-denying as Jesus was, and as full of love. May I be willing to leave my family, lifestyle, and personal goals in favor of the lost who need to be brought in. And may I always make a sharp distinction between separation from men and separation from their fallen nature. The greatest joy of self-separation is: "They have believed" (John 17:8, KJV). In the light of that, it will all have been worthwhile.

"For you know the grace of our Lord Jesus Christ, that though He was rich, yet for your sake He became poor, that you through His poverty might become rich" (2 Corinthians 8:9).

OCTOBER 31
Immortality by Works

I must realize that there are several kinds of immortality. First, there is *natural* immortality, the simple endless existence of all human beings, whether saved or lost. Second, there is *everlasting*, or eternal, *life*, which is referred to in the Bible as qualitative life, rather than simple duration. That is the kind of immortality every believer in Jesus Christ receives the moment he is "born again" (John 3:3). It is a "gift of God," apart from any good works (Ephesians 2:8–9).

The third kind of immortality is the *immortality of works*. That kind of immortality is an achievement by my own effort. It is said of Abel that because he offered his sacrifice by faith, he, being dead, "yet speaketh" (Hebrews 11:4, KJV). Men can achieve an immortality of works that are violent, cruel, and merciless, but God's men can achieve an immortality of works only by faith. That is, the life that is lived in simple dependence upon God carries in it the seeds of its own immortality. God will "testify" of that simple life forever. Good works done in simple dependence upon God will live forever. That is the kind of "forever" John referred to when he said, "The one who does the will of God abides forever" (1 John 2:17). That kind of immortality is better than either the natural or the eternal because it carries God's peculiar honor; it is "better" (Hebrews 11:35).

I must not merely live; I must live so that I will be remembered after I die. The only way to do so is the way of Abel, a man who lived by faith and is remembered with honor—God's honor and men's. That way I will earn another one of the blesseds: "Blessed are the dead who [keep the commandments of God, and] die in the Lord . . . [for] their works do follow them" (Revelation 14:13, NSRB).

"I have set the Lord continually before me; because He is at my right hand, I will not be shaken. Therefore my heart is glad, and my glory rejoices; my flesh also will dwell securely" (Psalm 16:8–9).

NOVEMBER 1
The Savior of Our Bodies

My body is included in Christ's redemption of me. "Body redemption" has two aspects: *glorification*, which will occur when Christ returns, and *deliverance*, which occurs now in this life. Too often I have been occupied with the future glorification of my body and have not given enough attention to its present need of deliverance.

The Holy Spirit is in charge of my body (Romans 8:11). He "quickens" (gives life to) my body when it flags and sinks under the load of ill health, fatigue, satanic opposition, or old age. The Holy Spirit is under orders to keep my body functioning until my work on earth is done. He is also under orders to give whatever level of life my body needs to accomplish a particular command of God. Abraham and Sarah had "old" bodies, bodies that by nature had ceased to produce children; yet God had promised them a son, Isaac. Their faith in God's revealed word, plus the activating power of the Holy Spirit, rejuvenated their bodies to such an extent that Isaac was conceived and brought to birth (Hebrews 11:11–12).

Body deliverance is not automatic; it must be claimed by faith and appropriation. Whenever I feel myself physically overwhelmed, I must "wait for the Lord" (Isaiah 40:31). He then renews my strength and makes me soar like an eagle. However, I must realize that sometimes God refuses deliverance and allows my body to suffer in order to give me some new understanding or perception of His ways. In either case, I am to allow the Master of my body to have His way with me. Of this I am sure, He is as concerned about my body as He is about my spirit. Whenever necessary, the same Savior who was Himself strengthened in His severest agony (Luke 22:43) will not fail me in mine.

"Who will transform the body of our humble state into conformity with the body of His glory, by the exertion of the power that He has even to subject all things to Himself" (Philippians 3:21).

NOVEMBER 2
The Great Inexplicable

When I ask God to help me, I must let Him choose the method. Long ago He said He would deliver Judah "not . . . by bow, or sword, or war, or horses, or horsemen" (Hosea 1:7, Berkeley). A strange way to wage war, with no weapons! And yet God in His sovereign power chooses His own way to fight, even as He did one night when He destroyed Sennacherib's army of 185,000 men around Jerusalem (Isaiah 37:36). How did He do it? To this day, nobody knows.

God must be God, and He must be God in His own way. John the Baptist said to Jesus, "Are you the Coming One or should we look for someone else?" (Matthew 11:3, Berkeley). What a surprising question from the man who introduced Jesus to the Jewish people as their Messiah! Because Jesus had not set up His Kingdom and mounted the throne, John thought maybe Jesus was not the long-awaited One. But it was John who made the mistake. His job was to *announce* Jesus, not *explain* Him. Jesus is the great inexplicable who moves by His own will.

Anyone can buy a "porcelain Jesus" from a novelty store, but we will never find that kind of Jesus in the Bible. There He is Someone who is living, moving, vital, and sovereign. Try to reduce Him to porcelain or plaster and He will be gone.

His message to me is always "Follow *Me*," and that is exactly what I must do—follow, follow, follow. If I try to bend Him toward my way for my purposes, He will pay no attention. I must learn this lesson carefully and say, "Whither *thou* goest, I will go" (Ruth 1:16, KJV, italics added). Less than that is painful loss. But to do it affords me life's great attainment, not necessarily to understand Jesus, but to be rightly related to Him (John 12:26). That means that when I serve and obey, He assures me of His company and His praise.

"Blessed be the God and Father of our Lord Jesus Christ, who according to His great mercy has caused us to be born again to a living hope through the resurrection of Jesus Christ from the dead" (1 Peter 1:3).

NOVEMBER 3
Brinkmanship and Discipleship

The life of victory begins, not with a sense of fullness, but with a sense of emptiness. Too often I am occupied with victory instead of being occupied with need. I will never develop strong, vibrant faith without a feeling of helplessness and, sometimes, despair. When Jesus rebuked His disciples with "O ye of little faith" (Matthew 8:26, KJV), He implied that they had failed to recognize their great need; hence, they felt no compunction to beg from God. People who are self-satisfied never have great faith.

How do I become filled with righteousness? By hungering and thirsting after it (Matthew 5:6). If I take care of the need, God will take care of the supply. The men who joined David's rebel army were men who were "in distress . . . in debt, and . . . discontented" (1 Samuel 22:2). They cherished visions of victory, triumph, and justice; but their road to those aspirations was made possible by a realization of their distress. So I cannot achieve victory in my personal discipleship for Jesus Christ until I have come to the end of myself. In that sense I am a "brinkmanship disciple" who is delivered from the edge and rendered victorious by His power.

I sense a need when I take a good look at myself—a good, honest look and not an idealistic one. I am admonished, "Look within and be distressed." Of course, but I need to be distressed; how else would I ever "look to Jesus and be at rest"? I must see my sin, my emptiness, my corruption. Once I really see it, it will not be long before I cry to heaven for help, and that help will not be long in coming. The vacuum created by my need will draw all the supplies that I desperately long for from heaven. The beginning of thirst is the beginning of blessing!

"Why are you in despair, O my soul? And why are you disturbed within me? Hope in God, for I shall again praise Him, the help of my countenance, and my God" (Psalm 43:5).

NOVEMBER 4
Friendship with God

I must not be satisfied with being a *follower* of God; I must become a *friend* of God. Friendship is a polarization of interests, and I must get beyond the point of simply using God as an insurance policy or a life preserver. Friends do not exploit each other, and I must never use my relationship with God as a handy ticket to success or an easy means out of a messy situation.

"Can two walk together, except they be agreed?" (Amos 3:3, NSRB). It is possible for a man and woman to be organically related (one flesh) in marriage and yet not be friends. It is possible for two people to be economically related (master and servant) and not be friends. That is why Jesus told His disciples, "No longer do I call you servants . . . but . . . friends" (John 15:15, ASV). They were no longer merely to follow directives, but to be "in" on the plans and purposes of the Father; their interests were polarized. Jesus made it clear that friendship with Him is not automatic; not all believers are His "friends." Only those who are willing to abandon their interests for His are accepted into the inner circle.

Friendship with God carries its own honor. Israel was God's "servant," Jacob was God's "chosen one," but Abraham was God's "friend" (Isaiah 41:8). The difference is not one of relationship, since all belonged to God, but of intimacy, for only Abraham was admitted to God's inner councils. I must convince God that His interests are mine, that His welfare is my welfare, and that His plans and purposes for this world are mine also. If God prizes holiness, so must I. If He delights in His Son, I must delight in Him also. In short, whatever is of interest, moment, and importance to God must be so to me. Then, and only then, will I become God's *friend*.

"Draw near to God and He will draw near to you. Cleanse your hands, you sinners; and purify your hearts, you double-minded" (James 4:8).

NOVEMBER 5
Friendship with the World

I must realize that friendship is a choice, and the act of choosing is a sword that cuts two ways. I cannot choose a friend without at the same time choosing an enemy. If I choose holiness, I reject sin, and vice versa. I understand now what James meant when he said, "Do you not know that friendship with the world is hostility toward God? Therefore whoever wishes to be a friend of the world makes himself an enemy of God" (James 4:4).

The Jews said to Pilate, "If you release this Man [Jesus], you are no friend of Caesar" (John 19:12). I am known not only by my friends, but also by my enemies. Pilate and Herod were bitter enemies until they both rejected Jesus; the rejection of their common enemy, Jesus, forced them into each other's arms of friendship (Luke 23:12).

I see now why God becomes so heated when His people get chummy with the world or idols or with the mammon of unrighteousness. To accept *them* is to reject *Him*. Friendship by its very nature denies a universal, all-inclusive embrace. Friendship is selective. It thrives on exclusive choices. So it is natural that God, who desires the warmth and love of my heart, should become "jealous" when He sees me consorting with those who hate Him.

Jesus Christ is constantly looking for friends. When He called Judas "friend" in the moment of his betrayal, He was revealing an innate yearning. Even for those who oppose Him, the door of friendship is always open, but always of course on the conditions He lays down. Judas was a friend in invitation only. I must go beyond; I must be a friend to Him in reality. The *condition* of being Christ's friend is to "do what I command you" (John 15:14, Berkeley). The *honor* of being His friend is to talk to Him "face to face" in sublime intimacy (Exodus 33:11).

"Or do you think that the Scripture speaks to no purpose: 'He jealously desires the Spirit which He has made to dwell in us'?" (James 4:5).

NOVEMBER 6
Fitness for Service

Lord, I need to understand the difference between being *called* to service and *fitness* for service. I have nothing to do with the call. It is beyond me and lies deep in the sovereign will of God. When it comes to fitness for service I must remember that there are two aspects to it: First, God's provision for my fitness is by equipping me with the gifts of the Spirit (1 Corinthians 12:4–11). These gifts, like the call, are God's prerogative alone; I am merely their channel. Second, my provision for my fitness is by being at my spiritual best at all times.

I take my cue from the Old Testament priest. He could not be blind (Leviticus 21:18). No sightless man was allowed to minister in the holy place, and the implications of that are pertinent to *me*; I may not minister God's truth to others unless I *see*—see Him, and them, and it. I have no business talking about something that is not really part of me; I may not be a "professional" disciple. I love that word from the Ascent Psalms, "Her priests . . . I will clothe with salvation" (Psalm 132:16). My whole business as God's priest is to be about "salvation." I am to be engaged in salvaging people from their sins, their failures, their evil desires, and their corrupted habits. But I must remember that to be a spokesman for salvation means I must be an example of it, right down to my "clothing."

I cannot call myself to minister, nor can I endow myself with the spiritual necessities; but I can make myself fit by knowing God, walking with Him, and keeping myself spiritually clean and effective. Who is sufficient for these things? No one! But "our sufficiency is God-given. And He has qualified us to be ministers of a new covenant" (2 Corinthians 3:5–6, Berkeley).

"Who gave Himself for us, that He might redeem us from every lawless deed and purify for Himself a people for His own possession, zealous for good deeds" (Titus 2:14).

NOVEMBER 7
Developing an Ear for God

I pray that God will enable me to become a good *listener*. I must understand that God does not speak to me in the storm, the earthquake, or the fire, but in the "still small voice" (1 Kings 19:9–12, KJV). That is another way of saying that God does not speak to me through circumstances or through others *unless* there is an inner confirmation and explanation of what comes from the outside. Eli, the old priest, was wise enough to know that God's will for Samuel, his aide, had to come directly from God to Samuel: "Speak, Lord, for Thy servant is listening" (1 Samuel 3:9).

Today's complex life is the deadliest enemy of listening. The result of our complexity is fragmentation, thinness, and the inability to concentrate or become deep about anything. Satan is the happiest heir of our technological age, and he enjoys slapping us about like a handball. I must resist him by deliberately choosing essentials and rejecting the gadfly activities that render me ineffective.

How do I learn to be a good listener to God? I must begin by giving Him *time* and *attention*. That is the crucial part of the battle. I must reject the siren calls that tell me to be everything to everybody, and simply concentrate on God. Next I must develop a sense of *awe and reverence* for God, which is a natural preparation for silence, which in turn is essential to proper listening. Once I develop an ear for God, I will be able to hear Him even in crowds and, as Brother Lawrence says, "Go forward even in sleep."

Listening to God is difficult to master, but the results will be beyond my greatest longings. He says, "Listen carefully to Me, and eat what is good, and delight yourself in abundance" (Isaiah 55:2). God knows that listening is but the first step of a process that ends in my eternal good.

"I will stand on my guard post and station myself on the rampart; and I will keep watch to see what He will speak to me, and how I may reply when I am reproved" (Habakkuk 2:1).

NOVEMBER 8
God's Tender Care for Us

I am impressed, Lord, by the tenderness of Your care for Your overworked servants. How sharply You know the difference between laziness and fatigue! Your treatment of Your servant Elijah is a revelation and a comfort to me.

After his tense confrontation with the priests of Baal on Mount Carmel, Elijah fled for his life, with the threats of Jezebel still ringing in his ears. "He was afraid" (1 Kings 19:3). His weariness and fatigue had invaded his spirit, and his faith fled. That led to depression: "Lord, take away my life" (v. 4, KJV). The intense, highly strung prophet was in the midst of an emotional collapse. He had overextended himself in God's work.

How did God respond to his broken faith, his anxiety, his depression? "Arise and eat" (v. 5, KJV). Twice the Lord told him to partake of food, "or the journey will be too much for you" (v. 7, Berkeley). God began His ministry to Elijah by ministering to his body. How often it is my body, instead of my spirit, that needs help. I must look upon both—body and spirit—as an integral, closely knit team. When one of them suffers, so does the other; and when breakdown occurs, I must ask, Where did it begin? I must not, of course, let my body become my all-demanding king before which everything must bow. On the other hand, I must not neglect my body as if it were an inconsequential bundle of rags.

God began with Elijah's body—with his spent energy, his strained nerves, and his weary muscles. Once the cup of physical strength began to fill, God could go on to minister to Elijah's other needs.

God the nursemaid! And why not? Is He not called *El Shaddai*, the "God with breasts" (Genesis 17:1, ASV margin)? How often I need the nursing ministry of God when body or spirit become tired in His service!

"So Jacob named the place Peniel, for he said, 'I have seen God face to face, yet my life has been preserved'" (Genesis 32:30).

NOVEMBER 9
God's Conscious Presence Revealed

God's tender care for Elijah extended to more than the body, even though ministry to his body was the first necessity. God also ministered to his spirit. The voice of the Lord, that "still small voice," came to him to assure him of God's continued presence with him. One of the results of an emotional breakdown in God's servants is a feeling of isolation from God. It seems as if the spirit is unable to apprehend God's presence, even though He is just as close as always. The cause is a defect in the spirit's *function*, like a clock whose mainspring is broken.

The remedy is an extra amount of attention from God, who makes His presence more peculiarly evident to His people in such distressing times. So He came to Elijah several times and made His "word" and His "voice" known to Him (1 Kings 19:9, 12, 13, 15). God knew that Elijah needed more than water and bread; he needed the conscious presence of the One he loved most. So God came, and Elijah was comforted.

There was one other aspect of God's care for Elijah, and that was in reference to his *vocation*. Was God finished with him? Did his breakdown mean the end of his ministry? Could he ever function again as a prophet? After a period of rest and refreshing, God's word came again to His servant: "Go, return . . . and . . . anoint Hazael king over Aram; and Jehu . . . king over Israel" (vv. 15–16). His ministry was to continue as his strength returned. He was still of great value to the Most High. What a comfort that must have been to Elijah after his bitter bout with nerves!

How assuring it is to me to see God's minute, individual care for one of His tired prophets! I serve a Master who is infinite in *heart* as in *mind*, and I rest in the center of both.

"The Lord is my strength and my shield; my heart trusts in Him, and I am helped; therefore my heart exults, and with my song I shall thank Him" (Psalm 28:7).

NOVEMBER 10
Weak and Assured Faith

I must remember that while all faith is the same in essence, it is not the same in *level*. The level of faith is like the level of a river; sometimes it is high and sometimes low, depending upon the circumstances. The first level of faith is *weak faith*. That is the kind the disciples seemed to have frequently; hence, the word of Jesus, "O ye of little faith" (Matthew 8:26, KJV). This kind of faith is like a sapling that needs lots of care and attention. It takes only a *little* storm to bend or twist it. It is not chronological, for old disciples may suffer from it just as much as young ones. It is caused by two things: lack of comprehension of what God's about, and lack of commitment to what God is doing. The disciples did not lack commitment, but they lacked understanding; hence, their faith was weak. On the other hand, the man "weak in faith" to whom Paul refers (Romans 14:1) simply had an immature commitment to God.

The second level of faith is *assured faith*. That is the kind of faith that God has underpinned. For example, God told Abraham specifically that despite his lack of progeny he would be the father of many peoples. The moment God underpinned his "hope" his faith became strong and assured; he no longer had "weak . . . faith" (Romans 4:18–19). Assured faith means that I no longer doubt because God has said that it will be so.

While I can do something about weak faith, there is nothing I can do about assured faith; it is, in the truest sense, a "gift of God" (Ephesians 2:8). It means that God has sovereignly chosen to do something and He has graciously included me in the work. When He does, I rejoice.

My rejoicing of faith, like Mary's, then becomes contagious and others rejoice also (Luke 1:44–46). Lord, lead us on to faith in its certainty and its rejoicing!

"When I am afraid, I will put my trust in Thee" (Psalm 56:3).

NOVEMBER 11
Authoritative Faith

The third level of faith, after *weak* faith and *assured* faith, is *authoritative* faith. That level of faith, closely allied with intercessory prayer, is the position in which God puts Himself at our disposal, so to speak. It is a position in which, in the words of Rees Howells, founder of the Bible College of Wales, the objective is "gained" and no further prayer needs to be offered. In gaining that position, God gives us a kind of carte blanche in which we may ask anything we wish in the area of our victory.

The example of that kind of faith is Moses interceding for Israel (Exodus 32:7–14). Because of Israel's sin in making a golden calf, God determined to destroy the people and make a new nation out of Moses. But Moses prayed agonizingly for his people and reached the place where God, in a sense, put Himself in Moses' hands to do whatever Moses asked. The position was gained, the authority was reached, the key was granted. Then Moses, using his new authority, asked God to restore Israel to His favor and grace, which God did—for Moses' sake.

Examples could be multiplied: Peter's authority with the Gentiles, the disciples' authority over demons, Paul's authority with rulers, and Elijah's authority over his enemies. Only trusted men are given such authority, and it is given in only one specific area. Such people are the extended fingers and hands of God on earth.

On the bottom of the ladder of faith are the words "Climb as high as you can." God encourages me to become a great believer in Him, and to grow so strong in the discipline that He will be able to trust me with responsible functions in His great, eternal plan. When He glances over His army to find responsible people, may He find me like Abraham, "strong in faith, giving glory to God" (Romans 4:20).

"Ask Me about the things to come concerning My sons, and you shall commit to Me the work of My hands" (Isaiah 45:11).

NOVEMBER 12
The Self-Restraint of Jesus

I must be aware that my life of discipleship will normally be a pull between self-expression and self-restraint. There are times when shyness is a sin and I must express myself unashamedly for His sake. On the other hand, there are times when I must exert every effort to be self-restrained, otherwise I sin.

Jesus exerted the most amazing self-restraint of all. He was "born of a woman, born under the Law" (Galatians 4:4). He restrained Himself *physically* by being "born of a woman." By assuming a physical form, Jesus Christ learned for the first time what hunger, thirst, and weariness were. He also learned what it meant to be confined to one spot at a time and to travel one step at a time. Perhaps an illustration would be for an adult to resort to crawling like a baby once again, and to live his life that way. However we look at it, the result is limitation; and in Jesus' case the cause of it was His unfathomable love for us.

He also restrained Himself *morally* by being "born under the Law." The Law was given, Paul says, to make us aware of our sins (Romans 7:7). Yet Jesus Christ, who had no sin, willingly endured the irritating reminders of a sinful nature for the sake of us who break the Law repeatedly.

Deep in the heart of Jesus Christ was the willingness to be curbed, limited, and contained *of rightful expressions* of Himself, in order that by doing so He might save us. I must learn the "mind" of Christ and realize that if I am to "save" others, I must follow His way. The path of service is the path of self-restraint. Jesus Christ has shown me so, and thank God He will help me to do so.

"Come, let us go up to the mountain of the Lord, to the house of the God of Jacob; that He may teach us concerning His ways, and that we may walk in His paths" (Isaiah 2:3).

NOVEMBER 13
Bound by the Father's Will

I am reminded on every hand that I must express myself, that I must be the real me that I was meant to be, that God's gifts are to be used and not neglected. Well and good. Yet I see a strong contrast to that idea in Jesus Christ, who restrained Himself *spiritually* for me. What can I say of the cross on which He died, which was a *necessity* to Him (Matthew 3:15; Luke 12:50)? He put Himself under the restraint of His Father's will and of our need, and both of them together bound Him so effectively that the cross was the result.

I also am bound by the Father's will. There are many things pleasurable to me that I may not do, even those things that in themselves are ethically acceptable. I also am bound by my brother's needs; I must go beyond the appealing ideology of socialism: "If anyone is hungry, I am hungry; if anyone is cold, I am cold; if anyone is in prison, I am not free." I must put into practice the ideology of Jesus Christ, who is the embodiment of self-restraint for the salvation of others, not simply from economic deprivation but from spiritual bankruptcy!

What a reward awaits the self-restrained person! It was because Jesus was willing to come "into the world" that God commanded all His angels to "worship [do reverence to] Him" (Hebrews 1:6), and for that reason He has a "better" name than they. The plaudits of heaven are reserved for those who hand their lives over to others, who spend their lives "handwriting" themselves on the souls of others, and who gain nothing except cost and pain in the process. For them, heaven has the highest praise and angels sing their sweetest songs. God, make me worthy to be included!

"Therefore let us not judge one another anymore, but rather determine this—not to put an obstacle or a stumbling block in a brother's way" (Romans 14:13).

NOVEMBER 14
The Flaw of Impatience

I must be on the alert against the sin of *impatience*. The great fault of the prodigal son was not the request "Give me," but the impatience with which he sought what ultimately would become his, "Give me *now*." He could not wait for the father's time, the father's plan; it had to be *his* time and that time was right now!

How often I repeat the same mistake with my heavenly Father! I must learn that all impatience is a denial of God's time. It says to Him, "I do not trust Your time; my time is better." Moses sinned with impatience when he struck the rock instead of speaking to it (Numbers 20:10–13). His impatience caused him to disobey a direct order of the Lord, thus publicly insulting God before the assembly of Israel (v. 12). For that impatient outburst Moses lost his lifelong desire—to lead Israel into the Promised Land. How often I will lose my goals and ambitions because my impatience makes a fool out of God in the eyes of the people!

Impatience is seizing God's *means* and substituting my own. God has promised His strength for every task, which means I cannot receive that help until God's time to act arrives. If I impatiently precipitate the action on my own, it means I must use my own resources instead of God's. By my impatience I am left nakedly to myself before my enemies.

Impatience is telling God what is important, and that is a sorry mistake. God will act when the purpose is mature and the time is ripe, not before. I cannot afford to seize green opportunities, lest I dishonor God and frustrate my own hopes. I can only afford to wait and let Him be "gracious" to me (Isaiah 30:18). May my testimony always be, "I waited patiently for the Lord; and He . . . heard my cry" (Psalm 40:1).

"And let endurance have its perfect result, that you may be perfect and complete, lacking in nothing" (James 1:4).

NOVEMBER 15
God's Perfect Plan for Us

The Christian life, properly lived, is perfectionism of a sort. David alluded to that when he said, "As for God, his way is perfect" (Psalm 18:30, KJV). Then he followed that statement with its necessary corollary, "[He] maketh *my* way perfect" (v. 32, KJV, italics added). God Himself is perfect, both in Himself and in all that He does, and His perfection has relevance to me; He is perfect not only for His sake, but for mine. The plan He has in mind for me is absolutely perfect, both for Himself and for me. The way He executes the plan and its many details also has the stamp of perfection upon it. The result is perfection in heaven, perfection on earth.

The word *perfect* has two meanings: to bring to an end, and to make mature. God brings to an end every phase, every detail of His plan for me, whether painful or pleasurable. He tailors His plan to me; it fits me like a glove. He knows so thoroughly and plans for me so carefully that no one in the universe can improve upon it. When each stage is completed, He blows the whistle and brings it to a halt. The time is up; that stage is done, complete, perfect.

Because God is in charge of my life and because He is the Master Architect, I must not fix my attention on things, circumstances, people, or events. Those are only passing elements in the drama of my life. In a certain sense, they are really illusions, not realities, and therefore they make a poor foundation for faith. Only God is my "constant," my abiding One, as the Bible stresses, and all else is "for a season." The Bible overcomer is tied to God the rock, undisturbed by the passing stream, and he knows that every time God touches him it is for perfection.

"He brought me up out of the pit of destruction, out of the miry clay; and He set my feet upon a rock making my footsteps firm" (Psalm 40:2).

NOVEMBER 16
Justification by Life

I must not entertain a shortsighted view of justification by faith. I must believe in *justification by life* also. Too often I have held the opinion that justification only has to do with my sins, whereas the Bible very clearly says, "The just [one] shall live by [his] faith" (Hebrews 10:38, KJV). That means more than just the initial act of faith whereby I come alive in Jesus Christ and my sins are justified in God's sight. True enough, thank God, but there is more! I am called upon by God to justify more than my *sins*; I am called upon to justify my way of life before men.

It is relatively easy to justify my sins. One believing look at Calvary's cross is sufficient for that. But God calls upon me to keep believing on Him as I believed at Calvary so that He can effectively demonstrate in me that He is capable of handling my life. By continually trusting His Word with wholehearted reliance, I justify God before the eyes of the world. Too often I have been lulled into the temptation to trust God to pardon my sins, only to refuse to trust Him in the mechanical, everyday matters of my life—whom do I marry, where do I work, what should I buy, how shall I serve, what should I do with my leisure, and hundreds of similar details. In short, I have justified my sins but I do not justify my life by faith.

Justification by life works both ways, manward and Godward. Can I justify before God my worry, my anxiety about money matters, my fretting about the future, or my frustration about my children? Or does my simple reliance on Him and His Word make my life "justified," that is, God saying yes to every attitude and bent of mind? "Justified by faith," yes, but not once and for all but every day and in every way. The result of justification by life is, "The Lord . . . delighteth in his way" (Psalm 37:23, KJV).

"What use is it, my brethren, if a man says he has faith, but he has no works? Can that faith save him?" (James 2:14).

NOVEMBER 17
God Is the Opposite of Us

I will be a better servant of God if I understand what my relationship to Him is. He is my Maker, my Lord, my Deliverer; but He is also my *opposite*. He is my opposite just as male and female are opposite, except of course on a much higher and grander scale. For my finiteness there is His infiniteness; for my weakness there is His omnipotence; for my limited eyesight there is His omniscience; for my confinement to a body there is His omnipresence. Even if man had not sinned, God would still be his opposite. Now, add the dimension of sin, and God becomes all the more opposite—for man's sin there are His mercy and forgiveness.

The greatest insult I can offer God is to try to be equal with Him, as Satan did when he sinned, and as Adam and Eve did when they sinned: "Ye shall be as *gods*" (Genesis 3:5, KJV, italics added). On the other hand, I please God the most when I am truly human—truly the opposite of Him, as He intended me to be. The great sin of the human race is to eliminate the oppositeness between man and God. As a Christian, I am guilty of that sin whenever I usurp God's rule in my life and put myself in His place. Only one Person ever lived who rightfully claimed equality with God and who therefore could say, "I and my Father are one" (John 10:30, KJV).

I must truly let God be God and me be me, which means a creature dependence upon Him at all times. When I am weak or hurt or sorrowful or sinful, I must come to Him for His opposites: strength, healing, joy, and mercy. I was made for Him, and He is a happy God when He ministers to my needs. "The Lord Himself is God; . . . we are His people and the sheep of His pasture" (Psalm 100:3).

"May it never be! Rather, let God be found true, though every man be found a liar, as it is written, 'That Thou mightest be justified in Thy words, and mightest prevail when Thou art judged'" (Romans 3:4).

NOVEMBER 18

The Luxury of Frustration

As a disciple of Jesus Christ I cannot afford the luxury of frustration. If I lie down at the end of the day and feel at loose ends, I am not up to my commitment. Why didn't that letter come? Why didn't I telephone so-and-so? Why did I leave some things out of that interview? Why did my talk before the group flop? And so on. In such a state I feel cheated, robbed, dissatisfied. And there is no peace whatever.

That condition is both *unbelief* and *rebellion*. Unbelief, because if all things are mine, as Paul said (1 Corinthians 3:21), why do I not simply believe it and rest? And rebellion because I have quarreled with God's portion for me today. I must learn that I cannot gain any more than what God has planned to give me in a given day. All the striving, yearning, and even praying will not yield one sliver more of the blessing God has decreed for me. My attitude ought to be: Thy will, not my will; let Thy portion come; not, give me the portion I demand. I must learn to yield, not resist.

Nothing in heaven or earth can stop or delay the blessing that God has reserved for me today. There is no Delayed Blessings Office in God's economy. The word *delay* does not even appear in His vocabulary. Anything that is delayed is simply not His will for me at the particular moment. Therefore, why fret? My days may not always be characterized by pleasureful delight, but they will always be characterized by His specially chosen portion, which will never fail to arrive. So why should I fear?

Yet I always seem to fear God—fearing that He will refuse to give me what I ought to have. The result? I live miserably rather than joyfully. God, give me a heart to accept Your portion—with joy! I rest in this: "No good thing does He withhold from those who walk uprightly" (Psalm 84:11).

"Cease striving and know that I am God; I will be exalted among the nations, I will be exalted in the earth" (Psalm 46:10).

NOVEMBER 19
Is God Hard?

I must remember that my service for God is determined by my attitude about God. The man with one talent buried it in the ground because, to him, his master was "a hard man, reaping where [he] did not sow, and gathering where [he] scattered no seed" (Matthew 25:24). Whenever I see God as a "hard man," it will affect my work for Him. I will see it as unrewarding toil, joyless slavery, and service without compensation.

Simon Peter practically insulted Jesus when he said, "We have left everything and followed You; what then will there be for us?" (Matthew 19:27). That was almost calling Jesus "a hard man" because the question indicated a doubt in Peter's mind as to whether he would ever receive a reward for his work. I am often a contradictory Christian. I believe in God's love and fairness; yet I treat Him as a "hard man" because I doubt that He will take care of me.

David established a law in Israel's military code that the men who guarded the supplies were to share and share alike with those who fought the battle (1 Samuel 30:24–25). I admire David's fairness and charity! But is God less fair and less charitable than David? Will He treat me, a soldier in His army, less considerately than David treated his men?

I read, "Seek first His kingdom and His righteousness; and all these things shall be added to you" (Matthew 6:33). Are those the words of "a hard man" or of a loving Master who will never deprive me of anything that He has designed for me? When God asks me, "Am I hard?" I must answer, "Never, Lord," and then let faith confirm that "Never!" I stand with Abraham: "Will not the Judge of all the earth *do right?*" (Genesis 18:25, NIV, italics added).

"For God is not unjust so as to forget your work and the love which you have shown toward His name, in having ministered and in still ministering to the saints" (Hebrews 6:10).

NOVEMBER 20
The Secret of Spiritual Growth

I will save myself a great deal of disappointment in my discipleship if I learn the secret of Christian growth. The secret lies in the word *maturing*. All natural, organic growth follows that pattern; so also does spiritual growth. Not even salvation is instantaneous, except the pinpoint moment of decision. But before that electric moment comes, a chunk of time has elapsed, preparing me for the reception of the new life.

If the preparation is long and sometimes tedious, it goes without saying that the fruits of salvation are also long awaited. That is because the new life operates within me on a time schedule, like a growing child. When the organism is ready, the child will walk and talk, not before. So it is with the newborn child of God. Assuming that I surround myself with the proper means of growth, I should then expect the new life within me to develop toward the image of Christ, not in one sudden burst, but in a series of maturity stages.

Much of the emphasis I have heard on Christian growth is on "crisis." I am to "make a decision" and then instantly manifest maturity. Wrong! That leads to frustration.

When Jesus said to Simon, "Thou shalt be . . . Cephas" (John 1:42, KJV), He was looking a long way down the road. So it is with me. Accepting Christ puts the package inside me, but walking with Christ allows the life to unfold within me, bringing about the changes God wants for me.

How glorious to have God as our Gardener! "A vineyard of delight . . . I, the Lord, am its keeper; I water it every moment" (Isaiah 27:2–3, margin). Then we "take root . . . blossom and sprout; and they will fill the whole world with fruit" (v. 6).

"Therefore, my brethren, you also were made to die to the Law through the body of Christ, that you might be joined to another, to Him who was raised from the dead, that we might bear fruit for God" (Romans 7:4).

NOVEMBER 21
Self-Deception

I am told that the greatest of all deceptions is self-deception, and that is true. But God will not allow any of His disciples the privilege of self-deception forever. Sooner or later He will force the mask off and let us see ourselves as we really are. He is the great mask remover.

I remember the story of Naaman and Elisha quite well. But do I remember the story of Gehazi? He is just as much a part of the picture as the other two (2 Kings 5). Naaman, the Syrian leper, came to Elisha to be cured. Elisha told him to dip seven times in the Jordan River, which he did, and his flesh became as the flesh of a child. He wanted to reward Elisha for his cure, but Elisha refused. Gehazi, Elisha's servant, ran after Naaman and asked for the silver and clothing that had been refused. Elisha rebuked Gehazi for his disobedience and he became, as Naaman had been, leprous.

The tragedy of Gehazi was that he never recognized he was first a leper in *heart*. He assumed that because his *environment* was right, he was right. Elisha was always before him, the prophetic school always around him, and the service of the Lord always by his side. With such surroundings, who could possibly be ungodly?

The truth is, with such surroundings it is easier to be self-deceived! Self-deception always works on the principle that God is as fuzzy-eyed as people are; we think that because they do not see, He does not see. However, Gehazi reminds me that God sees all too well, and sooner or later people will see what He has been seeing all along.

What is God telling me here? I must root out inward leprosy lest God make it painfully public. He will help me to do it, for what I voluntarily expose to Him, He will never expose to the world (1 John 1:9).

"But prove yourselves doers of the word, and not merely hearers who delude themselves" (James 1:22).

NOVEMBER 22
The Sin of Indispensability

Nature abhors a vacuum, says the scientist; so does God, says the Bible. When the invited ones failed to show up for the banquet, the host said to his servants, "Go out into the highways . . . and compel them to come in, that my house may be filled" (Luke 14:23). God's *will* is, "My house will be filled." God's *way* is, "If the people don't respond, get others." When Israel would not respond to Christ's message, God turned to the Gentiles and gave them the "vineyard that the Israelites violated." If John Doe does not respond to the gospel invitation, Jane Doe will; God's house must be "filled." If Judas will not become an apostle, Saul of Tarsus will. If the church at Ephesus grows lukewarm and cold and leaves its first love, Christ will remove the light from it and give it to another church that will manifest it (Revelation 2:5).

I have often been guilty of the sin of indispensability. I have treated potential converts as converts, church leaders as indispensable leaders, friends as indispensable friends. In God's eyes there are no indispensable people. All are expendable. I cannot claim such a privileged position with God that He cannot afford to bypass me in the ongoing of His work. I must at all times prove to Him that I am not castaway material (1 Corinthians 9:27). I must never abandon the conditions on which fruitful servantship rests, and never give myself the luxury of feeling that God's work will die when I die. God abhors that kind of a vacuum, and He will quickly fill it with someone else. My joy in all this is that God's purpose will never fall short: "He will not fail or be discouraged until He brings justice to victory" (Isaiah 42:4, author's trans.; cf. Matthew 12:20). His victory is my rest, and His unfailing purpose my delight.

"If I speak with the tongues of men and of angels, but do not have love, I have become a noisy gong or a clanging cymbal" (1 Corinthians 13:1).

NOVEMBER 23
Crisis Discipleship

Much of the time God deals with His disciples on a "crisis" basis. There is a certain quick kind of reaction generated by a crisis that never happens in the long, slow process. That happened to Nicodemus and Joseph of Arimathea. They were "secret" disciples, not of the Twelve, the Seventy, or the One Hundred and Twenty. They followed Jesus from the shadows and at a distance.

Then suddenly God sent a crisis, the crisis of the cross, and the two hidden disciples had to come out in the open. They identified themselves publicly as belonging to Jesus and begged the officials for His body for burial (John 19:38–42). So God often uses the crisis as a "do or die" tool to declare, strengthen, or purify a disciple.

As I study the wilderness journey of the Israelites, I am impressed by the number of crises they had to go through: thirst, hunger, snakes, enemies, rebellions. Yet God declares that the reason He led them through such experiences was to "prove . . . what was in [their] heart" (Deuteronomy 8:2–6, KJV). Thus, the wilderness was educational and cathartic; it was designed to show them the evil tendencies of their hearts and to purify them of such tendencies. For me, also, life will be a series of crises in which my commitment will either become strong and dependable or else will slowly shrink until it will be consumed by weakness.

Yet the theme of Deuteronomy 8 is not crisis but *guidance.* Over and over God assures His people that He led them, fed them, cared for them, fought for them, and guided them to His chosen goal. I must remember that! I am not living at the whim of mindless fate, but as the chosen son of a wise, loving Father. He leads me thus because He set His love upon me and chose me (see Deuteronomy 7:7).

"I know, O Lord, that Thy judgments are righteous, and that in faithfulness Thou hast afflicted me" (Psalm 119:75).

NOVEMBER 24
Learning Christ Secondhand

I must be careful not to "know" Christ in a natural way. Paul said, "Even though we have known Christ according to the flesh, yet now we know Him thus no longer" (2 Corinthians 5:16). To know Christ "according to the flesh" means to know Him in a natural way, or to know Him secondhand.

To know Christ "according to the flesh" means to be associated with Him on a natural basis, as the disciples were. We sometimes say, "Oh, if I had only been there," as if being in the physical presence of Jesus somehow creates faith. The disciples had been with Him for more than three years; yet they did not believe Him; they forsook Him and fled. But when the Holy Spirit entered them on Pentecost, suddenly all that Christ had taught them became amazingly alive and true. Then they knew Christ "after the Spirit." I must refuse to learn of Christ after the laws of reason, research, or history. I must see Him only through the eyes of the Holy Spirit. There are too many "Christians" who see Christ naturally. A natural Christ will transform no one.

Also, I must not learn of Jesus Christ secondhand. I must not be a "sucker" and live off someone else's faith. I must not "me too" the gospel, for such people shrivel and die when their source of life is removed from them.

If I let the Holy Spirit teach me *directly* of Jesus Christ, that knowledge will become richer and sweeter as time goes on; but if I learn of Him any other way, that knowledge will decay as surely as my body and brain will. I must never let Jesus be interpreted to me in any other way than spiritually; that is the only way He abides with me forever. I love Paul's prayer: "May [God] give to you a spirit of wisdom and of revelation in the knowledge of Him [Christ]" (Ephesians 1:17). How wonderful when answered!

"Therefore be careful how you walk, not as unwise men, but as wise, making the most of your time, because the days are evil" (Ephesians 5:15–16).

NOVEMBER 25

The Natural Beauty of Jesus Christ

I must learn to have the "eyes of God" in all things, to see things as He sees them, and to appreciate them as He appreciates them. For example, God has a special way of looking at His Son, Jesus Christ. He sees Him as a "tender plant," rich and beautiful, while the world sees Jesus only as a "root [stump] out of a dry ground," with no "comeliness" or "beauty" (Isaiah 53:2, KJV).

Do I see Jesus Christ as "altogether lovely" or as someone who is unattractive? We tend to look for our counterparts in everyone. That is why God looks at Jesus and finds great delight in Him; He sees Himself reflected in His Son. Natural people do not find Jesus attractive; in fact, they scarcely give Him a thought; but when we receive the Holy Spirit, suddenly Jesus Christ takes on a new attractiveness. We see Him in a new light; His hidden glories come bursting forth, all because it is the Spirit who is seeing Jesus through us.

From the other standpoint, God sees us human beings as stumps out of a dry ground, without natural beauty, until we receive His Son; then we become tender plants to Him because Jesus Christ makes us beautiful to God. So we Christians also delight in one another because the Spirit who is in each of us recognizes the Christ who is in the other person and rejoices in what He sees. The thrilling thing about being a Christian is that not only is Christ in us, but He by His Spirit is changing us more and more into His likeness every day (2 Corinthians 3:18). To the extent that we become more and more like the Christ who is in us, God rejoices over us; thus, little by little the beauty of Jesus becomes *our* beauty and God's heart overflows.

I say it reverently, Jesus Christ is my natural beauty kit. No one else will make me as attractive and beautiful to God as He.

"He is also head of the body, the church; and He is the beginning, the first-born from the dead; so that He Himself might come to have first place in everything" (Colossians 1:18).

NOVEMBER 26
Claiming Our Inheritance

I must remember that merely to proclaim what Christ has done for me is not enough; I must *claim* it also. The blessings of the Christian life are not automatic; they must be staked out and walked over just as the Israelites had to lay claim to the land of Canaan. One of the saddest things the Lord said to Joshua was, "Very much of the land remains to be possessed" (Joshua 13:1). The land as a whole had been conquered. Now it was up to each individual tribe to move in foot by foot, claim possession of its particular territory, drive out its enemies, and set up authority over it.

I make a mistake when I equate living by faith with living in laziness. God never intended that I should be "carried to the skies on flowery beds of ease." I must adopt an aggressive stance in my determination to possess everything Jesus died for. Satan will see to it that if he cannot keep me from accepting Jesus, he will do everything he can to keep me from using Jesus. If he cannot keep me out of the land of Canaan, he will do everything possible to keep the victories of Canaan out of me. Satan is the greatest "blowfish" of all time; he will blow himself immensely out of proportion just to frighten me out of the blessings Christ has bought for me. I may be living at the poverty level right now, not because I am not rich, but because Satan has convinced me I am not.

Just as God gave Israel the land of Canaan, so He has given me "all spiritual blessings . . . in Christ" (Ephesians 1:3, KJV). Therefore, I have the *authority* to claim everything I need from Him. But He promises something more: the *ability* to drive out the enemy, who keeps me from possessing my possessions. God, make me more than a conqueror (Romans 8:37)!

"Blessed be the God and Father of our Lord Jesus Christ, who has blessed us with every spiritual blessing in the heavenly places in Christ" (Ephesians 1:3).

NOVEMBER 27
Working to Conquer Canaan

A disciple must understand the difference between "rest" and "works" if he is to be successful. The Bible says, "We who have believed enter that rest" (Hebrews 4:3), but that refers to the rest of not having to strive for our *salvation*. It does not refer to the rest of not having to strive for our *victory*. That is why we read, "Let us . . . be diligent to enter that rest" (v. 11).

Too often we evangelicals have a carry-over attitude toward our Christian life. Because we are saved through faith alone, we feel that victory comes to us the same way. While of course we trust God to help us and see us through, we are not exempt from suffering, struggling, and striving in order to achieve victory. The land of Canaan, while promised to the Israelites, had to be fought for, maintained, and worked before it began to yield its fruit of possession to them. So it is with me. Christ has provided me all the provisions I will ever need for my Christian life (and more), but those provisions will never become mine practically simply by believing that they are there. They will become mine as I need them in the struggle, just as Canaan became Israel's by warfare and hard work.

I conquer my Canaan by working it. I work it by hard work in prayer, in self-denial, in witnessing to a hostile world, in facing opposition, in living according to the Bible, in obeying God's Word regardless of the obstacles, in challenging Satan's right to trespass.

That way of life is anything but easy. But when Canaan begins to yield its fruits, what blessing and what glory! The victory will not come without a battle, but my faith is like Caleb's: "Give me this mountain . . . the Lord will be with me, then I shall be able to drive them [the enemy] out, as the Lord said" (Joshua 14:12, KJV).

"Therefore, let us fear lest, while a promise remains of entering His rest, any one of you should seem to have come short of it" (Hebrews 4:1).

NOVEMBER 28
The Need for Vacations

I must tend my spiritual Canaan as faithfully as the Israelites did their physical land. Tending my blessing means two things: resting it and redeeming it. The Israelites "rested" their land each week on the Sabbath day, each seventh year, and each fiftieth year, the year of jubilee (Leviticus 25:1–12). Resting the land was necessary to its longevity and its fruitfulness. So I must "rest" myself occasionally as God did on the seventh day, and as Jesus did on several occasions (Mark 6:31). I must not goad myself into ceaseless activity because "Satan never vacations." Everybody vacations, including God, though He is exhaustless.

Spiritual rest involves rest from my enemy and rest for my spirit. Only God can give me rest from my enemy; therefore, I must concern myself with rest for my spirit, which is my responsibility. Since I am responsible for the use of my time, body, and talents, I am also responsible for my rest. Neither my body nor my spirit can grind on continually, because they were never meant to. Spiritual growth is like physical growth; it comes in spurts and pauses. I must always have the mind-set of Jesus, who, despite the overwhelming crush of needs around Him, took His rest.

Every spiritual blessing I actualize in my life must take time to mature. I must not only learn a lesson; I must absorb it. Perhaps that explains why there are so few real saints today, and an overabundance of managers and promoters. I must remember that my spiritual refreshment is vitally tied to a Person. "My presence shall go with you, and I will give you rest" (Exodus 33:14). I do not vacation *from* God but *in* God; that is, my being is in Him even though my faculties may be coasting.

"And He said to them, 'Come away by yourselves to a lonely place and rest a while.' (For there were many people coming and going, and they did not even have time to eat.)" (Mark 6:31).

NOVEMBER 29

The Kinsman Redeemer

In my quest for spiritual victory, I must realize that ground can be gained and lost. That is where the *law of redemption* comes in. The Old Testament Israelite could lose his inheritance through neglect or unfortunate reverses, so God provided him with a right of redemption by which his lost property could be restored to him in the fiftieth year (Leviticus 25:23–34). So it is with me. I may lose my spiritual blessing by neglect (Matthew 25:26–30) or by being taken unaware by the world or Satan, snatching it away (Matthew 13:4). However, God has provided a means whereby the blessing may be restored to me by my Kinsman Redeemer, Jesus Christ.

The duty of the kinsman redeemer was to deliver from poverty, to restore land to its original owner, and to secure justice for the oppressed relative. So Jesus Christ now functions as the Restorer of my lost blessing and power. He intercedes for me on the basis of His redemptive work on Calvary, thus securing for me a "clearing" at the throne of God. He gives me the right to be heard, the right to confess, and the right to be forgiven and restored (1 John 1:5–10). If it were not for Christ's present intercession for me, every loss in my Christian walk would be *permanent*; but the moment I find myself in distress, a quick appeal to my Kinsman Redeemer immediately brings the law of redemption, and the possibility of loss is removed.

I rejoice in the provision for continual redemption that God has made for me, but it must be asked for. Not to ask for it is to lose the blessing even as Esau lost his, and with all his sorrow. I must get a grip on myself and make my appeal, then my Kinsman Redeemer will do the rest. He says to us, "I will seek the lost . . . bring back the strayed . . . bind up the wounded . . . [and] strengthen the sick" (Ezekiel 34:16, Berkeley). He is a perfect Kinsman Restorer!

"Let us therefore draw near with confidence to the throne of grace, that we may receive mercy and may find grace to help in time of need" (Hebrews 4:16).

NOVEMBER 30
The Ministry of a Clear Name

I must at all times engage in the "ministry of a clear name." But it must be God's name, not mine. The clear name ministry is one in which I represent God as He truly is. I must not spend my time clearing my name, for that is God's responsibility.

The sin of Moses that kept him out of the Promised Land was dishonoring God before the people (Numbers 20:10–13). He struck the rock instead of just speaking to it, thus disbelieving God and desanctifying Him in the eyes of the Israelites (v. 12). To deliberately disobey God is to disbelieve Him, and that, especially on the part of a *leader*, is to humiliate Him before His people. God will not tolerate humiliation by any of His servants because it is a shadow of Lucifer's sin of elevating himself above God (Isaiah 14:14).

My duty is to elevate, sanctify, honor, and clear God's name before the people at all times, as Jesus did: "I have glorified thee on the earth" (John 17:4, KJV). Now I understand why God punished Moses so severely: he was a leader, his sin was public, and he sorely wounded God's glory.

If I spend my time clearing God's name, I will have no time to clear my own. I must never be willing to justify myself, as the young lawyer did (Luke 10:29). There is a time, of course, to "reason together" with God (Isaiah 1:18), during which God is willing to hear all my arguments and reasons for a certain thing. But once God has given His verdict, self justification should stop and God justification should begin. This is the mark of a mature disciple: do I make my brief for God, or do I plead my own case in the eyes of men? If I "fulfill the royal law" I will know the "worthy name by . . . which [I am] called" (James 2:7–8, NSRB); if I "let [my] light . . . shine before men . . . [I will] glorify [my] Father, who is in heaven" (Matthew 5:16, NSRB).

"O Lord, open my lips, that my mouth may declare Thy praise" (Psalm 51:15).

DECEMBER 1
The Cult of Success

Imust be careful to avoid the temptations of the "cult of success" in God's work. When Jesus announced to His disciples that He was going to Jerusalem to be betrayed into the hands of sinners and be crucified, Peter shouted: "Be it far from thee, Lord" (Matthew 16:22, KJV). Satan cannot stand the cross in any form, whether as an instrument of death or a way of life, and he will do anything to keep Jesus—and us—from it.

The "cult of success," not the cross, is Satan's ideal religion. When Peter saw Jesus transfigured on the mountain, in company with Moses and Elijah, he was overwhelmed. What a scenario! Eagerly he said to Jesus: "I will make three tabernacles here, one for You, and one for Moses, and one for Elijah" (Matthew 17:4). Peter was a promoter, a publicist. He had an eye for crowd appeal and knew how to build something that would cause excitement, noise, and fanfare. Unwittingly, Peter was on the wrong track. Jesus, with Moses and Elijah, was thinking of the cross. And God, as if to answer the satanic desire of Peter, said to the disciples, "This is My beloved Son . . . listen to Him!" (v. 5).

I must not build tabernacles; I must look for my cross. I must not plan for success; I must be obedient daily to my heavenly Father. Jesus did not plan for crowds; they simply materialized out of His obedience to His Father's will. He did not memorialize or historicize His ministry; He simply left the fruits to the disposition of His Father. I must resist all efforts to build an empire or to preserve the fruits of my ministry. He is the God who works for us (1 Samuel 14:6), which means He begins at our initiative and ends at His accomplished purpose. May God make me faithful in obeying, and may I leave the aftermath to Him.

"Forgetting what lies behind and reaching forward to what lies ahead, I press on toward the goal for the prize of the upward call of God in Christ Jesus" (Philippians 3:13–14).

DECEMBER 2
The Aftermath of Victory

I must be careful never to let a victory over Satan become my weakness, for his prime targets are not victims, but victors. Paul reminds me of this when he says, "And having done all, to stand" (Ephesians 6:13, KJV). In other words, after a notable victory, be all the more on your guard. Satan is the great "spoiler," and he loves to suck the honey out of a sweet victory we have won over him.

Think of Sanballat and Nehemiah. After his threats, bombast, and harassment failed, Sanballat said to Nehemiah, "Come, let us meet together . . . in the plain of Ono" (Nehemiah 6:2). He meant, "Why fight each other any longer? I tried to prevent the walls from going up, but I failed. Now let's be good sports, forget the past, and plan something harmonious for the future." Satan never quits when he loses. If Nehemiah had listened to Sanballat, all his previous efforts would have been washed away.

I love the word Nehemiah gave in reply: "I am doing a great work and I cannot come down" (Nehemiah 6:3). When Satan comes to neutralize my victory, I am to ignore, slight, and refuse him. Never must I turn from God's directive (to build walls for His work) to think about Satan's suggestions. More than that, I must never gloat over my victory over Satan, for gloating represents an abnormal preoccupation with the victory itself, rather than with the work God has given me to do. The victory is only an incident, a battle in the eternal war, and I must quickly arm myself against the next visit from the evil one. Having done that, I must *stand*, not nakedly, but "in the strength of His might" (Ephesians 6:10), for my all-Conqueror has blunted Satan's darts and crushed his armory forever.

"He who overcomes, I will grant to him to sit down with Me on My throne, as I also overcame and sat down with My Father on His throne" (Revelation 3:21).

DECEMBER 3
Mannequin Christianity

The one thing that God wants to see above all else in me, and that He prizes above all else, is *spiritual life*. So highly does He prize this in me that He makes it a condition of service. Aaron was chosen as high priest of Israel because his rod "budded" (Numbers 17:8, KJV); it sprouted with blossom and fruit because God had miraculously given it life. The lesson is obvious: unless I possess spiritual life, I will be fruitless.

God's people have institutionalized spiritual service. We call a man to be a pastor, and because he is officially a pastor, we expect him to be a mouthpiece for God. Not necessarily. The title is not the life, and the office is not the fruit. God does not bless an office or a title; He blesses a person, and He blesses him because he evidences the flow of spiritual life in his life.

Jesus Christ was a Priest after the order of Melchizedek (Hebrews 5:6). Why? Because Melchizedek was a priest in function, not office. He had no temple, no sanctuary, no ritual; but his life was a continuous outpouring of the life of God in his heart, which blessed others, including Abraham.

Spiritual life is what God requires and what the world craves. Nobody, not even the outspoken agnostic, will refuse the life and fruit that God gives through His church; but everyone will bitterly denounce the "mannequin" aspect of Christianity, form without life. If I am to minister to the world I must have life, the "more abundant" life that Jesus came to offer. Men have no use for "rods" or "sticks" that are beautiful in appearance but helpless to make things new. God is the Reviver of dry bones and the Restorer of parched deserts; He is the Giver of His Spirit, by whom I become gloriously, overflowingly alive (Ezekiel 37:14).

"The thief comes only to steal, and kill, and destroy; I came that they might have life, and might have it abundantly" (John 10:10).

DECEMBER 4
Discarded Talent

Just as the rod of Aaron represented life, the rod of Moses represented power and authority (Exodus 4:1–3). When Moses threw his rod on the ground, it became a writhing snake. The lesson was a potent one to Moses—God had called him to deliver the Israelites from Egypt. If he refused, if he threw away his rod, it would become an ugly, despised, and fearful thing.

The New Testament speaks of the "buried" talent. But what of the "discarded" talent? The discarded talent is responsibility shunned, power unexpressed, authority unused. It is the curse of Meroz, who refused to come "to the help of the Lord, to the help of the Lord against the mighty" (Judges 5:23, KJV). It is the sin of John Mark, who refused to enter Asia Minor with Paul and Barnabas and turned and went home (Acts 13:13). It is the sin of Ephraim, who "equipped with the bow, retreated in the day of battle. They did not keep God's covenant" (Psalm 78:9–10, Berkeley).

I owe my life to those who did not discard their call from God. Paul brought the message to Europe and (in time) I heard the story of Jesus. Luther braved opposition and freed the gospel from unbiblical entanglements (for me). And what shall I say of Jesus Christ, who did not discard either the cup or the baptism (for me)? Shall I renege on my responsibility to God's call, which could mean life to others? Do I dare throw down the rod, or put my hand back inside my bosom where it can be safe and uncommitted?

Of the heroes who do *not* discard their talent and who fulfill their responsibilities courageously, God says, "Of whom the world was not worthy" (Hebrews 11:38). That is His goal for me—and all His disciples—to make the world unworthy of us! God, make me worthy of that unworthiness!

"That I may know Him, and the power of His resurrection and the fellowship of His sufferings, being conformed to His death" (Philippians 3:10).

DECEMBER 5

The Presentness of Heaven

I must not let my view of heaven and hell become blurred by believing that they are only *future*. I have always been taught that heaven and hell are locations, which is true, but not altogether true. They are also *relationships*, and that is where the qualities of both existences can be experienced now.

Paul says, "The widow who lives for pleasure [self-indulgence] is dead even while she lives" (1 Timothy 5:6, NIV). That means, if my will is out of harmony with God, a miniature hell is set up in my heart. Horace Fenton, former director of the Latin American Mission, says, "Hell is God giving to men what they have wanted all their lives—freedom from Him." If so, then to the extent any person—even a Christian—pulls away from God to his own way, to that extent he sips the misery of the one who will be forever and completely independent of God.

But heaven also can be mine *now*, at least partially and in foretaste. To say, "Lord, Thy will be done," is to transplant heaven to earth, from a location to an experience. It is to make what is normal in heaven normal for me on earth, thus producing a taste of its joys before time. The Christian who longs for heaven, who cannot wait for it, is missing a valuable opportunity to enjoy it now. I can walk with heaven's attraction (Jesus), think heaven's thoughts, do heaven's bidding, and sing heaven's praises *now*. The materials that produce a heavenly atmosphere are already at my disposal; I need not wait till I get there to use them.

Lord, teach me how to walk the "enveloped" life, enveloped by the perfume of heaven in the midst of this contaminated world. For that is what God has promised me: a taste "of the world to come" (Hebrews 6:5, KJV).

"But if we walk in the light as He Himself is in the light, we have fellowship with one another, and the blood of Jesus His Son cleanses us from all sin" (1 John 1:7).

DECEMBER 6
Christ Means Adequacy and Peace

Peace is one of the fruits of the Spirit and is always the result of a previously devised set of conditions. Peace is the possession and realization of adequate resources. The work of Jesus Christ is to *provide* those adequate resources, and the work of the Holy Spirit is to make me *realize* them. Since Jesus Christ has done a perfect work in my redemption, the problem in obtaining peace is not His, it is mine. The Holy Spirit's frustration with me (being "grieved" or "quenched") is because I resist His attempts to get me to act upon what Christ has provided me.

There are only two ways in which I can be without peace: by not knowing what Christ has provided me, and/or by not availing myself of what He has provided. "I can do all things through Christ, who strengtheneth me" (Philippians 4:13, NSRB). Wonderfully true, but only if I avail myself of His strength!

I arrive at peace by knowing what Christ has done for me, and that means saturation with the Word. To live constantly in the Word is to be constantly reminded of everything Jesus Christ has put at my disposal. That constant reminder is a stimulus to faith, for "faith comes from hearing, and hearing by the word of Christ" (Romans 10:17). As I read the marvelous provisions that Jesus Christ has bought for me, faith is brought into action to use those provisions. Soon I am cashing in on my merchandise, and the result is a feeling of adequacy, which leads to peace.

I will always feel distressed, and depressed, whenever I feel that the resources within are inadequate to meet the problems without. Jesus Christ came to make me adequate! I must honor Him by believing it, and I must let peace be the manifestation of it.

"Peace I leave with you; My peace I give to you; not as the world gives, do I give to you. Let not your heart be troubled, nor let it be fearful" (John 14:27).

DECEMBER 7
Developing a Sensitivity to God

Much of my Christian life will make no sense unless I realize that God is trying to develop my sensitivity to Him. It is true that He wants me to be a more faithful witness, a user of my gifts, a sharper image of His Son; but before He can develop those things, He must develop my threshold of sensitivity to His delicate guidance.

He wants to guide me, not by "bit guidance" but by "eye guidance" (Psalm 32:8–9). "Bit guidance" means He needs to get rough with me, as we do with recalcitrant horses; but "eye guidance" means that we respond to the merest flick of God's eye. God can guide me with His eye only when I have a trained eye fixed on Him at all times in order to catch His sudden and slightest indications.

I must also develop a sensitive ear. "Morning by morning, He awakens My ear" (Isaiah 50:4). That beautifully expresses the function of the "opened" and "cleansed" ear, to keep tuned in to God's voice. While the bride of Solomon slept, her "heart was awake" (Song of Solomon 5:2), a characteristic that should be true of all lovers of God. God speaks to us continually in the Spirit's voice, and if my heart is fixed on Him I will hear.

My tongue must also develop a keen sensitivity for God. "The Lord God hath given me the tongue of the learned [those who are taught]" (Isaiah 50:4, KJV). The spiritually sensitive tongue is conditioned to speak only God's thoughts and ideas; it is "at home" talking about God and uncomfortable talking about self and sin. God wants me as sensitive to Him as a violin to the musician, an instrument for His glory. Then I will sing to Him a new song, and praise Him with loud shouts (Psalm 33:2–3).

"The mouth of the righteous utters wisdom, and his tongue speaks justice. The law of his God is in his heart; his steps do not slip" (Psalm 37:30–31).

DECEMBER 8
Godly Grief

I will never know God well until I learn His "grief." I read, "It pleased the Lord to bruise him [Christ]; he hath put him to grief" (Isaiah 53:10, KJV). But the grief that Jesus suffered was my grief, a grief that came His way because of my sin. Grief always touches me at the point of sin, either mine or someone else's. That is why Paul could suffer grief over the lost members of his own Jewish race (Romans 9:1–3).

When I am convicted of sin, I feel the grief of sin, which is really the grief of God over sin. The heaviness in my heart is simply the overflow of the sorrow of God concerning my sin. The moment I confess that sin, God is no longer sorrowful, and therefore I am no longer in grief. Christ is constantly probing us to find a nerve in us that is sensitive to sin. He said to Peter, "Lovest thou me?" and Peter was "grieved" because Christ had reached the very center of his soreness (John 21:17, KJV). He is no disciple who has not felt the probing finger of Jesus Christ on his heart. That is the "godly grief" that Paul mentions as being good for us (2 Corinthians 7:7). How much better to be grieved by God than grieved by the world!

The life of discipleship itself is a life of grief. How can God deal with me without correcting me, and how can He correct me without hurt? No discipline is pleasant; it is "grievous" . . . but it yields to the joy of mature, dependable discipleship (Hebrews 12:11, KJV). My grief is therefore my joy and I should shout "Hallelujah" because God is producing a better me.

At all costs I must avoid the grief of the world, a bitter sorrow with no promise of a brighter tomorrow. How sweet is the Lord's grief when accepted, and how eternal the consequences! My hope is in Him "who wounds, but He binds up, He smites but His hands bring healing" (Job 5:18, Berkeley).

"For I am afflicted and needy, and my heart is wounded within me" *(Psalm 109:22).*

DECEMBER 9
The Glory of Earning It

I must settle once and for all the differences between my *rights* and my *privileges*. To be called a "son of God" is my right (John 1:12, KJV), but the expression of that sonship is a privilege that I must earn. Even Jesus, the eternal Son of God, had to *earn* a better name than the angels (Hebrews 1:4). Sonship with God comes to me when I express faith in Jesus Christ, but the glory of my sonship comes to me only when I am faithful to my calling.

How I love the "overcomings" of Revelation 2 and 3: "To him who overcomes," said Jesus to His followers, "I will give . . ." What wonderful things He grants, or bestows on, His servants: the tree of life, hidden manna, power over nations, open praise, a new name, and a throne of glory. And yet each of these is not given unconditionally; it is bestowed upon me as I overcome. The overcomer earns the privilege; and unless he does indeed earn it, none will be given, even though he is a son of God.

That is what I read about Jesus. "Therefore . . . God highly exalted Him, and bestowed on Him the name which is above every name" (Philippians 2:9). The glory that Jesus now enjoys is an *earned* glory, a glory that the Father bestowed upon Him only after He made Himself of no reputation, took upon Himself the form of a servant, became a man, and obeyed even to the cross.

So it must be with me. My sonship with God is merely the seed out of which I am to reap a harvest of dedicated discipleship, the result of which will be reward, recognition, honor, and praise. God forbid that it should ever be said of me, "He did not live up to his birth promise!" Rather, by God's help, may I hear Him say: "I have counted you worthy of the Kingdom" (cf. 2 Thessalonians 1:5). I am in the Kingdom by grace; I am *worthy* of the Kingdom by obedient sonship.

"Although He was a Son, He learned obedience from the things which He suffered" (Hebrews 5:8).

DECEMBER 10
Having an Uncondemned Heart

I must at all times strive to maintain a good conscience before God. A good conscience is one in which I am not conscious of anything in me that is offensive to God. A good conscience is cultivated by a close walk with God; the farther from God I live, the more I will tend to have a weak conscience, one that is weakened by too much contact with the world. Thank God, no disciple ever has a dead conscience, one that is calloused or "past feeling" (Ephesians 4:19, KJV). Nor will the disciple ever have an evil conscience, one that is twisted by doing much evil.

A good conscience is not automatic. It is the result of the habit of bringing my "condemned heart" before God, who is greater than my conscience, and who by His power gradually brings my conscience into the same sensitive state that He is in (1 John 3:19–21). My aim must be to live before God with an "uncondemned heart" (clear conscience) so that I may "have confidence before God" (v. 21). Nothing weakens my conscience and destroys my effectiveness in service more than having God stare at some things in my life that do not meet His approval. I must live the life of the uncondemned heart.

I can afford the criticism of the world, and even my Christian friends, if my heart is clean before God. I must never bow to criticism at the expense of my conscience, for that is the denial of my conscience. Nor must I ever allow the consciences of others to dictate what my conscience ought to be before God. For that reason I must repel social pressure to conform, and never lose my individual accounting before God. To become social clay is to deny my "good conscience" before God. I must always let Him be my shaper and molder (Jeremiah 18:6) so that I become not only a usable vessel, but a person made sensitive toward sin as He Himself is.

"Therefore, let those also who suffer according to the will of God entrust their souls to a faithful Creator in doing what is right" (1 Peter 4:19).

DECEMBER 11
In the Valley, a Door of Hope

There is no difference whatever between the circumstances of the unsaved and my circumstances, if that is all there is to consider. The difference is not outward, but inward, for the disciple of Jesus Christ has what the world can never offer—*hope*. Paul says, "We are saved by hope" (Romans 8:24, KJV), which means we expect a better outcome to our sufferings and circumstances than the unsaved man does. Apart from that godly expectation that God will bring us through to comfort, safety, and victory, we would be just as miserable as the worldling.

God said to Israel, "I will . . . bring [you] into the wilderness, and speak kindly [tenderly] to [you] . . . and [make] the valley of Achor [sorrow] as a door of hope" (Hosea 2:14–15). Sooner or later I will find myself in the valley of Achor; it is one of God's favorite stopping places for His children. But when I find myself in that valley, I must cling to hope, not lapse into despair, for the valley itself is the beginning of a new, exhilarating relationship with God, a relationship so rich in meaning that it is like a marriage (v. 16). God purposely leads me into sorrow and distress in order to bring my hope into a mature, healthy condition, for without a strong hope I will never enjoy the consummation of my salvation (Romans 5:4).

What a marvelous God! Sometimes His ways are bitter, but they are always *right*. He treats me as a dearly loved person for whose well-being He would change everything but His nature. He will lead me into the valley of Achor for His name's sake, but for His love's sake He will turn it into a door of hope. Are my clouds black today? Then it is time for God to take over, and soon I will discover how much He loves me—enough to move mountains and let me pass through! Think of that!

"For I consider that the sufferings of this present time are not worthy to be compared with the glory that is to be revealed to us" (Romans 8:18).

DECEMBER 12
Keeping the Interior Strong

I must discard the idea once and for all that Satan wants me in the junk heap. Quite the contrary! He wants me the best possible specimen of uprightness and morality, with one exception, that I do it without the life of God inside me. Satan does not care a fig about my outside appearance, but he will not tolerate my vital link with God inside.

When he tempted Jesus, Satan did not try to change His outside. He still wanted Him popular, esteemed, even a miracle worker. What he really wanted was to crack His interior, like ultrasonic waves, until the inside of Him crumbled. I make a mistake if I think Satan wants me an alcoholic, a dealer in white slavery, or a con man in a carnival. He wants me outwardly acceptable, a pillar of the community, a respected citizen. But most of all, he wants me dead to God, cut off from the lifeline to the Almighty.

Satan jumps for joy when my lifeline to God shrivels from lack of use. He becomes positively ecstatic when he sees me go through the form of godliness but without its power. Is he not doing the same himself? Is he not an "angel of light"? Is he not the master hypocrite who masquerades as one of God's choicest messengers, and yet possesses nothing of the life of God?

What does that say to me right now? I believe that no matter how plaster perfect my outside may be, I may be seriously hurting my heavenly Father on the inside. After all, the refined sins (such as pride, indifference, and lovelessness) are inside sins, and they are the deadliest of all. I must not give Satan comfort regarding me; I must keep my interior strong. I praise Him who teaches me "to know wisdom in my inmost heart" because He desires "truth in [my] inward being" (Psalm 51:6, Amp.). Such a God will help me keep the inside of the cup as sparkling clear as the outside!

"And he must have a good reputation with those outside the church, so that he may not fall into reproach and the snare of the devil" (1 Timothy 3:7).

DECEMBER 13
A Plain-Path Christian

I must avoid the temptation to be a "plain-path Christian." The psalmist, surrounded by enemies, asked God to lead him in a *"plain* path" (Psalm 27:11, KJV, italics added). I feel sure God answered his prayer, for there are times when all of us need help and deliverance, when it is necessary for us to see where God is leading us. But most of the time God leads us along an *unknown* path on which we do not have the foggiest notion of where we are going. In fact, there are times when we desperately need His guidance, but it is not there. Listen to Jeremiah: "He has blocked my ways with hewn stone; He has made my paths crooked" (Lamentations 3:9). What a statement! Instead of being the God who opens my path, He blocks it; instead of leading me in a plain, understandable way, He makes my paths crooked and twisted. Is that our God?

Fortunately, yes. The fact that He blocks our way or leads us along a twisted road does not mean that He no longer sees or loves or cares. If we understood everything God was doing to us, something would be wrong. "The secret things belong to the Lord our God, but the things revealed belong to us" (Deuteronomy 29:29). God does not explain to us His daily dealings with us; He only promises to lead us in the good and wise way, and asks that we trust Him to be true to His Word.

I must not pray for the "plain path"; I must pray for the compassing God who "searchest out my path" and is "acquainted with all my ways" (Psalm 139:3, ASV). The fact that He is there, with me and beside me on the path, is all I need for peace of mind and heart. I need not see Him or feel Him; His Word is good enough for both. It is when I *believe* that "the path of the righteous [just] . . . shines brighter and brighter until the full day" (Proverbs 4:18). God, give me faith for dark days and twisted paths!

"I will instruct you and teach you in the way which you should go; I will counsel you with My eye upon you" (Psalm 32:8).

DECEMBER 14
The Bible Is a Life-Giving Book

I must realize that the Bible is not a book of *magic* but a book of *miracle*. God not only spoke to the writers of the sixty-six books, but He continues to speak *through* them to me today. Jesus called the words of the Bible "life" (John 6:63), and Peter called them "seed" (1 Peter 1:23–25). The Word of God is seed that contains the life principle of God Himself; and when that Word is read, digested, and obeyed, it manifests itself in a living reproduction of God, just as the seed will manifest itself again in the new plant. The Bible is not history, biography, or anthology; it is God's life in the crystalline form of words that, when read and obeyed, releases that life for the benefit and blessing of the reader.

The Bible is food (Deuteronomy 8:3), and food is nothing more than the chemical continuation of life. Unless the Holy Spirit has food to give me, He cannot maintain the level of spiritual life in me that He desires. That is why He pleads with me not to live off experience, service, ritual, dogma, or fellowship, but to live off the Word, which alone carries the capability of sustaining my spiritual life.

The Bible is a life-giving book! It is a drugstore loaded with tonics of every description, all waiting to be used. There is enough resource to take care of all my needs, for both soul and body, for today, tomorrow, and forever.

Have I found His Word a delight to my heart? Do I read it as one searching for a love message and not just "doing my daily dozen"? Have I gone past dates, facts, numbers, and events and found God Himself there? Have I made the Bible a rendezvous with infinity and eternity, and is my soul satisfied? Praise God for the "angels' food" He supplies for us in His Word (Psalm 78:25, KJV), which nourishes and satisfies the new man!

"And do not take the word of truth utterly out of my mouth, for I wait for Thine ordinances" (Psalm 119:43).

DECEMBER 15
Living the Gentle Life

As a disciple of Jesus Christ I am committed to live the "gentle" life. The words of the psalmist, "Thy gentleness makes me great" (Psalm 18:35), are no idle remark. It is through gentleness that God develops strong saints. Jesus Christ made it clear in His Sermon on the Mount that gentleness was expected of His followers; hence, the other cheek, the second mile, and the coat as well as the shirt (Matthew 5:39–41). Jesus became the best example of His own teaching when He stood before Pilate, condemned by lies; yet He offered no resistance and submitted His case to God the Father.

Jesus teaches me that the gentle way is the way of victory. I am not to push, make exertions, be ambitious or aggressive. I must never resort to the sword or the fist to gain my ends; nor must I resort to legal undertakings, because I must be willing to suffer loss, if necessary, as Christ did. Naturally, I will be taken advantage of, as God's people have been in all ages. "For thy sake we are killed all the day long; we are accounted as sheep for the slaughter" (Romans 8:36, KJV). Nevertheless, by being gentle I am actually pleading my case before God; by acting the way He wants, I am placing the responsibility of my welfare on Him. He is able to help.

The gentle life is the most difficult to live because it is not natural. Further, we have been taught to "stand up for your rights," "assert yourself," "be your own person," until the gentle life seems almost like heresy. We Christians, like the world, are sometimes shameful in pulling strings, politicking, and using influence and other carnal ways to reach our goals. How can we be so unlike Him who "when he suffered, he made no threats" (1 Peter 2:23, NIV)? He was the true *Gentleman*, and He wants me to be like Him so that I can say, "Thy gentleness hath made me great" (Psalm 18:35, KJV).

"Nevertheless I am continually with Thee; Thou hast taken hold of my right hand. With Thy counsel Thou wilt guide me, and afterward receive me to glory" (Psalm 73:23–24).

DECEMBER 16
Loving Ourselves

I must at all times maintain the delicate balance of attitudes toward my *"self."* I must respect and love myself without becoming egocentric, for egocentricity is sin. Why not love myself? There is nothing wrong with self—as self. Jesus died for me, myself, and He did so because He loved me, that is, *myself.* Self becomes a problem only when I allow it to become self *first,* when it becomes preoccupied with itself, when it wants the attention and worship that are due only to God.

I cannot be truly joyful if I am not at peace with myself. I do incalculable harm to my personality if I hate, despise, and reject myself. The gospel that enables me to love others also enables me to love and accept myself. To be crucified with Christ does not mean that the self literally dies. It simply means that I must always die to my own desires if they conflict with the will of Christ or run counter to the well-being of others. When I surrender my will to Jesus Christ, I am doing the very opposite of bruising or afflicting myself; I am freeing myself to be the kind of person God intended me to be.

I must not delight in self-punishment, as if it were a virtue. It is not true that the more I suffer, the more God is glorified. Of course I must realize that my natural born self is permeated with sin, a legacy from Adam; but God's redemptive purpose for me is to rescue me *from* sin, not to destroy me *with* sin. Spiritual victory is the proper relationship of these three things: to love God first and seek His glory; to love my fellow men and seek their highest good; and to love myself and seek my highest expression in company with God.

"There is no fear in love; but perfect love casts out fear, because fear involves punishment, and the one who fears is not perfected in love" (1 John 4:18).

DECEMBER 17
The Responsibility of Prayer

If I try to live by a rule of thumb, I may as well say goodbye to my prayer life. God is never interested in delivering me from trouble if I am going to be delivered by natural means anyway. It is only when I dare to dream about the unheard of, and trust God for the incredible, that I begin to understand the power of prayer. "Call to Me, and I will answer you, and I will tell you great and mighty things, which you do not know" (Jeremiah 33:3). Is that not an invitation to become spiritually daring? Is it not the kind of prayer giant that God loves to bless?

Prayer is the most unpredictable and unexplainable of all my spiritual responsibilities. God never promises to answer my large requests *my* way, only *the* way. A father prayed that his sons might become Christians, and God seemed to ignore that prayer. His death came with great agony and suffering. Afterward, his children said, "If Father, who was a Christian, died like that, what about us who are not Christians?" That led them all to make the very decision for which their father had prayed so long. It is the mark of *trust* as well as *sense* to leave the method of answering prayer entirely in God's hands.

I must remember that prayer is not an option; it is a command. But do I need the command? If my tears, my shrinking strength, my stricken land, my sorrowing loved ones, my hardened neighbors, my indifferent fellow Christians, and my calloused world are not enough to drive me to my knees, there is little hope for them—or for me—as a disciple. I must immediately "call" to Him in order that He may answer with "great and mighty things, which [I] do not know." God, enable me to call!

"Cast your burden upon the Lord, and He will sustain you; He will never allow the righteous to be shaken" (Psalm 55:22).

DECEMBER 18
Making Spiritual Reversals

God calls His disciples into existence in order to reverse the natural order of things. When God told Abraham that his first-born son, Ishmael, would become a "wild man," Abraham immediately began to struggle against the natural course of Ishmael's life and, by prayer, sought to bring his son over to the spiritual side. He was successful; the "wild man" (Genesis 16:12, KJV) became "the father of . . . princes" (17:20).

That is God's ministry for all disciples—to change wild men into princes, to turn the natural into the spiritual. How often parents complain, "My children aren't spiritual." Of course. It is our responsibility to make them spiritual. A pastor will wail, "My church is so unspiritual." What else? That is the direction of the natural man; and wherever it is unopposed by spiritual forces, it will always be unspiritual. We should look on natural people, with their disobedience, perverseness, and indifference, not as incorrigible deviants, but as opportunities for grace. We should not condemn; we should deliver.

How encouraged I am by Hezekiah's action: "He opened the doors of the house of the Lord and repaired them" (2 Chronicles 29:3). He reopened what had been shut by his father, Ahaz, and repaired what had been broken. He relit the lamps that Ahaz had put out, and cleansed and reused the altar. That is my ministry—to reverse the natural trend. That is what Jesus did to Adam's trend. That is what Jesus wants to do through me to help all sons and daughters of Adam. The story of Christ and His gospel is the redoing, remaking, and renewing of men. If Christ is alive in me, I will make spiritual reversals; the old will go and the new will come. How the church needs an army to make spiritual "reversals"!

"Therefore if any man is in Christ, he is a new creature; the old things passed away; behold, new things have come" (2 Corinthians 5:17).

DECEMBER 19
The Old and the New Obligations

I must always understand what *really* happened at Calvary and not entertain merely a flimsy estimate. When Christ died He freed me from the guilt of my sins, but He did not free me from obligation. He brought me out from the authority of Satan, but He did not set me free to choose for myself. My ownership was only *transferred* at Calvary, not terminated. I am now just as liable to the authority of my new Master as I had been to the old. I am to become subject to Him and Him alone. I am no longer obligated to serve the kingdom of darkness, but neither am I free to decide what I shall do, eat, or what I shall wear. I may not go where I want, say what I want, or even think what I want. The fact that I so often please *myself* does not mean that I have the *right* to do so.

However, there is a difference between my present obligation to Jesus and my former obligation to Satan. When I served Satan I had no choice, I "walked according to the course of this world, according to the prince of the power of the air" (Ephesians 2:2). Even so, I was content that way because I knew no better. I was natural, uninhibited, and selfish, and I did not try to buck the stream. So there was no conflict, just natural existence.

But now under Jesus, even though He has all rights to me, He lets me *choose* to serve Him: "I beg you, therefore, brothers . . . present your bodies a living sacrifice" (Romans 12:1, Berkeley). That is amazing! He owns me, and yet He begs me; He bought me completely, and yet He waits upon my decision. Why? It must be because He wants no legal love, no rubber stamp obedience. He wants me to want Him for *Himself*, not because I have no other choice. Thus, our relationship is a love relationship, the kind Satan could never offer and the natural man could never produce.

"So then, brethren, we are under obligation, not to the flesh, to live according to the flesh—for if you are living according to the flesh, you must die; but if by the Spirit you are putting to death the deeds of the body, you will live" (Romans 8:12–13).

DECEMBER 20
Signing Away Our Rights

It sobers me to realize that I can deny Jesus Christ the possession of my life, even though I have no *right* to refuse Him. I can, if I choose, reduce myself to the level of the Corinthians and become as fleshly and quarrelsome as they. But if I do, something will happen. My refusal to allow Him His possession makes it impossible for Him to do with me what He longs to do. He longs to give us—who have no right to it—everything!

Paul said, "All things are yours" (1 Corinthians 3:21, KJV). God has made us "joint heirs" with Christ, and He wants to dominate us in order to make that inheritance practical in our daily lives. The more I yield to Christ, the more I will be a "conqueror"; and the more I conquer, the more I will yield, until it becomes an upward spiral of continual conquest and victory. It is one of heaven's strange laws that if I resign all rights of possession to Jesus Christ, I begin that very moment to possess all that I have surrendered.

So I must not cheat Jesus Christ—or myself. I must never bring myself down to the place where I say dismally, "He bought my heart and I didn't love Him; He bought my body and I didn't serve Him; He bought my mind and I didn't think of Him; He bought my will and I didn't yield to Him." Oswald Chambers said, "The passion of Christianity is that I deliberately sign away my own rights and become a bond-slave of Jesus Christ. Until I do that, I do not begin to be a saint." This is why Jesus died: "that those who live should no longer live for themselves but for him who died for them" (2 Corinthians 5:15, NIV). The cross of Christ—and its power—is fulfilled in me the moment I say yes to the sovereignty of Jesus Christ over me.

"That at the name of Jesus every knee should bow, of those who are in heaven, and on earth, and under the earth, and that every tongue should confess that Jesus Christ is Lord, to the glory of God the Father" (Philippians 2:10–11).

DECEMBER 21

Salvation Is Not Cheap

My discipleship for Jesus Christ will mean nothing unless I consider my life *cheap* for Him. Paul said, "I consider my life worth nothing to me" (Acts 20:24, NIV). He was willing to cheapen himself for the gospel, and that cheap view of his own welfare and safety resulted in homelessness, danger, and finally death. If I regard my life of infinite value and protect and pamper it, I will certainly be more comfortable, and more fruitless.

Abraham Lincoln said, "Love destroys." He was right. I cannot love Jesus Christ without destroying many things, one of which is the price tag I put on my life. "The love of Christ . . . constrains [presses] me" (2 Corinthians 5:14, Williams). If I still think of my salvation as a security blanket or a comfort station, I have sadly missed the meaning of Christ's weeping over Jerusalem, the agony of Calvary, and the lostness of men.

Our emphasis on "the gospel of grace" has led us to think of our salvation as cheap and easy, the very opposite of what God intended. We think in terms of safety, preservation, and escape. Our faith is often a device to escape the eternal darkness, nothing more. Can we say that our attachment to God is due to our insatiable desire for Him as a person and our overwhelming desire to do His will, regardless of the cost?

I cannot expect to come to the end of my life fruit-laden unless I have shed tears, and perhaps blood, in the field. God will not examine me for jolliness or agreeableness, but for scars, the marks of a love that was willing to bear the cost. If my salvation has not carried me *that* far, I may have to hang my head in shame. But, thank God, He is able to carry me farther, past "mere salvation" and on to the kind of life that becomes "more precious than gold that perisheth" (1 Peter 1:7, ASV) in His sight.

"But Jesus said to them, 'You do not know what you are asking for. Are you able to drink the cup that I drink, or to be baptized with the baptism with which I am baptized?'" (Mark 10:38).

DECEMBER 22
"Glory" and "Hallelujah"

Too often I have looked upon joy as one of God's special treats, one that delights me but also surprises me. I should not be surprised. I am *commanded* to be joyful: "Rejoice in the Lord always; and again I say, Rejoice" (Philippians 4:4, NSRB). Bible commands are always God's enablements; if I am commanded to rejoice, I can rejoice, regardless of circumstances.

I must realize that I can control my feelings far more than I think I can. The little boy who said, "I'd druther be mad," was admitting that he *could* control his emotions. Possibly with the exception of organic difficulties, our feelings are controllable if we put on the right dress of mind. In other words, God holds me responsible for the kind of thinking that enables me to rejoice.

Jesus said, "That my joy may be in you, and that your joy may be made full" (John 15:11, ASV). Jesus Christ was the most optimistic, confident, radiant Person the world ever saw. Can we imagine Him *now* being worried, harried, or depressed? If He is released to be free in us, joy will always result, for Jesus is the personal expression of joy. It is impossible for me to think of all that Christ has done for me, all that He is to me, and all that He has promised to do for me without feeling joy.

I am joyless only when I set my mind on my surrounding circumstances and/or set my mind on myself and begin to pity myself. The opposite of that is to keep Jesus Christ alive in my mind. Billy Bray called his left foot "glory" and his right one "hallelujah" so that as he walked it was "Glory, Hallelujah!" I also will walk in joy if I keep Christ in the center of my heart and my mind.

"Be glad in the Lord and rejoice you righteous ones, and shout for joy all you who are upright in heart" (Psalm 32:11).

DECEMBER 23
My Expectations of God

It is only fair that I ask myself, What is my expectation from God? The only satisfying answer is: That He be true to His Word. For if God has magnified "above all things [His] name and [His] word" (Psalm 138:2, NIV), then I have a right to depend upon that Word, and to expect He will do as He said. The Bible is clear in reminding me that not one word that the Lord utters will fail to come to pass (Joshua 23:14). Where God has clearly spoken, the answer will be clearly given.

But what about the times when God does not speak clearly? There is a difference between going according to principle and going according to an explicit word from the Lord. So many times in our lives there is no explicit word from God. What then? I find great help from the three Hebrew children who faced the furnace for refusing to bow to Nebuchadnezzar's image. Their answer to the king was, "God . . . is able to save us from the fire" (Daniel 3:17, Berkeley). That was their *expectation*, but they went beyond that to the personal equation—God Himself. They said, "But if not . . . we will [still] not serve [your] gods, nor worship the golden image" (v. 18). Lacking an explicit word from God, the Hebrews could only appeal to the nature, or character, of God and expect that He could never be other than what He was—holy, just, loving, merciful. They agreed with the psalmist, "My soul, look in stillness to God, for my expectation is from Him" (Psalm 62:5, Berkeley).

God does not always give me a particular message for every circumstance of my life, but He has given me Himself. That is the bottom line, the very bedrock of my relationship to Him. The man who works his way down to that solid foundation cannot be shattered by the storms of life.

"For the needy will not always be forgotten, nor the hope of the afflicted perish forever" (Psalm 9:18).

DECEMBER 24
God's Expectation of Us

If my expectation of God is His changeless nature and reliable Word, what is His expectation of me? Jesus said He chose us to "bear fruit" (John 15:16, NIV). That is always God's expectation of His people. God chose Israel to be a fruitful vine (Isaiah 5:1–2), and His purpose for His church is that it be "neither . . . barren nor unfruitful in the knowledge of . . . Jesus Christ" (2 Peter 1:8, KJV). When God wanted to reassert Aaron's priesthood, he instructed Moses to deposit twelve rods, or sticks, in the tabernacle, one for each tribe. On the next day, Aaron's rod was the only one that "sprouted and put forth buds and produced blossoms, and it bore ripe almonds" (Numbers 17:8). The production of fruit was the sign that Aaron was still the chosen priest, still the intercessor of God.

God accepts my service, but not because I am ordained, educated, or titled. He accepts me because I bear fruit. The office means nothing to God apart from that which He considers to be the first condition of service—fruitfulness. I am to avoid anything that substitutes for that fruit, and not pretend to be the genuine article unless the fruit itself vindicates me. Aaron's rod was a dead stick, nothing more, until activated by the Spirit of God. Then it became alive, and from that life it produced the bud, blossom, and fruit. So the source of my fruit is not myself, whether in the natural or educated self, but God. Apart from the life that He breathes into me, I will never be able to bear fruit for Him.

The fruitful man is an alive man, a man who offers God His own fruit strained through a human personality, which becomes an offering of endless pleasure to Him.

"He who tills his land will have plenty of food, but he who follows empty pursuits will have poverty in plenty" (Proverbs 28:19).

DECEMBER 25
The Poverty of Conditional Faith

I must beware of having a faith that is *conditional*. When Jacob fled from his father's house because of his brother Esau's threats, God met him at Bethel and promised him and his descendants the land of Canaan, just as He had promised it to Abraham, Jacob's grandfather (Genesis 28:10–17). The next day, Jacob made a conditional promise to God (vv. 20–22):

IF GOD WILL • be with me
   • keep me in the way
   • give me bread to eat
   • give me clothes to wear
   • bring me back to my father's house in peace

THEN: • the Lord shall be my God
   • this stone shall become God's house
   • I will tithe all my income

The weakness of Jacob's faith is all the more glaring in the light of God's *unconditional* promise to him the previous day. Conditional faith is cautious, timid faith. It asks for evidence before it will commit itself. Paul says, "Jews demand miraculous signs [before they will believe]" (1 Corinthians 1:22, NIV). But am I any better if I say that God must show Himself trustworthy before I will believe Him?

One of the saddest statements in the New Testament must be that of the father of the demon-possessed boy: "If You can do anything, take pity on us and help us!" To which Jesus replied, "'If You can!' All things are possible to him who believes" (Mark 9:22–23). Jesus puts the condition of faith squarely where it belongs—not on Him, but on us. I cannot blame God for the miracles He did *not* do; I can only blame myself for tying His hands.

"Why should I take my flesh in my teeth, and put my life in my hands? Though He slay me, I will hope in Him. Nevertheless I will argue my ways before Him" (Job 13:14–15).

DECEMBER 26

Holy Discomfort

Confession of sin is not only the means of restoring my fellowship with God, but also the means of keeping my sanity. A human being is so alien to sin, as God intended him to be, that unless God had given him the ability to confess, he would live in a perpetual asylum. As a believer in Jesus Christ, if I sin and do not confess, I am even more miserable than the natural man in the same state. "When I kept silent about [did not confess] my sin, my body wasted away" (Psalm 32:3); "My bones were broken" (Psalm 51:8, author's trans.). My sad spiritual state reaches to my body and affects it. How often has my body tried to tell me that my spirit was not right with God?

Thank God for His holy *discomfort!* A holy God believes in making me uncomfortable, for His name's sake. An indifferent, unloving God would leave me utterly comfortable in my sins, and that comfort, like leprosy, would be a sign of danger, not health. Of course God wants me to be comfortable, but not at the expense of my soul's well-being. Therefore He gives me the pain of guilt in order to drive me to repentance and confession, which in turn lead to the kind of comfort He truly desires for me.

If I refuse to acknowledge my sin, if I continue to repress my guilt, I may suffer from a disorder of the subconscious. It is possible that Christians may suffer from events long past in their lives, and therefore they may need the healing grace of God for their subconscious maladies. The cleansing power of God's Word reaches deeply into the "heart" (Psalm 119:11); and while we cannot consciously confess anything in the subconscious, we can trust the Holy Spirit to apply the cleansing Word there.

"Blessed is he whose transgression is forgiven" (Psalm 32:1). What a blessing confession is! Lord, may I never treat it with disdain.

"So now, our God, listen to the prayer of Thy servant and to his supplications, and for Thy sake, O Lord, let Thy face shine on Thy desolate sanctuary" (Daniel 9:17).

DECEMBER 27
The Appeal of Worldly Riches

I must be careful not to let the world enrich me. Abraham refused the spoils of Sodom, telling Bera, king of Sodom, "Lest you should say, 'I have made Abram rich'" (Genesis 14:23). Abraham saw clearly that once he began to accept Sodom's favors, it would not be long before he accepted its atmosphere and perhaps its sins.

The world longs to enrich me. Jesus felt its appeal when the people surged around Him near the Sea of Galilee and begged Him to accept the kingship (John 6:15). That was highly flattering. But the people did not want Jesus for His own sake; they wanted Him for *their* sake. They wanted His miracles, His bread, His notoriety. They did not want His *godliness*. So He refused them.

The subtle appeal of the world is not to the lurid, the grotesque, or the flamboyant. Many people, who would not give in to the gross temptations of the flesh, have surrendered to the intangible thing called worldliness—a selling of their heavenly hope for the enjoyment of the material, tangible, hard substance that is available now. For God to make Abraham rich was one thing; for Sodom to make him rich was entirely different.

The Bible commands me not to have anything to do with the riches offered me by Sodom. God wants me to move back into Canaan's highlands with Abraham and there quietly walk before Him who is my true treasure.

The riches of Sodom are *uncertain.* Suppose Abraham had accepted them, what then? Within twenty years Sodom became a lake of fire, and his investment would have gone up in smoke. I must not commit my destiny to smoke! So I will trust in God, who "giveth us richly all things to enjoy" (1 Timothy 6:17, KJV).

"Better is the little of the righteous than the abundance of many wicked. For the arms of the wicked will be broken; but the Lord sustains the righteous" (Psalm 37:16–17).

DECEMBER 28

The Meaning of Abiding in Him

Every disciple will pass through three levels of relationship with Jesus Christ, each one in response to an invitation. "Come to Me" (Matthew 11:28) is the first one. It is Christ's simple invitation to find rest and relief from the awesome burden of sin, the first and most necessary step in anyone's life. The second is "Follow Me" (Matthew 4:19), an invitation to a closer relationship, a relationship of master and servant. Christ needs workers to carry out His purposes for this age, and this second invitation is His plea for help. The third is "Abide in Me" (John 15:4), and it refers to the deepest relationship any human can have with Jesus. It is the key to victorious Christian living, and it is the greatest way in which we can glorify God.

What does it mean to abide in Him? I think it means three things: First, a *conscious awareness of His presence* at all times. That does not mean direct verbal communication with Him, but the feeling that He is there, as a child playing is aware of its mother's nearby presence. Second, it also means a *careful consultation with Him* about everything that affects us. That consultation may be in direct prayer, or else in scanning the Bible indirectly for any message He has for us there. The important thing is to keep the lines of communication open with Him so that we are instantly ready to receive any necessary message sent from Him. Third, it means a *continual enjoyment of Him as a person*. That means He is a joy, a delight to us at all times; the very thought of Him fills us with pleasure.

Lord, help me to graduate up the scale from convert, to ambassador, to confidant. To abide in You is to ride the high places of the earth.

"He who dwells in the shelter of the Most High will abide in the shadow of the Almighty" (Psalm 91:1).

DECEMBER 29
The Seeds of an Overcoming Life

Above all things, I must cultivate a "moment by moment" faith. My body lives one moment at a time, and so must my soul, for the same God created both. We are too apt to think of Christ's salvation work as a "once for all" thing, something static and fixed; in reality, it is a moment-by-moment thing as He keeps applying His Calvary work continually in heaven. He intercedes for us unceasingly and will continue in that ministry forever.

A man said in a testimony meeting, "Jesus saves me *now*." True! Jesus is saving all His followers now, for the effects of His salvation pour down continually from above on all His people. I am to see the saving power of Jesus Christ at work in me daily, even hourly, and see how the Christ who first cleansed me continues to cleanse, continues to heal, and continues to deliver.

I must not be preoccupied with the past. I should thank God for the lessons learned, the blessings received, and the prayers answered, but I need the same help *today*. Nor should I be unduly concerned about tomorrow. Jesus said, in effect, "Don't worry about tomorrow because you don't have tomorrow's salvation yet" (see Matthew 6:34). Christ's saving power is working for me on today's schedule, not tomorrow's. When tomorrow comes, that power will be there, but not before.

My prayer should not be, "Lord, make my life such and such," but, "Lord, help me *now* with today's problem." If I overcome today, tomorrow will take care of itself. The seeds of an overcoming life are found in today's victories.

Lord, I seek You for a present-tense salvation that will meet today's needs. For tomorrow, I will seek You again—and again—and again!

"The Lord God is my strength, and He has made my feet like hinds' feet, and makes me walk on my high places" (Habakkuk 3:19).

DECEMBER 30

Living as Never Seeing Death

God's purpose for me, His disciple, is that I should never "see" death. Enoch is the great example of a life lived so dependently on God that not even death could touch him. "By faith Enoch was taken up so that he should not see death" (Hebrews 11:5). There was no "dying grace" with Enoch, for dying grace is God's final act of charity toward a believer who needs a little extra help in his transition from earth to heaven. I must live so that no "dying grace" will ever be necessary.

Victory over death does not occur when death lays its hand upon me. It occurs in the continuous stream of life, where death continually shadows me and seeks to frighten me, even if it cannot claim me. I must live as Enoch did, by faith, which continually holds down death. By the time I reach my actual transition, death should be a slain giant dangling at my side. My immortality must be an immediate and continual thing. I must not *die* and go to heaven, but *live* and go to heaven; in fact, I must not go to heaven at all, but bring heaven down to my level and my sphere, so that the transition will simply be the continuation of an already heavenly walk.

I must get beyond the point where faith "saves my soul." Thank God, it does that, but it does infinitely more; it creates a way of life in which heaven has already come and is not just a distant hope. Some Christians say, "Oh, if I were only in heaven!" I *can* be in heaven, here and now, by faith. By living according to God's rules, by letting God visit me personally, and by thinking heaven's thoughts, I *can* be enwrapped by heaven *now*; then, when the transition comes, it will be just the further opening of everlasting glory.

"'O death, where is your victory? O death, where is your sting?' The sting of death is sin, and the power of sin is the law; but thanks be to God, who gives us the victory through our Lord Jesus Christ" (1 Corinthians 15:55–57).

DECEMBER 31
God's Final Morning

I must remember that one of the unwritten laws of Scripture is that night leads to morning. When I read the first page of the Bible I discover the "darkness" that was "upon the face of the deep" (Genesis 1:2, KJV), but the last page tells me of the God who will be my light forever (Revelation 22:5). There was darkness when Jesus was crucified, and He arose in the breaking light of the following Sunday morning (Luke 23:44; 24:1).

It was during the "fourth watch of the night" that Christ's disciples were struggling hard to bring their boat to the Galilee shore. Suddenly, at the blackest point of the night, they saw Him walking toward them on the water and they heard Him call, "It is I; do not be afraid" (Matthew 14:25, 27). The wind immediately ceased, the waters grew calm, and the disciples worshiped their all-powerful Lord again. How often have Christ's followers experienced this! Clement of Alexandria said, "Christ has turned all our sunsets into sunrises."

If Jesus delays His return, there is one sunset we must all face. Yet, even then we look confidently through the darkness to the coming dawn and say, "I shall not die, but live, and declare the works of the Lord" (Psalm 118:17, KJV). For that is the way God ends His beginnings.

> To Thee our morning song of praise,
> To Thee our evening prayer we raise;
> Thy glory suppliant we adore
> For ever and for evermore.
> *Ambrose of Milan*

"Thou makest the morning dawn and the evening sunset to shout for joy" (Psalm 65:8, Berkeley).

"And a voice came from the throne, saying, 'Give praise to our God, all you His bond-servants, you who fear Him, the small and the great'" (Revelation 19:5).